HUMAN RIGHTS IN EUROPE

HUMAN RIGHTS IN EUROPE

being an account of the
European Convention for the Protection of
Human Rights and Fundamental Freedoms
signed in Rome on 4 November 1950,
of the Protocols thereto
and of the machinery created thereby:
the European Commission of Human Rights
and
the European Court of Human Rights

Second edition
by
A. H. ROBERTSON, B.C.L. (Oxon.), S.J.D. (Harvard)
Professeur Associé at the University of Paris I,
former Simon Visiting Professor at the University of Manchester,
former Director of Human Rights, Council of Europe

MANCHESTER
UNIVERSITY PRESS

© A. H. Robertson 1977
Published by
. Manchester University Press
Oxford Road, Manchester M13 9PL

First edition 1963
Second (revised, expanded and reset) edition, 1977

ISBN 0 7190 0658 9

Distributed in the USA by
Humanities Press Inc
171 First Avenue, Atlantic Highlands, N.J. 07716

Printed in Great Britain
by Willmer Brothers Limited, Birkenhead
E 0473/6/2

CONTENTS

PREFACE

In May 1974 the Council of Europe celebrated its twenty-fifth anniversary, and in November 1975 a quarter of a century had passed since the European Convention on Human Rights was signed in Rome. There is, I believe, general agreement on two propositions: first, that the conclusion of the Convention and the establishment of a European system for the protection of human rights which results therefrom constitute the most important achievement of the Council of Europe; secondly, that this system is the most effective yet established by any international organisation and is likely to remain so for a considerable period of time. The purpose of this book is to describe that system by relating its origins, by explaining what are the rights and freedoms guaranteed, and by recounting the functions of the European Commission and Court of Human Rights – and also those of the Committee of Ministers of the Council of Europe when discharging its functions under the Convention; in short, how the system has operated over a period of more than twenty years since the Convention entered into force in September 1953.

The first edition of this book was written in 1962, when the system had been in operation for less than ten years; at that time only seven applications had been declared admissible by the Commission, two cases had been referred to the Court and three to the Committee of Ministers. By the end of 1974 nearly 140 cases had been declared admissible, fifteen had been referred to the Court and twenty to the Committee of Ministers. A second edition is therefore overdue.

Much has been written about the Convention in several languages. Indeed, it is (with the Charter of the United Nations and the Treaty of Rome) one of the three treaties which have aroused the greatest interest among international lawyers, and inspired the largest volume of literature, since the end of the Second World War. I have been assisted by the consultation of many books and articles, of which further particulars are given in the bibliography, particularly the book of Mr J. E. S. Fawcett and the publications of Mr A. B. McNulty and M. Karel Vasak. Having myself received and complied with frequent requests for articles about different aspects of the European Convention, I have in this book made extracts from or summaries of several articles previously published; the appropriate acknowledgements are made in the notes. Though this is essentially a second edition, about three-quarters of it is new. It is in some ways a companion volume to *Human Rights in the World* (also published by Manchester University Press, 1972) and frequent references are made to the latter work.

The book was written over a period of eighteen months running from the spring of 1974 to the autumn of 1975. Four chapters were written while I was Simon Visiting Professor at the University of Manchester and two while I was in residence at the Bellagio Conference and Study Centre; I express my thanks to the Simon trustees and to the Rockefeller Foundation for the wonderful facilities afforded to me both at Broomcroft Hall and at the Villa Serbelloni. I have tried to cover all important developments in the life of the Convention down to the end of 1974 and also some cases considered by the Commission and the Court in the first half of 1975.

My gratitude is also expressed to M. Pierre-Henri Teitgen, the *rapporteur* who proposed the conclusion of the Convention in 1949; twenty-five years later, as Director of the University Centre for Studies of the European Communities, he arranged for me to give a series of lectures on the subject in the University of Paris I, on which I have drawn considerably in writing this work.

Finally I express my thanks to Professor B. A. Wortley, under whose inspiration and guidance the Law Faculty of the University of Manchester has developed remarkably its international law programme in recent years, and to Manchester University Press, which has published many of the works resulting from this programme – particularly the Melland Schill lectures – among which a significant place has been given, in accordance with Manchester's liberal tradition, to human rights and fundamental freedoms.

Strasbourg, 1975   A. H. ROBERTSON

TABLE OF CASES

(Heavy type indicates principal references)

NOTE ON SOURCES

Since the source materials relating to the European Convention on Human Rights are numerous and not always simple to identify, the following indications may be useful. The publications listed are bilingual in English and French, or in separate volumes in the two languages, unless the contrary is indicated.

Yearbook of the European Convention on Human Rights
This is an official publication which contains the basic texts (including ratifications and optional declarations), the more important decisions of the Commission, the Court and the Committee of Ministers and other information about the work of the Council of Europe in the field of human rights.

The first two volumes covered the years 1955–59. Since 1960 it has been published annually. An extra volume was published in 1969 (XII *bis*) containing the report of the Commission and the decision of the Committee of Ministers in the *Greek case*. Sixteen volumes were published by 1975.

Since the *Yearbook* is available in most law libraries, references to it are given whenever possible.

Digest of Case Law (one volume)
The *Digest*, published in 1970, contains summaries or extracts from the more important decisions of the Commission, the Court and the Committee of Ministers during the period 1955–67, that is to say those published in the first ten volumes of the *Yearbook*.

European Convention on Human Rights: Collected Texts
This is a handbook published periodically (tenth edition in August 1975) which contains the basic texts, the Rules of Procedure of the Commission, the Court and the Committee of Ministers, lists of members of the Commission and the Court and certain other texts.

Publications of the Court
Series A *Judgements and Decisions*. The full text of all the judgements and decisions of the Court. Eighteen volumes published by 1975.
Series B *Pleadings, Oral Arguments, Documents*. In this series may be found, *inter alia*, the reports of the Commission on cases referred to the Court for decision. Sixteen volumes published by 1975.

Publications of the Commission
Collection of Decisions. From 1960 to 1974 the Commission published
(in roneotyped or offset form) forty-six volumes in this series, usually
three numbers a year. The series therefore includes a greater number
of decisions than the *Yearbook,* and they were published more
promptly; but the decisions are given only in the language in which
they were drafted (English or French) without translation.

An analytical summary of the decisions included in Nos. 1–30 was
published in 1973, in French only.

Decisions and Reports. As from July 1975 the *Collection of Decisions*
is replaced by a new series, *Decisions and Reports,* which is bilingual.
In addition to decisions on admissibility it will contain reports of the
Commission where they have been made public.

Annual Review. Since 1972 the Commission publishes an *Annual
Review* which contains information and statistics on its activities,
and surveys of the most important applications examined.

Case Law Topics. These are separate volumes grouping together various
decisions of the Commission according to the subject-matter to which
they relate. The first four numbers relate to: human rights in prison;
family life; the procedure for bringing an application; and limitations
on human rights.

'Stocktaking'. This is an unofficial publication compiled periodically
(once or twice a year) by the Secretary of the Commission, which
summarises the more important cases. It is particularly useful as a
source of information about cases which have not yet been decided
by the Court or the Committee of Ministers. Roneotyped or offset.

Other Publications
Reports of cases decided by the Committee of Ministers:
> the report of the Commission and the resolution of the Committee
> of Ministers on cases submitted to the Committee for decision.
> Roneotyped.

Travaux préparatoires of the Convention and First Protocol:
> six volumes published in a roneotyped edition (1963–65); printed
> edition in press (see Chapter 1, n. 24).

Travaux préparatoires of the Second and Third Protocols:
> roneotyped edition, published in 1966 and 1968.

'Explanatory reports on the Second to Fifth Protocols': Document
> H(71)11. Offset.

'Collection of decisions of national courts referring to the Convention',
> published in 1970, with annual supplements thereafter.

'Bibliography relating to the Convention': Document H(73)13, Nov-
> ember 1973, with annual supplements thereafter.

Reports of conferences and colloquies
La Protection internationale des Droits de l'homme dans le cadre
européen, Paris, 1961. In French only. Proceedings of the Strasbourg
Colloquy, 1960.
Human Rights in National and International Law, Manchester, 1968.
Proceedings of the Vienna conference, 1965.
Symposium on Human Rights and Mass Communications, Strasbourg,
1969. Proceedings of the Salzbourg Symposium, 1968.
Privacy and Human Rights, Manchester, 1973. Proceedings of the
Brussels Conference, 1970.
Parliamentary Conference on Human Rights, Strasbourg, 1972. Pro-
ceedings of the Vienna Conference, 1971.

CHAPTER I

THE ORIGINS AND HISTORY
OF THE CONVENTION

1. HUMAN RIGHTS AS THE GUARANTEE
OF DEMOCRACY

Human rights have a very special place in the philosophy of the Council of Europe. The reason is not far to seek and may be stated quite simply: respect for human rights is a pre-condition of democracy and the rule of law.[1]

The preambles to treaties frequently constitute a rewarding object of study. We often tend to ignore them, on the ground that they have no legal effect and are little more than 'window dressing' for the operative clauses. But this is a mistake, because in many cases they reveal the political objectives of the contracting parties and enable us to place in perspective, that is to say in their historical context, the legal obligations that follow.

The Covenant of the League of Nations was drafted after the war of 1914–18, and the principal object of its authors was to prevent the repetition of such a catastrophe; their main concern was thus for the maintenance of international relations on a peaceful basis, and this is reflected in the words of the Preamble: 'to promote international co-operation and to achieve international peace and security...'

In 1945 the situation was broadly similar and the Preamble to the Charter of the United Nations is thus mainly concerned with international relations: 'to save succeeding generations from the scourge of war... to establish conditions under which justice and the respect for the obligations arising from treaties and other sources of international law can be maintained ... to unite our strength to maintain international peace and security...' – and so on. But something new is introduced in the second paragraph of the Preamble, which expresses the determination of the peoples of the United Nations:

> to reaffirm faith in fundamental human rights, in the dignity and worth of the human person, in the equal rights of men and women and of nations large and small.

Human rights are mentioned almost for the first time in an international treaty,[2] presumably because the drafters of the Charter were looking behind the facts of war to its causes, one of which had been shown by experience to be the existence of dictatorships. An international order which can effectively secure human rights is thereby taking a major step towards the prevention of war.[3] The Charter therefore includes among the purposes of the United Nations set out in Article 1: 'to achieve international co-operation ... in promoting and encouraging respect for human rights and for fundamental freedoms for all without distinction ...' Later articles (particularly Articles 55, 56 and 76) contain undertakings to 'promote' or 'encourage' respect for human rights and fundamental freedoms for all without distinction, and to take joint and separate action in co-operation with the Organisation for the achievement of this purpose. But these are all undertakings aimed at action in the future.[4]

It was left to the regional organisations in Europe to carry the matter further by providing for obligations of immediate application. In the Brussels treaty of 17 March 1948 the five signatories (Belgium, France, Luxembourg, the Netherlands and the United Kingdom), after reaffirming their faith in the ideals proclaimed in the Charter of the United Nations, stated that they were resolved:

> To fortify and preserve the principles of democracy, personal freedom and political liberty, the constitutional traditions and the rule of law, which are their common heritage.

The same ideas were reproduced, with a slight rearrangement, in the North Atlantic Treaty of 4 April 1949, in which the Parties declare that they are:

> determined to safeguard their freedom, common heritage and civilisation of their peoples, founded on the principles of democracy, individual liberty and the rule of law.

Another variant was enshrined in the Statute of the Council of Europe, which was signed in St James's Palace on 5 May 1949. In the Preamble the Contracting Parties declare that they are:

> Reaffirming their devotion to the spiritual and moral values which are the common heritage of their peoples and the true source of individual freedom, political liberty and the rule of law, principles which form the basis of all genuine democracy;

Thereafter come two important provisions. The first article of the Statute sets out the aim of the organisation as 'to achieve a greater unity between its Members' and then specifies as one of the means by which this aim shall be pursued 'the maintenance and further realisation of human rights and fundamental freedoms'. This, of course, is broadly similar to the coresponding provision in Article 1 of the Charter.

However, Article 3 of the Statute continues:

> Every Member of the Council of Europe must accept the principles of the rule of law and of the enjoyment by all persons within its jurisdiction of human rights and fundamental freedoms, and collaborate sincerely and effectively in the realisation of the aim of the Council as specified in Chapter I.

It thus appears that the maintenance of human rights and respect for the rule of law are not only included among the objectives of the Council of Europe, they are actually made a condition of membership. It was in this respect that the Statute went much further than any earlier treaty. Moreover the violation of this condition is a reason for the suspension or expulsion of a member, in accordance with Article 8 of the Statute, so that the obligation is evidently meant to be taken seriously.

Why was the cause of human rights espoused so ardently by the Council of Europe? There were, it is believed, two main reasons. The first of these resulted from the grim experiences through which Europe had passed during the years immediately preceding the creation of the Council. 1949 was very close to 1945. Many of the leading statesmen of the immediate post-war epoch had been in the resistance or in prison during the Second World War and were acutely conscious of the need to prevent any recrudescence of dictatorship in Western Europe. They knew that as long as human rights are respected democracy is secure and the danger of dictatorship and war is remote; but that the first steps towards dictatorship are the gradual suppression of individual rights – infringement of the freedom of the press, prohibition of public meetings, trials behind closed doors, and so on – and that once this process has started it is increasingly difficult to bring it to a halt. What is necessary, therefore, is to lay down in advance what are the standards of rights and freedoms that must be respected in a democratic society and institute machinery to ensure that they are observed. If any member State should then start on the path which leads to dictatorship, the alarm would be sounded and international machinery put in motion to restore the rule of law. Pierre-Henri Teitgen (a leader of the French Mouvement Républicain Populaire and a former Minister of Justice) expressed this graphically in a speech to the Consultative Assembly in August 1949: [5]

> Many of our colleagues have pointed out that our countries are democratic and are deeply impregnated with a sense of freedom; they believe in morality and in natural law ... Why is it necessary to build such a system?
>
> Democracies do not become Nazi countries in one day. Evil progresses cunningly, with a minority operating, as it were, to remove the levers of control. One by one, freedoms are suppressed, in one sphere after another. Public opinion and the entire national conscience are asphyxiated. And then, when everything is in order, the 'Führer' is installed and the evolution continues even to the oven of the crematorium.
>
> It is necessary to intervene before it is too late. A conscience must exist somewhere which will sound the alarm to the minds of a nation menaced by this progressive corruption, to warn them of the peril and to show them that they are progressing down a long road which leads far, sometimes even to Buchenwald or to Dachau.
>
> An international Court, within the Council of Europe, and a system of supervision and guarantees could be the conscience of which we all have need, and of which other countries have perhaps a special need.

The second main reason which inspired the Council's concern for human rights was the ideological conflict between East and West which surrounded its creation. The post-war movement for European unity was not only the result of a conviction that this was a desirable political goal; it was also a reaction to the Communist threat, which was very real at that time. The year which elapsed between the Hague Congress in May 1948, which led to the establishment of the Council of Europe,[6] and the signature of the Statute in the following spring witnessed the seizure of power by the Communists in Czechoslovakia, the civil war in Greece and the Berlin blockade. M. Paul-Henri Spaak once remarked that the man who did most for the union of Western Europe was Josef Stalin. It was when the European countries were acutely aware of the challenge of Communism that they felt the need to reaffirm the principles of their own political faith; it was the danger of dictatorship that made them conscious of the value of democracy. The Council of Europe was thus a peaceful association of democratic States (not, be it noted, a military alliance – that was NATO) which proclaimed their faith in the rule of law and 'their devotion to the spiritual and moral values which are the common heritage of their peoples'. This aspect of the matter was well summarised when the Convention on Human Rights was signed at the sixth session of the Committee of Ministers in Rome in November 1950. Mr Sean MacBride, the Irish Minister for External Affairs, said on that occasion:

> The present struggle is one which is largely being fought in the minds and consciences of mankind. In this struggle, I have always felt that we lacked a clearly defined charter which set out unambiguously the rights which we democrats guarantee to our people. This Convention is a step in that direction.

and M. Robert Schuman added:

> This Convention which we are signing is not as full or as precise as many of us would have wished. However, we have thought it our duty to subscribe to it as it stands. It provides foundations on which to base the defence of human personality against all tryannies and against all forms of totalitarianism.

The provisions about human rights in the Statute of the Council of Europe, the obligations undertaken in the European Convention and the machinery of the Commission and the Court are thus designed primarily to preserve the rule of law and the principles of democracy in the member States and, should the danger arise, forestall any trend to dictatorship before it is too late.

2. THE HISTORY OF THE CONVENTION AND OF THE FIRST PROTOCOL

The history of the Convention goes back to a period antedating the Council of Europe. The Congress of Europe convened by the International Committee of Movements for European Unity was held at the Hague from 8 to 10 May 1948; it included 663 delegates from sixteen countries[7] and observers (of whom many were refugees) from ten others.[8] The purposes of the congress were to demonstrate the wide support for the cause of European unity, to provide fresh impetus to this movement and to make practical recommendations for the accomplishment of its objectives. The participants included a number of former Prime Ministers and Foreign Ministers, many members of parliament and leading citizens from different sectors of the community. Not a few of them were later to become prominent members of the Consultative Assembly. The President of Honour was Sir Winston Churchill, and the chairmen of the three committees of the congress were M. Paul Ramadier, a former Prime Minister

of France, M. Paul van Zeeland, a former Prime Minister of
Belgium, and Professor Salvador de Madariaga, a former Spanish
Foreign Minister living in exile in Oxford. In the *Message to
Europeans* adopted at the final plenary session the delegates pro-
claimed:

> We desire a United Europe, throughout whose area the free move-
> ment of persons, ideas and goods is restored;
> We desire a Charter of Human Rights guaranteeing liberty of
> thought, assembly and expression as well as the right to form a
> political opposition;
> We desire a Court of Justice with adequate sanctions for the imple-
> mentation of this Charter;
> We desire a European Assembly where the live forces of all our
> nations shall be represented;
> And pledge ourselves in our homes and in public, in our political
> and religious life, in our professional and trade union circles, to
> give our fullest support to all persons and governments working
> for this lofty cause, which offers the last chance of peace and the
> one promise of a great future for this generation and those that
> will succeed it.

The desire for a Charter of Human Rights and for a Court of Justice
with adequate sanctions for its implementation subsequently formed
the subject of more detailed study. Early in 1949 the International
Juridical Section of the European Movement was set up under the
chairmanship of M. Pierre-Henri Teitgen, former French Minister
of Justice, with Sir David Maxwell Fyfe (later Lord Chancellor
Kilmuir) and Professor Fernand Dehousse of Belgium (later President of the Consultative Assembly) as joint *rapporteurs*. This group
set to work to prepare a draft Convention in which the Contracting
Parties would undertake to uphold the fundamental liberties of their
citizens and establish a European Court to adjudicate in cases of
alleged violation. The draft thus prepared was submitted to the
Committee of Ministers of the Council of Europe in July 1949, with
a recommendation that the matter should be placed on the agenda
of the first session of the Consultative Assembly, which was about
to take place during the following month.[9]

The other progenitor of the European Convention was, of course,
the *Universal Declaration of Human Rights*, proclaimed by the
General Assembly of the United Nations on 10 December 1948.
The Declaration did not contain legally binding obligations, but its
authors intended it to have 'a moral value and authority which is
without precedent in the history of the world';[10] it 'gave expression

to what, in the fullness of time, ought to become principles of law recognised and acted upon by States members of the United Nations'.[11] Once the Declaration had been proclaimed, the General Assembly, in its Resolution 217 (III) of 10 December 1948, instructed the Commission on Human Rights to give priority to the drafting of the two other parts of the proposed Bill of Rights: a Covenant containing legal obligations to be assumed by States, and 'measures of implementation'. In 1952 the General Assembly decided that there should be two separate Covenants, to be concluded simultaneously, relating to economic, social and cultural rights, on the one hand, and to civil and political rights, on the other. The Commission on Human Rights submitted its draft texts to ECOSOC and the General Assembly in 1954; in due course the two Covenants and the Optional Protocol to the Covenant on Civil and Political Rights were approved by the General Assembly on 16 December 1966.[12]

What is important in the present context is that when the Council of Europe started work on the subject in 1949 it found ready to hand the statement of rights contained in the Universal Declaration, while there was already available the first draft of the UN Covenant prepared by the Commission on Human Rights of the United Nations. In spite of the recommendation of the European Movement, the Committee of Ministers of the Council of Europe did not include the question of human rights on the draft agenda which it drew up for the first session of the Assembly in 1949.[13] Consequently three separate proposals relating to human rights were tabled by different groups of representatives, and the Assembly itself then proposed to include on its agenda the study of 'measures for the fulfilment of the declared aim of the Council of Europe in accordance with Article 1 of the Statute in regard to the maintenance and further realisation of human rights and fundamental freedoms'.[14] The Committee of Ministers' consent was then required for the inclusion of an item on the Assembly's agenda in accordance with the original text of Article 23 of the Statute, and the Ministers at first would not agree, fearing duplication of work with the United Nations, and possibly confusion if the two organisations set about drafting two separate treaties relating to the same matter at the same time. This led Sir Winston Churchill to remark that 'a European Assembly forbidden to discuss human rights would indeed have been a ludicrous proposition to put to the world'.[15] Finally, when the Assembly insisted, the Ministers acquiesced and asked the Assembly to devote particular attention to the question of the definition of human rights.[16]

The Assembly held a general debate on the subject on 19 August 1949, and a formal proposal was made for the establishment of 'an organisation within the Council of Europe to ensure the collective guarantee of human rights'.[17] This was referred to the Committee on Legal and Administrative Questions, presided over by Sir David Maxwell Fyfe, with M. Antonio Azara (Italy) as vice-chairman and M. Pierre-Henri Teitgen (France) as *rapporteur*. The committee's discussions resulted in the famous Teitgen report of 5 September 1949,[18] which was debated by the Assembly on 7 and 8 September, discussed in detail (more than twenty amendments were proposed and voted on), and led to the adoption of the Assembly's *Recommendation 38* on 8 September.[19]

The first question which the committee considered was that of the rights which should be protected. Should they be limited to the 'classic' rights and freedoms set out in such hallowed texts as the English and American Bills of Rights and the French Declaration of 1789? Or should they extend to the rights of an economic and social character which found their way into several of the new constitutions elaborated after the Second World War, such as the French constitution of 1946, the Italian constitution of 1947 and the Basic Law of the Federal Republic of Germany of 23 May 1949? M. Teitgen answered this question as follows:[20]

> The Committee on Legal and Administrative Questions had first to draw up a list of freedoms which are to be guaranteed. It considered that, for the moment, it is preferable to limit the collective guarantee to those rights and essential freedoms which are practised after long usage and experience in all the democratic countries. While they are the first triumph of democratic regimes, they are also the necessary condition under which they operate.
>
> Certainly, professional freedoms and social rights, which have themselves an intrinsic value, must also, in the future, be defined and protected. Everyone will, however, understand that it is necessary to begin at the beginning and to guarantee political democracy in the European Union and then to co-ordinate our economies, before undertaking the generalisation of social democracy.

The committee therefore 'began at the beginning' and listed twelve basic civil and political rights which it proposed should be the subject of a collective guarantee. In spite of the Ministers' recommendation, the committee did not attempt to define the rights in detail. The rights which it proposed were the following (taken from the articles indicated of the Universal Declaration):

1. Security of person (Arts. 3, 5 and 8).
2. Freedom from slavery and servitude (Art. 4).
3. Freedom from arbitrary arrest, detention or exile (Arts. 9, 10 and 11).
4. Freedom from arbitrary interference in private and family life, home and correspondence (Art. 12).
5. Freedom of thought, conscience and religion (Art. 18).
6. Freedom of opinion and expression (Art. 19).
7. Freedom of assembly (Art. 20).
8. Freedom of association (Art. 20).
9. Freedom to unite in trade unions (Art. 23, para. 4).
10. The right to marry and found a family (Art. 16).
11. The right of parents to choose the kind of education to be given to their children (Art. 26, para. 3).
12. The right to own property (Art. 17).

When this list of rights was considered by the Assembly, an amendment was tabled by Lord Layton to delete the last three on the list – not, of course, that he was opposed to the rights as such, but because he foresaw difficulties of drafting and of interpretation (particularly as regards the right to own property) and considered that these rights were not fundamental requirements of a democratic regime. After a lively debate on 8 September 1949, in which twenty-six speakers participated, the Assembly decided to include in the list the right to marry and to found a family but to refer back to the committee for further consideration the right of parents as regards the education of their children and the right to own property.

The Assembly then considered how the collective guarantee should be established. In the first place, it proposed that all member States should bind themselves to respect the fundamental principles of democracy, and to hold free elections at reasonable intervals with universal suffrage and by secret ballot; it was then to be left to each signatory State, subject to certain safeguards, to determine the rules by which the guaranteed rights and freedoms should be established and protected within its territory. The object of the collective guarantee was 'to ensure that the laws of each State in which are embodied the guaranteed rights and freedoms, as well as the application of these laws, are in accordance with 'the general principles of law as recognised by civilised nations' referred to in Article 38(c) of the Statute of the International Court of Justice'. Secondly, in order to implement the collective guarantee of human rights, it was proposed to create a European Commission for Human Rights and a European Court of Justice.

The committee proposed – and the proposal was accepted by the Assembly – that member States might bring any alleged breach of the Convention before the Commission, which would endeavour to settle the matter by conciliation. A similar right was to be granted to private individuals or associations after exhausting domestic remedies. If conciliation failed, the Commission itself, or a member State, might refer the matter to the European Court of Justice, though this right was not to be accorded to private parties. The Court would take decisions as to whether a violation had occurred; these decisions would be transmitted to the Committee of Ministers of the Council of Europe, with which would rest responsibility for further action. This plan, then, to recapitulate, proposed for the first time the institution of an international remedy for the individual whose rights were infringed by a sovereign State: he would, in his individual capacity, have a direct recourse to an international organ (the Commission) and, though he could not himself appeal to the European Court, a State could be made answerable before the Court if the individual's case were championed by the Commission or by another signatory State. As an alternative remedy, a member State might, if it preferred, submit the case to the International Court of Justice.

Under the Statute of the Council of Europe the Consultative Assembly is a deliberative organ which has no powers of decision but makes recommendations to the Committee of Ministers; the latter, as the executive organ of the Council, then acts on them as it thinks fit.[21] Accordingly the Assembly's *Recommendation 38* was submitted to the member governments of the Council of Europe.[22] The Ministers at their meeting in November 1949 decided to appoint a committee of governmental experts to prepare a draft Convention, 'due attention being paid to the progress achieved in this matter by the competent organs of the United Nations'. The committee thus appointed met in Strasbourg in February and March 1950 under the chairmanship of M. de la Vallée Poussin (a Belgian senator and member of the Consultative Assembly) and prepared a draft Convention, taking as the basis of its work the proposals made by the Assembly. It made considerable progress and had no difficulty in accepting the list of rights proposed by the Assembly, with some rearrangement,[23] but was unable to reach agreement on certain questions (such as the problem whether the rights to be protected should be merely enumerated or defined in detail) and did not attempt to reach agreement on others (including the right of individual petition and the creation of a European Court) which it considered to be of a political rather than of a legal character; it therefore submitted to the Committee of Ministers a report containing a number of alternative texts.[24]

The Ministers considered this report in April 1950 and decided to convene a meeting of senior officials to take the political decisions necessitated by the report of the Committee of Experts. The 'Conference of Senior Officials' met in June 1950, under the chairmanship of Mr Sture Petrén, Legal Adviser in the Swedish Foreign Office (and later President of the Commission of Human Rights and judge both on the European Court of Human Rights and on the International Court of Justice). It prepared a draft Convention incorporating the greater part of the texts submitted by the Experts. The conference accepted the view that the rights to be protected should be defined in detail and not merely enumerated in the Convention; in the majority of cases the definitions followed closely those already worked out by the Commission on Human Rights of the United Nations in preparing the early drafts of the Covenants. The decision to establish detailed definitions of the rights to be protected was indeed a wise one, because otherwise it would have been difficult for governments to know whether or not their internal law was in conformity with the Convention and impossible for the Commission and the Court to answer the same question. As regards the creation of a European Court, the Senior Officials took a positive view, subject to the rider that its jurisdiction should apply only to States which expressly accepted that jurisdiction in a separate declaration, and that the Court would be established only when nine States had done so. When it came to the Assembly's proposal for a right of individual petition to the Commission of Human Rights, opinions were sharply divided between those delegations which considered that this procedure was essential if the protection accorded by the Convention was to be effective and other delegations which took the view that this would be a revolutionary development in international law whose acceptance would be dangerous for States and whose utilisation could be easily abused to their detriment. A decision on this point was therefore referred to the Ministers themselves.

At the request of the Assembly the report of the Conference of Senior Officials was communicated to the Assembly's Committee on Legal and Administrative Questions, whose comments were submitted to the Committee of Ministers at the same time as the report itself. On behalf of his committee Sir David Maxwell Fyfe urgently requested that the right to free elections should be re-inserted in the draft Convention; he reminded the Ministers that his committee was continuing to study the right to own property and the right of parents to choose the kind of education to be given to their children; and he emphasised the importance which the committee attached to the right of individual petition, which he preferred to describe as 'the right of individuals to seek a remedy directly'.[25]

The Committee of Ministers, during the fifth session in August 1950, considered the report of the Senior Officials, together with the comments thereon of the Assembly's Legal Committee. On 7 August they adopted a revised text of the draft Convention; they accepted without difficulty the definition of the rights proposed by the Senior Officials and the proposal to create a Court of Human Rights with optional jurisdiction. Before the insistence of the Assembly on the inclusion of the right of individual petition, they achieved a compromise similar to that already accepted for the Court, that is to say that the competence of the Commission to examine individual petitions should be established in the Convention, but that it should apply only in relation to States which expressly accepted that competence in a separate declaration.

The new draft of 7 August 1950 was then submitted to the Assembly at its second session, held during the same month, and again considered by the Committee on Legal and Administrative Questions, whose report was approved by the Assembly on 25 August 1950.[26] On this occasion the parliamentary organ of the Council of Europe substantially accepted the Ministers' draft, but made several suggestions to improve it. The first of these was for the insertion in the Convention of a Preamble, a draft for which was prepared by Mr G. R. Mitchison, MP; the second was that the Court of Human Rights should be established when eight Contracting Parties had accepted its jurisdiction as compulsory (instead of nine); thirdly, the Assembly proposed an amendment of the 'colonial clause' (Article 63), which permits a metropolitan country to extend the application of the Convention to its overseas territories;[27] finally the Assembly called for the addition of three further articles to protect the three other rights which it had discussed the year before but which had not been included: the right of property, the right of parents to choose the kind of education to be given to their children, and the right to free elections.

These proposals were considered by the Committee of Ministers at its sixth session in Rome in November of the same year. Once more a number of the Ministers brought with them their legal advisers, who reviewed the amendments proposed by the Assembly and undertook a final revision of the text.[28] They added a Preamble to the Convention based on the Assembly's draft and agreed to reduce from nine to eight the number of acceptances of the compulsory jurisdiction of the Court which would be required before the Court was set up; but they were unable to reach agreement on accepting the majority of the amendments proposed, with the result that the Convention was finally signed on 4 November 1950 substantially in the form which had been approved by the Ministers in August.[29]

Later in the same month Count Sforza, the chairman of the committee of Ministers, came to Strasbourg to present a report on the results achieved by the Committee of Ministers since the adjournment of the Assembly's session in August.[30] He had little to report except the signature of the Convention on Human Rights. Even the satisfaction recorded by the parliamentarians on that achievement was tempered by disappointment – even strong criticism – at the fact that the Ministers had not accepted the Assembly's proposal to add to the earlier draft the three additional rights of property, of education and of free elections.[31] However, Lord Layton felt able to state that 'in spite of its defects ... I regard the Convention, watered down as it is, as a most important landmark in European history'.[32]

The criticism of the Committee of Ministers as regards the failure to include the three additional rights was rather exaggerated. The Ministers had not rejected the proposal; but they required more time to study it. Indeed, it was obvious that any clause designed to guarantee the individual's enjoyment of his possessions and protect them from confiscation would be unacceptable to socialist governments unless it was made quite clear that this would not prevent the State from nationalising private property. At the same time it was a matter of some delicacy to draft a clause which would permit a democratic socialist government to nationalise private property 'in accordance with the general interest' but would not allow a totalitarian government to confiscate private property in acordance with a policy which it claimed to be in the general interest but which democratic countries would regard as unacceptable.

The right to education trod on equally delicate ground. The

Assembly proposed recognition of the right of parents to choose the kind of education to be given to their children. In modern society, where the education of children is primarily the function of the State, recognition of the right of parents to choose the education to be given to their children might be held to involve as a corollary the duty of the State to furnish education in accordance with the individual convictions of its nationals. How far is this duty to be carried? Must schools of all denominations be provided in every village? If not, where is the line to be drawn? These questions immediately evoked in certain Continental countries the long and bitter dispute between Church and State over education and the support of Church schools.

The text on free elections also raised difficulties. Clearly all member States of the Council of Europe are by definition advocates of political liberties and free elections. This was established beyond doubt in the Statute of the Council of Europe, which reaffirmed their 'devotion to the spiritual and moral values which are the common heritage of their peoples and the true source of individual freedom, political liberty and the rule of law, principles which form the basis of all genuine democracy'. Again, under Article 3 of the Statute 'every Member of the Council of Europe must accept the principle of the rule of law and of the enjoyment by all persons within its jurisdiction of human rights and fundamental freedoms'. It is, however, quite a different question to draft a short paragraph which contains a legal guarantee of the right to free elections.

It was in the light of these difficulties that the Committee of Ministers, when it came to consider the proposals of the Assembly on the three rights of property, education and free elections as part of a heavy agenda at their two-day session in Rome in November 1950, decided to refer them for further study to their legal experts. They were then faced with the choice of deferring signature of the Convention until these proposals had been more carefully examined or, on the other hand, of signing the Convention without them. In view of the extended negotiations which had already been necessary to produce the text of the Convention as it then was, there was unanimous agreement among the Foreign Ministers that it was preferable to sign it immediately without these additional articles and to conclude a protocol at a later date, if agreement thereon proved possible.

In fact a series of meetings of the legal experts took place during the year 1951, and the Assembly's Legal Committee was consulted on two occasions in August and November about the drafts which had been prepared.[33] The First Protocol to the Convention covering the three further rights of property, education and free elections was duly concluded and signed on 22 March 1952.[34]

The history of the Convention and of the First Protocol has been described at some length, partly because a knowledge of its origins is useful to an understanding of its contents and partly because there was developed on this occasion a new technique in the drafting of treaties which resulted from the dual nature of the Council of Europe. It was the parliamentary organ of the Council, the Consultative Assembly, which proposed the conclusion of the Convention and it was the governmental organ, the Committee of Ministers, which acted on that proposal. Each organ was assisted by a specialised committee which was responsible for the detailed work (the Ministers, in fact, by two) and a dialogue was established between them, as we have seen, the aim of which was to co-ordinate the views of the two sides and produce a final text which would be acceptable both to the governments and to the parliaments. We shall have occasion to return to this subject at a later stage;[35] for the moment it is sufficient to record that the Council of Europe's technique of convention-making has been one of its more successful achievements and has resulted in the conclusion of over eighty conventions and agreements during the first twenty-five years of the organisation's existence.[36]

The necessity for the governments to consult, and take account of the views of, the Consultative Assembly and its Committee on Legal and Administrative Questions protracted the negotiations somewhat, but brought into play a more liberal and more European parliamentary point of view than is commonly found among government officials. It is doubtful whether the right of individual petition to the European Commission of Human Rights, which is often described as the 'cornerstone' of the Convention, would ever have been included had it not been for the insistence of the Consultative Assembly. And if the negotiations seemed slow and protracted at the time, continuing as they did from August 1949 to November 1950, that period of fifteen months seems in retrospect astonishingly short when it is compared with the period of gestation of eighteen years (from 1948 to 1966) that was required to give birth to the United Nations Covenants.

The first ratification of the Convention was that of the United Kingdom, which was deposited on 8 March 1951; its ratification of the First Protocol followed on 3 November 1952. In other countries, where positive action by the parliament was a prerequisite to ratification, the procedure was inevitably slower; three further ratifications were received in the course of 1952 (Norway, Sweden and the Federal Republic of Germany) and the Convention entered into force on 3 September 1953, when the necessary ten instruments of ratification had been deposited. By the end of 1974 the Convention had been ratified by eighteen States, that is to say by all members of the Council of Europe.[37]

The First Protocol entered into force on 18 May 1954, when the tenth instrument of ratification was deposited. By the end of 1974 it had been ratified by the same eighteen States as the Convention.[38]

Once the Convention and the First Protocol had entered into force the next task was to secure the acceptance of the optional provisions: the right of individual petition to the Commission and the compulsory jurisdiction of the Court.

Sweden was the first country to accept the right of individual petition, on 4 February 1952, followed by Ireland and Denmark a year later. Six acceptances were necessary for this procedure to become operative, but there was some delay. The Consultative Assembly then adopted its *Recommendation 52* in September 1953 urging all member States to ratify the Convention and the First Protocol and to make the various optional declarations. Iceland accepted the right of individual petition in March 1955, followed by the Federal Republic of Germany and Belgium four months later. The Commission was then competent to receive individual applications directed against the six States which had accepted this procedure.

Gradually other countries followed suit: Norway (1957), Luxembourg (1958), Austria (1958), the Netherlands (1960), the United Kingdom (1966), Italy (1973) and Switzerland (1974), so that by December 1974 all Contracting Parties had accepted this procedure except Cyprus, France, Greece, Malta and Turkey.

The acceptance of the compulsory jurisdiction of the Court took longer, which was all the more important in that the Court could not be established until eight Contracting Parties had accepted its jurisdiction as compulsory. Ireland led the way in February 1953, followed by Denmark two months later and by the Netherlands in August 1954. It took until September 1958 to obtain eight acceptances,[39] and the Court was then constituted in January 1959. By 1974 its jurisdiction had been accepted as compulsory by fourteen of the eighteen Contracting Parties.[40]

3. THE SECOND TO FIFTH PROTOCOLS AND THE AGREEMENT OF 1969

The next development after the conclusion of the First Protocol to the Convention related to 'the generalisation of social democracy', or, in other words, to what are usually called 'economic and social rights'. In 1954 the Committee of Ministers informed the Assembly of its decision to tackle this problem:

> Our Committee will endeavour to elaborate a European Social Charter which would define the social objectives aimed at by Members and would guide the policy of the Council in the social field, in which it would be complementary to the European Convention on Human Rights and Fundamental Freedoms.

Owing to the complexity of the issues involved and to the different levels of economic and social progress in the member States, which made agreement on common standards all the harder, the negotiations were more difficult and progress was slower than with the Convention on Human Rights. But on 18 October 1961 the European Social Charter was signed in Turin. It lists nineteen economic and social rights and principles which the Contracting Parties 'accept as the aim of their policy, to be pursued by all appropriate means, both national and international in character . . .'; while Part II of the Charter contains more precise commitments which the Contracting Parties assume with a view to ensuring the effective exercise of these rights. The Charter also institutes an elaborate system of international control, based on the submission of reports by governments and the examination of these reports by a Committee of Independent Experts, by the governmental Social Committee, by the Consultative Assembly and finally by the Committee of Ministers of the Council of Europe.[41]

While the negotiations for the Social Charter were still continuing the Assembly and its Legal Committee turned their attention once more to civil and political rights. This was the more natural because the Preamble to the Convention stated that the Contracting Parties were resolved 'to take the first steps for the collective enforcement of certain of the Rights stated in Universal Declaration'. It was therefore only appropriate that further steps should be taken, when circumstances permitted, for the enforcement of other rights.

In 1959 the Legal Committee presented a report to the Assembly (Document 1057) which proposed the conclusion of a second protocol to the Convention to guarantee a number of additional rights not already included in the Convention itself and its First

Protocol. As the result of the adopted of *Recommendation 234* (*1960*) the Committee of Ministers appointed a Committee of Experts on Human Rights with a wide mandate of studying problems relating to the European Convention. This committee, meeting under the chairmanship of M. Ugo Caldarera (Italy), undertook the necessary drafting work, and the result was the Fourth Protocol, signed on 16 September 1963. (It had been overtaken, in the meantime, by two others.) It protects four additional rights and freedoms: freedom from imprisonment for civil debt; freedom of movement and choice of residence; the right to enter one's own country and freedom from expulsion therefrom; prohibition of the collective expulsion of aliens.[42] The Fourth Protocol entered into force on 2 May 1968, and by the end of June 1975 had been ratified by ten member States.[43]

When the European Court of Human Rights was established in 1959, after eight States had recognised its jurisdiction as compulsory, this event led the Legal Committee to consider whether further steps could be taken to make use of this new judicial body and enhance its standing. One means of doing so which the committee proposed was to confer on the Court a further power not given to it by the Convention but possessed by the International Court of Justice at The Hague and the Court of Justice of the Communities, that is to say competence to give advisory opinions. In November 1959 the committee submitted to the Assembly a report on this subject (Document 1061) which led to the adoption of *Recommendation 232 (1960)* and to the drafting of another instrument, which became the Second Protocol when it was signed on 6 May 1963.[44] In passing we may note that this protocol was so narrowly conceived by the Committee of Experts that it is hard to imagine the circumstances in which the competence to give advisory opinions could be exercised. We will, however, return to this question in a later chapter.[45]

The Third Protocol to the Convention was also concluded in 1963. Its origin was a proposal of the European Commission of Human Rights, and it relates to the procedure of that body. Article 29 of the Convention, as drafted in 1950, provided that the functions of establishing the facts in any particular case and of attempting to reach a friendly settlement should be discharged by a sub-commission of seven members; but subsequently, if no friendly settlement is reached, the Commission as a whole is required to draw up a report setting out the facts and expressing an opinion on the question of violation (Article 31). The Commission had found this 'two-tier' system inconvenient and time-wasting, and proposed that all these functions should be discharged by the Commission in plenary session. The Third Protocol therefore abolished the system of sub-commissions.[46]

The Fifth Protocol to the Convention was concluded three years later, in 1966. It related to the question of the election of members of the Commission and the Court. The Convention provides in its Articles 22 and 40 for the partial renewal of each body every three years. However, experience had shown that the admission of new member States of the Council of Europe and the deposit of new instruments of ratification had necessitated the holding of other elections at other times not coincidental with the triennial system. This situation, indeed, had been foreseen by the Legal Experts who met in Rome on the eve of signature of the Convention.[47] The purpose of the Fifth Protocol is to bring these 'occasional' elections into the triennial rhythm established by Articles 22 and 40 of the Convention.[48]

The last instrument to be mentioned in this connection is not a protocol to the Convention but the *Agreement relating to Persons participating in Proceedings of the European Commission and Court of Human Rights*, concluded on 6 May 1969. Its preparation took nearly ten years, which may seem surprising having regard to its fairly modest content. Its interest lies in the fact that it attempts to deal for the first time on a conventional basis with certain problems largely untouched previously under international law: it is concerned with the facilities and immunities to be granted to those who take part in the proceedings of the Commission and the Court; its novelty lies in the fact that, by reason of the nature of those proceedings, the participants include a much greater variety of persons (including, on occasion, convicted criminals) who may find themselves in a greater variety of circumstances (including detention) than those concerned in the proceedings of other international courts. It was no doubt for this reason that the negotiations were so protracted.[49]

After the Court of Human Rights was established in 1959 its first task was to work out its Rules of Procedure. When engaged on this work the judges quickly realised that no national or international court can fulfil its functions properly unless persons summoned to appear before it can do so freely, under its authority alone and without the interference of any extra-judicial authority. In the case of national courts this is secured by appropriate national legislation. In the case of international courts there are already certain conventional provisions: as regards the International Court of Justice, the agents, counsel and advocates of the parties – as well as witnesses and experts – enjoy the necessary immunities and facilities by virtue of a resolution of the General Assembly and an exchange of letters between the President of the Court and the Foreign Minister of the Netherlands.[50] Similar immunities and facilities are accorded to persons summoned to appear before the Court of Justice of the European Communities under the Protocol of 17 April 1957 and the Rules of Procedure of the Court of 11 November 1959.[51]

It was clearly desirable that similar provision should be made for persons summoned to appear before the European Court of Human Rights; the same considerations made it desirable that these provisions should also apply to persons appearing before the Commission. Indeed, the latter need was greater than the former, not only on account of the much greater volume of cases handled by the Commission but also by reason of the fact that, of necessity, the hearing of witnesses and experts occurs more frequently during the Commission's proceedings than during the hearings of the Court.

Since this was a matter which concerned both organs, the Commission and the Court set up a joint working party to study the problem and make suitable proposals. The result was the preparation in March 1960 of a first draft for a text designed to confer certain privileges and immunities on agents, advocates, advisers and other persons taking part in cases brought before the European Commission and Court of Human Rights.

There were, of course, already texts conferring privileges and immunities on the members of the Commission and the Court.[52] The working party which met in 1960 therefore proposed the conclusion of a further protocol to the General Agreement on Privileges and Immunities of the Council of Europe which would relate to persons participating in proceedings of the Commission and the Court. The draft thus elaborated was discussed by the two parent bodies and revised on several occasions. In August 1962 it was submitted by the Secretary General to the Committee of Ministers with a request that the governments should approve this text and proceed to its signature and ratification.

This event was interesting in itself as constituting an attempt to produce an international treaty by a quite new procedure. The normal practice of the Council of Europe – as indeed of other international organisation – is that conventions and agreements are drafted by representatives of governments who meet together in the framework of the appropriate committee of the organisation concerned; they then proceed to discuss, to draft and to negotiate, each member of the committee acting on behalf of, and with the instructions of, his government. The preparation of a draft by the Commission and the Court marked a new departure, because the members of these bodies sit in complete independence and are in no way representatives of governments. This is perhaps the reason why the first stage of the negotiations was not successful. The draft submitted to the Committee of Ministers formed the subject of discussion during the following months; amendments were proposed by a number of governments; further consultations of the Commission and the Court took place; but a satisfactory text was not achieved in this way, and in April 1963 the whole matter was referred to the Committee of Experts on Human Rights.

The Experts had just finished drafting the Second and Third Protocols to the Convention and had nearly completed their work on the Fourth Protocol. In 1964 and 1965 they worked on the Fifth Protocol and thereafter turned their attention to the problem under discussion, meeting under the chairmanship of Sir Samuel Hoare (United Kingdom). They decided that the new instrument should not be conceived as a protocol to the Agreement on Privileges and Immunities of the Council of Europe, on the ground that that form is appropriate for persons (such as permanent representatives, members of the Commission and the judges) who enjoy a continuing status and have diplomatic or similar functions, but that it was not the proper form for dealing with persons whose functions in relation to the Commission and the Court are of a transitory nature. Moreover, they were opposed to the idea of conferring 'privileges' on such persons; all that was required was to grant them the 'facilities' necessary for the proper conduct of the proceedings. It was therefore decided to conclude a new and independent agreement and not a protocol to an existing text.

The Committee of Experts reported their conclusions to the Committee of Ministers in November 1967. After some minor revisions during the following year the 'Agreement relating to persons participating in proceedings of the European Commission and Court of Human Rights' was signed on 6 May 1969. Its provisions are discussed below.[53]

NOTES

1 For some reflections on the history of human rights see A. H. Robertson, *Human Rights in the World*, Manchester, 1972, pp. 1–14.
2 The treaties for the protection of minorities concluded after the First World

War related to the rights of special groups, but not to human rights in general, though the German–Polish Convention on Upper Silesia, 1922, did contain a provision (Article 4) for the international protection of the rights of the individual even against the State of which he was a national. *Cf. Human Rights in the World*, pp. 20–2; C. A. Macartney, 'League of Nations' protection of minority rights', in *The International Protection of Human Rights*, ed. Luard, London, 1967, pp. 22–37.

3 *Cf.* President Truman's closing speech to the San Francisco conference, in which he said: 'Under this document [the Charter] we have good reason to expect an international Bill of Rights acceptable to all the nations involved. That Bill of Rights will be as much a part of international life as our own Bill of Rights is part of our Constitution. The Charter is dedicated to the achievement and observance of fundamental freedoms. Unless we can attain those objectives for all men and women everywhere – without regard to race, language or religion – we cannot have permanent peace and security in the world.'

On the inclusion in the Charter of provisions relating to human rights see John P. Humphrey, 'The UN Charter and the Universal Declaration of Human Rights', in *The International Protection of Human Rights* (note 2), pp. 39–58, and references given in n. 4.

4 There is an immense literature about the human rights provision of the Charter, among which may be mentioned H. Lauterpacht, *International Law and Human Rights*, London, 1950, pp. 145–65; Hans Kelsen, *The Law of the United Nations*, pp. 27–50; John P. Humphrey, *op. cit.*, n. 3; Egon Schwelb, *Human Rights and the International Community*; Louis B. Sohn, 'A short history of United Nations documents on human rights', in *The United Nations and Human Rights*, New York, 1968. See also Sohn and Buergenthal, *International Protection of Human Rights*, New York, 1973; and *Human Rights in the World*, pp. 23–8.

5 Consultative Assembly, *Official Reports*, August 1949, p. 1158.

6 See A. H. Robertson, *The Council of Europe*, second edition, 1961, pp. 1–9.

7 Austria twelve, Belgium eighteen, Britain 140, Denmark thirty-two, Ireland five, France 185, Germany fifty-one, Greece eighteen, Italy fifty-seven, Liechtenstein three, Luxembourg eight, the Netherlands fifty-nine, Norway twelve, Saar five, Sweden nineteen, Switzerland thirty-nine.

8 Bulgaria, Canada, Czechoslovakia, Finland, Hungary, Poland, Roumania, Spain, the USA and Yugoslavia.

9 *The European Movement and the Council of Europe*, 1949, p. 114. The draft Convention worked out by the European Movement is to be found therein at pp. 115–19, and the draft Statute for the Court at pp. 184–98. They may also be found in *European Convention on Human Rights: Collected Edition of the 'Travaux Préparatoires'*, The Hague, Vol. I, 1975, pp. 296 and 302.

10 The words quoted are from the speech of the Belgian delegate on the occasion of the adoption of the Declaration (A/PV 181, p. 47).

11 H. Lauterpacht, 'The Universal Declaration of Human Rights', *British Yearbook of International Law*, 25, 1948, p. 354. With the passage of time the Declaration has acquired greatly increased authority by virtue of its reaffirmation by the General Assembly on several occasions, its incorporation by reference into national constitutions and otherwise. Some authors now consider it as a statement of customary international law. See *Human Rights in the World*, pp. 27–8.

12 The drafting history is summarised in *Human Rights in the World*, Chapter II, pp. 23–32. See also the references given in n. 4 above and R. Cassin, 'La Déclaration Universelle et la mise en oeuvre des droits de l'homme', *Recueil des Cours de l'Académie de Droit International*, 1951, pp. 241–367.

13 Consultative Assembly, *Minutes of Proceedings of the Second Sitting*, 11 August 1949, Appendix I.

14 Consultative Assembly, *Minutes of Proceedings of the Fourth Sitting*,

13 August 1949, Appendix I.

15 Consultative Assembly, *Official Report* of 17 August 1949, *Debates of the Assembly*, 1949, Vol. I, p. 284.

16 Consultative Assembly, *Minutes of Proceedings of the Fifth Sitting*, 16 August 1949, Appendices II and III.

17 Motion of M. Teitgen, Sir David Maxwell Fyfe and others, *Documents of the Assembly*, 1949, Document 3.

18 *Documents of the Assembly*, 1949, Document 77.

19 *Texts adopted by the Assembly*, 1949, p. 49. The recommendation was adopted by sixty-four votes to one, with twenty-one abstentions.

20 Consultative Assembly, Official Report of 7 September 1949, p. 127; *Documents of the Assembly*, Document 77, paras 4–5.

21 The functions and powers of the Assembly and of the Committee of Ministers are explained in A. H. Robertson, *The Council of Europe*, second edition, 1961, Chapters 3 and 4.

22 Recommendation 38, *Texts adopted by the Assembly*, 1949, p. 49.

23 The committee did not include in its draft, however, the undertaking to hold free elections at reasonable intervals with universal suffrage and secret ballot – nor the two rights (education and property) which had been referred back to the Committee on Legal and Administrative Questions for further consideration.

24 In accordance with the general practice of the Council of Europe the documents and reports of governmental committees are considered confidential and are therefore not available to the general public. This rule has applied for many years to the work of the Committee of Experts and of the Conference of Senior Officials which drafted the Convention on Human Rights in 1950. The present author was, however, authorised to publish a brief summary of the negotiations, which appeared in the *British Yearbook of International Law*, 1950, pp. 145–63, and 1951, pp. 359–65.

A collected edition of the *travaux préparatoires* was prepared in 1963 but remained confidential. In 1966 the Committee of Ministers was asked to authorise the publication of the *travaux préparatoires*, and the matter was referred to the Committee of Experts on Human Rights (*Yearbook of the Convention*, Vol. IX, 1966, p. 72). In 1972, on the proposal of the Committee of Experts, the Ministers agreed that the *travaux préparatoires* should be published. At the time of writing they are in the press; the first volume appeared in the spring of 1975.

25 *Documents of the Assembly*, 1950, Document 6, Appendix 5.

26 Recommendation 24, Texts adopted, 1950, p.33

27 The amendment, proposed by M. Léopold Senghor (then a member of the French National Assembly and later President of Senegal), was designed to secure that the Convention should apply automatically to the overseas territories without the need for a separate declaration to that effect.

28 The 'final revision of the text' undertaken in Rome on the eve of the signature of the Convention led to the insertion of two new paragraphs relating to the election of judges in the event of the admission of new members of the Council of Europe (Article 39, para. 2) and to the duration of the term of office of a judge elected to replace a judge whose term of office has not expired (Article 40, para. 3). On 11 November 1950 the present author wrote a note recording some of the points discussed by the legal advisers in Rome on 3 November 1950; it is reproduced in *La Protection internationale des droits de l'homme dans le cadre européen*, Paris, 1961, pp. 362–7.

The final revision of the text also related to certain points of translation and was designed to secure a better concordance of the English and French texts of the Convention. The greater part (though by no means all) of the drafting work had been done in French, and in many cases the English text had been subsequently modified to bring it into conformity with the French text. Anyone with experience of the drafting of treaties in more than one language will readily understand the difficulties involved in establishing a perfect concordance. In September 1950 the present author was given the task of revising the English text in order to improve the concordance with the French text, and made a number of suggestions for this purpose. They were communicated to the British Foreign Office in the first place and then submitted to the Legal Advisers in Rome. (They will be included in the published edition of the *travaux préparatoires* – see n. 24 *supra*.) The most important suggestion related to the English text of Article 6 ('in the determination of his civil rights and obligations'), which is discussed in Chapter II, at p. 68–72. Some examples of imperfect concordance between the two texts remain, however. It was suggested at the time that another meeting of experts should be held in order to improve further the concordance of the two texts, but this suggestion was rejected on account of the time that would be taken and of the political necessity to complete the work on the Convention during the course of 1950. Indeed, the conclusion of the Convention on Human Rights was practically the only positive achievement of the Committee of Ministers of the Council of Europe during the first eighteen months of the existence of the organisation, and it was considered imperative to complete it without delay.

29 The text of the Convention is given in Appendix 1.

30 Debate of 18 November 1950, *Official Reports*, 1950, Part III, pp. 674–5.

31 See particularly the speech of M. P.-H. Teitgen, *ibid.*, pp. 680–1.

32 *Ibid.*, p. 696.

33 The negotiations are summarised in A. H. Robertson, 'The European Convention on Human Rights – recent developments', *British Yearbook of International Law*, 1951, pp. 359–65.

34 The First Protocol is reproduced in Appendix 2. The rights contained in the Protocol are discussed below in Chapter III, section 3.

35 See below, Chapter VIII.

36 Two volumes entitled *European Conventions and Agreements* were published by the Council of Europe in 1971–2; they contain seventy-two of these texts. See also *Manual of the Council of Europe*, London, 1970, Chapter XIII and Appendix II. The texts of the various conventions and agreements are also, for the most part, published in the successive volumes of the *European Yearbook* (annual since 1953).

37 The dates of ratification are given after the text of the Convention in Appendix 1. The ratification by France was deposited on 3 May 1974 after discussions which had continued over a period of twenty years and included a number of debates in the National Assembly and the Senate. *Yearbook of the Convention*, Vol. III, 1960, p. 528; Vol. VII, 1964, p. 446; Vol. XIV, 1971, p. 910; Vol. XV, 1972, p. 718. A colloquy in Besançon in November 1970 was devoted entirely to this subject; its proceedings are reported in *Human Rights Journal*, 1970, No. 4.

38 The dates of ratification are given after the text of the First Procol in Appendix 2.

39 Other acceptances of the compulsory jurisdiction of the Court were by Belgium and the Federal Republic in July 1955 and by Luxembourg, Austria and Iceland in 1958.

40 The other acceptances were by Norway (1964), Sweden (1966), the United Kingdom (1966), Italy (1973), France (1974) and Switzerland (1974).

41 The drafting of the Social Charter and its provisions are described more fully in the first edition of this book, Chapter VIII, pp. 140–50. The text of the Social Charter may be found *ibid.*, Appendix 6; also in the *European Yearbook*, Vol. IX, 1961, pp. 247–77, and in *European Conventions and Agreements*, Vol. I, 1971, p. 338.

42 The text of the Fourth Protocol is given in Appendix 4. The explanatory reports of the Committee of Experts on Human Rights which drafted the Second, Third, Fourth and Fifth Protocols are published in a separate volume

by the Directorate of Human Rights (1971) and contain fuller information about their history and their contents.

43 Austria, Belgium, Denmark, France, the Federal Republic of Germany, Iceland, Ireland, Luxembourg, Norway and Sweden.

44 The text is given in Appendix 3. By 1974 the Second Protocol had been ratified by all Contracting Parties except France. See also n. 42 above.

45 See Chapter V, section 5.

46 The amendments to Articles 29, 30 and 34 are incorporated in the text of the convention given in Appendix 1. By 1974 the Third Protocol had been ratified by all Contracting Parties. It also contains a provision permitting the Commission, in certain circumstances, to reject a petition even after it has been declared admissible. This is discussed below in Chapter IV. See also n. 42.

47 See n. 28 above.

48 The amendments to Articles 22 and 40 are incorporated in the text of the Convention given in Appendix 1. By 1974 it had been ratified by all Contracting Parties to the Convention. See also n. 42.

49 The history and content of the Agreement of 1969 are explained more fully in an article on the same subject by the present author published in *Miscellanea in honour of W. J. Ganshof van der Meersch*, Brussels, 1972, Vol. I, p. 545, from which the present text is an extract.

50 'Acts and documents relating to the organisation of the International Court of Justice', Series D, pp. 84–90.

51 *Official Gazette* of the European Communities, 1959, pp. 349–78, and also 1960, pp. 13–17.

52 Second and Fourth Protocols to the General Agreement on Privileges and Immunities of the Council of Europe of 15 December 1956 and 16 December 1961, *Yearbook of the Convention*, Vol. I, 1955–57, p. 86, and Vol. IV, 1961, p. 16.

53 The text of the Agreement is given in the *Yearbook of the Convention*, Vol. XII, p. 2. By June 1975 it had been ratified by all Contracting Parties to the Convention except Austria, Denmark, France, the Federal Republic, Greece, Iceland, Italy and Turkey. Its substantive provisions are discussed below in Chapter IV, section 4.

CHAPTER II

THE RIGHTS GUARANTEED I

ARTICLE 1. THE GENERAL OBLIGATION

Article 1 of the Convention reads as follows:

> The High Contracting Parties shall secure to everyone within their juridiction the rights and freedoms defined in Section I of this Convention.

Though this article consists of only three lines, it raises three important questions of principle, which will now be considered separately.

(a) THE RELATIONSHIP BETWEEN THE EUROPEAN CONVENTION AND INTERNAL LAW. The first thing to be noted about Article 1 is that it contains an immediate obligation on the Contracting Parties to secure the rights and freedoms guaranteed, and not merely an undertaking to do so at some future date, possibly after the amendment of their law.

The earlier drafts of the Convention used the expression, common in international treaties, 'The High Contracting Parties undertake to secure . . .' But on 24 June 1950 the late Professor Henri Rolin (then vice-chairman of the Assembly's Committee on Legal and Administrative Questions and later President of the European Court of Human Rights) proposed an amendment, which was accepted by the committee, to delete the words 'undertake to secure' and substitute 'shall secure'. (The sense of the amendment is even clearer in the French text. Previously it had read: 'Les Hautes Parties Contractantes s'engagent à reconnaître . . .'. As amended it read: 'Les Hautes Parties Contractantes *reconnaissent* . . . les droits et libertés définis . . .'.) This amendment was accepted by the Committee of Ministers on 7 August 1950, and the amended text remained unchanged in the Convention as signed.

Subsequently M. Rolin explained his amendment as follows:[1]

> By virtue of the first Article, for instance — and this at the suggestion of our own Committee — the countries do not 'undertake to recognise' these rights in their laws. They have already recognised them. That

is the big difference. Once this Convention has been approved by our Parliaments, and ratified, our Courts of Law will be fully within their rights, without waiting for any further legislation, in implementing the terms of this Convention.

Though the issue raised here is perhaps more familiar to Continental than to common lawyers, it will be seen that it concerns the relationship between a treaty and internal law.[2]

It is generally agreed that there are two well established principles or rules relevant to the matter under consideration. The first of these is that a State which is a party to a treaty is under an obligation to ensure that its national law conforms to its international obligations. Thus the Permanent Court of International Justice in 1925 restated 'a principle which is self-evident, according to which a State which has contracted valid international obligations is bound to make in its legislation such modifications as may be necessary to ensure the fulfilment of the obligations undertaken'.[3] This principle is indeed 'self-evident'; otherwise the conclusion of treaties would be without effect and the basic principle of international law, *pacta sunt servanda,* would be rendered nugatory. The principle applies, moreover, not only to legislation in the narrower sense of the term but also to national law in its widest connotation; a State cannot invoke the provisions of its constitution with a view to evading its treaty obligations.[4]

But if the duty to bring municipal law into line with treaty obligations is clear, international law is silent as regards the means by which this object is to be achieved. Individual States are free to secure the conformity of their municipal law with their international obligations in the way which seems to them most appropriate; international law does not enjoin any particular method of doing so. The method of securing such conformity is a matter within the domain of national sovereignty; normally it depends on the constitutional provisions and practice of each State.

In fact national practice varies considerably in this respect. In some countries the treaty itself has no effect on municipal law unless the legislature passes a law for the purpose. This is the case in the United Kingdom, Ireland and the Scandinavian countries. The doctrine was clearly stated by the Supreme Court of Ireland in the case of *The State (Lawless)* v. *O'Sullivan and the Minister for Justice.* The appellant claimed that his detention by order of the Minister for Justice, even if legal under domestic law, was illegal as contrary to the provisions of the Convention on Human Rights. The Supreme Court said in its judgement:[5]

The insuperable obstacle to importing the provisions of the Convention for the Protection of Human Rights and Fundamental Freedoms into the domestic law of Ireland – if they be at variance with the law – is however the terms of the Constitution of Ireland. By Article 15(2)(1) of the Constitution it is provided that the sole and exclusive power of making laws for the State is hereby vested in the Oireachtas; no other legislative authority has power to make laws for the State'. Moreover, Article 29, the Article dealing with international relations, provides at Section 6 that 'no international agreement shall be part of the domestic law of the State save as may be determined by the Oireachtas.

The Oireachtas has not determined that the Convention on Human Rights and Fundamental Freedoms is to be part of the domestic law of the State, and accordingly this Court cannot give effect to the Convention if it be contrary to domestic law or purports to grant rights or impose obligations additional to those of domestic law.

No argument can prevail against the express command of Section 6 of Article 29 of the Constitution before judges whose declared duty it is to uphold the Constitution and the laws.

In the countries which follow this system it is necessary, in order to comply with the international obligations of the State, for the legislature to adopt a new law to give effect to the treaty – unless it is satisfied that its domestic law is already in conformity therewith. Normally the question whether this is so will be considered at the time when the legislature authorises ratification. If it does approve the treaty and adopt the necessary implementing legislation, then the rules of domestic law will, as a result, correspond to the rules laid down in the treaty; but the rules binding on domestic courts will derive their force of law from the act of the legislature and not directly from the treaty itself. The international rules will have been transformed or converted by a specific act into national rules; this is known as the method of 'special transformation' or 'special conversion'.

Quite a different method is followed by the Romanist systems of law, according to which – though with certain variations – the treaty, once it is duly ratified, is directly binding in national law. Publication in the official gazette is usually a necessary prerequisite. When this method is followed it is usually as the result of constitutional provisions to that effect; the terms of the treaty may then be cited before, and applied by, the national judge, without any implementing legislation being required. The legal systems which adopt this method are sometimes said to provide for the 'general transformation' or 'general conversion' of international rules into national rules;[6] it may, however, be questioned whether the term 'transformation' is the most appropriate, since the fundamental notion is that the international rules are not changed or modified but are directly binding in national law without the need for implementing legislation. In these circumstances 'incorporation' would seem a more accurate description than 'transformation'.

This aspect of the problem leads one to mention briefly the classic controversy between the monist and dualist theories. The former holds that international law and municipal law constitute a single legal system, with the generally recognised rules of international law constituting an integral part of municipal law,[7] while the dualist theory holds that there are two separate and independent legal systems, one national and one international. The latter regulates relations between States, based on customary law and treaty law, whereas the former attributes rights and duties to individuals and legal persons, deriving its force from the national constitution. This discussion certainly affords a fascinating intellectual exercise, but may seem of limited relevance to the practising lawyer.[8] What is more important to him is that the rules of a treaty can – and, under certain systems of law, must – be applied directly by the national courts.

Even this must be limited, however, to the provisions of the treaty which are sufficiently explicit as to be capable of enforcement by the national courts. The provisions of a treaty which express quite general obligations of the contracting parties cannot be directly enforced by the courts; this can be done only as regards those clauses which are sufficiently explicit. 'If the provision is so worded that it can be regarded as addressing itself not only to the Contracting States but also to subjects of municipal law, it is ready to be applied immediately by national courts and may accordingly be called 'self-executing'.[9] While this principle is generally recognised, there is room for much discussion as to what is 'self-executing'. National courts may, and sometimes do, take a restrictive view as to what rules fall into this category. Once again, moreover, on the question of terminology, some doubt may be felt as to the appropriateness of the expression 'self-executing'. The essence of the concept is not that the rule in question secures its own execution or enforcement by the national judge. One may wonder whether the expression 'directly enforceable' would not be more accurate than 'self-executing'; though it must be admitted that the latter term has come to be commonly used, in English, in countries where English is not the national language, and that it had its origin in the United States.

As regards the European Convention on Human Rights, the acceptance by the Contracting Parties of the obligation to ensure the conformity of their law with the provisions of the treaty can be shown in another way. Article 57 of the Convention provides:

> On receipt of a request from the Secretary General of the Council of Europe any High Contracting Party shall furnish an explanation of the manner in which its internal law ensures the effective implementation of any of the provisions of this Convention.

Acting in accordance with this provision, the Secretary General, on 9 October 1964, addressed an enquiry to the Contracting Parties as to the way in which their national law ensured the application of the Convention. The replies received[10] show that, before ratifying, the Contracting Parties were at pains to make sure that their national law was in conformity with its provisions. The following extract from the Belgian reply is perhaps typical:

> Before the Convention on Human Rights was ratified by Belgium, the Conseil d'Etat was consulted and expressed the opinion that ratification raised no legal difficulties, since the rights and freedoms set out in the Convention were already either guaranteed by the Constitution itself or enshrined in Belgian law. This view was shared by the Senate and the Chamber when they passed the bill authorising ratification.

As regards the way in which the obligation is carried out, the position varies from country to country. In the Scandinavian countries, Iceland, Ireland and the United Kingdom, where no question of direct enforceability arose, the question was simple. The government satisfied itself that its law was in conformity with the Convention, in many cases relying in whole or in part on the national constitution,[11] and then complied with the national requirements for ratification without the necessity of further implementing legislation; in a few cases where there was incompatibility, reservations were made.[12] The position was similar, at a later date, for Cyprus and Malta.[13] In other countries where the treaty, once ratified, would be directly applicable in municipal law it was necessary to go through the necessary formalities for this purpose. In several cases a further question then arose: the place of the Convention in the 'hierarchy' of legal rules. Did it rank as an ordinary law, in which case later legislation could change the rules thus adopted, under the principle of *lex posterior derogat legi priori*? Or did it, since it related to matters which normally form the object of constitutional guarantees, have the status of a constitutional law? Or could it even prevail over the provisions of the constitution itself? It would be outside the scope of this chapter to examine these questions in detail; learned dissertations on the subject have already been published.[14] It will suffice for our present purposes to say that in Austria, Belgium, France, Italy, Luxembourg and the Federal Republic of Germany the provisions of the Convention have the force of law. The same would appear to be the case in Turkey.[15] In Austria, after a certain period of doubt, they were accorded the status of constitutional law by an Act of 4 March 1964.[16] In the Netherlands, under the provisions of the constitution of 1956, they would appear to take precedence, in case of conflict, even over the constitution itself.

It thus appears that the normative provisions of the European Convention, provided that they are sufficiently precise as to be capable of direct enforcement (commonly, but erroneously, called 'self-executing'), are binding rules in internal law in a number of European countries. This, of course, gives the Convention much greater importance and practical effect than a treaty which merely creates obligations between States. In fact more than 400 national decisions referring to – and in some cases directly applying – the provisions of the European Convention have now been recorded.[17] Moreover even in countries where a treaty is not directly applicable in internal law those provisions may nevertheless have considerable persuasive force, as when they were cited (together with the Universal Declaration) by the House of Lords in the case of *Waddington* v. *Miah alias Ullah* as supporting the proposition that 'it was hardly credible that any government department would promote or that Parliament would pass retrospective criminal legislation'.[18] It is necessary that the provisions of the European Convention should be cited with increasing frequency by national courts and that the standards it lays down should be recognised as rules of municipal law. Only thus can the Convention have its full effect; in this way it will reinforce the principle that the first line of defence of human rights is in the national legal systems and that international remedies should be contingent and subsidiary.[19]

(b) THE BENEFICIARIES OF THE CONVENTION. The second important principle announced in Article 1 is one of universality in the application of the Convention.

National constitutions normally guarantee fundamental rights to all citizens. In an international treaty about human rights the contracting parties might well have guaranteed those rights to their own citizens and to the citizens of the other contracting parties. This, indeed, would have been consistent with the principle of reciprocity on which so many treaties – particularly those relating to establishment – are based.

Such an approach, however, was not acceptable to the authors of the Convention. The rights set out in Section I are secured 'to everyone within the jurisdiction'. The basic conception of human rights is that they pertain to everyone by virtue of their personality, that is to say by virtue of their nature as human beings. If this is so, it follows that international measures to secure their protection cannot be limited in their effect to the citizens of one country or of a group of countries. Fundamental rights must be secured to 'everyone'. They are a matter of *ordre public* or public policy.[20]

In this respect the European Convention follows the Universal Declaration. 'All human beings are born free and equal in dignity and rights. Everyone is entitled to all the rights and freedoms set forth in this Declaration without distinction of any kind . . .'. The same principle is reproduced in Article 1 of the European Convention, which secures the rights and freedoms set out therein 'to everyone within the jurisdiction', while Article 14 makes this even more explicit:

> The enjoyment of the rights and freedoms set forth in this Convention shall be secured without discrimination on any ground such as sex, race, colour, language, religion, political or other opinion, national or social origin, association with a national minority, property, birth, or other status.

This principle of the general applicability of the Convention to all categories of beneficiaries on the widest possible basis was well stated by the European Commission of Human Rights in the case of *Austria* v. *Italy*:[21]

> . . . the purpose of the High Contracting Parties in concluding the convention was not to concede to each other reciprocal rights and obligations in pursuance of their individual national interests, but to realise the aims and ideals of the Council of Europe, as expressed in its Statute, and to establish a common public order of the free democracies of Europe with the object of safeguarding their common heritage of political traditions, ideals, freedom and the rule of law.

The fact that the benefit of the Convention is not limited to nationals of the Contracting Parties has considerable practical importance, as may be seen from the applications which are filed. The Commission's statistics show forty-nine applications filed in 1971 by persons who were nationals of non-member States or stateless, and fifty-six in 1972. The latter figure included six Hungarians, five Israelis, eight Moroccans and three each from Czechoslovakia, Nigeria, Poland and Tunisia. The fact that applications can be considered from nationals of other countries has had particular importance in relation to aliens who have been served with deportation orders or otherwise threatened with expulsion in circumstances which endangered their life or liberty.[22]

Another point to be noted as regards the beneficiaries of the Convention is that the phrase 'everyone within their jurisdiction' does not contain any territorial limitation. It is wider than the expression used in the United Nations Covenant on Civil and Political Rights, Article 2 of which begins as follows:

> Each State Party to the present Covenant undertakes to respect and ensure to all individuals *within its territory* and subject to its jurisdiction the rights recognised in the present Covenant. ...

The absence of the words 'within its territory' in the European Convention means that the measure of protection is wider.[23] Of course, the great majority of persons subject to the jurisdiction of a State are also within its territory. But this is not necessarily so, and cases may be brought by persons who consider that they have been injured by the agents of a State when they were not within its territory. Examples of this have been complaints about the actions of a consular official of a Contracting Party in the territory of a non-member State[24] and the complaint of a Pole living in Germany that he was refused an entry permit by the Swedish authorities which he had requested in order to take part in legal proceedings before the Swedish courts about divorce and the custody of his child.[25]

(c) RESTRICTIVE CHARACTER OF THE LIST OF RIGHTS GUARANTEED. The third important principle which results from the first article of the Convention is that the Contracting Parties will secure to everyone within their jurisdiction *the rights and freedoms defined in Section I* of the Convention, but their undertaking is limited to those rights and freedoms. Of course, other rights may be guaranteed in national constitutions, or otherwise under domestic law – Article 60 specifically envisages this possibility – but the European Convention will not serve to protect such other rights because they are outside the scope of its provisions. The treaty means what it says, and no more.

Section I of the Convention in fact sets out, in Articles 2–13, twelve rights and freedoms. Three more are included in the First Protocol, Article 5 of which specifies that they shall be regarded as additional articles to the Convention; the same is true of four further rights contained in the Fourth Protocol, by virtue of its Article 6. We thus have nineteen rights and freedoms which are the object of the European system of protection – and no more.

It may be thought that this is a statement of the obvious. But if it is obvious to lawyers that the Convention protects only the rights and freedoms which are specifically enumerated and defined, it is far from obvious to the public in general and, more particularly, to very many people who write to the Commission to complain of the alleged violation of other rights.

Applications relating to rights not guaranteed by the Convention and its Protocols have to be rejected by the Commission as inadmissible. Such applications are commonly declared inadmissible as being 'incompatible with the provisions of the ... Convention', which (as we shall see in Chapter IV) is one of the grounds of inadmissibility set out in Article 27. The Commission sometimes characterises them as inadmissible *ratione materiae* – terminology which it used frequently during the early years of its existence. However the ground of inadmissibility is expressed, the principle is clear. Its importance is shown by the fact that scores of applications have been rejected on this ground. *The Digest of Case Law* lists thirty-seven different rights which have been invoked (some of them many times) in applications which the Commission was obliged to declare inadmissible because the rights concerned are not protected by the Convention and its Protocols.[26]

Before proceeding to an examination of the rights and freedoms set out in the separate articles of the Convention it will be convenient at this stage to consider one further general point, which concerns the technique of drafting international treaties. A problem which caused much discussion while the Convention was being drafted was whether the rights and freedoms to be protected should be simply enumerated or whether they should be defined in detail. As we have seen in Chapter I, the Assembly's *Recommendation 38* of September 1949 simply listed ten rights and freedoms, indicating the corresponding articles of the Universal Declaration, without attempting any detailed definitions; indeed, paragraph 4 of the

Recommendation provided that each Contracting Party 'shall have full and entire freedom to establish the rules by which the guaranteed rights and liberties shall be organised and protected within its territory'. The *rapporteur* explained that the Committee on Legal and Administrative Questions had proceeded in this way because it considered that an attempt to define in detail the rights and freedoms to be protected would require an international codification not only of the rights and freedoms themselves but also of the methods and conditions in which they would be exercised in each country. This would in any event take too long and might well prove impossible.[27]

The question was reconsidered by the Legal Experts when they met in February 1950. Two conflicting views were then expressed. One school of thought favoured the method of 'enumeration' of human rights, as statements of general principle, which each member government would implement within its jurisdiction in accordance with its own law; it was argued that, as the Assembly committee had stated, it would be extremely difficult to codify human rights and that, if the attempt were to be made, it would be better to await the conclusions of the United Nations Commission on Human Rights, which had already started on this work. The opposing point of view was that an essential prerequisite to any Convention was the precise definition of the rights to be safeguarded and of the permitted limitations on those rights; unless this were done it would not be possible for a State to know whether its existing laws were consistent with the obligations imposed by the Convention, nor what amendments to its laws should be introduced. Moreover it would be extremely difficult to decide whether a State had violated its obligations under the Convention if they were not precisely defined.

The Legal Experts were unable to agree on either of these conflicting principles as a basis for drafting the Convention. Consequently they agreed to differ, and decided to submit two alternative texts. The first was based on an enumeration of general principles, reproducing verbatim the relevant texts of the United Nations Declaration; the second contained detailed definitions of the rights and freedoms, and of the limitations to which they might be subjected, which had been proposed by the United Kingdom expert. When the Committee of Senior Officials met in June 1950 it decided in favour of a 'compromise solution'. The result was to start each article with a general statement of the right to be guaranteed and then, in the majority of cases, to set out in later paragraphs a more detailed definition of the right and of the restrictions which may be permitted. This 'compromise', which in fact largely followed the British proposal to the Committee of Experts, remained substantially unaltered in the final text of the Convention as signed in November.

The human rights and freedoms involved were the same as those originally proposed by the Assembly in August 1949 and listed above. Their treatment, however, differed considerably. As a result of the method of definition that was adopted, some rights were spelt out in considerable detail, though for others this was not considered necessary. Thus freedom from torture (Article 3) and the right to marry and found a family (Article 12) each occupy only two lines. Again, the Assembly included as three separate rights: freedom of assembly, freedom of association, and freedom to unite in trade unions. It was found possible to combine all three in the first paragraph of Article 11 of the Convention, which reads: 'Everyone has the right to freedom of peaceful assembly and to freedom of association with others, including the right to form and to join trade unions for the protection of his interests.'

Certain rights, on the other hand, required more detailed treatment. Article 9 of the United Nations Declaration reads: 'No one shall be subjected to arbitrary arrest, detention or exile.' The civilians proposed to incorporate this *verbatim* in the draft Convention. To a common lawyer it immediately implied the necessity of defining the circumstances in which detention is lawful. This meant listing the following cases: detention after conviction by a competent court or for non-compliance with the lawful order of a court; arrest or detention to bring a suspect before a magistrate; detention of minors; detention of persons of unsound mind or suffering from infectious diseases, etc. The result was to expand a phrase of two lines into a page of print, which may be found in Article 5 of the Convention. Similarly, the right to a fair trial, which is expressed in three lines in the United Nations Declaration, involved, when the subject of detailed definition, inclusion of the following: the presumption of innocence until guilt is proved; the public nature of the hearing, including admission of the press and definition of the circumstances in which it may be excluded; adequate time and facilities for the defence; free legal assistance; production and examination of witnesses; and, when necessary, free interpretation (Article 6 of the Convention). In both cases, of course, extensive use was made of the draft articles of the UN Covenants then under negotiation in New York.

In retrospect it appears evident that this system of detailed definition is a fundamental and essential element of the system instituted by the European Convention. Without it the task of the Commission and Court of Human Rights would be well nigh impossible – and, in any event, vastly different from, and less effective than, what it has been in practice. Fortunately the task of 'codification' – that is to say of drafting detailed definitions – proved much less difficult in practice than the Assembly committee had supposed.

ARTICLE 2. THE RIGHT TO LIFE

Article 2 of the Convention provides another apt illustration of the difference between the two methods: enumeration and definition. The Universal Declaration provides in one article: 'Everyone has the right to life, liberty and security of person' (Article 3). When it came to defining the first part of this trilogy in the European Convention it was necessary to affirm the right in the first sentence and then make an exception in the second sentence to cover the case of imposition of a death sentence by a court after conviction of a crime for which this penalty is provided by law.[28] A second paragraph then lists three cases in which deprivation of life may occur accidentally without constituting a violation of the Convention: when it results from the use of force which is no more than absolutely necessary in self-defence or defence of another, in order to affect a lawful arrest or prevent escape, or in quelling a riot or insurrection.

While the European Convention is careful to protect the legality of capital punishment, the UN Covenant on Civil and Political Rights adopts a rather different approach in its Article 6, which, while admitting the possibility of the death penalty, seems to treat it as something which should disappear before long and prohibits it expressly for persons below the age of eighteen and for pregnant women.[29]

There is little case law relating to Article 2. An application against Norway in 1960 claimed that the Norwegian law of 12 October 1960 authorising interruption of pregnancy in certain circumstances violated the right to life, but it was declared inadmissible under Article 25 because the applicant did not claim to be a victim of the law in question and the Commission was not competent to examine the question in abstracto.[30]

In the case of Ireland v. United Kingdom (5310/71) the Irish government alleged, *inter alia,* that the deaths of twenty-two persons which had occurred in Northern Ireland in August and October 1971 constituted a violation of Article 2. This part of the application was declared inadmissible on 1 October 1972. The Commission did not consider that substantial evidence had been produced to show an administrative practice which was responsible for these deaths (in which case the rule of exhaustion of domestic remedies would not have applied); nor had the domestic remedies been exhausted. Consequently these allegations were inadmissible by reason of Article 26 and Article 27(3) of the Convention.[31]

ARTICLE 3. FREEDOM FROM TORTURE AND FROM INHUMAN OR DEGRADING TREATMENT OR PUNISHMENT

This short article of two lines states: 'No one shall be subjected to torture or to inhuman or degrading treatment or punishment'. It has been taken *verbatim* from Article 5 of the Universal Declaration, except that the word 'cruel' in the UN text has been omitted. The omission has no importance, since the sense of 'cruel' is equally covered by 'inhuman'. The text of the Universal Declaration is also used in Article 7 of the Covenant on Civil and Political Rights, which continues by prohibiting medical or scientific experimentation on a person without his consent. But the Covenant also goes further than the Declaration or the Convention, because, while their provisions are in the negative form of prohibitions, the Covenant imposes a positive obligation, at least in relation to detained persons, for Article 10(1) provides that 'All persons deprived of their liberty shall be treated with humanity and with respect for the inherent dignity of the human person'.

Several cases have been brought before the European Commission in which it has considered whether various forms of treatment practised in prisons in different countries constitute violations of the prohibition of inhuman or degrading treatment. In *X* v. *Austria* (462/59) the Commission itself raised the question whether the punishment of 'sleeping hard' once in three months inflicted in an Austrian prison violated Article 3; it concluded in the negative.[32] It reached the same conclusion in 1967 as regards solitary confinement for twenty hours a day for a period of ten months;[33] and in 1968 as regards the use of force and of a straitjacket after a violent scene in prison.[34]

In 1973 the Commission considered two applications alleging that the punishment of birching, ordered by a court in the Isle of Man, violated Article 3 of the Convention, as amounting to inhuman or degrading treatment; one application was declared admissible, though the other was rejected for non-exhaustion of domestic remedies.[35]

The question of physical punishment was one of the issues raised in the two inter-State cases brought by *Greece against the United Kingdom* in 1956 and 1957, relating to the situation in Cyprus while the island was still a British colony. The first application alleged, *inter alia*, that legislation providing for the penalty of whipping and various forms of collective punishment violated Article 3 of the Convention; the second application made a similar claim as regards 49 cases of 'torture or maltreatment amounting to torture' for which the British government was alleged to be responsible.[36] The first case was declared admissible on 2 June 1956, and the second on 12 October 1957 as regards twenty-nine of the incidents complained of.[37] However, after the Commission had drawn up its report on the first case, but before it had done so in the second case, a political settlement was reached about the status of Cyprus and the Parties requested that the proceedings should be terminated; the Committee of Ministers then decided, on 20 April and 14 December 1959, that no further action was called for.[38] The report of the Commission on the first case has never been published and the second case was terminated before this stage of the procedure had been reached, so that it is not possible to consult them for further interpretation of Article 3.

The situation is very different, however, with the case brought by *Denmark, Norway, Sweden and the Netherlands against Greece*, relating to the situation in that country after the *coup d'état* of the Greek army officers in April 1967.[39] Since there will be many references to the 'Greek case' in this book, it will be convenient to summarise it briefly at this stage.

On 3 May 1967 the permanent representative of Greece addressed a letter to the Secretary General of the Council of Europe in which, invoking Article 15 of the Convention on Human Rights, he stated that, by royal decree No. 280 of 21 April 1967, the application of Articles 5, 6, 8, 10, 11, 12, 14, 20, 95 and 97 of the Greek constitution had been suspended in view of internal dangers threatening public order and the security of the State. In subsequent letters of 25 May and 19 September 1967 the Greek government gave further information in regard to Article 15.[40]

In identical applications of 20 September 1967 to the European Commission of Human Rights the applicant Governments of Denmark, Norway and Sweden, after referring to the suspension of the above provisions of the Greek constitution, submitted that, by royal decree No. 280 and other legislative measures, and by certain administrative practices, the respondent government had violated Articles 5, 6, 8, 9, 10, 11, 13 and 14 of the Convention. In relation to all these allegations they contended that the respondent government had failed to show that the conditions of Article 15 of the Convention permitting measures of derogation were satisfied. The government of the Netherlands, in its application of 27 September 1967, made submissions which corresponded in substance to those of the first three applicant governments. The four applications were joined by the Commission on 2 October 1967.

The respondent government, in its written observations in reply of 16 December 1967, submitted primarily that the Commission was not competent to examine the applications because they concerned the actions of a revolutionary government. It also stated with regard to Article 15 of the Convention that, in accordance with the Commission's jurisprudence, a government enjoyed a 'margin of appreciation' in deciding whether there existed a public emergency threatening the life of the nation and, if so, what exceptional measures were required.

On 24 January 1968 the Commission declared the four applications admissible.[41]

The three Scandinavian governments in their joint memorial of 25 March 1968 extended their original allegations to Articles 3 and 7 of the Convention and Articles 1 and 3 of the First Protocol. On 31 May 1968 these further allegations were also declared admissible.[42]

After protracted hearings during the next eighteen months the Commission of Human Rights, on 18 November 1969, transmitted to the Committee of Ministers the report which it had drawn up in accordance with Article 31 of the Convention.[43] After three months had elapsed without the case having been referred to the European Court of Human Rights, the Committee of Ministers took the decision required by Article 32 of the Convention; in particular it decided that Greece had violated nine articles of the Convention, including Article 3, and also Article 3 of the First Protocol (the undertaking to hold free elections).[44]

As mentioned above, the allegations of torture and ill treatment of political prisoners were contained in the new allegations made by the Scandinavian governments in March 1968. They were examined by the Commission with great care; many witnesses were heard; an inspection was made – and photographs were taken – of the Security Police building in Athens;[45] more than 300 pages of the report were devoted to the question of torture. It is impossible to read the report without being impressed by the objective manner in which the Commission required corroboration of the allegations made, offered the government every opportunity to rebut the evidence produced and even examined the possibility that (as alleged) many of the accounts of torture were deliberately fabricated as part of a plot to discredit the government. The Commission took as its point of departure that 'the notion of inhuman treatment covers at least such treatment as deliberately causes severe suffering, mental or physical, which, in the particular situation, is unjustifiable'.[46] The following passage in the report is particularly significant:[47]

> Further, the Commission cannot ignore the sheer number of complaints. The International Red Cross reported that, at one stage, out of 131 prisoners, forty-six complained of torture or ill-treatment, and it apparently later investigated certain further torture allegations, but the respondent Government has failed to submit the report on those investigations. In the present proceedings allegations have been made concerning the treatment of 213 named detainees; thirty of these cases had been examined to some substantial degree before the proceedings were terminated following the respondent Government's refusal to make possible the hearing of a number of further witnesses detained in Greece.
>
> Since the Commission considers that in eleven of the cases which were examined torture or ill-treatment has been established and that in seventeen others there is at least some evidence corroborating the complaint, it is not able to reject the whole as a conspiracy by Communist and anti-Government groups to discredit the Government and the police. It cannot but regard the actual number of complaints brought before it as strong indication that acts of torture or ill-treatment are not isolated or exceptional, nor limited to one place.

After carefully reviewing all the evidence at its disposal the Commission concluded that torture had been inflicted in eleven cases; that there were indications, *prima facie* cases or strong indications in seventeen other cases, with regard to which the sub-commission had been prevented from completing its investigation; that there was a practice of torture and ill treatment by the Athens Security Police of persons arrested for political reasons; and that the Greek authorities, confronted with numerous and substantial complaints and allegations of torture and ill treatment, had failed to take any effective steps to investigate them or remedy the situation.[48]

Happily the situation in Greece has been corrected with the restoration of democratic government in 1974, after which Greece was invited to resume its membership in the Council of Europe and again ratified the Convention on Human Rights, which the military government had denounced in December 1969.

Physical maltreatment was also one of the issues raised in the case of *Ireland* v. *United Kingdom*.[49] The Irish government lodged this application in December 1971 and filed two supplementary memorials in March 1972. The Commission decided to treat the first supplementary memorial as part of the original application, but to register the second memorial as a new application (No. 5451/72).

The government referred to the Civil Authorities (Special Powers) Act, Northern Ireland, 1922, and the connected statutory rules, regulations and orders and submitted that this legislation was in itself a failure by the United Kingdom to comply with the obligation in Article 1 of the Convention to secure to everybody within its jurisdiction the rights and freedoms defined in Section I of the Convention. They also submitted that the methods employed or permitted by the United Kingdom government in the implementation of this legislation constituted an administrative practice in breach of Article 1.

The application then referred to certain deaths in Northern Ireland in August and October 1971, and submitted that they constituted a breach of Article 2, which guarantees the right to life. (On this point, see above under Article 2.)

The application further referred to the taking into custody of persons on or after 9 August 1971 under the Special Powers Act and alleged that they were subjected to treatment which constituted torture and inhuman and degrading treatment and punishment contrary to Article 3 of the Convention. In support of this allegation, and particularly as regards about ninety cases, the Irish Government submitted statements, medical evidence and the text of the 'Compton report' (referred to below).

The Irish government also claimed that internment without trial, as carried out in Northern Ireland subsequent to 9 August 1971, constituted a violation of Article 5 (the right to liberty and security of person) and Article 6 (the right to a fair trial). In addition the applicant government alleged that the powers of detention and internment were exercised in a discriminatory manner, contrary to Article 14 of the Convention, while the derogation made by the

British government under Article 15 of the Convention could not justify a derogation from Article 2 (the right to life) nor the suspension of Articles 5 and 6 to an extent which was greater than that permitted under Article 15.

On the question of torture or inhuman treatment the Irish government complained particularly about the methods of interrogation used by the British security forces in Northern Ireland, including hooding, noise, standing against a wall, deprivation of sleep and limited diet. In this respect the British government was a victim of its own good faith. The Home Secretary appointed in 1971 a committee of enquiry to look into allegations of brutality in Northern Ireland in the course of procedures known as 'interrogation in depth'; in its report, known as the 'Compton report', the committee described in detail the techniques used by the security forces.[50] As the result of a further report of Privy Counsellors, known as the 'Parker report',[51] the Prime Minister announced in the House of Commons on 2 March 1972 that the government had decided that the use of the techniques in question would be discontinued; he added that if the government should wish to reintroduce the use of these techniques at some future date it would first consult the House of Commons before doing so. This action to stop the use of the methods of interrogation in question was commendable in itself, but it put a powerful argument in the hands of the Irish government in its case before the European Commission, because it could quote official British sources as to the methods utilised, the criticism of them by, among others, a former Lord Chancellor, the decision to stop their use and the possibility (even if remote) of further recurrence to them in future.

After considering the Irish memorials of December 1971 and March 1972 and the British government's observations of May 1972, the Commission heard the Parties (each represented by its Attorney General) in September of that year – on the question of admissibility. On 1 October 1972 the Commission declared the first application admissible (except as regards Article 2 of the Convention)[52] but decided to strike the second application off the list.[53]

The decision on admissibility was, of course, without prejudice to the merits of the case. Examination of the merits then began. After an exchange of memorials, hearings on the merits took place in October 1973, and again in December of that year. Witnesses proposed by the Irish government were heard by three delegates of the Commission in December 1973 and February 1974 and those proposed by the British government on several occasions in 1974 –

at an air force base at Stavanger in Norway – and in London in February 1975. By March 1975 118 witnesses had been heard by the delegates in the course of nine sessions, but the Commission had not completed its work on this case.[54]

Related – one might say parallel – to this inter-State case were a number of individual applications, seven of which, filed in July 1972, were grouped together as *Donnelly* et al. v. *United Kingdom*.[55] The applicants complained that they were the victims of an administrative practice of ill treatment in violation of Article 3. After an exchange of written observations the applications were declared admissible in April 1973.[56] The Commission then proceeded to an examination of the merits, which involved an exchange of memorials and hearing of witnesses in 1974. The proceedings had not been completed by the end of that year.

These applications raised two separate issues. Was there an administrative practice in violation of Article 3? If there was not, were the applicants individually victims of inhuman treatment in violation of Article 3? The distinction is important, because the rule of exhaustion of domestic remedies does not apply where the application raises the issue of an administrative practice; in such cases domestic remedies are likely to be non-existent or ineffective.[57] In its decision the Commission declared both issues admissible, and joined to the merits the question of exhaustion of domestic remedies in relation to specific acts as distinct from an administrative practice.[58] In fact the existence of effective domestic remedies appears to have been established by the courts: by December 1974 a total of £76,000 had been awarded to six men who had sued for damages on account of ill treatment during 'deep interrogation' by the army and police in Northern Ireland.[59]

The question of torture or inhuman treatment was also one of the issues raised in the inter-State case brought by *Cyprus against Turkey* in September 1974, after the Turkish occupation of part of that island. A second application was lodged in March 1975. After a hearing of the parties the two applications were declared admissible on 26 May 1975.[60]

The expression 'inhuman or degrading treatment' may also have a quite different meaning not directly related to physical injury. Two different categories of cases may be cited as illustrations.

The first category concerns measures of extradition or expulsion from a country. The Convention contains no provision on the right of asylum.[61] Nevertheless, if a person is in danger of expulsion from one country to another where his life (or, in certain circumstances, his liberty) would be in danger, such an act of expulsion could constitute a violation of human rights amounting to inhuman treatment. Thus in the case of *Kerkoub* v. *Belgium* the Commission said: [62]

> ... the extradition of an individual can, in certain exceptional cases, be seen to be contrary to the Convention, and particularly to its Article 3, when there are serious reasons to believe that, in the country to which he will be sent, he will be subjected to treatment which is prohibited by that article.

Though this statement was made in relation to extradition proceedings, the same principle would apply in relation to expulsion.[63] In a number of cases of threatened extradition or expulsion the Commission has worked out an informal procedure to delay or prevent such measures, which is described by the Secretary of the Commission in a statement reproduced below.[64]

One of the most striking cases relating to expulsion and Article 3 of the Convention is *Amekrane* v. *United Kingdom* (5961/72). It was brought by the widow of a Moroccan air force officer who took part in an attempted putsch against the Moroccan government which included an attempt to assassinate the King. When the attempt failed, Lieutenant Colonel Amekrane fled to Gibraltar, where he requested political asylum. This was refused. On the following day he was sent back to Morocco, where he was tried and executed. Mrs Amekrane's application to the European Commission alleged violation of Article 3, (Artice 5(4) (right of a detained person to take proceedings to determine the legality of his detention) and Article 8 (right to family life). The case was declared admissible in October 1973;[65] a friendly settlement was achieved in July 1974 whereby the British government, without admitting violation of the Convention, agreed to make a payment of £37,500 in settlement of the complaint.[66]

Other important cases which relate to the meaning of 'degrading treatment' are those of twenty-five *East African Asians* v. *the United Kingdom*. During the years 1970 to 1972 nearly three hundred applications were filed by holders of British passports who were citizens of the United Kingdom from Uganda or Kenya, or British-protected persons, whose continued residence in those countries had become difficult or illegal; they sought to settle in England, but the British government refused to allow them to enter, or remain in, the country by reason of the provisions of the Commonwealth Immigrants Act, 1968. They alleged that this action violated Article

8 of the Convention (right to respect for family life) – in cases where members of their families were already in the United Kingdom – also Article 14 (prohibition of discrimination) and Article 3. The various applications were divided into sixteen groups. Detailed examination of the majority of the cases was adjourned pending the outcome of the proceedings relating to the first two groups, which were declared admissible in October and December 1970.[67] While the proceedings continued the great majority of the applicants were admitted to the United Kingdom, but in many cases on a temporary basis with no assurance of permanency.

The Convention itself contains no guarantee of the right to enter the country of which one is a national. Such a right is protected by Article 3(2) of the Fourth Protocol, but the Preamble thereto makes it clear that it protects 'certain rights and freedoms other than those already included in ... the Convention ... and ... the First Protocol ...' Moreover the United Kingdom has not ratified the Fourth Protocol. Consequently it was argued that the United Kingdom was under no obligation to admit the East African Asians to its territory. On the other side, it was argued that the treatment accorded to the applicants amounted to taking away their rights as citizens and making them, in effect, stateless – which constituted 'degrading treatment' within the meaning of Article 3, more particularly as the same treatment would not be applied to citizens of the white countries of the Commonwealth. It was admitted that the intention and the effect of the Commonwealth Immigrants Act, 1968, were discriminatory.

In its decision on the admissibility of the first group of twenty-five cases, in October 1970, the Commission reached the conclusion that 'discrimination based on race could, in certain circumstances, of itself amount to degrading treatment within the meaning of Article 3 of the Convention'.[68] In September 1971 the Commission held hearings on the merits and during the next two years endeavoured to reach a friendly settlement. In 1971 and 1972 the British government took various measures to increase the number of entry vouchers granted to East African Asians, and also granted entry to some 25,000 holders of British passports expelled by General Amin in 1974. In December 1973 the Commission adopted its report on the first twenty-five cases and transmitted it to the Committee of Ministers. The case was not referred to the Court. The committee had not taken a decision on these cases by June 1975.

ARTICLE 4. FREEDOM FROM SLAVERY OR SERVITUDE AND FROM
FORCED OR COMPULSORY LABOUR

The prohibition of slavery or servitude in paragraph 1 of Article 4
corresponds to Article 4 of the Universal Declaration. The latter
text continues: 'slavery and the slave trade shall be prohibited in
all their forms', but the omission of this phrase in the European
Convention has no significance, since it already contains a categorical
prohibition of slavery.

The European text continues with the prohibition of forced or
compulsory labour, which is not found in the Universal Declaration
but does exist in Article 8(3) of the Covenant on Civil and Political
Rights. This prohibition reaffirms the principle set out in various
conventions and resolutions of the International Labour Organisation, particularly the Forced Labour Convention of 1930 and the
Abolition of Forced Labour Convention of 1957.[69] It also represents,
in the European context, a reaction against the horrors of concentra-
tion camps and forced labour during the Second World War.

The notion was explained as follows by four members of the
Commission in the case of *Iversen* v. *Norway*:[70]

> these elements of forced or compulsory labour are, first, that the
> work or service is performed by the worker against his will and,
> secondly, that the requirement that the work or service be performed
> is unjust or oppressive or the work or service itself involves avoid-
> able hardship.

Paragraph 3 of Article 4 sets out four kinds of work or service
which are not to be considered as 'forced or compulsory labour'.
They are:

(a) work done during detention or conditional release from
    detention;
(b) military service or service in lieu thereof required of con-
    scientious objectors;
(c) service exacted in the event of emergency or calamity;
(d) work or service which forms part of normal civic obligations.

The leading case on Article 4 is *Iversen* v. *Norway*.[71] Iversen was
a Norwegian dentist who was ordered by the Ministry of Social
Affairs to exercise his profession in a remote village in the north
of the country in accordance with a law of 21 June 1956 relating
to obligatory public service for dentists. The law was adopted
because a public dental service had been established in Norway in
1949 but it was found difficult to find practitioners willing to serve in

C

certain regions, particularly in the far north. The law authorised the
Ministry to direct young dentists who had recently qualified to
occupy, for a period of up to two years, vacant posts which could
not otherwise be filled. The Act was adopted in the parliament by
a majority vote of the government party over the objections of the
opposition, who argued that it authorised the compulsory direction
of labour, which was contrary to the Norwegian constitution and
Article 4 of the European Convention.

.Iversen, after being accepted by the Norwegian Dental College
as qualified, was ordered in December 1959 to take up a position
at Moskenes, in the region of Nordland. He did so in January 1960
but left his post in May and refused to return. He was condemned
by the court to pay a fine of 2,000 krone or serve thirty days in
prison. The sentence was confirmed, on appeal, by the Supreme
Court. Iversen paid the fine, but then filed an application with the
European Commission of Human Rights in June 1962, alleging
violation of Article 4 of the Convention. The Commission thus had
to consider whether the service he was required to perform was
'forced or compulsory labour' within the meaning of Article 4 and,
if so, whether it fell within one of the four exceptions set out in
paragraph 3 of that article.

The Commission, by a majority of six members out of ten, dismissed the application as manifestly ill founded. Four members of
the majority held that the service which Iversen was required to
perform did not constitute 'forced or compulsory labour' within the
meaning of Article 4, 'since such service was for a short period,
provided favourable remuneration, did not involve any diversion
from chosen professional work ... and did not involve any discriminatory, arbitrary or punitive application'.[72] Two members of
the majority arrived at the same conclusion by a different reasoning;
they considered that the service in question fell within the third
exception set out in paragraph 3 of Article 4 and 'was service
reasonably required of him in an emergency threatening the well-
being of the community and was not forced or compulsory labour'.[73]
The majority therefore rejected the application under Article 27(2)
of the Convention as being manifestly ill founded.

The minority of four members of the Commission did not reach
the conclusion that the application was justified and revealed a
violation of the Convention. That question had not arisen, because
the proceedings had not yet reached that stage. The Commission
was discussing the question of admissibility: was there a *prima
facie* case of violation? The minority was of the opinion that the

case was not *manifestly* ill founded and that therefore it should be declared admissible, which would permit a detailed examination of the merits.[74]

It seems reasonable to believe that, if the case had been declared admissible, the reasoning of the four members of the majority should, and would, have prevailed, i.e. that the service required of Iversen was not 'forced or compulsory labour' in the sense in which those words are used in Article 4 of the Convention. Nevertheless it is straining the meaning of words to hold that the application was 'manifestly ill founded' when there was room for much argument on important issues of interpretation of the Convention, and four members of the Commission were of a contrary opinion. This difficult question of the mean of 'manifestly ill founded' is further discussed in Chapter IV, section 5.

The exception recognised in paragraph 3(b) of Article 4 relating to military service or service in lieu thereof required of conscientious objectors in countries where they are recognised came up in the case of *Grandrath* v. *Federal Republic of Germany*.[75] Grandrath was a member of the sect of Jehovah's Witnesses and exercised the functions of a Bible study director within that sect. When he was called up for military service in 1960 his status as a conscientious objector was recognised. When instructed to do substitute service in a hospital he asked for exemption, as he had conscientious objections not only to military service but also to substitute service. This request was refused. His appeal to the courts against the decision was rejected. When he still refused to do substitute service he was condemned in 1963 to eight months' imprisonment. After two appeals, which confirmed the conviction but reduced the sentence to six months, he tried unsuccessfully to lodge an appeal with the Federal Constitutional Court. On 1 September 1964 he lodged an application with the European Commission of Human Rights. He served his sentence from October 1964 to April 1965. In the latter month his application was declared admissible.[76]

Grandrath based his application on Article 9 of the Convention, which guarantees the right to freedom of thought, conscience and religion; the case is therefore considered below under Article 9. When examining his case the Commission pointed out that it was also necessary to look at Article 4, which clearly admits the legality of military service and other service in lieu thereof. The Commission said:[77]

As in this provision it is expressly recognised that civilian service may be imposed on conscientious objectors as a substitute for military service, it must be concluded that objections of conscience do not, under the Convention, entitle a person to exemption from such service.

In fact it is generally admitted that the Convention does not guarantee the right of conscientious objection; attempts to add a provision protecting this right are referred to in Chapter VIII, section 1.[78]

ARTICLE 5. THE RIGHT TO LIBERTY AND SECURITY

Article 3 of the Universal Declaration provides that 'Everyone has the right to life, liberty and security of person'. The European Convention, after protecting the right to life in Article 2, deals with liberty and security of person in Article 5; it incorporates in the same article freedom from arbitrary arrest and detention, to which the Declaration devotes a separate article – together with freedom from exile (Article 9).

As explained earlier in this chapter, Article 5 furnishes a clear illustration of the difference between two drafting techniques: two lines of the Universal Declaration are expanded to nearly a page of the European Convention when one uses the method of detailed definition.

Article 5 starts off with the affirmative 'Everyone has the right to liberty and security of person' and then continues by defining the circumstances in which someone may be deprived of his liberty, provided this is done 'in accordance with a procedure prescribed by law'. These circumstances include the following cases:

(*a*) detention after conviction by a competent court;
(*b*) arrest or detention for non-compliance with the order of a court;
(*c*) arrest or detention on reasonable suspicion for the purpose of bringing a person before the competent legal authority or as a preventive measure to prevent the commission of an offence;
(*d*) the detention of minors by lawful order for stated purposes;
(*e*) detention to prevent the spread of infectious diseases, of persons of unsound mind, alcoholics, drug addicts or vagrants;
(*f*) detention to prevent unauthorised entry into a country or to permit deportation or extradition.

The following paragraphs of Article 5 provide that anyone who is arrested or detained shall be informed promptly in a language which he understands of the reasons therefor (para. 2); that a person arrested or detained on suspicion or as a preventive measure shall be entitled to trial within a reasonable time or release pending trial (para. 3); that anyone arrested or detained shall have the right to take proceedings by which the lawfulness of his detention shall be decided speedily by a court and his release ordered if the detention is not lawful – the principle of *habeas corpus* (para. 4). Finally, anyone arrested or detained in contravention of this article shall have an enforceable right to compensation (para. 5).

It will be observed that this article deals with two distinct questions: it defines in paragraph 1 the cases in which arrest or detention are permitted; secondly, it goes on to define the rights of a person who has been arrested or detained. The experience of twenty years' application of the Convention has shown that this is one of its most important provisions and one of those which have given rise to the greatest number of cases filed with the Commission.

One of the first important cases relating to Article 5 of the Convention, which was also the first case to be brought before the European Court of Human Rights, was *Lawless* v. *Ireland*.[79] Since many references will be made to this case, it will be convenient to set out the facts at this stage.[80]

Gerard Richard Lawless was arrested by agents of the government of Ireland on 11 July 1957 and was detained without trial in a military detention camp (the Curragh) between 13 July and 11 December 1957 in pursuance of an order made by the Minister for Justice under section 4 of the Offences Against the State (Amendment) Act, 1940. This Act empowered the government to arrest and detain persons without trial when it considered that the exercise of such powers was necessary to preserve peace and public order and after it had made a proclamation to that effect. Such a proclamation had been made on 5 July 1957 after a series of incidents disturbing the peace; and it was in accordance with the powers thus conferred on the government that Lawless was arrested as being a suspected member of an illegal organisation, namely the Irish Republican Army.

Lawless took *habeas corpus* proceedings before the Irish courts, but his application was rejected by the High Court in October 1957 and, on appeal, by the Supreme Court in November.[81] Two days later he transmitted an application to the European Commission of Human Rights alleging violation of the Convention, more particularly of Article 5, and claiming immediate release, compensation and damages, and payment of his costs. In December he was released from detention, having given an undertaking that he would not engage in any illegal activity, but continued the proceedings before the Commission in order to obtain compensation, damages and costs.

The Commission of Human Rights was unanimous in holding that Lawless's arrest and detention without trial were in violation of Article 5 of the Convention. (Various other questions then arose relating to the validity of the Irish government's derogation under Article 15 of the Convention and – after the case had been referred to the Court – as to the procedure to be followed in obtaining and making known to the Court the views of the applicant. These questions are discussed below.[82]) As regards Article 5, the issue submitted to the Court related to the interpretation of paragraph 1(c) thereof.

The relevant passages of Article 5 are as follows:

1. Everyone has the right to liberty and security of person. No one shall be deprived of his liberty save in the following cases and in accordance with a procedure prescribed by law:
    (a) ...
    (b) ...
    (c) the lawful arrest or detention of a person effected for the purpose of bringing him before the competent legal authority on reasonable suspicion of having committed an offence or when it is reasonably considered necessary to prevent his committing an offence or fleeing after having done so;
2. ...
3. Everyone arrested or detained in accordance with the provisions of paragraph 1(c) of this article shall be brought promptly before a judge or other officer authorised by law to exercise judicial power and shall be entitled to trial within a reasonable time or to release pending trial. Release may be conditioned by guarantees to appear for trial.

As stated above, the Commission of Human Rights was unanimous in holding that arrest and detention without trial under the 1940 Act were not in accordance with Article 5. The government nevertheless challenged this in the proceedings before the Court, on the ground that paragraph 1(c) of Article 5 'permits the lawful arrest or detention of a person ... when it is reasonably considered necessary to prevent his committing an offence ...' and that Lawless had in fact been detained precisely for this reason. The Commission in reply argued that it was necessary to look at the whole of paragraph 1(c), which permits the arrest or detention of a person, in order to prevent his committing an offence, *when this is effected for the purpose of bringing him before the competent legal authority.* Paragraph 3 of Article 5, moreover, the Commission argued, made it perfectly clear that arrest or detention as authorised in paragraph 1 must be only a preliminary stage before the person detained is brought before a judge for trial. In reply to this argument the government claimed that the clear meaning of Article 5 could be found in the *travaux préparatoires.* The original text of paragraph 1(c) of Article 5 (which had been proposed by the United Kingdom) read 'the lawful arrest or detention of a person effected for the purpose of bringing him before the competent legal authority etc. *or which* it is reasonably considered necessary to prevent his committing an offence . . .' This showed, in the government's submission, that the words 'effected for the purpose of bringing him before the competent legal authority' related only to cases of reasonable suspicion that an offence has been committed and *not* to cases of reasonable suspicion that an offence is about to be committed. Moreover, as regards paragraph 3 of Article 5, the earlier text limited this *expressis verbis* to cases of arrest or detention 'on a charge of having committed a crime'. Admittedly both texts had subsequently been altered, but, the government claimed, this was done only in the course of final comparison of the English and French texts and revision of the translation. No intention to change the sense of the earlier text could be traced in the *travaux préparatoires.* Therefore it was argued that the clear sense of the earlier text must be held to prevail over the Commission's interpretation of the final ambiguous text.

As the Commission pointed out, the *travaux préparatoires* of Article 5, when closely examined, do not appear to bear out the government's deduction from them. The Court, however, did not find it necessary to examine the *travaux préparatoires,* for it upheld the Commission's interpretation of Article 5, on the ground that the plain and natural meaning of the words used was that which the Commission gave to them; and it further pointed out that the construction advocated by the government would open the door wide to arrest and detention on suspicion without the requirement of bringing to trial. Consequently the Court held that the arrest and detention of Lawless were incompatible with Article 5. (The case failed on other grounds, as recounted below under Article 15.[83])

In 1968 and 1969 the Court of Human Rights heard four cases concerning the length of detention on remand awaiting trial in Germany and Austria. These were *Stögmüller* v. *Austria,*[84] *Neumeister* v. *Austria,*[85] *Matznetter* v. *Austria*[86] and *Wemhoff* v.

Federal Republic of Germany.[87] In the three Austrian cases the applicants had been detained for periods of twenty-four or twenty-six months awaiting trial, while in the Wemhoff case the period was three years. In all four cases the applicants complained that their prolonged detention violated the requirement of paragraph 3 of Article 5 that 'Everyone arrested or detained . . . shall be entitled to trial within a reasonable time or to release pending trial'. They also alleged violation of Article 6(1): 'In the determination . . . of any criminal charge against him everyone is entitled to a fair and public hearing within a reasonable time by an independent and impartial tribunal established by law.'

It is to be noted, in the first place, that a 'reasonable time' within the meaning of Article 5(3) is not necessarily the same as a 'reasonable time' within the meaning of Article 6(1). Article 5(3) relates to a situation in which the person to be tried is under detention, that is to say deprived of his liberty; stricter criteria may be required to justify continued detention (when there is an alternative of release pending trial) than would be the case in the simple preparation of a case for trial. As the Court has said, there must be special diligence in the conduct of the prosecution concerning persons under detention.[88]

In the Wemhoff and Neumeister cases the Commission expressed the opinion that there had been violation of Article 5(3) and, in the Neumeister case, also of Article 6(1). In the other two cases it considered that there was no violation. In view of the importance of the issues involved, and in order to have them clarified for the future, the Commission decided to refer all four cases to the Court; the Austrian government did the same for the three cases in which it was concerned.

The essence of the problem is the difficulty of deciding what is a 'reasonable time' during which a person may be detained awaiting trial. It was common ground that no fixed period of time can be established as a yardstick to apply to all cases; it is necessary to judge what is reasonable in the light of all the circumstances, including the complexity of the case, the difficulty of obtaining evidence, the volume of the evidence, the length and nature of the charge, and so on. But does this mean that there are no objective criteria? The Commission thought not. In its report on the *Wemhoff case* it set out a summary of its 'jurisprudence' in nineteen earlier cases in support of the proposition that the meaning of 'reasonable time' must be determined in the light of the concrete facts of each case,[89] and continued by listing seven elements or factors which are relevant to an evaluation of the circumstances : the actual length of detention; the length of detention on remand in relation to the penalty to be expected in the event of conviction; material, moral or other effects on the person detained; the conduct of the accused – in particular whether he contributed to the delay of the investigation; the difficulties in the investigation; the manner in which the investigation was conducted; and the conduct of the judicial authorities. The Commission considered that all these factors should be evaluated. Some of them might point in opposite directions; the conclusion would depend on their relative importance.[90]

The Court did not accept this method of approaching the problem. It pointed out that an application, before being filed with the Commission, must have been the subject of domestic remedies and therefore of reasoned decisions by national judicial authorities. It is for them to state the reasons why they considered continued detention necessary; the applicant must have invoked his reasons in the opposite sense. This led to the conclusion : [91]

> It is in the light of these pointers that the Court must judge whether the reasons given by the national authorities to justify continued detention are relevant and sufficient to show that detention was not unreasonably prolonged and contrary to Article 5(3) of the Convention.

The facts of the Wemhoff case showed that it was quite extraordinarily complex. The investigation concerned thirteen persons and lasted twenty-seven months. It involved the examination of 169 bank accounts in fifty-six banks and of transactions totalling DM 776 million. The reports of the financial experts ran to 1,500 pages, the court's records comprised forty-five volumes of some 10,000 pages and the indictment was a document of 855 pages.[92] The Court, like the Commission, considered that no criticism could be made of the conduct of the judicial authorities.[93] It examined the reasons given by the German courts for prolonging the detention, namely the danger of flight, of destroying evidence and of contaminating witnesses; it considered these reasons justified. The Court therefore held that there was no violation of Article 5(3) of the Convention. Equally, there was no breach of Article 6(1).[94]

In the *Neumeister case,* on the other hand, which was also a complicated case of fraud involving large sums of money, the Court decided – in accordance with the opinion of the Commission – that there had been a violation of Article 5(3), though (contrary to the opinion of the Commission) not of Article 6(1). Among the elements which contributed to this conclusion were the fact that during a period of detention lasting over two years fifteen months elapsed during which the accused was not interrogated at all; also that the alleged danger of flight (if he were released on remand) was not substantiated and the investigating judge himself did not believe that Neumeister intended to abscond.[95] Three years later, in 1971, Neumeister asked, via the Commission, for compensation under Article 50 of the Convention, on the ground that he had failed to obtain any compensation in Austria in spite of the judgement of the Court of Human Rights in 1968. In 1974 the Court awarded him 30,000 Austrian schillings for his costs but rejected his claim for compensation.[96]

As regards the other two cases in this group, the Court gave judgement in November 1969. It held that there was no violation in the Matznetter case,[97] but that the detention of Stögmüller for twenty-four months exceeded the limits of a reasonable time permitted under Article 5(3) of the Convention. Once more the Court examined the reasons given by the Austrian courts for prolonging his detention on remand: the danger of repetition of the offences and the danger of absconding. It did not find that these reasons were substantiated and therefore concluded that there was violation.[98]

The proceedings in these cases led the governments concerned to take a new look at their law and practice as regards detention on remand. Both in the Federal Republic (in 1964) and in Austria (in 1971) the Code of Criminal Procedure was amended so as to provide that remand in custody should not exceed six months except in special circumstances.[99]

A fifth case relating to prolonged detention on remand was *Ringeisen* v. *Austria*.[100] The Commission was of the opinion that the applicant's detention (for two periods amounting together to twenty-two months) constituted a violation of Article 5(3) of the Convention, but that the length of the criminal proceedings did not violate Article 6(1). The Court in its judgement so decided. This case is of interest principally for two reasons: the interpretation given by the Court to Article 6(1) of the Convention, which will be considered in the following section; and the fact that in this case the Court for the first time awarded compensation to an applicant under Article 50 of the Convention, which is discussed below in Chapter V, section 3.

A separate question arising under Article 5 is whether, and to what extent, its provisions apply to military discipline. The further question arises whether the provisions of Article 6 on the right to a fair trial are applicable to disciplinary proceedings in the armed forces. These questions were raised in the cases filed in 1971 by *Five Dutch soldiers* v. *The Netherlands*.[101] The applicants were conscripts in the Dutch army and were punished by their company commanders for breaches of military discipline: absence without leave, reckless driving and publishing articles in the press without authorisation. They received various sentences of light, aggravated or strict arrest; after complaining unsuccessfully to the complaints officer they had taken their case to the Supreme Military Court, which had confirmed the penalties. They complained of violation of Articles 5 and 6 of the Convention – and also of Article 14, prohibiting discrimination, because the same penalties would not have been imposed on civilians or on officers. Certain applications also alleged violation of Article 10 on freedom of expression, on account of punishment for publishing an article in the press, and of Article 11 on freedom of assembly and association, by reason of punishment for attending a meeting of a Servicemen's Association.

The Commission decided to join the applications and declared them admissible in July 1972, when the issues raised had already been discussed in the Dutch parliament and a Bill tabled to amend the law on military discipline and the military penal code. It then became necessary to examine the substance of the questions raised, in particular whether the rules set out in Articles 5 and 6 apply to military discipline – a question which it is probable that no one even considered when the Convention was drafted. (France was careful to make a reservation on this point when she ratified the Convention in May 1974.) Moreover, do the permitted limitations on freedom of expression and freedom of association set out in Articles 10 and 11 of the Convention authorise such stringent restrictions as are normally imposed on members of the armed forces? If the applications were held to be justified, what would be the effect on military discipline in the member States of the Council of Europe?

The Commission adopted its report in July 1974 and expressed the opinion that there had been violation of Article 5 as regards 'aggravated' or 'strict' arrest, but that 'light arrest' did not constitute deprivation of liberty within the meaning of Article 5. Further, the Commission considered that Article 6 was not applicable to the disciplinary proceedings in question and that no other violation of the Convention had been established. In the following October it referred these cases to the Court. After an exchange of memorials, oral hearings were held by the Court in October 1975, but judgement had not been given by the end of the year.

Paragraph 4 of Article 5 enshrines, as mentioned above, the principle of *habeas corpus*:

> Everyone who is deprived of his liberty by arrest or detention shall be entitled to take proceedings by which the lawfulness of his detention shall be decided speedily by a court and his release ordered if the detention is not lawful.

The leading cases relating to this provision are the so-called 'First vagrancy cases'. There were three separate applications filed in 1966 by *De Wilde, Ooms* and *Versyp* v. *Belgium*,[102] which were joined. They related to the applicants' detention in centres for vagrants by order of a magistrate (*juge de paix*) under an Act of 1891 for the suppression of vagrancy and begging. Their principal complaint was that, as the magistrate acted in an administrative capacity, they had no possibility of obtaining a decision by a court as to the lawfulness of their detention, as required by Article 5(4) of the Convention. The Commission granted them legal aid.

It will be remembered that 'the lawful detention of ... vagrants' is one of the grounds of detention specifically permitted by paragraph (1) of Article 5. Nevertheless that does not obviate the requirement of paragraph (4) that a detained person should be able to 'take proceedings by which the lawfulness of his detention shall be decided speedily by a court.'

The Commission expressed the opinion, and the Court decided in 1971, that there was violation of Article 5(4) because the applicants had no right to appeal to a court of law against the administrative decisions ordering their detention. The Court reserved for the applicants the right to apply for 'just satisfaction' under the terms of Article 50 of the Convention. The applicants did so apply, through the intermediary of the Commission, but in a further judgement of 10 March 1972 the Court decided that the request for compensation was not justified and therefore made no award.[103]

In the meantime, after the judgement on the merits of the case in June 1971, a new law was adopted in August of that year amending the Act of 1891 so as to confer a right of appeal to the criminal courts from a magistrate's order of detention for vagrancy; as a transitional measure a similar right was given to vagrants already detained. As a result, when the Committee of Ministers came to supervise the execution of the judgement of the Court in accordance with Article 54 of the Convention, it was able to take note of the new law and 'express its satisfaction with the legislative measures introduced by the Belgian authorities with a view to securing the application of the Convention ... in Belgium'.[104]

Four other cases raised the same issue: *La Haye, de Wilde, Nys* and *Swalens* v. *Belgium,* known as the 'Second vagrancy cases'.[105] Once the question of principle had been settled by the Court in June 1971, the Commission transmitted its report on the second group of cases to the Committee of Ministers in April 1972, and the latter, by its Resolution DH(72)1 of 16 October 1972, decided that there had been a violation of Article 5(4) but that it was now remedied and no further action was required.[106]

Paragraph 5 of Article 5 provides that:

> Everyone who has been the victim of arrest or detention in contravention of the provisions of this Article shall have an enforceable right to compensation.

To date this provision has been rarely invoked before the Convention organs. It is not free from difficulties. Domestic law in most – probably all – member States provides for compensation in various cases of unlawful detention, particularly if there has been negligence or malice. But do the circumstances in which compensation is payable under national law correspond closely to the circumstances in which detention violates Article 5 of the Convention? It is possible to answer this question only by a careful examination of the national law of the different Contracting Parties.

With this in mind, the Secretary General of the Council of Europe, acting in accordance with Article 57, asked the governments in 1972 to explain the way in which their internal law ensured the effective implementation of this provision of the Convention. The results of this enquiry are referred to in Chapter VII below.

ARTICLE 6. THE RIGHT TO A FAIR TRIAL

Article 6 constitutes, like Article 5, one of the most important provisions in the Convention. Nor is this hard to understand. The right to a fair trial has roots which go back to Magna Carta and to King Edward III's undertaking, in his reaffirmation of the Charter, that no man, of whatever estate or condition he be, should be harmed except *par due process de ley*. This right evokes the long history of the two notions of 'the law of the land' and 'due process of law', as explained by Coke in 1628, the part played by the latter principle in the American constitution and in the Fifth and Fourteenth Amendments, and the presumption of innocence proclaimed in Article 7 of the French Declaration of the Rights of Man of 1789.[107]

The right to a fair trial was of course included in the Universal Declaration, as Article 10:

> Everyone is entitled in full equality to a fair and public hearing by an independent and impartial tribunal, in the determination of his rights and obligations and of any criminal charge against him.

The presumption of innocence followed immediately after, in the first paragraph of Article 11. The rights incorporated in both articles were among those which the Assembly proposed in 1949 for inclusion in the European Convention.[108]

Utilisation of the method of detailed definition of the rights set out in the Convention made it necessary to elaborate Article 6 in much greater detail than the brief statement in Article 10 of the Universal Declaration quoted above. The first paragraph of Article 6 begins with a general statement of the right which follows closely, though not exactly, Article 10 of the Universal Declaration. (There are four differences, which will be explained below.) This paragraph continues by defining the circumstances in which the press and the public may be excluded from a trial. Paragraph 2 of Article 6 then sets out the presumption of innocence, while paragraph 3 sets out (but not limitatively) five separate rights of the defence in a criminal case. Article 14 of the UN Covenant on Civil and Political Rights follows a similar method (with certain variations) but adds four more paragraphs relating to the procedure in the trial of juveniles, the right of appeal, the right to compensation for miscarriage of justice and the principle of *ne bis in idem*.[109]

As regards the general statement of the right to a fair trial set out at the beginning of Article 6, the four differences between that text and Article 10 of the Universal Declaration are (apart from a change in the order of the words) the following. First, that the Declaration states 'Everyone is entitled *in full equality* to a fair and public hearing ...'. The words italicised are omitted in the Convention. This has no importance, because 'everyone' is entitled to the same right, and Article 14 of the Convention prohibits discrimination. Secondly, the Convention has inserted the word 'civil' in the phrase 'in the determination of his *civil* rights and obligations'. This is important and necessitates further consideration below. Thirdly, the Convention (unlike the Declaration) requires that the hearing should take place 'within a reasonable time', which is very important. Indeed, it is surprising that this requirement of reasonable expedition in the administration of justice is not included in the UN Covenant on Civil and Political Rights.[110] One recalls that in 1215 King John promised '. . . to none will we deny *or defer* right or justice'. It is recognised that 'justice delayed is justice denied'. It was therefore only right that the European Convention made this important addition to the UN text.

The fourth difference between the Declaration and the Convention in the general definition of the right to a fair trial is that both texts require that the hearing should be by an 'independent and impartial tribunal' but the Convention adds the words 'established by law'. This addition may also have some importance. It is no doubt directed against *ad hoc* or emergency tribunals which may be established by executive action in times of crisis, though some may think that the requirement that a court should be 'independent and impartial' would constitute a sufficient guarantee. The UN Covenant on Civil and Political Rights adds the requirement, in its Article 14, that the tribunal must be 'competent', though it is doubtful whether this is an addition of substance.

No one will be surprised that there is much case law interpreting Article 6 of the Convention. Some earlier decisions which may be mentioned are the following.

This Commission has held that Article 6(1) does not guarantee the right to be present in person at all civil proceedings, but has indicated that it does imply the right to be present in certain classes of cases, such as 'where the personal character and manner of life of the party concerned is directly relevant to the formation of the Court's opinion on the point which it is called upon to decide; and . . . a case in which a parent, following upon a divorce, makes an application to the Court for a right of access to a child of the marriage is without doubt a case of this kind'. The Commission has also held that the provision in paragraph 2 of Article 6 that 'everyone charged with a criminal offence shall be presumed innocent until proved guilty according to law' does not apply to a request for a retrial by a person already convicted.[111]

Another decision of the Commission has interpreted paragraph 3(a) of Article 6, which provides that an accused person has the right 'to be informed promptly in a language which he understands, and in detail, of the nature and cause of the accusation against him'. 'It follows from this provision,' says the Commission, 'that as part of the right to a fair trial guaranteed by the provisions of Article 6 as a whole, an accused person has the right to be informed not only of the grounds for the accusation, that is not only the acts with which he is charged and on which his indictment is based, but also of the *nature* of the accusation, namely the legal classification of the acts in question.'[112]

It has also been held that the right to free legal assistance is limited to persons charged with a criminal offence and does not apply in civil proceedings.[113] Furthermore that the right to call witnesses 'does not permit an accused person to obtain the attendance of any and every person and in particular of one who is not in a position by his evidence to assist in establishing the truth'. A court is therefore entitled to refuse to call witnesses if it considers that they could not prove the accuracy of quite general statements made by the accused.[114] The Commission has also held that the requirement of paragraph 1 of Article 6 that 'judgement shall be pronounced publicly' applies in civil and criminal matters but not in an administrative court determining a matter which is not a civil right.[115]

One of the first cases referred to the Committee of Ministers for final decision related to the provisions of Article 6 guaranteeing the right to a fair trial; this was *Nielsen* v. *Denmark*.[116] It aroused a good deal of interest at the time, *inter alia* because Nielsen was sentenced to life imprisonment for robbery, attempted robbery and homicide, and the jury found him guilty of planning and instigating the commission of these offences by another person through the use of hynotism.[117] After Nielsen had been convicted and his appeal rejected by the Danish Supreme Court the other person's allegation that he had been hypnotised by Nielsen was withdrawn, but a request for reopening the case was refused. Nielsen, in his application to the Commission, complained that he had not had a fair trial and, in particular, that he had not been informed in detail of the accusation against him, because the charge of hypnosis was not contained in the indictment.

The Commission examined these allegations in detail, after a sub-commission had established the facts, and reached the unanimous conclusion, which was endorsed by the Committee of Ministers, that he had been informed of the accusation against him in sufficient detail and that 'considered as a whole, the criminal proceedings brought against Nielsen in the Danish courts ... do not fall short of the standards required by Article 6(1) as to the right of every accused to have a fair trial'.[118]

This right was also the principal issue raised in the inter-State case of *Austria* v. *Italy*,[119] lodged in 1960. It concerned the sentences passed successively by the Assize Court of Bolzano (16 July 1957), the Court of Appeal of Trent (27 March 1958) and the Italian Court of Cassation (16 January 1960) on six young men of the village of Fundres/Pfunders in the South Tyrol (Upper Adige) accused of murdering a customs officer during the night of 15–16 August 1956. The Austrian government alleged various violations of Article 6, particularly as regards the refusal to hear two witnesses for the defence and as regards an investigation at the scene of the crime in the absence of the accused. The Commission declared the application admissible in January 1961 as regards the alleged violations of Article 6(2) of the Convention (presumption of innocence) and Article 6(3)(d) (hearing of witnesses for the defence under the same conditions as witnesses for the prosecution) and also of Article 14 (non-discrimination). On the other hand the Commission declared the application inadmissible in regard to the allegation of a violation of Article 6(1), based on the composition of the courts of Bolzano and Trent, because the convicted persons had not in that respect exhausted all the domestic remedies available to them, as required by Article 26 of the Convention.

Some interesting points came up for consideration by the Commission before it gave its decision on the admissibility of the application. The Italian government claimed that it was inadmissible *ratione temporis,* because Austria had become a Party to the Convention only on 3 September 1958 and the trial of the six young men had taken place in July 1957 and, on appeal, in March 1958. It was only the final appeal to the Court of Cassation in Rome in January 1960 that was subsequent to the Austrian ratification of the Convention, and no complaint had been made about the procedure on that occasion. The Commission rejected this contention on the ground that the whole conception of the Convention was to provide a collective guarantee of the rights and freedoms set forth therein, which the Contracting Parties undertake to secure 'to everyone within their jurisdiction' without condition of reciprocity; consequently 'it follows that a High Contracting Party, when it refers an alleged breach of the Convention to the Commission under Article 24, is not to be regarded as exercising a right of action for the purpose of enforcing its own rights, but rather as bringing before the Commission an alleged violation of the public order of Europe'.[120]

A second point considered by the Commission at this stage was the application of the rule about the exhaustion of domestic remedies in Article 26 of the Convention. The Austrian government, while admitting the full application of the rule in relation to individual petitions under Article 25, argued that it did not apply to inter-State applications under Article 24; it drew a distinction between individual petitions, for which the applicant cannot seize the Commission before he has exhausted his domestic remedies, and inter-State applications, to which this condition should not apply because, it was said, the applicant State does not normally have access to the national courts of the respondent State. The Commission rejected this argument, holding that the provisions of Article 26 of the Convention apply equally to inter-State and individual applications; in so doing it followed its own precedent in the Cyprus case, where it had rejected a part of the Greek government's application on the ground that domestic remedies had not been exhausted.[121]

The sub-commission appointed in accordance with Article 29 of the Convention (in the original version), after an exchange of memorials in 1961, held a number of sittings during the first half of 1962 and then reported to the plenary Commission. The latter held hearings during the second half of that year, during which a number of procedural points were evoked – in particular as regards the right of the Commission to hear additional witnesses and consider issues which had not been raised in the sub-commission's report.[122] The Commission heard eight further witnesses in November 1962, the representatives of the Parties in January 1973 and then adopted its report in March of that year. (It was as a result of its experience in this case that the Commission proposed the abolition of the system of sub-commissions, which led to the conclusion of the Third Protocol, as explained in Chapter I, section 3.)

On the points of substance raised in this case, the Commission established that the Italian Code of Penal Procedure makes the acceptance of witnesses dependent on the relevance of their evidence, and that this rule applies equally to witnesses for the prosecution and for the defence; in this particular case the Court of Appeal at Trent had reasonable grounds for holding that it was not necessary to call the two witnesses about whose absence the applicant government complained.[123] Secondly, the fact that the accused were not personally present when an investigation was carried out at the scene of the crime did not constitute a violation of the right to a fair trial, because their lawyers were present and they had already stated that they had themselves no knowledge of the facts to be clarified at the investigation on the spot.[124] Thirdly, the Commission found no evidence to establish that the Italian court committed a breach of the rule of presumption of innocence.[125] Finally, the

Commission concluded that there was no violation of the provisions of Article 6. At the same time it expressed the wish that for humanitarian reasons, among which might be counted the youth of the prisoners, measures of clemency should be taken in their favour. The Committee of Ministers took a formal decision in the sense of the Commission's conclusion and instructed the Secretary General of the Council of Europe to inform the two governments concerned of the wish expressed by the Commission.[126]

The rights of the defence in a criminal trial were also raised in four cases filed in 1959 and 1960 concerning the *Austrian Code of Criminal Procedure.*

The two cases of *Ofner* v. *Austria* and *Hopfinger* v. *Austria* were very similar.[127] Ofner was condemned to four years' imprisonment on six charges of fraud and misappropriation and appealed against the judgement, entering at the same time a plea of nullity. The Supreme Court heard the appeal and the plea at a non-public hearing, in the absence of both parties but having 'heard' the Attorney General to the extent of taking note of his formal agreement to the draft decision. The court dismissed the plea of nullity but allowed the appeal and reduced the sentence. Hopfinger was sentenced to seven years' imprisonment for fraud. He appealed against his conviction and also entered a plea of nullity. Again, the Supreme Court heard the appeal at a non-public hearing in the absence of the parties, but having 'heard' the Attorney General; it dismissed the appeal and the plea of nullity.

In the case of *Pataki* v. *Austria* the applicant was sentenced to three years' imprisonment on several charges of theft and fraud. He stated that he was not allowed to call medical evidence in his defence, which would have shown that there were extenuating circumstances, but he did not appeal, since the court took such circumstances into account and fixed a lighter sentence than would have been normal. The Public Prosecutor, however, did appeal, and the Court of Appeal increased the sentence from three to six years' imprisonment. Again the hearing was not in public, the applicant and his lawyer were not present, but the Public Prosecutor was present and was heard.[128]

In *Dunshirn* v. *Austria* the applicant was convicted on several charges of larceny and sentenced to fourteen months' imprisonment, the court taking into account as an extenuating circumstance that he had made restitution as to 90 per cent of the money stolen. The Public Prosecutor appealed against the sentence and the Court of Appeal, stating that it did not accept the existence of extenuating circumstances, increased the sentence from fourteen to thirty months' imprisonment. Once again, the Court of Appeal heard the Public Prosecutor *in camera*, without the presence of the applicant or his lawyer.[128]

All four cases raised the question whether the Austrian Code of Criminal Procedure of 1873 – which required in its Articles 294 and 296 that the Court of Appeal and Supreme Court should give judgement on an appeal, sitting *in camera,* after hearing the Public Prosecutor – was in conformity with Article 6 of the European Convention. The applicants alleged that these proceedings were contrary to the principle of 'equality of arms' between the prosecution and the defence. But that principle is not mentioned in Article 6 of the Convention. The Commission had already held in *Nielsen* v. *Denmark*[129] that paragraph 3 of Article 6, which sets out five separate rights of the defence, is not limitative. (It starts with the following phrase: 'Everyone charged with a criminal offence has the following minimum rights:'.[130]) 'Equality of arms' could reasonably be deduced from sub-paragraph (b) of paragraph 3 ('to have adequate time and facilities for the preparation of his defence') or from sub-paragraph (c) ('to defend himself in person or through legal assistance'). But the Commission did not consider that this was necessary, 'since it is beyond doubt that in any case the wider and general provision for a fair trial, contained in paragraph 1 of Article 6, embodies the notion of "equality of arms"'.

Having thus established an important principle, which has subsequently been approved expressly by the Court,[131] the Commission turned to the facts of the particular cases. In *Ofner* and *Hopfinger* v. *Austria,* which had been joined, it reached the conclusion that there had been no violation, because in the course of the written procedure of the Supreme Court the Attorney General had merely expressed in writing his agreement with the report of the Judge Rapporteur. He had not attempted to influence the decision to the disadvantage of the accused without the latter being heard, and his action could not be said to violate the principle of equality.[132] The Committee of Ministers endorsed this opinion of the Commission.[133] In *Pataki* and *Dunshirn* v. *Austria* (which had also been joined), on the other hand, the Public Prosecutor was present when the case was examined by the Court of Appeal and had an opportunity of influencing the members of the court, without the accused or his counsel having a similar opportunity. The Commission concluded that this constituted a violation of Article 6 of the Convention.[134]

In 1962, while the Commission was examining the cases of *Pataki* and *Dunshirn,* the Austrian Minister of Justice proposed, and the parliament approved, an amendment to the Code of Criminal Procedure the effect of which is to give an accused person the right to be present or to be represented during the hearing of a criminal appeal.[135] The Minister's explanatory memorandum made it clear that this was the direct result of the proceedings in Strasbourg.[136] This amendment of the Austrian law regulated the problem for the future. But it did not remedy the violation in the particular cases of *Pataki* and *Dunshirn.* Consequently, as a result of a further proposal by the Minister of Justice, the parliament approved on 26 March 1963 a further Act giving a right to a new hearing to persons whose appeals had been rejected under the old procedure and whose applications to the European Commission of Human Rights had been declared admissible.[137]

In the light of these developments the Commission concluded that there had been a violation in the cases of *Pataki* and *Dunshirn,* but that a remedy was now afforded to them which was in accordance with the Convention.[138] The Committee of Ministers, for its part, took a formal decision to this effect in September 1963 and expressed its satisfaction at the legislative measures introduced in Austria to ensure the full application of the European Convention on Human Rights.[139]

A similar decision was taken in the following year on fourteen other applications against Austria which raised the same issue.[140] And in 1965 the circle was completed with the case of *Plischke* v. *Austria,* in which the applicant had taken advantage of the Act of 1963 in order to have his case reopened before the Austrian Supreme Court, which then reduced his sentence from three to two and a half years' imprisonment.[141]

The *Delcourt case* raised a similar issue to that considered in the various cases about the Austrian Code of Criminal Procedure. Delcourt was convicted of various offences by the Criminal Court at Bruges in 1964 and sentenced to one year's imprisonment. Both he and the Public Prosecutor appealed to the Court of Appeal in Ghent, which in March 1965 increased the sentence to five years' imprisonment and in addition ordered that after serving his sentence he should be detained at the government's discretion for a period of ten years. He appealed to the Court of Cassation in Brussels, which dismissed the appeal in June 1965. Later that year he filed an application with the European Commission of Human Rights, alleging that a number of provisions of the Convention had been violated concerning the right to a fair trial.[142]

Only one of the applicant's complaints was declared admissible: it concerned the presence of a member of the Attorney General's Department attached to the Court of Cassation at the deliberations of that court, when it was considering in chambers its decision on Delcourt's appeal. In accordance with a Belgian law of 1815 an *Avocat Général* had in fact participated in a consultative capacity in the deliberations of the court, which raised the question of 'equality of arms' which had been the central issue in the Austrian cases. The Commission by seven votes to six expressed the opinion that there was no violation of the Convention in the Delcourt case, because the role of the Attorney General's Department attached to the Court of Cassation is not similar to that of the prosecuting officers in lower courts; the Attorney General attached to the Court of Cassation does not bring criminal proceedings and is not a party to cases before that court; his function is to make submissions to the Court of Cassation, stating his reasons for considering that a decision of a lower court is consistent with or contrary to the law. Six members of the Commission, however, considered that the principle of equality of arms had been violated because the presence of the *Avocat Général* at the deliberations of the Court of Cassation violated the principle of equality of arms and was likely to affect the impartiality of the court.[143] The Commission referred the case to the European Court of Human Rights.

The Court, in its judgement of 17 January 1970, held unanimously that there was no violation of the Convention. Substantially it adopted the reasoning of the majority of the Commission. It pointed out that the Attorney General's Department attached to the Court of Cassation is not a party to a case, enjoys complete independence of the Minister of Justice, and advises the court with a view to ensuring the uniformity of judicial precedent. It found that there were no grounds for holding that the department had failed to observe the duty of independence and impartiality to the detriment of the applicant.[144]

The right to a fair trial is guaranteed by Article 6 of the Convention to everyone *in the determination of his civil rights and obligations or of any criminal charge against him*. The cases mentioned above have related to criminal proceedings; it is now time to consider the meaning of the phrase 'in the determination of his civil rights and obligations'.

First, a word about the legislative history. As mentioned at the beginning of this section, the Universal Declaration of Human Rights of 10 December 1948 used, in its Article 10, the phrase 'in the determination of his rights and obligations' (in French, 'de ses droits et obligations'). When the UN Commission on Human Rights was drafting the UN Covenants a discussion of the corresponding article (which became Article 14 of the UN Covenant on Civil and Political Rights) took place in December 1947. The US delegate proposed to use the expression 'civil rights and obligations' (in French, 'ses droits et obligations civils'). This was agreed. However, on 1 June 1949 Mrs Eleanor Roosevelt proposed to amend this by using the phrase 'in a civil suit', apparently intending to exclude various matters (such as those connected with military service and taxation) which are generally determined by administrative officers rather than by courts. When several delegates, including Dr Garcia Bauer and Professor René Cassin, objected that this was too narrow, as it would exclude, for example, commercial and labour questions, and fiscal and administrative questions, Mrs Roosevelt suggested using the phrase 'in a suit at law'. M. René Cassin then proposed 'ses droits et obligations de caractère civil' in French and 'his rights and obligations in a suit at law' in English.[145] This was agreed. He added that the question of the administration of justice between individuals and the State had not been fully thrashed out and should be examined more thoroughly; but it never was. It seems, however, that the phrase he proposed was not intended to exclude administrative adjudication.[146]

The Committee of Experts which prepared the first draft of the European Convention in 1950 utilised the text of the draft UN Covenant as it then stood, so that the right to a fair trial would be guaranteed to everyone 'in the determination of any criminal charge against him or of his rights and obligations in a suit at law', while the French text read 'des contestations sur ses droits et obligations de caractère civil, soit du bien-fondé de toute accusation en matière pénale dirigée contre elle'. This formulation was adopted (as one of two alternatives) by the Committee of Experts in March 1950, and approved by the conference of Senior Officials in June of that year and by a sub-committee of the Committee of Ministers on 7 August 1950. It will be observed that at that stage the English text put 'the determination of any criminal charge' in the first place and 'his rights and obligations in a suit at law' second, whereas in the French text the order of these two categories was reversed. In the final revision of the text of the European Convention in Rome on 3 November 1950, on the eve of its signature, two changes were made to this sentence: (1) to substitute the phrase 'civil rights and obligations' for 'rights and obligations in a suit at law'; and (2) to change the order of the words in the English text, so that 'the determination of his civil rights and obligations' should precede '[the determination of] any criminal charge against him', as in French. Both changes were inspired by a desire to secure a closer concordance between the two texts.[147]

This explanation of the legislative history has been given (even though it is inconclusive) because both the European Commission and the Court have had occasion to examine it when considering on a number of occasions the meaning of the phrase 'civil rights and obligations' and, in particular, whether the rules set out in Article 6 apply to proceedings before administrative tribunals.

In general, the Commission has stated that 'the term "civil rights and obligations" .·.. cannot be construed as a mere reference to the domestic law of the High Contracting Party concerned, but, on the contrary, relates to an autonomous concept which must be interpreted independently of the rights existing in the law of the High Contracting Parties . . .'.[148] In relation to that 'autonomous concept', the following have been held by the Commission not to concern 'civil rights and obligations' within the meaning of Article 6(1): proceedings concerning the imposition of a tax or the execution of tax decisions;[149] proceedings relating to social security contributions;[150] a request to be released on probation;[151] an application to enter and reside in a country.[152]

In a statement to the Court on 12 February 1968 in the *Neumeister case* the then President of the Commission, Professor Max Sørensen, analysed the concept of 'civil right' within the meaning of Article 6. He concluded rather tentatively, from an examination of the legislative history, that the intention of the Parties was best reflected in the French text ('droits et obligations de caractère civil'), which would justify considering the word 'civil' as relating in some way to the classical distinction between civil law and public law and would exclude the meaning used in the phrase 'civil rights and liberties', namely the rights of the citizens against the State.[153] In that case the Commission considered, by a majority of seven to five, that 'the right to personal liberty and the restrictions which may be imposed on a suspected criminal pending trial are not questions of civil rights within the meaning of Article 6'.[154] The Court in its judgement noted that certain members of the Commission expressed the view that requests by a detained person for provisional release relate to 'civil rights and obligations' within the meaning of Article 6; but the Court rejected that view, which it conisdered would give an excessively wide scope to the concept of 'civil rights'.[155]

The meaning of 'civil rights and obligations' was discussed again in the *Ringeisen case*. Ringeisen complained of a violation of Article 6(1) in proceedings which he introduced before a Regional Land Commission in Austria, requesting authorisation for a transfer of real property consisting of farmland, which he wished to develop as a building site. The Regional Land Commission was an administrative tribunal and not a court of law. The question therefore arose whether the proceedings before the Commission related to a 'civil right', in which case the standards of a fair trial set out in Article 6(1) would apply.

The Commission examined at some length the meaning of 'civil rights and obligations' in Article 6(1), including the *travaux préparatoires*, and reached the conclusion that:

> the term 'civil rights and obligations' must be interpreted restrictively so as to comprise such legal relationships only as are typical of relations between private individuals, to the exclusion of such legal relations in which the citizen is confronted with those who exercise public authority.

Consequently it reached the conclusion that the proceedings before the Regional Land Commission were not concerned with determining Ringeisen's civil rights within the meaning of Article 6(1).[156] This conclusion, however, was reached by seven votes against five, the minority holding that a civil right was in issue, namely the right to acquire by contractual agreement, under the conditions provided by law, the property in question.[157] It was common ground that the characterisation of the tribunal as administrative in Austrian law was not determinant; what mattered was the nature of the right in dispute.

The Ringeisen case was also referred to the Court, and once again the President of the Commission, now Mr J. E. S. Fawcett, analysed the notion of 'civil rights and obligations'.[158] In its judgement the Court adopted a wider interpretation of this notion than the majority of the Commission and made this important statement:[159]

> *As to the question whether the present complaint involves the determination of civil rights and obligations:*
> For Article 6(1) to be applicable to a case ('contestation') it is not necessary that both parties to the proceedings should be private persons, which is the view of the majority of the Commission and of the Government. The wording of Article 6(1) is far wider; the French expression 'contestations sur (des) droits et obligations de

caractère civil' covers all proceedings the result of which is decisive for private rights and obligations. The English text 'determination of ... civil rights and obligations', confirms this interpretation.

The character of the legislation which governs how the matter is to be determined (civil, commercial, administrative law, etc.) and that of the authority which is invested with jurisdiction in the matter (ordinary court, administrative body, etc.) are therefore of little consequence.

In the present case, when Ringeisen purchased property from the Roth couple, he had a right to have the contract for sale which they had made with him approved if he fulfilled, as he claimed to do, the conditions laid down in the Act. Although it was applying rules of administrative law, the Regional Commission's decision was to be decisive for the relations in civil law ('de caractère civil') between Ringeisen and the Roth couple. This is enough to make it necessary for the Court to decide whether or not the proceedings in this case complied with the requirements of Article 6(1) of the Convention.

One may conclude, therefore, that the expression 'determination of ... civil rights and obligations' covers all proceedings the result of which is decisive for private rights and obligations, and that the standards of a fair trial set out in Article 6(1) apply to all such proceedings.[160]

The most recent, and in certain respects the most important, case concerning Article 6 and the right to a fair trial is *Golder* v. *United Kingdom*.[161] The applicant was convicted of robbery with violence in 1965 and sentenced to fifteen years' imprisonment. While he was serving his sentence in Parkhurst Prison, Isle of Wight, a disturbance and demonstration by the prisoners took place on 24 October 1969, in which he played no part, which fact was corroborated by two prison officers. Another prison officer mistakenly stated that Golder was actively concerned in the riot. He was taken, with other prisoners said to be involved in the disturbance, to a separate wing of the prison and kept there for two weeks; on 30 October he was charged with assaulting a prison officer.

Golder wrote two letters to his Member of Parliament and one to the Chief Constable, protesting his innocence, but the letters were stopped. He was cleared of the charge on 7 November, but was still concerned that his prison record would show that he was suspected of participation in the riot, that this would affect his chances of release on parole and lead to refusal of permission to continue his technical education – he had already passed eight examinations while in prison and was due to take others. On 20 March 1970, in order to clear his record, he petitioned the Home Secretary for permission to consult a solicitor about bringing an action against the prison officer who had wrongly accused him; this request was refused on 6 April. He alleged that this refusal constituted a violation of Article 6(1) of the Convention, because, though a prisoner, he had the same civil rights in other respects as a free man and should be allowed to consult a solicitor about his rights.

The Commission declared his application admissible on 30 March 1971 and in a report transmitted on 5 July 1973 expressed the opinion that there had been violation of Article 6 of the Convention and also of Article 8 (right to respect for one's private and family life, one's home and one's correspondence). The British government referred the case to the Court of Human Rights on 27 September 1973, expressing its disagreement with the opinion of the Commission and with the latter's approach to the interpretation of the Convention. The chamber of the Court selected to hear the case decided on 7 May 1974, in view of the importance of the questions of interpretation of the Convention involved, to relinquish jurisdiction in favour of the plenary Court.

This case raised three separate issues. (1) Does Article 6(1) of the Convention secure a right of access to the courts? (2) If so, are there limitations on this right which apply to a convicted prisoner? (3) Does Article 8 of the Convention confer on a convicted prisoner the right to correspond with a lawyer with a view to institute civil proceedings?

The most important issue for the future application of the Convention is the first one: does Article 6(1) secure a right of access to the courts? At first sight it may seem surprising that the question is asked at all. 'Everyone is entitled to a fair and public hearing . . . by an independent and impartial tribunal established by law.' Does that not mean necessarily that everyone has the right to a fair and public hearing? If so, does not the right to a hearing imply necessarily the right of access to a court? This would seem to be the normal construction of the words.

But another interpretation is possible. This starts from a comparison of Article 6(1) with two other provisions of the Convention. Article 5(4) provides that 'Everyone who is deprived of his liberty . . . shall be entitled to take proceedings by which the lawfulness of his detention shall be decided . . .'; and Article 13 states that 'Everyone whose rights and freedoms as set forth in this Convention are violated shall have an effective remedy before a national authority . . .' If in those two cases the right to take proceedings and the right to an effective remedy are stated explicitly, is it not surprising that such a right is not stated explicitly in Article 6(1) – if it is meant to be protected by Article 6(1)? The latter provision could be interpreted to mean that *when* anybody's civil rights and obligations ... are to be determined, *then* he is entitled to a fair and public hearing by an independent and impartial tribunal established by law. If this interpretation is adopted, Article 6(1) sets out the conditions of a fair trial *in the event that* there is a trial, but it does not in itself guarantee the right to a trial, because there are not found in that article words guaranteeing access to a court such as there are in Article 5(4) and in Article 13. It will be seen that this issue is fundamental to the whole notion of the right to a fair trial enshrined in Article 6 of the Convention.

The Court in its judgement in the *Golder case* of 21 February 1975 examined these and other arguments. It based its position on Articles 31–33 of the Vienna Convention on the Law of Treaties of 23 May 1969. It observed that the phrase 'in the determination of his civil rights and obligations' does not necessarily refer only to judicial proceedings already pending; as the Commission had stated, it may be taken as synonymous with 'wherever his civil rights and obligations are being determined'. The Court relied heavily on the Preamble to the Convention, which forms an integral part of the context (*cf.* Article 31(2) of the Vienna Convention). In the Preamble the Contracting Parties declared that they are 'resolved, as the Governments of European countries which ... have a common heritage of political traditions, ideals, freedom and the rule of law, to take the first steps for the collective enforcement of certain of the Rights stated in the Universal Declaration ...' Their devotion to the rule of law, moreover, is twice affirmed in the Statute of the Council of Europe, both in the Preamble and in Article 3; the latter makes acceptance of the rule of law a condition of membership in the Council. 'In civil matters,' said the Court, 'one can scarcely conceive of the rule of law without there being a possibility of access to the Courts. ... The principle whereby a civil claim must be capable of being submitted to a judge ranks as one of the universally recognised fundamental principles of law; the same is true of the principle of international law which forbids the denial of justice. Article 6(1) must be read in the light of these principles.'

The Court therefore concluded: [162]

It would be inconceivable, in the opinion of the Court, that Article 6(1) should describe in detail the procedural guarantees afforded to parties in a pending lawsuit and should not first protect that which alone makes it in fact possible to benefit from such guarantees, that is access to a court. The fair, public and expeditious characteristics of judicial proceedings are of no value at all if there are no judicial proceedings.

Taking all the preceding considerations together, it follows that the right of access constitutes an element which is inherent in the right stated by Article 6(1). This is not an extensive interpretation forcing new obligations on the Contracting States: it is based on the very terms of the first sentence of Article 6(1) read in its context and having regard to the object and purpose of the Convention, a lawmaking treaty (see the Wemhoff judgment of 27 June 1968, Series A, No. 7, p. 23, §8), and to general principles of law.

The Court thus reaches the conclusion, without needing to resort to 'supplementary means of interpretation' as envisaged at Article 32 of the Vienna Convention, that Article 6(1) secures to everyone the right to have any claim relating to his civil rights and obligations brought before a court or tribunal. In this way the Article embodies the 'right to a court', of which the right of access, that is the right to institute proceedings before courts in civil matters, constitutes one aspect only. To this are added the guarantees laid down by Article 6(1) as regards both the organisation and composition of the court, and the conduct of the proceedings. In sum, the whole makes up the right to a fair hearing.

Having thus established clearly that Article 6(1) of the Convention guarantees the right of access to a court, the European Court of Human Rights considered whether there were limitations on this right in the case of a convicted prisoner in the situation of Golder. It recognised that the right of access was not absolute and that there might be limitations thereon. Nevertheless Golder could justifiably wish to consult a solicitor with a view to instituting proceedings; it was for a court to rule on any claim that might be made; in preventing Golder from presenting his claim the Home Secretary failed to respect Golder's right to go before a court as guaranteed by Article 6(1).

In the third place the Court considered whether there was a violation of Article 8 of the Convention, which protects, *inter alia,* the right of correspondence. This right is not absolute; various permissible limitations are set out in the second paragraph of that article. But they must be 'in accordance with the law and necessary in a democratic society'. The Court held that the refusal to allow

Golder to correspond with a solicitor was not so necessary and that therefore there was violation of Article 8.

In conclusion the Court held by nine votes to three that there was a violation of Article 6(1) and unanimously that there was a violation of Article 8.[163] It did not award damages under Article 50 of the Convention because it held that its decision in itself constituted adequate just satisfaction.

The Ringeisen judgement, in elucidating the notion of 'civil rights and obligations', and the Golder judgement, in establishing that Article 6(1) ensures not only the conditions of a fair trial but also the right of access to a court, will have great importance for the future in clarifying the content of one of the most fundamental rights guaranteed in the European Convention. Professor A. L. Goodhart once wrote, 'in three words "the fair trial" we can sum up the outstanding contribution that the common law has made to civilisation'.[164] We can conclude with satisfaction that this notion is an outstanding contribution not only of one system of law but of the European system enshrined in the Convention on Human Rights, which is the expression of the 'heritage of political traditions, ideals, freedom and the rule of law' common to the member States of the Council of Europe.

NOTES

1 Consultative Assembly, *Official Report*, 18 September 1953, p. 341. *Cf.* Jacques Velu, in *Human Rights in National and International Law*, 1968, pp. 44–6.

2 This question was discussed at some length during the second International Conference on the European Convention on Human Rights, organised in Vienna in October 1965 under the joint auspices of the Council of Europe and the University of Vienna. The proceedings of the Vienna Conference have been published in three editions: *Menschenrechte im Staatsrecht und im Völkerrecht*, Karlsruhe, 1967; *Human Rights in National and International Law*, Manchester, 1968; and *Les Droits de l'homme en droit interne et en droit international*, Institut d'Etudes européennes, Brussels, 1968. See particularly the reports of Professors Sørensen, Verdross and Ganshof van der Meersch, *ibid.*, pp. 15, 45 and 93 (German edition); pp. 11, 47 and 97 (English edition); pp. 35, 83 and 155 (French edition). See also A. H. Robertson, 'The relationship between the European Convention on Human Rights and internal law in general', in *Droit pénal européen*, Brussels, 1972, on which the text is partly based.

3 *PCIJ*, Series B, No. 10, p. 20, quoted Sørensen, *op. cit.*, p. 12.

4 *PCIJ*, Series A/B, No. 44, p. 24, quoted *ibid.*

5 The judgment is reproduced in the *Yearbook of the Convention on Human Rights*, Vol. II (1958–59) at pp. 608–26.

6 *Cf.* Sørensen, *op. cit.*, pp. 13–15, and Verdross, *op. cit.*, pp. 49–51.

7 There are variants postulating the primacy of municipal law or the primacy of international law; there are also differences between radical and moderate monism. On this whole question see Verdross, *op. cit.*, pp. 47–50, and the references given there.

8 Fitzmaurice denies the relevance of both theories in his lectures 'The general principles of international law considered from the standpoint of the rule of law', ADI, *Recueil des Cours*, 1957, Vol. II, pp. 70–80.

9 Sørensen, *op. cit.*, p. 24.

10 Summaries of the replies have been published by the Directorate of Human Rights of the Council of Europe in document H(67)2 of 2 January 1967. On the application of Article 57 see further Chapter VII, below.

11 Since this could not be done in the United Kingdom, the examination covered an extensive body of common law and statute law. The reply of the United Kingdom to the Secretary General enquiry under Article 57 annexed over fifty statutes, beginning with Magna Carta, 1215, and including several others more than two centuries old.

12 Article 64 of the Convention permits specific, but not general, reservations. Of the countires here considered, such reservations were made by Ireland, Norway, Sweden and the United Kingdom. (*Yearbook of the Convention*, Vol. I, pp. 40–5.)

13 In the case of Cyprus there are extensive constitutional provisions based in part on the terms of the Convention. (*Yearbook* III, 1960, pp. 678–704.)

14 T. Buergenthal, 'The effect of the European Convention on the internal law of member States', *ICLQ Supplement*, No. 11 (1965), pp. 79–106; M. Sørensen, *Proceedings of the Vienna Colloquy*, pp. 14–17; W. J. Ganshof van der Meersch, *ibid.* (French edition), pp. 196–202.

15 *Cf.* T. Buergenthal, *op. cit.*, n. 14, pp. 88–9.

16 *Yearbook*, VII p. 444.

17 A 'Collection of national decisions referring to the European Convention on Human Rights' is published annually by the Directorate of Human Rights of the Council of Europe. Lists of such decisions are published each year in the *Yearbook of the Convention*, Part III.

18 1974 All E.R. 377. *Cf. Hubbard* v. *Pitt*, which cited Article 11 of the European Convention as guaranteeing the right to hold public meetings. (1975 All E.R. 1506.)

19 It is, of course, highly desirable that the normative provisions of the Convention should be accorded the force of rules of internal law in all member States. The Consultative Assembly so proposed in its *Recommendation 683 (1972)* – see below, Chapter VIII, section 1. Several proposals to this effect have been made in the United Kingdom in recent years: see M. Zander, *A Bill of Rights?*, London, 1975, pp. 5–18.

20 *Cf.* W. J. Ganshof van der Meersch, 'Does the Convention have the force of *ordre public* in municipal law?', in *Human Rights in National and International Law*, 1968, pp. 97–143.

21 *Yearbook* IV, 1961, p. 138.

22 See references in nn. 62–4. A national decision affording the benefit of the European Convention to a foreigner (not a European) is that of the District Court of Bremerhaven of 18 October 1962. (*Yearbook* V, 1962, p. 362.) (The right of the accused to free interpretation if he does not understand the language used in Court.) See also H. Golsong, 'The European Convention . . . in a German court', *BYIL*, 1957, pp. 317–21.

23 In the American Convention on Human Rights the States Parties undertake '. . . to ensure to all persons subject to their jurisdiction the free and full exercise of those rights and freedoms . . .' without any territorial limitation. (*Human Rights in the World*, pp. 249–50.)

24 X v. Federal Republic of Germany, Application 1197/61, *Yearbook* V, p. 88. See also application 1611/62, in which the Commission said, 'in certain respects the nationals of a contracting State are within its "jurisdiction" even when domiciled or resident abroad'. (*Yearbook* VIII, 158, at p. 168.)

In its decision of 26 May 1975 on the admissibility of two applications brought by *Cyprus against Turkey* (6780/74 and 6950/75) the Commission said, '. . . the

. . . Parties are bound to secure the said rights and freedoms to all persons under their actual authority and responsibility, whether that authority is exercised within their own territory or abroad'.

25 *Yearbook* I, 1955–57, pp. 211–19.

26 The *Digest of Case Law* (Editions UGA, Heule, Belgium, 1970) contains summaries of, or extracts from, the more important decisions of the Commission, the Court and the Committee of Ministers during the period from 1955 to 1967, that is to say those published in the first ten volumes of the *Yearbook of the Convention*. (A second volume of the *Digest* will cover volumes XI–XV of the *Yearbook*.) The list of applications relating to rights not protected by the Convention and Protocols is given at pp. 314–20. For further discussion of grounds of inadmissibility see below, Chapter IV, section 5.

27 See speech of M. P.-H. Teitgen on 7 September 1949, *Travaux préparatoires*, Vol. I, p. 266, at p. 274.

28 The full text of each article is to be found in Appendix 1.

29 *Cf. Human Rights in the World*, pp. 88–90. The death penalty has been abolished, or is not carried out in peacetime, in the majority of member States of the Council of Europe. The position is reviewed in J. E. S. Fawcett, *The Application of the European Convention on Human Rights*, Oxford, 1969, pp. 31–2.

30 X *v*. Norway (867/60), *Yearbook* IV, p. 270. Incompatibility with Article 2 of the European Convention was a ground invoked by a group of seventy-eight French Deputies who in December 1974 filed a suit with the *Conseil Constitutionnel* asking for a declaration that the new law authorising abortion was unconstitutional. (*The Times*, 21 December 1974.) The suit was unsuccessful.

31 *Yearbook* XV, p. 76, at p. 242.

32 *Yearbook* II, 382, at p. 385.

33 Kenneth de Courcy *v*. U.K. (2749/66), *Yearbook* X, p. 382.

34 Zeidler-Kornmann *v*. Federal Republic of Germany (2686/65), *Yearbook* XI, p. 1020. The case is described more fully in Chapter IV, section 6.

35 X and Y *v*. United Kingdom (5775/72 and 5856/72), *Collection of Decisions*, No. 46, p. 128. The respondent government did not contest the admissibility of the question whether birching constituted a degrading treatment within the meaning of Article 3 of the Convention.

36 *Yearbook* II, pp. 174–80. For the investigation in Cyprus see Chapter IV, section 6.

37 *Ibid.*, pp. 182 and 186.

38 *Ibid.*, pp. 186 and 196.

39 Applications 3321/67, 3322/67, 3323/67 and 3344/67, filed in September 1967. A special volume of the *Yearbook* of the Convention on Human Rights – Vol. XII, 1969, Part II, or XII *bis* – contains the report of the Commission on this case and the resolution of the Committee of Ministers of 15 April 1970.

40 *Ibid.*, pp. 33–9.

41 *Yearbook* XI, pp. 690–728.

42 *Ibid.*, pp. 730–80.

43 See n. 39.

44 Resolution DH(70)1 of the Committee of Ministers, *Yearbook* XII *bis*, pp. 511–14.

45 For the hearing of witnesses and investigation on the spot see below, Chapter IV, section 6.

46 *Op. cit.* n. 39, p. 186.

47 *Ibid.*, p. 502.

48 *Ibid.*, pp. 504–5.

49 Application 5310/71. The summary which follows is based on 'Stocktaking', October 1974, pp. 9–10.

50 'Report of the enquiry into allegations against the security forces of physical brutality in Northern Ireland', Cmnd. 4823.

51 'Report of the committee of Privy Counsellors appointed to consider

authorised procedures for the interrogation of persons suspected of terrorism', Cmnd. 4901.

52 The decision on admissibility is published in *Yearbook* XV, pp. 76–258.

53 The second application (5451/72), arising out of the second memorial of the Irish government of March 1972, alleged that the Northern Ireland Act, 1972, violated Article 7 of the Convention because it enacted that failures to comply with orders of the security forces were criminal offences although they did not constitute criminal offences at the time they took place. During the hearings the UK Attorney General gave an undertaking that this Act would not be applied retroactively (*ibid.*, p. 236). The Irish Attorney General accepted this statement and withdrew the second application (*ibid.*, p. 240).

54 Council of Europe press communiqué C(75)9 of 21 March 1975. For the problems involved in this investigation see Chapter IV, section 6 (*in fine*).

55 Applications 5577–5583/72. Summary taken from 'Stocktaking', October 1974, pp. 36–7, which also summarises other individual applications relating to the situation in Northern Ireland, including that of Miss Bernadette Devlin, MP, which was declared inadmissible in 1971. Nearly 200 such applications had been filed by December 1974 (*Annual Review*, 1974, p. 22).

56 *Collection of Decisions*, No. 43, October 1973, pp. 122–49.

57 *Ibid.*, pp. 146–8.

58 *Ibid.*, p. 149.

59 *The Guardian*, 11 December 1974.

60 Council of Europe press communiqué C(75)19 of 30 May 1975.

61 For various attempts to protect the right of asylum see Chapter VIII, section 1.

62 *Collection of Decisions*, No. 40, 1972, p. 53, at p. 62 (unofficial translation). In the same sense *X* v. *Federal Republic of Germany* (1802/62), *Yearbook* VI, p. 462, at p. 480. See also (4763/71), *Collection of Decisions*, No. 37, p. 157.

63 *Baouya* v. *Federal Republic of Germany* (2396/65). See also *Dolani* v. *Belgium*, 'Stocktaking', 1975, p. 32, 'Stocktaking', October 1975, p. 30; *Yearbook* XIII, p. 1094.

64 'Stocktaking', October 1974, pp. 54–6, quoted at pp. 170–1.

65 *Collection of Decisions*, No. 44, February 1973, p. 101.

66 Report of the Commission of 19 July 1974.

67 The cases are summarised in 'Stocktaking', October 1974, pp. 37–9. For decision on admissibility see following note.

68 *Yearbook* XIII, p. 928, at p. 994. On 'inhuman or degrading treatment' see also *Simon-Herold* v. *Austria* (4340/69), Chapter IV, section 6, nn. 75–6.

69 *Cf.* C. W. Jenks, *Human Rights and International Labour Standards*, London, 1960, pp. 25–46.

70 *Iversen* v. *Norway* (1468/62), *Yearbook* VI, p. 278, at p. 328.

71 See previous note.

72 *Ibid.*, p. 328.

73 *Ibid.*, p. 330.

74 *Ibid.*, p. 332.

75 Application 2299/64. Decision on admissibility in *Yearbook* VIII, p. 324. Report of the Commission in *Yearbook* X, p. 626; decision of the Committee of Ministers, *ibid.*, p. 694.

76 See previous note.

77 *Yearbook* X, p. 674. The Commission also considered the question whether there was a violation of Article 14 (the non-discrimination clause) on the ground that the total exemption which would be accorded to a Catholic priest or a Protestant minister was not granted to a 'minister' of the sect of Jehovah's Witnesses. It rejected this argument because Grandrath's work as a Bible study director was carried out in his spare time and on Sundays; he could have done the same if he had complied with the order to do substitute service. The Com-

mittee of Ministers endorsed the opinion of the Commission that no violation had occurred (reference in n. 75).

78 See also reference in Chapter III, n. 11, at pp. 553–4.

79 *Lawless* v. *Ireland* (332/57): decision of the Commission on admissibility of 30 August 1958 in *Yearbook* II, p. 308. The *Lawless case*: Judgement of the Court on the preliminary objections, 14 November 1960, in *Yearbook* III, p. 492; judgement of the Court on the merits, 1 July 1961, in *Yearbook* IV, p. 438. The judgements of the Court are also published in separate volumes in the series *Publications of the European Court of Human Rights*, Series A. The report of the Commission, the pleadings and the oral arguments are published in *Publications of the European Court of Human Rights*, Series B, 1960–61.

80 A more complete account of the *Lawless case* by the present author is given in *British Yearbook of International Law*, Vols. XXXVI, 1960, p. 343, and XXXVII, 1961, p. 536; also in Chapter VII of the first edition of this book. More than a dozen articles about the case are listed in *Bibliography* (November 1973), pp. 107–11. For other aspects of the case see Chapter III, under Article 15, and Chapter V, section 4.

81 The judgement of the Supreme Court is given in *Yearbook* II, p. 608. An extract is given in the first section of this chapter.

82 See section of Chapter III *infra* on Article 15 and Chapter V, section 4, on the position of the applicant before the Court.

83 See previous note.

84 Application 1602/62. Decision of the Commission on admissibility, *Yearbook* VII, p. 168; judgement of the Court, *Yearbook* XII, p. 364.

85 Application 1936/63. Decision of the Commission on admissibility, *Yearbook* XII, p. 224; judgement of the Court, *Yearbook* XI, p. 812.

86 Application 2178/64. Decision of the Commission on admissibility, *Yearbook* VII, p. 330; judgement of the Court, *Yearbook* XII, p. 406.

87 Application 2122/64. Decision of the Commission on admissibility, *Yearbook* VII, p. 280; judgement of the Court, *Yearbook* XI, p. 796.

88 Stögmüller judgement (see n. 84), at p. 394.

89 Report of the Commission in *Publications of the Court*, Series B, 'Wemhoff case', 1969, pp. 184–201.

90 *Ibid.*, pp. 65–6.

91 *Publications of the Court*, Series A, 'Wemhoff case', judgement of 27 June 1968, p. 24; *Yearbook* XI, p. 796, at p. 804.

92 Judgement, p. 9.

93 Judgement, p. 26; *Yearbook* XI, p. 808.

94 Judgement, pp. 25 and 27; *Yearbook* XI, pp. 806 and 810. On length of detention pending trial see also *Jentzsch* v. *Federal Republic of Germany*, *Yearbook* XIV, pp. 876–902.

95 Neumeister case, judgement of 27 June 1968, pp. 38–9; *Yearbook* XI, pp. 818–20.

96 Neumeister case, judgement of 7 May 1974, p. 21.

97 Matznetter case, judgement of 10 November 1969; *Yearbook* XII, p. 406.

98 Stögmüller case, judgement of 10 November 1969, pp. 43–5; *Yearbook* XII, p. 364, at pp. 400–04.

99 'Stocktaking', October 1964, p. 16. *Bundesgesetzblatt*, 1964, Part I, p. 1067 (European Court of Human Rights, Series B, Wemhoff case, 1969, p. 19); Austrian *Bundesgesetzblatt*, 1971, No. 273.

100 Application 2614/65. Decision on admissibility in *Yearbook* XI, 268. Report of the Commission in *Publications of the Court*, Series B, 1970, No. 11, pp. 10–150. Judgement of the Court of 16 July 1961 (merits), *Yearbook* XIV, p. 838; judgement of 22 June 1972 (compensation, Article 50), *Yearbook* XV, p. 678; judgement of 23 June 1973 (interpretation of judgement of 22 June 1972). A later case on prolonged detention pending trial (over three years) was Levy *v.* Federal Republic of Germany (6066/73), declared admissible in 1973; *Col-*

lection of Decisions No. 45, p. 99. The Commission sent its report to the Committee of Ministers in July 1975.
101 *Engel, van der Wiel, de Wit, Dona and Schul* v. *the Netherlands.* Decision on admissibility of 17 July 1972 in *Yearbook* XV, pp. 508–58. Summary of the cases in 'Stocktaking', October 1975, pp. 53–5.
102 Applications 2832/66, 2835/66 and 2899/66. Decision on admissibility in *Yearbook* X, p. 420. Judgements of the Court of 18 November 1970 (on hearing of the applicant's lawyer) and 18 June 1971 (merits) in *Yearbook* XIV, p. 788. Judgement of 10 March 1972 (compensation, Article 50), *Yearbook* XV, p. 662.
103 See last reference in preceding note.
104 *Yearbook* XV, p. 62. On the functions of the Committee of Ministers under Article 54 of the Convention see below, Chapter VI, section 4.
105 Applications 2551/65, 3155/67, 3174/67 and 3499/68. Decision on admissibility in *Yearbook* XIV, p. 138; decision of the Committee of Ministers, *Yearbook* XV, p. 694.
106 *Yearbook* XV, p. 694. The case of *Binet* v. *Belgium* (2208/64) raised similar issues. It was declared admissible in 1966 (*Yearbook* IX, p. 392) but was struck off the list owing to the disappearance of the applicant.
107 The development of the notion of 'due process of law' is discussed in *Human Rights in the World*, pp. 10–14.
108 Article 2(3) of Recommendation 38 (1949). The Assembly grouped with these two articles of the Declaration Article 9 (freedom from arbitrary arrest, detention or exile).
109 These differences are explained more fully in *Human Rights in the World*, pp. 90–3. For the attempt to add the rule *ne bis in idem* to the European Convention see below, Chapter VIII, section 1.
110 These words were added to Article 8 of the American Convention on Human Rights during the San José conference in 1969 at the suggestion of the present author. *Cf. Human Rights in the World*, p. 125.
111 Application 434/58, *Yearbook* II, p. 354, at p. 370, and application 914/60, *Yearbook* IV, p. 372, at p. 378.
112 Application 524/59, Ofner v. Austria, *Yearbook* III, 1960, p. 322, at p. 344.
113 Application 250/57, German Communist Party v. Federal Republic of Germany, *Yearbook* I, p. 222, at p. 228. See also application 134/55, *ibid.*, p. 232; application 180/56, *ibid.*, p. 236; application 265/57, *ibid.*, p. 192.
114 Application 753/60, *Yearbook* III, 1960, p. 310, at p. 320.
115 Application 423/58, *Collection of Decisions*, No. 1, January 1960.
116 Application 343/57. Decision of the Commission on admissibility in *Yearbook* II, p. 412. Report of the Commission and decision of the Committee of Ministers in *Yearbook* IV, pp. 494 and 590.
117 A fuller summary of the case is given in the first edition of this book at pp. 68–72.
118 See second reference in n. 116, at p. 592. See also *Köplinger* v. *Austria* as regards adequate opportunities for consulting a lawyer. *Yearbook* XII, pp. 438–94.
119 Application 788/60. Decision of the Commission on admissibility in *Yearbook* IV, p. 116. Report of the Commission and decision of the Committee of Ministers in *Yearbook* VI, pp. 742 and 796.
120 *Yearbook* IV, p. 140.
121 *Ibid.*, pp. 150–2. On this point see further Chapter IV, section 5.
122 *Yearbook* VI, pp. 758–64.
123 *Ibid.*, pp. 772–8.
124 *Ibid.*, p. 780.
125 *Ibid.*, pp. 782–90.
126 *Ibid.*, pp. 796–800. The youngest of the accused was in fact pardoned and released. On the question whether the Commission is entitled to make suggestions

or recommendations if it has reached the conclusion that no violation has occurred, see Chapter VI, section 3.

127 Applications 524/59 and 617/59, which were joined. Decisions of the Commission on admissibility in *Yearbook* III, pp. 323 and 370. Report of the Commission and decision of the Committee of Ministers, *Yearbook* VI, pp. 680 and 708.

128 Pataki *v*. Austria, application 596/59, and Dunshirn *v*. Austria, application 789/60, which were joined. Decisions of the Commission on admissibility in *Yearbook* III, p. 356, and *Yearbook* IV, p. 186. Report of the Commission and decision of the Committee of Ministers, *Yearbook* VI, pp. 718 and 736.

129 See n. 116 above, para. 52 of the report.

130 In French, 'Tout accusé a droit notamment à:'.

131 Neumeister judgement, *Yearbook* XI, p. 812, at p. 828.

132 *Yearbook* VI, p. 704.

133 *Ibid*., p. 708.

134 *Ibid*., p. 732.

135 *Yearbook* V, p. 344.

136 *Ibid*., p. 340.

137 *Yearbook* VI, p. 804. A proposal to this effect had been made by the Minister in the Bill which he had submitted to the parliament in the previous year, but it was not accepted at that time.

138 *Ibid*., p. 734.

139 *Ibid*., p. 738.

140 *Glaser* et al. v. *Austria*. Decision of the Commission on admissibility in *Yearbook* VI, p. 140. Report of the Commission in *Yearbook* VII, p. 386; decision of the Committee of Ministers, *ibid*., p. 434.

141 Application 1446/62. Decision of the Commission on admissibility in *Yearbook* VI, p. 252. Report of the Commission and decision of the Committee of Ministers in *Yearbook* VIII, pp. 426 and 464.

142 Application 2689/65. Decisions of the Commission on admissibility in *Yearbook* X, pp. 238 and 282.

143 Report of the Commission in *Publications of the Court*, Series B, 'Delcourt case', p. 11 and pp. 58 and 63.

144 Judgement of the Court of 17 January 1970, *Yearbook* XIII, p. 1100, at pp. 1122–32.

145 This summary is based on an article by Professor Frank C. Newman, 'Natural justice, due process and the new international covenants on human rights' in *Public Law*, 1967, pp. 274–313, which examines the legislative history of this provision in detail. See also references in nn. 150 and 155.

146 Newman, *op. cit*., p. 304.

147 As regards the final revision of the text on the eve of signature, see Chapter I, n. 28. The *travaux préparatoires* show that the two changes in the text referred to were suggested by the present author in a letter to the British Foreign Office of 21 October 1950 and approved by the Legal Advisers who accompanied their Foreign Ministers to the sixth session of the Committee of Ministers in Rome. On the publication of the *travaux préparatoires* see Chapter I, n. 24.

148 *X* v. *Austria*, application 1931/63, *Yearbook* XII, p. 212, at p. 222. The right to be enrolled as a probationer barrister was held not to be a 'civil right' within the meaning of Article 6. *Idem* for the right to be admitted to the public service.

149 Applications 1904/63, etc, *A, B, C* and *D* v. *the Netherlands, Yearbook* XI, p. 268, at p. 284.

150 Application 2248/64, *X* v. *the Netherlands, Yearbook* X, p. 170.

151 Application 606/59, *X* v. *Austria, Yearbook* IV, p. 340.

152 Application 3325/67, *X* et al. v. *United Kingdom, Yearbook* X, p. 528, at p. 538. But see also *Alam and Khan* v. *United Kingdom* (2991/66), *ibid*., p. 470, at p. 504. In the case of *X* et al. v. *United Kingdom* the applicants claimed that

the action of an immigration officer in refusing to the first applicant the right of entry into the United Kingdom by an administrative procedure which did not correspond to the requirements of Article 6 constituted a violation of that article. The Commission said, 'the right to enter and reside in a country is determined by public law, through acts of public administration, from which it follows that the term "civil rights" in Article 6(1) does not include any such right . . .'. (*Yearbook* X, p. 528, at p. 538.) On the other hand in the case of *Alam and Khan* v. *United Kingdom* the Commission declared admissible, and decided to examine the merits of, an allegation that the refusal of admission to England of a minor child who wished to join his father was a violation of Article 8; the Commission added, 'the determination of a right to respect for family life under Article 8 may well be considered as the determination of a civil right within the meaning of article 6'. (*Yearbook* X, p. 478, at p. 504.) In fact the Commission did not reach the stage of expressing an opinion on these two issues because a friendly settlement of the case was achieved. (*Yearbook* XI, p. 788.)

153 *Publications of the Court*, Series B, 'Neumeister case'. Hearing of 12 February 1968, p. 216.

154 *Ibid.*, p. 217.

155 Neumeister judgement, *Yearbook* XI, p. 812, at p. 828.

156 See references given in n. 100 above.

157 Report of the Commission in *Publications of the Court*, Series B, 'Ringeisen case', 1970–71, p. 75.

158 *Ibid.*, pp. 236–45. Mr Fawcett suggested the following definition: 'Civil rights and obligations in Article 6(1) and in the equivalent French text are narrower in scope than civil and political liberties; but they embrace those rights and obligations which are established by law for the individual in his relations with other persons or with the State and its various agencies in such matters as personal status, property, contract and fault. To give a simple example, the compulsory acquisition of private property for public purposes would, on this view, involve civil rights and obligations.' (*Ibid.*, p. 241.)

159 *Yearbook* XIV, p. 850.

160 In the Ringeisen case the Court found no evidence of violation of Article 6(1). For its finding of violation of Article 5(3) see above under 'Article 5' and n. 100.

161 Application 4451/70. Decision of the Commission on admissibility in *Yearbook* XIV, p. 416. Judgement of the Court of 21 February 1975 in *Publications of the Court*, Series A, Vol. 18 (1975).

162 Judgement (see n. 161), p. 18.

163 Judges Verdross, Zekia and Sir Gerald Fitzmaurice appended dissenting opinions as regards Article 6(1). That of Sir Gerald Fitzmaurice was particularly long and interesting. Judgement (see n. 161), pp. 32–63.

164 Quoted by Newman, *op. cit.* n. 145, p. 277.

CHAPTER III

THE RIGHTS GUARANTEED II

1. ARTICLES 7–13 OF THE CONVENTION

ARTICLE 7. PROTECTION AGAINST RETROACTIVITY
OF THE CRIMINAL LAW

This article is based on paragraph 2 of Article 11 of the United Nations Declaration. Its first paragraph sets out the general principle of non-retroactivity of the law: 'No one shall be held guilty of any criminal offence on account of any act or omission which did not constitute a criminal offence under national or international law at the time when it was committed.' It continues by providing that no heavier penalty shall be imposed than was applicable at the time when an offence was committed. In fact the text of the European Convention follows *verbatim* that of the Universal Declaration, except for the use of the phrase 'criminal offence' instead of 'penal offence', which is used in the UN text. (The Fench text uses 'acte délictueux' in the Declaration and 'infraction' in the Convention.) Article 15(1) of the UN Convenant on Civil and Political Rights follows Article 7(1) of the European Convention in English (with minor differences in the French text, which uses both 'acte délictueux' and 'infraction'); it continues with a further provision: 'If, subsequent to the commission of the offence, provision is made by law for the imposition of a lighter penalty, the offender shall benefit thereby.' This additional safeguard is not found in the European Convention, though the principle would probably be respected in European States should occasion arise.

The second paragraph of Article 7 of the Convention has a saving clause:

> This article shall not prejudice the trial and punishment of any person for any act or omission which, at the time when it was committed, was criminal according to the general principles of law recognised by civilised nations.

This saving clause was introduced in order to make it clear that the trial of war criminals for acts which were criminal according to the general principles of law recognised by civilised nations 'was not inconsistent with the Convention and not contrary to the general guarantee against retroactivity of the law'.

The government of the Federal Republic of Germany, at the time of ratifying the Convention, made a reservation as regards paragraph 2 of Article 7. It stated that it could apply this provision only within the limits of paragraph 2 of Article 103 of the Basic Law, which provides that an act can be punished only if the law declared it to be an offence before it was committed.[1]

In the case of *De Becker* v. *Belgium* one of the allegations of the applicant was that the penalty imposed on him after the war on account of his wartime activities as a collaborator, by which he was deprived of the right to exercise his profession as a journalist, was contrary to Article 7. The Commission held that the offence committed by the applicant clearly fell within the exception contained in the second paragraph of that article.[2]

Article 7 was also invoked by the applicant in the case of *Lawless* v. *Ireland*.[3] Both the Commission and the Court held that it did not apply to the circumstances of the case, because Lawless was detained in order to prevent him from engaging in activities prejudicial to public order or the security of the State, and not as a result of a conviction on a criminal charge.[4]

The most important case involving Article 7 of the Convention to date has been the second inter-State application in 1972 by *Ireland* v. *the United Kingdom*.[5] The Irish government alleged that the Northern Ireland Act, 1972, concerning the legislative powers of the Northern Ireland parliament with regard to the armed forces constituted a violation of Article 7, in that it provided that persons would be held guilty of criminal offences for acts which did not constitute offences at the time they were committed, in particular by reason of failure to comply with the orders of a member of the security forces. During the proceedings the Attorney General of the United Kingdom gave an undertaking on behalf of his government to the effect that no one had been and no one would, by reason of the Act of 1972, be held guilty of a criminal offence on account of an act or omission which did not constitute a criminal offence at the time when it was committed. The Attorney General of Ireland, on behalf of his government, accepted this undertaking and stated that he would withdraw his allegations relating to violation of Article 7. In the light of these two statements the Commission decided to strike this case off the list.[6]

ARTICLE 8. THE RIGHT TO RESPECT FOR ONE'S PRIVATE AND FAMILY LIFE, ONE'S HOME AND ONE'S CORRESPONDENCE

Article 8 starts, in the first paragraph, with the affirmation of the right: 'Everyone has the right to respect for his private and family life, his home and his correspondence.' This is based on Article 12 of the Universal Declaration: 'No one shall be subjected to arbitrary interference with his privacy, family, home or correspondence'; the UN text continues, 'nor to attacks on his honour and reputation', which has been omitted in the European Convention. It will be observed that whereas the Declaration uses the single word 'privacy' the Convention uses 'private ... life'; this does not reflect any difference of substance, however, but rather an attempt to secure concordance between the English and French texts. The same expression 'vie privée' is used in French both in the Declaration and in the Convention. Article 17 of the UN Covenant on Civil and Political Rights follows closely Article 12 of the Declaration, but is more emphatic in prohibiting 'arbitrary *or unlawful* interference'.

Article 8 of the Convention – like a number of later articles – then includes a second paragraph which sets out the limitations which may be imposed on the right proclaimed in the first paragraph. It must be admitted that the net is widely cast. Paragraph 2 reads as follows:

> There shall be no interference by a public authority with the exercise of this right except such as is in accordance with the law and is necessary in a democratic society in the interests of national security, public safety or the economic well-being of the country, for the prevention of disorder or crime, for the protection of health or morals, or for the protection of the rights and feedoms of others.

The majority of these limitations are easy to understand, though it may seem surprising that it should be thought necessary to insert a restriction on the grounds of 'the economic well-being of the country'. The explanation is that at the time when the Convention was drafted in 1950 a number of countries still had in force exchange control regulations and wished to reserve the right to open correspondence for the purpose of enforcing these regulations. This restriction might now be invoked in justifying restrictions on immigration which have the effect of separating families.[7]

A great variety of problems have arisen in relation to Article 8 of the Convention; it is proposed to consider them separately under the four headings of privacy, family life, home and correspondence. Before doing so it is right to recall that the *Third International*

Colloquy about the European Convention on Human Rights, organised by the Belgian universities and the Council of Europe,
which was held in Brussels from 30 September to 3 October 1970,
took as its theme 'Privacy and Human Rights' and examined in
greater detail a number of questions relating to Article 8 of the
Convention;[8] in particular the report of Professor Jacques Velu
analysed in depth the question of respect for private life, home and
communications, while that of Professor Torkel Opsahl did the
same as regards respect for family life.[9]

(a) PRIVACY. The Convention does not attempt to define the notion
of 'privacy' or 'private life', and it is very hard to do so. Professor
Velu has discussed a number of definitions,[10] and the present author
has done so elsewhere.[11] Professor Velu has singled out the following aspects:

1. Protection of the individual's physical and mental inviolability
   and his moral and intellectual freedom.
2. Protection against attacks on an individual's honour or reputation
   and assimilated torts.
3. Protection of an individual's name, identity or likeness against
   unauthorised use.
4. Protection of the individual against being spied on, watched or
   harassed.
5. Protection against disclosure of information covered by the duty
   of professional secrecy.

The European Commission of Human Rights has not had to
consider many cases dealing with this aspect of Article 8. It has
been argued that the German law which punishes homosexuality
is an infringement of the right to respect for private life; but the
Commission has rejected this contention on the ground that the
public authorities are entitled, under paragraph 2, to limit the right
in accordance with the law for the protection of health or morals.[12]
Similarly the Commission has rejected as inadmissible an application alleging that the German law about keeping criminal records,
including photographs and fingerprints, was in violation of Article
8.[13] The same application made the rather surprising claim that a
Federal Act on closing hours for shops violated this article because
it forced consumers to do their shopping at hours which might
inconvenience them; this also was rejected.[14]

In the case of *Scheichelbauer* v. *Austria* the Commission declared
admissible an allegation concerning the use as evidence in a criminal

trial of a tape-recording made of a conversation of the accused without his knowledge.[15] When it came to express its opinion on the merits the Commission considered that there was, on the facts of the case, no violation of the right to a fair trial, but it was careful to leave open the question whether the tape-recording of a private conversation, unbeknown to the participants, constitutes an interference with privacy. The Committee of Ministers endorsed this view, in its Resolution DH(71)3.[16]

This last case leads one on quite naturally to the wider question of protection of the right of privacy from interferences made possible by modern scientific and technical devices. In 1968 the Consultative Assembly of the Council of Europe, in its *Recommendation 509 (1968)*, called for a study of the question whether, having regard to Article 8 of the Convention, the national legislation in the member States adequately protects the right of privacy against violations which may be committed by such methods; and, if the answer to this question is in the negative, for measures to be taken to secure better protection of this right.[17] At about the same time the Assembly interested itself in the question of interference with privacy by the press and other mass media; in September 1968 it organised a symposium in Salzburg on this subject.[18] These discussions led the Assembly to adopt in due course a *Declaration on Mass Communication Media and Human Rights* and its *Recommendation 582 (1970)* on the same subject, making various proposals for action by the Council of Europe to secure the better protection of the right of privacy.[19] Further developments resulting from these initiatives are recounted elsewhere.[20]

One aspect of *Recommendation 582 (1970)* must be mentioned here, as it concerns directly the intepretation of Article 8 of the Convention. The Assembly asked for 'an agreed interpretation of the right to privacy provided for in Article 8 of the Convention ... , by the conclusion of a Protocol or otherwise, so as to make it clear that this right is effectively protected against interference not only by public authorities but also by private persons or the mass media'. Can one so interpret Article 8? Is the protection afforded by that article *erga omnes* or only against the public authorities? Paragraph 2 of Article 8 enumerates the circumstances in which it is legitimate for the public authorities to interfere with the right of privacy but says nothing about interference by private persons or legal persons. Does that mean that no interference by third parties is permissible or simply that the Convention is silent on this point?[21] Generally speaking, the Convention is conceived as an instrument for the protection of the rights of the individual against interference by the organs of the State; yet many of the dangers to privacy in the modern world (for example, from the mass media or industrial espionage) result from the acts of private persons or organisations. Many will consider that the right should be similarly protected against such interferences by third parties, but it is far from clear that such a form of protection is established by Article 8 of the European Convention. Hence the legitimate desire of the Assembly that Article 8 should be construed in that way.

(b) FAMILY LIFE. The protection of the right to family life has been invoked much more frequently before the European Commission. In a number of cases an applicant has claimed that refusal to allow him to enter or reside in a country of which he is not a national but where members of his family reside is an infringement of Article 8. The Commission has said that the right to reside in a country of which one is not a national is not guaranteed by the Convention; though, in certain circumstances, refusal of permission to enter or reside might raise problems under Article 8, no violation occurred as regards a German national living in Germany who was refused a residence permit in Denmark but was allowed to go to Denmark for reasonably long periods to visit his parents.[22] Similarly, with an applicant, an adult, who wished that his father should be allowed to come from India to join him in England after they had been living apart for a number of years.[23] The same conclusion was reached as regards a husband who wished to join his wife and children in the United Kingdom, where they had been resident for a short period; they could have joined him abroad; the refusal of permission to enter the country did not therefore constitute a separation of the family by the authorities and did not disclose a violation of Article 8.[24]

On the other hand, in the case of *Alam and Khan* v. *United Kingdom*, which concerned the refusal of the immigration authorities to allow a minor child to join his father in England, the Commission considered it necessary to examine the merits of the case and declared it admissible;[25] subsequently a friendly settlement was achieved and the boy was admitted to the United Kingdom.[26]

A German decision of the Higher Administrative Court of Münster on 2 August 1960 is interesting in this context. The court set aside an expulsion order against a Belgian living in Germany who was bigamously married to a German woman (apparently believing that his first marriage had been dissolved) on the ground that this would break up the family in violation of Article 8 of the Convention, since, being unemployed, he might not be able to take with him to Belgium his German 'wife' and children.[27]

Interference with the right to family life has been alleged in a number of other cases considered by the Commission. It was one of the issues raised in *East African Asians* v. *United Kingdom*.[28] In two of the twenty-five cases joined together in the first group the allegations of violation of Article 8 were declared admissible.[29] Other applicants have made the same allegation.[30] Again in *Amekrane* v. *United Kingdom* one of the complaints of the applicant was that her husband's forced repatriation from Gibraltar to Morocco (after which he was tried and executed for his participation in a plot to assassinate the king of Morocco) violated her rights under Article 8; this allegation was declared admissible by the Commission.[31]

Interference with the right to family life was one of the issues raised in the 'Case relating to certain aspects of the laws on the use of languages in education in Belgium', generally known as the *Belgian linguistic case*.[32] The principal issues, concerning Article 2 of the First Protocol (right to education) and Article 14 of the Convention (non-discrimination) are discussed later in this chapter. It will suffice for the present to say that the applicants were French-speaking Belgians living in the Flemish (and therefore Dutch-speaking) region of Belgium, and on the periphery of Brussels, who complained that the education of their children in the local schools was carried on in the Dutch language, whereas they wished them to be educated in French. This, they claimed, violated several articles of the Convention. One of the arguments on which they based their case was that the system introduced by the Belgian education acts of 1932 and 1963 interfered with their right to family life because it threatened the children's intellectual and emotional development, prevented the head of the family from deciding in which language his children should be taught and interfered with the unity of the family.[33] The Court of Human Rights, in its judgement of 23 July 1968, rejected this argument; it held that Article 8 of the Convention 'in no way guarantees the right to be educated in the language of one's parents by the public authorities or with their aid. Furthermore, in so far as the legislation leads certain parents to separate themselves from their children, such a separation is not imposed by the legislation; it results from the choice of the parents . . .'[34]

(c) INVIOLABILITY OF THE HOME. There has been very little case law about this aspect of Article 8. It was one of the matters invoked in the *Greek case*, when the applicant governments alleged that the suspension of Article 12 of the constitution of 1952, guaranteeing inviolability of the home (and also of Article 20 on secrecy of correspondence) constituted a violation of Article 8 of the Convention. Evidence was given that the Law on the State of Siege of 1967 authorised the military authorities to search a house by day or night, that such searches in fact took place frequently without a warrant and that arrests of suspects normally occurred in their homes at night. The Commission considered that there was violation of Article 8 and the Committee of Ministers so decided.[35]

(d) FREEDOM OF CORRESPONDENCE. The question of everyone's right to respect for his correspondence has arisen chiefly in relation to the correspondence of detained persons. The Commission has held that the control and stopping of letters written by a prisoner 'are consistent with the Convention, since the limitation of the right of a detained person to conduct correspondence is a necessary part of his deprivation of liberty which is inherent in the punishment of imprisonment'.[36] Similarly 'the practice of prison authorities in examining the correspondence of detained persons is covered by the exceptions authorised in Article 8(2) of the Convention. This principle may also apply, should the occasion arise, to persons detained for the purpose of extradition or expulsion.'[37]

In the 'Vagrancy cases' the Commission reaffirmed the principle that the control of prisoners' correspondence 'can be considered as an inherent feature of the concept of deprivation of liberty in the case of a punishment entailing such deprivation' but went on to conclude that, since the detention of the applicants was unlawful, the censorship of their correspondence during their detention constituted a violation of Article 8.[38] The Court of Human Rights, however, took a different view on this point, holding that the Belgian authorities did not transgress the limits of the power of appreciation given to them by paragraph 2 of Article 8, which permits restrictions for 'the prevention of disorder or crime, for the protection of health or morals, or for the protection of the rights and freedoms of others'.[39]

A particular problem concerns the right of detained persons to correspond with a lawyer. This was indeed one of the central issues in the case of *Golder* v. *the United Kingdom* which has been recounted above.[40] Though the Court of Human Rights was divided on the question of violation of Article 6(1), it was unanimous in holding that the action of the Home Secretary in refusing to allow Golder to write to a solicitor with a view to bringing an action against a prison officer constituted a violation of Article 8; the government was not able to show that that refusal was necessary on any of the grounds set out in paragraph 2 of that article.[41]

Another special problem is raised by the right of detained persons to correspond with the European Commission of Human Rights. Their claim to do so may be based not only on Article 8 of the Convention but also on Article 25(1), the last sentence of which provides that Contracting Parties which have made a declaration recognising the right of individual petition 'undertake not to hinder in any way the effective exercise of this right'. This matter is discussed fully below in Chapter IV, section 4. It will suffice for the present to note that Article 3 of the *European Agreement relating to Persons Participating in Proceedings of the European Commission and Court of Human Rights* provides expressly for the right of the persons to whom the agreement applies (i.e. applicants, their lawyers and others) to correspond freely with the Commission and the Court and continues by providing, as regards persons under detention, that if their correspondence is examined it shall be despatched without undue delay and without alteration.[42]

ARTICLE 9. FREEDOM OF THOUGHT, CONSCIENCE AND RELIGION

The first paragraph of Article 9 is taken *verbatim* from Article 18 of the Universal Declaration (except for a change in the order of the final words) and guarantees not only freedom of thought, conscience and religion but also freedom to practise in public or in private and to change one's religion or belief. The second paragraph sets out the limitations on this freedom which may be necessary in the public interest; such limitations must be prescribed by law and necessary in a democratic society.

Article 18 of the UN Covenant on Civil and Political Rights contains a very similar text and adds two further provisions, of which one (para. 2) provides that no one shall be subject to coercion which would impair his religious freedom, while the second (para. 4) contains an undertaking by States to respect the liberty of parents (and, when applicable, legal guardians) to ensure the religious and moral education of their children in conformity with their own convictions. (This corresponds to the undertaking in Article 2 of the First Protocol to the European Convention.)

Article 9 formed the subject of a reservation by Norway when she ratified the Convention in 1952. Article 2 of the Norwegian constitution of 1814 contained a provision prohibiting the Jesuits in Norway; a corresponding reservation was therefore made as regards freedom of religion in that country But this led the Norwegians to reflect that if such a prohibition had seemed reasonable in 1814 it was no longer acceptable nearly 150 years later. They therefore amended their constitution to bring it into conformity with the Convention and withdrew the reservation in 1956. (*Yearbook of the Convention*, I, pp. 41–2.) A somewhat similar problem arose in Switzerland, where there was not a complete ban on the Jesuits but a prohibition on their opening educational establishments. The Swiss constitution was amended in this respect (as well as in relation to the right to vote for women) before Switzerland ratified the Convention in 1974.

In considering one of the applications in the *Belgian linguistic case* the Commission examined whether Article 9 of the Convention was applicable to the facts of the case. The applicants argued that their children 'risk permanent harm to the development and exercise of their intellectual faculties through being obliged to study in a language other than that of their family'; the Commission considered that this amounted, in the last analysis, to a claim by the applicants 'to have the imprint of their own personality and of [their] culture ... take first place among the factors conditioning the education of their children, in order that their children's thinking should not become alien to their own'. It concluded that this right was outside the scope of Articles 9 and 10 of the Convention.[43]

Article 9 formed the basis of the application introduced by *Grandrath* v. *the Federal Republic of Germany*.[44] Grandrath was a member of the sect of Jehovah's Witnesses who was recognised as a conscientious objector and as such was excused from military service but was required to do substitute civilian service in lieu thereof. This he also refused to do on grounds of conscience and was sentenced to a term of imprisonment. He contended that this was a violation of Article 9, quoting in support of his case the teachings of St Thomas Aquinas and Cardinal Newman; respect for the functions of ministers of religion, he claimed, constituted an essential part of religious freedom as guaranteed by that article.[45] The Commission, however, did not find it necessary to interpret Article 9 in relation to the facts of this case, because Article 4(3)(b) of the Convention expressly authorises the requirement of military service or, in the case of conscientious objectors, other service in lieu thereof. Consequently, the Commission concluded that objections of conscience do not, under the Convention, entitle a person to exemption from substitute service; and found it unnecessary to examine the interpretation of 'freedom of conscience and religion' in Article 9.[46]

The Netherlands Supreme Court was called upon in 1962 to consider whether Article 184 of the constitution of the Netherlands was in conformity with Article 9 of the Convention. The question arose because a Catholic priest organised an open-air procession in the town of Geertruidenberg, for which he was prosecuted and convicted by the court of first instance at Breda. Article 184 of the Dutch constitution authorises the practice of all religions *inside* buildings and permits their exercise *outside* buildings only subject to the laws and regulations in force at the date of the adoption of the constitution, that is to say in 1848; this meant, in fact, that religious processions which were already traditional at that date could continue but that the organisation of further religious ceremonies in the open air would not be allowed. On 8 March 1961 the Court of Appeal at Arnhem held that Article 184 of the constitution was in conflict with Article 9 of the European Convention; but the Supreme Court, on further appeal, held on 19 January 1962 that the limitation on the free practice of religion in public places contained in Article 184 of the constitution was intended to prevent tension between rival faiths and possible counter-demonstrations and was in the interests of public order – thus falling within one of the restrictions permitted by paragraph 2 of Article 9.[47]

As regards their substance there is a close connection between the right of freedom of religion and the right of parents to have their children educated in accordance with their own religious convictions – so much so that, as we have seen, both rights are included in the same article (Article 18) of the UN Covenant on Civil and Political Rights. In the Europeon system the second of these rights is protected by Article 2 of the First Protocol to the Convention (the article on the right to education). The case of *Karnell and Hardt* v. *Sweden*,[48] which raised the problem of the religious education of the applicants' children, is therefore recounted below in the text relating to the First Protocol, Article 2.

The question of the right of a prisoner to practise his religion was raised in the case of *X* v. *the United Kingdom*, which was examined by the Commission in 1974. The applicant, who was sentenced to five years' imprisonment, was a Buddhist; while in prison he wrote articles for a Buddhist magazine, but was refused permission to send them to the editor. He claimed that communication with other Buddhists was an important part of his religious practice and alleged violation, *inter alia*, of Article 9. The Commission ascertained that the prison authorities had tried to find a Buddhist minister who would visit him in prison; when the attempt was unsuccessful they allowed him to write extra letters to a fellow Buddhist. It concluded that there was no violation of Article 9 and dismissed the application as manifestly ill founded.[49]

ARTICLE 10. FREEDOM OF EXPRESSION AND FREEDOM OF INFORMATION

This article guarantees freedom of expression, including freedom to hold opinions and receive and impart information and ideas without interference by public authority and regardless of frontiers. The text is based fairly closely on Article 19 of the Universal Declaration, but continues with a rider not found in the Declaration: 'This Article shall not prevent States from requiring the licensing of broadcasting, television or cinema enterprises.'

Once more the general affirmation of principle contained in the first paragraph of the article is subject to the limitations and restrictions set out in the second paragraph. In this case they are particularly extensive and may be quoted in full:

> The exercise of these freedoms, since it carries with it duties and responsibilities, may be subject to such formalities, conditions, restrictions or penalties as are prescribed by law and are necessary in a democratic society, in the interests of national security, territorial integrity or public safety, for the prevention of disorder or crime, for the protection of health or morals, for the protection of the reputation or rights of others, for preventing the disclosure of information received in confidence, or for maintaining the authority and impartiality of the judiciary.

The UN Covenant on Civil and Political Rights contains a broadly similar text in Article 19. It is to be noted, however, that the Covenant (like the Declaration) refers to 'freedom to *seek*, receive and impart information', while the Convention omits the word 'seek'; the latter thus avoids raising the problem whether the right to seek information imposes on the public authorities any obligation to communicate information. It is also to be noted that the limitations and restrictions set out in Article 19 of the Covenant are less extensive than those found in Article 10 of the Convention; in particular, the prevention of disorder or crime and the main-

tenance of the authority and independence of the judiciary are
not mentioned in the UN text. It appears, therefore, that the authors
of the European Convention were particularly careful when they
came to draft this article. Freedom of information was one of the
principal subjects discussed at the Salzbourg symposium mentioned
above.[50]

Article 10 of the Convention was the principal basis of the case
of *De Becker* v. *Belgium*, for it was in respect of this article that
the Commission declared the application admissible.[51] De Becker
was a Belgian journalist who had collaborated with the enemy
during the war and thereafter was condemned initially to death and,
on appeal, to life imprisonment. In 1950 the sentence was reduced
to seventeen years' imprisonment, and in the following year he
was released on giving an undertaking to reside abroad and not to
engage in politics. He had been condemned under Article 123
sexies of the Belgian Penal Code, which provided that persons
sentenced to a penalty of more than five years' imprisonment for
certain offences committed in time of war should be deprived for
life of various rights, including:

. . .
   (e) the right to have a proprietary interest in or to take part in
      any capacity whatsoever in the administration, editing, printing
      or distribution of a newspaper or any other publication;
   (f) the right to take part in organising or managing any cultural,
      philanthropic or sporting activity or any public entertainment;
   (g) the right to have a proprietary interest in, or to be associated
      with the administration or any other aspect of the activity of
      any undertaking concerned with theatrical production, films or
      broadcasting.

The Commission considered, by eleven votes to one, that these
provisions of the Belgian code 'in so far as they affect freedom of
expression are not fully justified under the Convention . . . They are
not justifiable in so far as the deprivation of freedom of expression
in regard to non-political matters, which they contain, is imposed
inflexibly for life without any provision for its relaxation when, with
the passage of time, public morale and public order have been
re-established and the continued imposition of that particular in-
capacity has ceased to be a measure "necessary in a democratic
society" within the meaning of Article 10(2) of the Convention'.[52]

The Commission adopted its report in January 1960 and transmitted it to the Committee of Ministers on 1 February. In April
it referred the case to the Court, pointing out that the amendment

of Article 123 *sexies* of the Penal Code was under discussion in the Belgian parliament. After various procedural steps and an exchange of memorials and counter-memorials, the hearing of the Court was fixed for 3 July 1961. On 30 June the Belgian parliament adopted a law amending Article 123 in such a way that the disabilities imposed on De Becker would no longer apply. When the Court met on 3 July it was informed of this new development and adjourned the hearing until October. On that occasion the Court was informed by the delegates of the Commission that the applicant had communicated to them a declaration in which he made it known that he had no further claims to pursue and had withdrawn from the case.

Further hearings took place on 19 February 1962 at which the Commission, in its final submissions, suggested, *inter alia*, that the Court should strike the case off its list. The Belgian government, in its own final submission, made the same request.

The Court gave its judgement on 27 March 1962. It accepted the submissions submitted to it, mainly on account of two factors: the promulgation of the Belgian Act of 30 June 1961 amending Article 123 *sexies* of the Belgian Penal Code; De Becker's memorandum to the Commission, dated 5 October 1961, in which, finding that his application before the Commission had been met by the Act of 30 June 1961, he stated that he regarded it as 'unnecessary further to proceed with this case' and that he withdrew his application. As regards the first point, the Commission had emphasised in its final submissions of 30 June 1961 that the Act was in conformity with the Convention. The Belgian government, in its turn, having maintained throughout that even the former legislation was in conformity with the Convention, declared itself in agreement with the Commission.

In its judgement the Court recalled that to those submissions was added the above-mentioned statement by De Becker; the Court emphasised, however, that that statement had not come from a party represented before the Court and could not, therefore, possess the legal character or produce the effects of a notice of discontinuance of the proceedings. The Court nevertheless agreed that the Commission had the right to take the statement into account as a means of clarifying the issue before the Court.

On the basis of these facts and submissions the Court considered that the proceedings brought before it no longer served any purpose and that, on general principles, it was time to grant the request that the case be struck off the list.[53]

Three cases may be mentioned as illustrations of the restrictions which may be imposed on freedom of expression in accordance with paragraph 2 of Article 10. In *X* v. *Austria* the Commission, noting that the applicant had been convicted for activities aimed at the reintroduction into Austria of National Socialism, found that the restrictions imposed on him were necessary in a democratic society in the interests of public safety and national security and for the protection of the rights and freedoms of others; consequently the penal measures taken against the applicant were justified under Article 9(2) and Article 10(2).[54] In *X and the German Association of Z* v. *the Federal Republic* the applicant was sentenced under an Act of 1953 on the circulation of publications liable to corrupt the young; the Commission found that the provisions of this Act contained restrictions on the right of freedom of expression such as are authorised by paragraph 2 of Article 10, since they were provided for by law and represented measures necessary for the protection of morals of young persons.[55] In *X* v. *Austria* the Commission held that certain provisions of the Austrian Penal Code which penalise attacks on the honour of the army made through the medium of printed matter constitute restrictions on freedom of expression such as are authorised under paragraph 2 of Article 10, since they are provided for by law and constitute measures necessary for the protection of the reputation of others.[56]

In *NV Televizier* v. *the Netherlands* the applicant company published a weekly magazine containing information on forthcoming radio and television programmes – information which it obtained from other publications put out by a central bureau. This was held by the Dutch courts to be a breach of the latter's copyright. The applicants complained of violation of Article 10 (and also of Article 14, which prohibits discriminatory treatment) and their application was declared admissible.[57] Subsequently an arrangement was concluded whereby, after the adoption of a new broadcasting Act in 1967, Televizier was authorised to publish the programmes of all the Dutch broadcasting companies and the proceedings against them were discontinued. The applicants, in agreement with the government, stated that they wished to withdraw their application; the Commission then decided to strike the case off its list.[58]

Rather similar issues were raised in the case of *De Geillustreerde Pers NV* v. *the Netherlands*. The applicant company was the publisher of a weekly magazine in which it wished to publish the Dutch radio and television programmes, but it was prevented from doing so by the broadcasting Act of 1967. It complained that this violated

Article 10 of the Convention. The application was declared admissible in October 1973, but the Commission had not drawn up its report thereon by the end of 1974.[59] Another application relating to freedom of expression which was declared admissible in 1974 was *Handyside* v. *United Kingdom*. The applicant, who was the proprietor of a London publishing house, proposed to publish the *Little Red Book for Schoolchildren*, which was an English translation of a Danish original. The book was seized under the provisions of the Obscene Publications Acts of 1959 and 1964, and the applicant was prosecuted and convicted on a charge of possessing, with a view to publication for gain, an obscene book. He alleged the violation of several articles of the Convention, and the application was declared admissible in April 1974 in relation to Article10.[60]

Questions of wider interest are perhaps raised by the case of *Harold Evans, The Sunday Times and Times Newspapers Ltd* v. *United Kingdom*. The applicant claimed that a court order preventing the publication in *The Sunday Times* of an article concerning the 'thalidomide children' constituted a violation of Article 10 of the Convention. It was stated in the application that between 1959 and 1962 a number of children were born who were deformed allegedly by reason of their mothers having taken thalidomide as a tranquilliser or sleeping pill during pregnancy.

In September 1972 *The Sunday Times* published an article headed 'Our thalidomide children: a cause for national shame' and announced that it intended next to publish a long article tracing the history of the tragedy and of the manufacture and testing of thalidomide from 1958 to 1961. In October 1972 the maker and seller of thalidomide in the United Kingdom, Distillers Company (Biochemicals) Ltd, made formal representations to the Attorney General, claiming that the publication of this article would constitute contempt of court in view of the litigation still outstanding. The Attorney General subsequently decided to apply to the High Court for an injunction to restrain publication of the proposed article. This was granted in November 1972.

On appeal by Times Newspapers Ltd the Divisional Court's order was reversed by the Court of Appeal, but on a further appeal by the Attorney General to the House of Lords the Law Lords, on 18 July 1973, unanimously confirmed the order finding that the proposed article sought to interfere with pending court proceedings, including settlement negotiations, between the claimants and Distillers Company, and therefore constituted contempt of court.[61]

The application was declared admissible in April 1975.[62]

The last case to be mentioned as regards freedom of expression concerns the transmission of television programmes by cable. In the case of *Sacchi* v. *Italy* the applicant complained in January 1974 of the action of the Italian Minister of Posts and Telecommunications, who ordered him to close down his cable television business at Biella ('telebiella'), an order which was based on provisions in a decree of 1973 granting a monopoly to the Italian Radio and Television Corporation. The applicant alleged violation of Article 10 of the Convention.[63] Subsequently the Italian Constitutional Court declared unconstitutional the provisions on which the Minister's order was based.[64] By the end of the year no decision had been taken on the admissibility of the application, but a new decree had been submitted by the government to the Italian parliament.

The question whether a State monopoly of broadcasting or television is compatible with the Convention has been much discussed but not perhaps finally decided. The last sentence of the first paragraph of Article 10 expressly permits States to require the licensing of broadcasting, television or cinema enterprises. Does this authorise them simply to refuse licences to private enterprises if there is a State monopoly, or does the principle of non-discrimination enshrined in Article 14 of the Convention mean that the State may lay down certain conditions for obtaining a licence but that a licence must be granted to any enterprise, public or private, which satisfies those conditions? In the case of *X* v. *Sweden* in 1968 the applicant (a former Deputy Speaker of the Swedish parliament) attacked a Swedish statute of 1966 which established a monopoly of television and broadcasting as contrary to Article 10. The Commission, in interpreting the term 'licensing', observed that in a number of member States of the Council of Europe, both at the time of drafting the Convention and at the time when the application was filed, there was a system of public monopoly enterprises for radio and television; it therefore considered that the term licensing 'cannot be understood as excluding in any way a public television monopoly as such'.[65] While the position of the Commission is thus clear, there has been no final decision on the point by the Court or the Committee of Ministers. When the ratification of the Convention was under discussion in France one objection made was that the monopoly of the ORTF would be held inconsistent with Article 10.[66] When the French ratification was finally deposited in 1974 a declaration of interpretation was made to the effect that the government 'interprets the provisions of Article 10 as being compatible with the system established in France under Act No. 72,553 of 10 July 1972 determining the legal status of the French radio and television'.[67]

ARTICLE 11. FREEDOM OF ASSEMBLY AND FREEDOM OF ASSOCIATION

The Consultative Assembly, in its *Recommendation 38* of 8 September 1949, listed as two separate rights freedom of assembly and freedom of association. They were, however, the object of one article, Article 20, in the Universal Declaration. Similarly they were grouped together in Article 11 of the European Convention. The first paragraph affirms the right 'to freedom of peaceful assembly and to freedom of association with others' – in words which correspond closely to the UN text; it then continues with the words '. . . including the right to form and join trade unions for the protection of his interests', which relate to a right that is dealt with separately in Article 23, paragraph 4, of the Universal Declaration. It is significant that the second paragraph of Article 20 of the Universal Declaration is omitted from the Convention: 'No one may be compelled to belong to an association.' No doubt this was done with the 'closed shop' in mind; there is no protection against the closed shop in the European text.

The Convention has instead a second paragraph on the same lines as in the three previous articles, permitting restrictions in the interests of national security, public safety, for the prevention of disorder and crime, for the protection of health or morals or for the protection of the rights and freedoms of others. A specific restriction is then introduced: 'This Article shall not prevent the imposition of lawful restrictions on the exercise of these rights by members of the armed forces, of the police or of the administration of the State.'

In the UN Covenant on Civil and Political Rights the two rights are separated. Article 21 protects the right of peaceful assembly and Article 22 the right to freedom of association. Both articles include a list of permissible restrictions similar, but not identical, to the list in the European Convention. Restrictions on the right of association of members of the armed forces and of the police are specifically mentioned, but not of persons employed in the administration of the State. The Covenant contains an additional paragraph 3 referring to the *ILO Convention of 1948 on Freedom of Association and Protection of the Right to Organise*, which is not, of course, found in the European Convention.

Article 11 was hardly invoked before the Commission during the first fifteen years of its activity, but several interesting cases were filed in 1970 and 1972. The first of these was *Belgian National Police Union* v. *Belgium*.[68] An Act of 1961 introduced various changes affecting the staff structures, conditions of recruitment and promotion, and salary scales of provincial and communal employees in that country. The Act provided that various arrangements should be made 'after consulting representatives of those organisations that best represent the staff of the provinces and communes'. A trade unions' advisory committee was set up for this purpose, at to the Ministry of the Interior, but the only union representatives thereon were those of the three main poltical unions in Belgium. When the National Police Union objected at their exclusion the method of selection was changed; it was provided that the members of the advisory committee should be appointed by 'the organisations most representative of the staff of the provinces and communes'; but this was defined to mean 'organisations which are open to all staff of the provinces and communes and which defend such staff's professional interests,' which again meant that all professional organisations other than the three prinicipal political unions were excluded from the procedure of consultation. The Police Union objected, claiming that as a national federation of local police associations it represented three-quarters of the Belgian police force and should be accepted as representative of its members; if the benefit of consultation was restricted to the large professional political unions to the exclusion of non-political organisations, this would discriminate in favour of the former at the expense of the latter, whose members might in consequence tend to leave them. Article 11 of the Convention, they argued, protects the right to join or refrain from joining a union or association of one's choice without the Contracting Parties being entitled to place any restriction on this right by favouring one at the expense of another. This would also be required by the ILO Convention of 1949.

The central issue raised in this case was therefore whether Article 11 merely requires the State to abstain from interfering in trade union affairs – in which case it is enough that it does not prevent people from joining a union – or whether Article 11 requires a positive attitude on the part of the government (at least when the State is the employer) in accepting the union as an effective partner in collective negotiations. It will be apparent that to allow individuals to join a union but then to refuse to negotiate with it constitutes a very restricted notion of trade union freedom.

The Belgian National Police Union case was declared admissible in February 1972.[69] After hearings on the merits and an unsuccessful attempt at friendly settlement the Commission adopted its report in May 1974. It reached the conclusion that no violation had occurred, but in October of that year referred the case to the Court of Human Rights in view of the importance of the issues raised. Hearings by the Court took place in May 1975 and judgement was expected in the autumn.[70]

Similar issues were raised in two Swedish cases: *Swedish Pilots' Association* v. *Sweden* and *Swedish Engine Drivers' Union* v. *Sweden*. The Pilots' Association represented the majority of all Swedish pilots; until 1967 it was affiliated to one of the major Swedish labour organisations and was bound by a collective agreement concluded between that organisation and the National Collective Bargaining Office (SAV). When that agreement expired in 1968 the Pilots' Association sought to negotiate separately with the SAV; the latter refused, as its policy was to negotiate only with the four major labour organisations in Sweden. The application was declared inadmissible in July 1972 for failure to comply with the six-months rule in Article 26 of the Convention.[71] The application of the Engine Drivers' Union, on the other hand, was declared admissible, with the agreement of the Swedish government.[72] The Union's 1,200 members represent about 20 per cent of all engine drivers employed by the Swedish State Railways, but the Collective Bargaining Office refused to negotiate with them in accordance with the policy mentioned above. The applicants complained of violation of Article 11, and also of Article 14 (non-discrimination). After the failure of attempts to reach a friendly settlement, the Commission adopted its report in May 1974 and in October decided to refer the case to the Court of Human Rights at the same time as the Belgian Police Union case.[73] Concurrently it took similar action with the cases of *Schmidt* and *Dahlström* v. *Sweden*, which also raised problems concerning freedom of association. Professor Schmidt and Captain Dahlström belonged to unions which called a strike, in which they, however, did not participate. When a wage settlement was reached with the largest unions (in which theirs did not join) the Collective Bargaining Office gave retroactive effect to the settlement generally, but not as regards the members of their unions, since the latter had taken strike action. The applicants complained of violation of Article 11 and of discrimination against them on account of their trade union membership.[74] The cases were due to be heard in the autumn of 1975; it was expected that the judgements of the Court would clarify the meaning of the very general provisions of Article 11.

ARTICLE 12. THE RIGHT TO MARRY AND FOUND A FAMILY

This right is set out succinctly as follows: 'Men and women of marriageable age have the right to marry and to found a family, according to the national laws governing the exercise of this right.' This is based on Article 16 of the Universal Declaration, which also includes a prohibition of 'any limitation due to race, nationality or religion'. It was no doubt considered unnecessary to insert in Article 12 of the Convention a prohibition of discrimination since a general and wider prohibition is to be found in Article 14, which will be discussed shortly.

Article 16 of the Declaration is wider in scope than Article 12 of the Convention, because it continues by providing that men and women 'are entitled to equal rights as to marriage, during marriage and at its dissolution', while the following paragraph states, 'Marriage shall be entered into only with the free and full consent of the intending spouses.' A third paragraph of the Declaration continues: 'The family is the natural and fundamental unit of society and is entitled to protection by society and the State.' This last provision was no doubt considered an affirmation of principle rather than a statement of a right, and therefore suitable for inclusion in the Universal Declaration but not in the European Convention. The requirement of free and full consent of the intending spouses is certainly secured in European countries by the national law; but the same cannot be said of 'equal rights as to marriage, during marriage and at its dissolution', since nearly all systems of law contain certain provisions (for example, as regards domicile and maintenance) which impose unequal obligations.

Article 23 of the UN Covenant on Civil and Political Rights is based closely on Article 16 of the Universal Declaration, but its fourth paragraph is even more binding in requiring States Parties to take steps to ensure equality of rights and responsibilities as to marriage, during marriage and at its dissolution. Indeed, this is one of the four rights in the Covenant which contain important differences of definition when compared to the corresponding articles in the Convention.[75]

There is little case law of the European Commission of Human

Rights – and none of the Court or the Committee of Ministers – relating to Article 12. Three cases may be mentioned, all concerning the Federal Republic of Germany. In one of them the Commission considered that the refusal of the German authorities to allow the marriage of a man detained on remand, who had already been engaged for more than three years and could expect a long penal sentence (he was later sentenced to ten years' imprisonment) did not constitute a violation of Article 12.[76] In the second a German woman living in Berlin and married to an Austrian working in Germany complained that measures of expulsion against her husband, after his conviction for seven minor offences, would destroy her marriage and violate Article 12; the Commission dismissed the case as manifestly ill founded.[77] The third case concerned a German citizen who complained that the authorities would not recognise his marriage, which he had performed himself in accordance with provisions of the Book of Moses in the Old Testament, because he refused to contract a marriage in proper form before the registrar of marriages as required by German law. The Commission declared the application manifestly ill founded.[78]

ARTICLE 13. THE RIGHT TO AN EFFECTIVE REMEDY BEFORE A NATIONAL AUTHORITY

Article 13 provides that 'Everyone whose rights and freedoms as set forth in this Convention are violated shall have an effective remedy before a national authority notwithstanding that the violation has been committed by persons acting in an official capacity.' It is based on Article 8 of the Universal Declaration, which provides, 'Everyone has the right to an effective remedy by the competent national tribunals for acts violating the fundamental rights granted him by the constitution or by law.'

It will be observed that the UN text is wider, in that it applies to all rights guaranteed by the constitution or by law, whereas the European text is limited to rights and freedoms set forth in the Convention; on the other hand the Convention requires a remedy before *a national authority* (in French, *devant une instance nationale*), which could in certain circumstances be an authority other than a court or tribunal.

'The central question presented by Article 13,' writes Fawcett 'is whether it is concerned with the international or the domestic implementation of the Convention, with the collective guarantee, of with internal remedies.'[79] Does it come into play only after the

Convention organs have decided that there has been a violation of the Convention, or does it mean that the individual must be entitled to invoke effective domestic remedies if he considers that there has been a substantive breach of any of its provisions in his regard? The latter is what Fawcett calls the 'domestic view'. 'An allegation of a substantive breach of the Convention would then bring Article 13 into operation on the domestic plane.'[80]

In the present submission the latter interpretation – the 'domestic view' – is that which is most in accordance with the intention of those who drafted the Convention. It must not be forgotten that the proposals of the Assembly in 1949 envisaged that the formulation and definition of the rights to be protected would be left to the domestic law of each Contracting Party; but the Assembly insisted that, in the event of violation, there should be an effective remedy. Article 13 is based on a proposal of the United Kingdom delegation at the meeting of the Committee of Experts in February–March 1950; the UK was then opposed to the right of individual petition and to the creation of a European Court; the emphasis was on effective remedies at the national level. The words 'effective remedy before a national authority' are immediately followed by the phrase 'notwithstanding that the violation has been committed by persons acting in an official capacity', which also points to Article 13 coming into operation on the domestic plane. On this view the essence of Article 13 is to secure protection of the individual, by according him an effective remedy even, when necessary, against the *raison d'état*. The idea was expressed forcibly by M. Pierre-Henri Teitgen, the *rapporteur* of the Legal Committee, in a speech to the Assembly on 19 August 1949, when he said: [81]

> The first threat is the eternal reason of State. Behind the State, whatever its form, were it even democratic, there ever lurks as a permanent temptation this reason of State.
>   Montesquieu said, 'Whoever has power is tempted to abuse it.' Even Parliamentary majorities are in fact sometimes tempted to abuse their power. Even in our democratic countries we must be on guard against this temptation of succumbing to reasons of State.

The object of Article 13, therefore, is to ensure an effective remedy at the national level even against the organs of the State. In Article 1 the Contracting Parties assume the general obligation to ensure the rights and freedoms set out in the Convention; in Articles 2–12 they state which rights and freedoms are to be secured; in Article

13 they state that in case of violation an effective remedy shall be available at the national level.

It must be admitted, nevertheless, that a substantial difficulty remains in the interpretation of Article 13. When the Commission is seized of a complaint alleging violation of this article because the applicant had no effective remedy in domestic law for an alleged violation of a right protected by the Convention, the Commission will first enquire whether that right was in fact violated; if it was, a violation of the Convention has been established even without invoking Article 13; if it was not, then Article 13 does not apply. It appears, therefore, that before the Convention organs Article 13 is largely tautologous – though, in case of violation, the absence of an effective remedy at the national level might be considered relevant to an award of damages under Article 50. But Article 13 cannot stand alone. The importance of Article 13 lies principally in the obligation it imposes on States to ensure that an effective remedy is available in domestic law, particularly against decisions of the administration which may violate the rights and freedoms protected by the Convention.[82]

The Commission has repeatedly held that it cannot consider an alleged violation of Article 13 unless a violation has been established of a right set forth in another provision of the Convention. In *W, X, Y and Z* v. *United Kingdom* the Commission said, 'Article 13 relates exclusively to a remedy in respect of a violation of one of the rights and freedoms set forth in the Convention ... the applicants not having established even the appearance of a violation of one of the other rights invoked by them, there is in the present cases no basis for the application of Article 13.[83] In *Müller* v. *Austria* the Commission held in 1974 that Article 13, like Article 6, does not require that there should be several degrees of jurisdiction.[84] The Commission was of the opinion that Article 13 had been violated in the *Greek case*, both on account of the lack of independence of the judicial tribunals since May 1968 and because, in the case of complaints of political prisoners alleging torture or ill treatment, administrative enquiries either were not ordered or, if ordered, were not carried out effectively. The Committee of Ministers decided in its Resolution DH(70)1 that violation of Article 13 had occurred.[85]

2. ARTICLES RELATING TO THE EXERCISE OF THE RIGHTS GUARANTEED

Articles 14–18 of the Convention lay down a certain number of

rules which are designed not so much to secure additional rights
as to ensure the effective exercise of the rights enunciated in the
previous articles.

Article 14 is a non-discrimination clause. It provides that the
rights guaranteed by the Convention shall be secured without discrimination on any ground such as sex, race, colour, language,
religion, political or other opinion, national or social origin, association with a national minority, property, birth or other status. This
text follows closely paragraph 1 of Article 2 of the Universal
Declaration, but has added one new ground, which is 'association
with a national minority'. The text of the Universal Declaration
itself recalls the resolution on non-discrimination adopted at the
first session of the Council of the United Nations Relief and
Rehabilitation Administration at Atlantic City on 1 December
1943.[86] The UN Covenants (each in its Article 2) reproduce *verbatim*
the grounds of discrimination set out in the Declaration.

In the same way that Article 13 is not a guarantee of an effective
remedy for violation of all rights, but only of those set out in the
Convention, so Article 14 is not a general guarantee against discrimination but only of non-discrimination in respect of the rights
set forth in the preceding articles and in the Protocol.[87] Moreover
the Commission has held that Article 14 does permit certain
differences in the treatment accorded to men and women. It has
rejected the contention that the punishment of male homosexuals
but not of females is a contravention of this article.[88] Not all
differentiation is discrimination.

It is to be observed that there is an important difference between
the English and French texts of Article 14. The English text provides
that the enjoyment of the rights and freedoms set forth in the Convention shall be secured 'without *discrimination* on any ground . . .',
whereas the French text, following the Universal Declaration, uses
the words 'sans *distinction* aucune', which is clearly much wider
in meaning.[89] The Court of Human Rights drew attention to this
difference in its judgement of 23 July 1968 in the *Belgian linguistic
case*, when it said:[90]

> In spite of the very general wording of the French version ('sans
> distinction aucune') Article 14 does not forbid every difference in
> treatment in the exercise of the rights and freedoms recognised.
> This version must be read in the light of the more restrictive text
> of the English version ('without distinction').

The Court went on to observe that certain differences in treatment exist in many democratic countries, and that certain legal inequalities tend only to correct factual inequalities. The Court continued: [91]

the principle of equality of treatment is violated if the distinction has no objective and reasonable justification.

moreover:

Article 14 is likewise violated when it is clearly established that there is no reasonable relationship of proportionality between the means employed and the aim sought to be realised.

The Commission of Human Rights expressed the same idea in different words in the *Grandrath case* when it said: [92]

The notion of discrimination between individuals implies a comparison between two or more different groups or categories of individuals and the finding that one group or category is being treated differently from – and less favourably than – another group or category and, secondly, that such different treatment is based on grounds which are not acceptable.

It would appear, therefore, that in order to prove violation of Article 14 it is necessary not only to show that there is a difference or distinction as regards the treatment accorded to different groups in the enjoyment of one of the rights guaranteed in the Convention but also that the distinction has no reasonable justification or is not proportionate to the aim envisaged, even though that aim may be legitimate in itself.

It results from the text of Article 14 that this provision is not an autonomous concept; it has no independent existence on its own. Article 14 relates to the enjoyment of the rights and freedoms set forth in the Convention, and therefore comes into play only if it can be shown that one of those rights and freedoms is exercised in a manner which is discriminatory. Thus the Court said in the *Belgian linguistic case*: [93]

... persons subject to the jurisdiction of a Contracting State cannot draw from Article 2 of the Protocol the right to obtain from the public authorities the creation of a particular kind of educational establishment; nevertheless, a State which had set up such an establishment could not, in laying down entrance requirements, take discriminatory measures within the meaning of Article 14.

This explains why both the Commission and the Court frequently consider an alleged violation of some article of the Convention taken in conjunction with Article 14. The facts may not show a violation of a substantive right considered in isolation, but they may show a violation of that right considered in conjunction with Article 14 if the substantive right is exercised in a manner that is discriminatory. Equally, when the Convention permits certain limitations or restrictions on one of the rights guaranteed, as in Articles 8–11, those limitations or restrictions may not be imposed in a discriminatory manner. 'If a restriction which is in itself permissible under paragraph 2 of one of the above articles is imposed in a discriminatory manner, there would be a violation of Article 14 in conjunction with the article concerned.'[94]

ARTICLE 15

Article 15 then provides for the possibility of derogation 'in time of war or other public emergency threatening the life of the nation'. In such circumstances any High Contracting Party may take measures derogating from its obligations under the Convention 'to the extent strictly required by the exigencies of the situation', provided that such measures are not inconsistent with its other obligations under international law. It is to be noted, however, that under paragraph 2 of this article no derogations may be made from Article 2 of the Convention (right to life) except in respect of deaths resulting from lawful acts of war, nor from Article 3 (freedom from torture or degrading or inhuman treatment), Article 4(1) (freedom from slavery or servitude), nor from Article 7 (protection against retroactivity of the criminal law). Furthermore paragraph 3 of Article 15 requires any High Contracting Party which avails itself of this right of derogation to keep the Secretary General of the Council of Europe fully informed of the measures which it has taken and the reasons therefor.

A broadly similar provision is contained in Article 4 of the UN Covenant on Civil and Political Rights. Two differences, however, may be noted. The UN text requires that the 'public emergency which threatens the life of the nation' must be 'officially proclaimed' in order to bring into play the right of derogation. Secondly, while the European Convention lists four 'sacrosanct rights' which may not be suspended even in time of emergency, the UN Covenant adds three more to this list: freedom from imprisonment for civil debt, the right to recognition as a person before the law and the right to freedom of thought, conscience and religion. The Covenant therefore contains additional safeguards when compared to the European Convention.

Article 15 is, of course, a very important provision, because it permits a State which has complied with its terms to suspend the operation of the great majority of the rights and freedoms guaranteed in the Convention. Clearly it must not be invoked lightly; indeed, it can be invoked only 'in time of war or other public emergency threatening the life of the nation' and 'to the extent strictly required by the exigencies of the situation'. These are strong words. It is necessary to consider separately: (1) what constitutes an emergency threatening the life of the nation; (2) who may determine that such an emergency exists; and (3) what are the procedural requirements of paragraph 3 of Article 15 concerning the information to be communicated to the Secretary General. The leading cases on Article 15 are the first *Cyprus case* (Greece *v.* United Kingdom), the *Lawless case* (Lawless *v.* Ireland) and the *Greek case* (Denmark, Norway, Sweden and the Netherlands *v.* Greece).

On the first, substantive, question the Court of Human Rights laid it down in the *Lawless case* that the natural and customary meaning of the words 'public emergency threatening the life of the nation' is sufficiently clear; 'they refer to an exceptional situation of crisis or emergency which affects the whole population and constitutes a threat to the organised life of the Community of which the State is composed'.[95] This is now the accepted definition, as evidenced by the *Greek case*. In the latter the Commission distinguished four separate elements:[96]

1. The public emergency must be actual or imminent.
2. Its effects must involve the whole nation.
3. The continuance of the organised life of the community must be threatened.
4. The crisis or danger must be exceptional, in that the normal measures or restrictions permitted by the Convention for the maintenance of public safety, health and order are plainly inadequate.

The second question, namely who may determine the existence of a public emergency threatening the life of the nation, is more difficult. Of course, the decision must be made in the first place by the government of the country concerned. But is its decision final? On the one hand it may be claimed that only the government has the responsibility for the maintenance of public order and the information necessary to decide whether public order is seriously endangered; consequently it is only the government which can take a decision on a matter of such importance and, once it has done so, no one else is competent to question it. On the other hand it can be argued that an uncontrolled, unilateral power of decision would make it possible for any government to declare an emergency at any time when there is slight provocation, in which case the value of the collective guarantee established by the Convention would be seriously weakened; it would indeed cease to operate precisely at the time when it is most needed.

In the first *Cyprus case* the Commission laid down the following principles: [97]

> (a) The Commission always has the competence and the duty under Article 15 to examine and pronounce upon a Government's determination of the existence of a public emergency threatening the life of the nation for the purpose of that Article; but
> (b) some discretion and some margin of appreciation must be allowed to a Government in determining whether there exists a public emergency which threatens the life of the nation and which must be dealt with by exceptional measures derogating from its normal obligations under the Convention.

In the *Lawless case* the Irish government cited a series of facts from which they deduced the existence of a public emergency threatening the life of the nation. The question of general prinicple which arose was whether the Commission and the Court could question and pass judgement on the conclusions that the government had drawn.

This, the latter argued, was outside the competence of the Commission or the Court:

> No machinery is provided under the Convention to enable a Government to take the opinion of the Commission or of the Court as to the existence of a state of emergency, or as to the measures which are necessary to deal with such an emergency, and it is inconceivable that a Government acting in good faith should be held to be in breach of their obligations under the Convention merely because their appreciation of the circumstances which constitute an emergency, or of the measures necessary to deal with the emergency, should differ from the views of the Commission or of the Court.

The government recognised the danger that if a determination of this sort were left to the sole discretion of individual governments, then a government might falsely claim the existence of a state of emergency and thus improperly suspend a number of guarantees. But this danger, it argued, was countered by Article 18 of the Convention, which reads:

The restrictions permitted under this Convention to the said rights and freedoms shall not be applied for any purpose other than those for which they have been prescribed ...

It would therefore be possible for the Court to determine in the light of Article 18, whether or not a government was acting in good faith.

The point of view of the Commission was very different. It referred back to the attitude which it had adopted in the first Cyprus case; this led to what came to be known as the doctrine of 'margin of appreciation'. The Commission could and must look behind the government's own appraisal of the situation; nevertheless the government should be allowed a margin of discretion, having regard to its responsibilities for keeping law and order and to the fact that it was likely to have at its disposal sources of information which could not be available to the Commission. The President of the Commission explained this to the Court on 10 April 1961 as follows: [98]

> The concept behind this doctrine is that Article 15 has to be read in the context of the rather special subject matter with which it deals: the responsibilities of a Government for maintaining law and order in times of war or public emergency threatening the life of the nation. The concept of the margin of appreciation is that a Government's discharge of these responsibilities is essentially a delicate problem of appreciating complex factors and of balancing conflicting considerations of the public interest; and that, once the Commission or the Court is satisfied that the Government's appreciation is at least on the margin of the powers conferred by Article 15, then the interest which the public itself has in effective Government and in the maintenance of order justifies and requires a decision in favour of the legality of the Government's appreciation.

Its earlier attitude was reaffirmed by the Commission in the Lawless case but was strongly attacked by the Irish government, which asked the Court to declare that the Commission had 'erred in principle in its approach to the application of Article 15'.

The applicant, of course, took a wholly different view. He argued that when a government makes a derogation under Article 15 it has the obligation of satisfying the Commission first as to the existence of the emergency, and secondly that neither the ordinary courts nor any special criminal courts are able to function and deal with the threat to the life of the nation. The burden of proof, he argued, is on the government, and it should produce evidence that can satisfy the Commission or the Court objectively – such as sworn evidence by a responsible Minister or other public official, which could be tested in cross-examination. The applicant in fact submitted a sworn affidavit by the Lord Mayor of Dublin in support of his view that there was not an emergency threatening the life of the nation, which, he alleged, remained uncontroverted. He proposed four objective tests to determine whether such an emergency existed: whether (1) the government and parliament, (2) the courts and (3) the public administration were functioning normally; and (4) had there been any major upheaval or disaster in the country? He contended that the answers to these questions showed clearly that no emergency existed in Ireland of the gravity which had been alleged.

The Commission's reply to this was that there was little difference of opinion as to the general facts of the situation; the dispute was as to the proper interpretation of the facts. In order to interpret them it maintained its doctrine of margin of appreciation and left it to the Court to decide which approach was the right one.

On the general issue of principle the Court decided against the government's view that once its good faith was established neither the Commission nor the Court could look into the matter further. It held that 'it is for the Court to decide whether the conditions laid down in Article 15 for the exercise of the exceptional right of derogation have been fulfilled in the present case', and again 'the Court must determine whether the facts and circumstances which led the Irish government to make their proclamation of 7 July 1957 come within this conception' (i.e. of an emergency threatening the life of the nation). Nevertheless, on the facts of the case, the Court held that the government was justified in the conclusion which it reached; the existence at the time of a public emergency threatening the life of the nation was reasonably deduced by the Irish government from a combination of circumstances which had been explained to the Court.[99]

It then became necessary to consider whether the measures taken by the Irish government – particularly arrest and detention without trial – were 'strictly required by the exigencies of the situation' within the meaning of Article 15. This question also the Court answered in the affirmative,[100] and thus came to the conclusion that there was no violation of the Convention by the Irish government.[101]

Somewhat similar problems arose in the *Greek case* after the *coup d'état* of April 1967. But there was an important difference, because the proclamation of a state of emergency in the Lawless case had been made by a lawful and democratically elected government, whereas in the Greek case the 'Government of the Colonels' had itself seized power by military force and overthrown the legitimate government. It argued that its action was justified by the existence of a public emergency threatening the life of the nation.

The way in which the Commission examined this question, by sending a sub-commission to Greece to conduct an enquiry on the spot, which heard twenty witnesses on the question (including three former Prime Ministers), is recounted below in Chapter IV, section 6. As to the law, the plenary Commission referred to the definition of a 'public emergency threatening the life of the nation' given by the Court in the *Lawless case* and distinguished the four separate elements mentioned at the beginning of this section. It then considered three distinct factors which had been adduced by the respondent government: the threat of a Communist take-over of the government by force; the state of public order; and the constitutional crisis immediately preceding the general elections due to be held in the month of May 1967. On the first point, it did not find that the evidence adduced showed that a displacement of the lawful government by force of arms by the Communists and their allies was imminent on 21 April 1967. On the second point, the picture of strikes and work stoppages in Greece at that time did not differ markedly from that in many European countries over a similar period; indeed, it was more favourable than in some of them. On the third point, the Commission gave a negative answer to the question whether there was an imminent threat of such political instability and disorder that the organised life of the community could not be carried on.[102]

For these reasons the Commission expressed the opinion that there was not in Greece on 21 April 1967 a public emergency threatening the life of the nation, and that the Greek derogation was therefore not justified.[103] The Committee of Ministers so decided in its *Resolution DH(70)1* of 15 April 1970.[104]

The existence of the conditions laid down in Article 15 was also relevant to the inter-State case brought by *Ireland against the United Kingdom* in 1971, relating to the situation in Northern Ireland.[105] The British government had made a declaration under the terms of Article 15.[106] The Irish government did not contest the existence at all material times of a public emergency within the meaning of that article, but maintained that the measures taken exceeded what was strictly required by the exigencies of the situation.[107] This question was, in effect, joined to the merits.[108]

Paragraph 3 of Article 15 requires that any Contracting Party availing itself of the right of derogation 'shall keep the Secretary General of the Council of Europe fully informed of the measures which it has taken and of the reasons therefor'. In the *Lawless case* the applicant claimed that the Irish government's communication to the Secretary General of the Council of Europe of 20 July 1957 was not an effective notice of derogation within the meaning of that paragraph, because it did not state expressly that it was a notice of derogation and did not adduce the existence of a state of emergency threatening the life of the nation; moreover he claimed that, even if it was effective, it had been made public in Ireland only on 23 October 1957, and could not be enforced with respect to events occurring before that date.

On grounds of principle this last argument was not without force. Everyone should be in a position to know whether the rights to which he is entitled under the Convention have been modified by a government's recourse to its exceptional power to derogate from the Convention under Article 15. For more than three months after the emergency measures were in force it was not known in Ireland that the government had made a derogation under Article 15. If a derogation published in October was effective in July, could it not be argued that its application was retroactive? On the other hand it could be said on behalf of the government that its proclamation bringing into force the exceptional power to detain persons without trial under the 1940 Act had been made public in Ireland by being duly promulgated on 5 July 1957.

The Court held that the government's communication, whatever its exact wording, had in fact given the Secretary General sufficient information about the measures taken and the reasons therefor, and that the Convention did not require publication of the notice of derogation but merely its communication to the Secretary General of the Council of Europe.[109]

In the *Greek case* the Commission considered whether the government's notice of derogation complied adequately with the requirements of paragraph 3 of Article 15 and reached the conclusion that it did not, notably because the government did not communicate the reasons for the measures of derogation until more than four months after they were first taken.[110] This, however, was a subordinate point, since the conclusion that there did not exist a public emergency threatening the life of the nation meant that the derogation was invalid in any case.

Another point to be mentioned in connection with paragraph 3 of Article 15 concerns the action to be taken by the Secretary

General when he has received a notice of derogation. The Convention is silent on this point, but the Committee of Ministers in September 1956 adopted its *Resolution (56)16* to the effect that 'any information communicated to the Secretary General by a Contracting Party in pursuance of Article 15, paragraph 3, of the Convention must be communicated by him as soon as possible to the other Contracting Parties and to the European Commission of Human Rights'. Since the establishment of the Court in 1959 such information is, of course, also communicated to the judicial organ; it is also transmitted to the chairman of the Committee of Ministers and to the President of the Assembly of the Council of Europe.[111]

Finally mention must be made of the French reservation to the Convention, under the terms of Article 64, relating to Article 15. The sense of this reservation is that a decision made by the President of the Republic in accordance with Article 16 of the French constitution of 1958 proclaiming a state of emergency 'must be understood as complying with the purpose of Article 15 of the Convention'; and further that the words in Article 15 'to the extent strictly required by the exigencies of the situation' shall not restrict the power of the President of the Republic to take the measures which he considers to be required by the circumstances.[112] The effect of this reservation is that a decision of the President of the Republic proclaiming a state of emergency, which is valid under the French constitution and accompanied by a derogation under the European Convention, should not subsequently be questioned by the European Commission of Human Rights.[113]

ARTICLE 16

Article 16 is very short and makes it clear that Articles 10 (freedom of expression), 11 (freedom of association) and 14 (non-discrimination) do not prevent the Contracting Parties from imposing restrictions on the political activity of aliens.

Article 25 of the UN Covenant on Civil and Political Rights is conceived in the same spirit, because it provides that 'every citizen' shall enjoy certain political rights, namely to take part in the conduct of public affairs, to vote and to be elected to public office and to have access to public service in his country. But the Covenant does not contain any specific restrictions on the political activity of aliens.

It appears that Article 16 of the Convention has not yet been invoked in a case brought before the European Commission of Human Rights.

Article 17 is important. It reads as follows:

> Nothing in this Convention may be interpreted as implying for any State, group or person any right to engage in any activity or perform any act aimed at the destruction of any of the rights and freedoms set forth herein or at their limitation to a greater extent than is provided for in the Convention ...

This text is designed to prevent adherents to totalitarian doctrines from using the freedoms guaranteed by the Convention for the purpose of destroying human rights. The article was the basis for the rejection by the Commission in July 1957 of an application by the German Communist Party, which complained of a decision of the Federal Constitutional Court of 17 August 1956 that had declared the party illegal, dissolved it and confiscated its assets. The Commission considered that the declared aim of the Communist Party, according to its own declarations, was to establish a Communist society by means of a proletarian revolution and the dictatorship of the proletariat; that recourse to dictatorship would be inconsistent with the Convention, because it would involve the suppression of a number of the rights guaranteed thereby; and that the activities of the Communist Party therefore fell clearly within the terms of Article 17.[114]

There were certain features common to this case and to the later case of *Retimag SA* v. *the Federal Republic of Germany*, on which the Commission took a decision as to admissibility in December 1961. Retimag was a joint stock company registered under Swiss law in 1955. It owned property in Germany which included the local offices of the Communist Party in Mannheim, and a printing plant and publishing firm which worked partly for their account; also property in Munich allegedly intended to house the offices of a Communist newspaper. The penal chamber of the Federal Court of Justice at Karlsruhe in October 1959 ordered the confiscation of these two properties without compensation, on the ground that Retimag was a cover to conceal an organisation whose objects were to preserve the property of the outlawed Communist Party and to continue Communist subversive activities. The company lodged an application with the Commission of Human Rights, claiming that this decision violated Article 1 of the Protocol, on the ground that it was made in circumstances not provided for by law and contrary to the general principles of international law. After an exchange of pleadings and oral hearings, the Commission declared the application inadmissible for non-compliance with the requirement of Article 26 on the exhaustion of domestic remedies.[115]

Article 17 of the Convention also came up for consideration in the *Lawless case*. The Irish government argued that at the time of his arrest Lawless was engaged in the activities of the Irish Republican Army, that these activities were of the type referred to in Article 17, and that therefore he could not rely on the provisions of the Convention at all. The Court's decision on this point was as follows.[116]

Whereas in the opinion of the Court the purpose of Article 17, insofar as it refers to groups or to individuals, is to make it impossible for them to derive from the Convention a right to engage in any activity or perform any act aimed at destroying ... any of the rights and freedoms set forth in the Convention; whereas, therefore, no person may be able to take advantage of the provisions of the Convention to perform acts aimed at destroying the aforesaid rights and freedoms; whereas this provision, which is negative in scope cannot be construed *a contrario* as depriving a physical person of the fundamental individual rights guaranteed by Articles 5 and 6 of the Convention; whereas, in the present instance, G. R. Lawless has not relied on the Convention in order to justify or perform acts contrary to the rights and freedoms recognised therein but has complained of having been deprived of the guarantees granted in Articles 5 and 6 of the Convention; whereas, accordingly, the Court cannot, on this ground, accept the submissions of the Irish Government.

ARTICLE 18

Article 18, which concludes section I of the Convention, provides that the restrictions permitted on the rights and freedoms guaranteed shall not be applied for any purpose other than those for which they have been prescribed.

The first thing to note about this article is that, like Article 14, it does not have an independent character of its own but can come into play only in conjunction with some other article of the Convention protecting a certain right and specifying what restrictions may be placed on that right. The effect of Article 18 is then to make it clear that those restrictions may not be applied for any other purpose than that for which they have been prescribed.

There is little case law on Article 18. The leading case is *Kamma v. the Netherlands*.[117] The applicant had been arrested and remanded in custody on suspicion of having committed two offences of extortion and attempted robbery with violence. While he was held on remand on these charges a separate investigation was opened in a murder case in which he was suspected of having committed or participated in the commission of that crime. He was transferred from the remand prison where he was held to the police headquarters in another town for interrogation in connection with the murder charge. He complained that after the investigation had been completed on the charge of extortion he was held in detention on suspicion of another crime (the murder) without having been formally informed of this. In the event he was convicted of robbery with violence, but the preliminary investigations in the murder case were closed without his being charged. The essence of his complaint was that the police took advantage of his detention on remand on one charge in order to conduct investigations with a view to another charge, although he was not detained in connection with the latter.

The Commission declared this part of his application admissible, though other parts were rejected.[118] In its report the Commission noted that the interrogation of the applicant in connection with the murder case was not more prolonged than it would have been had he not been already under detention; further, the applicant had himself told certain persons that he was involved in the murder and indeed himself confessed to the murder at one stage of the interrogation; moreover there was no ground to question the validity of his detention at the police headquarters, the Convention containing no provision about the place of detention on remand. Having considered all the elements in the case, the Commission concluded that there had been no breach of Article 18 read in conjunction with Article 5 of the Convention.[119] The Committee of Ministers so decided in its Resolution DH(75)1.[120]

3. THE RIGHTS PROTECTED BY THE FIRST PROTOCOL

THE RIGHT OF PROPERTY

Article 1 of the First Protocol relates to the right of property. Once

again the point of departure was the Universal Declaration of
Human Rights, Article 17 of which proclaims very simply:

1. Everyone has the right to own property alone as well as in
   association with others.
2. No one shall be arbitrarily deprived of his property.

The kernel of the matter, of course, is the meaning of the word
'arbitrarily'; this text raised all the problems both of international
and of municipal law which are latent in the nationalisation or
confiscation of property. The right to nationalise private property
had to be recognised – particularly having regard to the programme
of the Labour government in power in Britain in 1951, when the
Protocol was drafted. It was, however – as pointed out in Chapter
I – a matter of some difficulty to draft a text which would, on the
one hand, assert the principle of the right to private property and,
on the other hand, permit a socialist government to nationalise
private property by legislation legitimately adopted in a democratic
society without, at the same time, permitting confiscation by a
totalitarian government on grounds which it claims to be in the
general interest but under conditions which democratic countries
would regard as unacceptable.[121] It is significant in this context
that, after prolonged discussion, the Commission on Human Rights
of the United Nations abandoned the attempt to include an article
on the right of property in the UN Covenants, since agreement
thereon proved impossible.[122]

Article 1 reads as follows:

Every natural or legal person is entitled to the peaceful enjoyment
of his possessions. No one shall be deprived of his possessions
except in the public interest and subject to the conditions provided for by law and by the general principles of international law.
    The preceding provisions shall not, however, in any way impair
the right of a State to enforce such laws as it deems necessary to
control the use of property in accordance with the general interest
or to secure the payment of taxes or other contributions or penalties.

It will be observed that one of the limitations on the right of the
State to deprive someone of his possessions is constituted by 'the
conditions provided for . . . by the general principles of international
law'. This provision was intended to guarantee compensation to
foreigners for the expropriation of their property, even if compensation is not paid, or an inadequate compensation is paid, to
nationals; it would make it impossible for a State which nationalises
foreign property without adequate compensation to justify its action

on the ground that the foreign owners of property were treated on a footing of equality with its own citizens. The rules of international law, however, do not apply to the measures taken by a State in relation to the property of its own nationals.[123]

In 1959 the Commission considered an interesting case arising under Article 1 of the Protocol. The Liability Equalisation Act of 1948 (*Lastenausgleichsgesetz*) of the Federal Republic of Germany imposed, as part of the financial reforms associated with the introduction of the Deutschemark, a special levy on all capital and also a levy on gains accruing to mortgagors from the reduction of their mortgages under the financial reform. The applicant in this case was subjected to a 100 per cent levy on his mortgage gains. He argued that his assets had been reduced to ten per cent of their former value, whereas his liabilities had not been subjected to any diminution, and that his right to the use of his property had been infringed in that the legislation imposing financial reform deprived him of a substantial part of his capital. The Commission rejected this contention in a decision which said, *inter alia*: [124]

> Whereas the Liability Equalisation Act was introduced by the competent authorities as a measure forming part of financial and monetary reforms in Germany after the Second World War, and considered to be necessary for establishing a sound economic basis for a new democratic society in that country; whereas, furthermore, it was an express purpose of the said financial and monetary reforms to ensure that the economic burdens arising out of the war and out of the changes in the value of German currency should be distributed proportionately amongst the citizens; whereas it follows that the financial measure of which the applicant complains was introduced in the public interest and was administered to the applicant subject to the conditions provided by the relevant law, namely the Liability Equalisation Act; whereas it follows that the measure in question complied with the conditions laid down in the second sentence of paragraph (1) of Article 1 of the Protocol, and was not inconsistent with the right to peaceful enjoyment of possessions guaranteed under Article 1 of the Protocol;

A somewhat similar problem arose in the case of *Gudmundsson* v. *Iceland* in connection with Icelandic law No. 44 of 3 June 1957, which provided for taxation on large properties and which imposed a special tax on the properties of individuals exceeding one million kronur (about $65,000). The tax was a progressive tax on capital, varying from 15 per cent to 25 per cent on the value in excess of the first million kronur. The applicant claimed that this law amounted to a measure for the expropriation of property by reason of its provisions for excessive and discriminatory taxation and that it violated Article 1 of the Protocol. The Commission rejected this contention on the ground that the law in question was a measure 'to secure the payment of taxes or other contributions' within the meaning of paragraph 2 of Article 1.[125]

Other decisions relating to 'the payment of taxes or other contributions' – and holding that they were in conformity with Article 1 of the Protocol – have concerned the tax imposed in the Netherlands under the Old Age Pensions Act;[126] additional income tax required of persons who have a conscientious objection to old-age insurance;[127] and other social security contributions.[128]

In one of the first individual applications brought against the United Kingdom after it had accepted the right of individual petition in December 1966, *A., B., C. and D.* v. *the United Kingdom*, the Commission declared inadmissible an application by debenture holders of the United Steel Companies Ltd arising out of the compulsory acquisition of their stock under the provisions of the Iron and Steel Act, 1967. The Commission considered that the measures in question had the purpose of 'serving a public interest, namely the establishment of a sound economic basis for the British iron and steel industry, and that, in applying them, the United Kingdom had not exceeded the margin of appreciation as to what measures were in the public interest'.[129]

In 1974 the Commission considered another application relating to Article 1 of the First Protocol: *Christian Müller* v. *Austria*. The applicant, a locksmith, had paid contributions to an Austrian old-age pension fund for thirty-seven years when he became unemployed. He was not then entitled to a full pension. In 1963 he found employment in Liechtenstein and paid contributions both to the Austrian fund (on a voluntary basis) and to the scheme in operation in Liechtenstein. When he retired at the age of sixty-five in 1970 the Austrian authorities treated his contributions paid since 1963 not as voluntary contributions to his pension but as contributions to a supplementary scheme, which resulted in a financial loss to the applicant of about 100 schillings a month. He claimed that the partial loss of the right to a full pension amounted to a violation of Article 1 of the First Protocol, social security contributions being equivalent to insurance premiums and conferring a right to a corresponding benefit; he claimed that he had been deprived in part of his acquired right to a full pension, which was a right of property under Article 1.

The Commission declared the application admissible in December 1974, the Austrian government not contesting its admissibility.[130]

The right of property was one of the rights invoked in the *Greek case*, on the ground that the Constitutional Act 'Eta' promulgated by the revolutionary government authorised the confiscation of the property of persons deprived of their citizenship for political reasons. The Commission of Human Rights, however, expressed the opinion that this article had not been violated, because Article 1 of the First Protocol permits the State 'to enforce such laws as it deems necessary ... to secure the payment of taxes or other contributions or penalties'. The Committee of Ministers so decided.[131]

Violation of this Article was also one of the allegations made in the case of *Cyprus* v. *Turkey*, which was declared admissible on 26 May 1975.[132]

THE RIGHT TO EDUCATION

This was one of the articles which gave rise to most difficulty during the drafting of the Convention and Protocol. Article 26 of the Universal Declaration is very extensive; it provides not only that 'Everyone has the right to education' but also that elementary education shall be free and compulsory, technical and professional education generally available and higher education equally accessible to all on the basis of merit. Paragraph 2 of Article 26 relates to the aim of education, which includes 'strengthening of respect for human rights and fundamental freedoms' and promoting 'understanding, tolerance and friendship among all nations ...'. Paragraph 5 of this article provides that 'Parents have a prior right to choose the kind of education that shall be given to their children'. The UN Covenant on Economic, Social and Cultural Rights also contains an Article 13 in which the same principles are set out in greater detail.

The text proposed by the Assembly in 1950 started off with the general statement 'Every person has the right to education' and continued by providing that the State shall not encroach on 'the right of parents to ensure the religious and moral education and teaching of their children in conformity with their own religious and philosophical convictions'.[133] The government experts who drafted the Protocol were fearful that this text went too far. Did the right of every person to education impose a corresponding duty on the State to ensure that everyone is educated? While that is the policy of all members of the Council of Europe, there are few countries where governments can make it completely effective. Consequently a negative formulation was adopted. The second part of the text also raised problems. As far as religious convictions were concerned it presented no particular problem, but an obligation to ensure the education and teaching of children in conformity with the religious *and philosophical* convictions of the parents is very elastic. Does it include vegetarianism, polygamy and nudism? Were governments to accept that children could be brought up as agnostics and atheists? The government experts proposed limiting this provision to 'the right of parents to ensure the religious education of their children in conformity with their own creeds'. A number of texts went back and forth between the Committee of Ministers and the Assembly's Legal Committee;[134] the parliamentarians insisted on the retention of the word 'philosophical'; and the governments finally agreed to the following formula:

> No person shall be denied the right to education. In the exercise of any functions which it assumes in relation to education and teaching, the State shall respect the right of parents to ensure such education and teaching in conformity with their own religious and philosophical convictions.

But, as a result, several governments made reservations relating to this article at the time of signature or ratification.[135]

The leading case on Article 2 of the First Protocol is that 'relating to certain aspects of the laws on the use of languages in education in Belgium', generally known as the *Belgian linguistic case*.[136]

A number of applications were lodged with the Commission in 1962, 1963 and 1964 claiming that the legislation in Belgium on the use of languages in schools was in violation of the Convention. The applicants concerned were French-speaking but lived in localities where the Dutch language predominates; therefore, under the Belgian legislation, teaching in the schools is given in Dutch, which is also used by the administration and the courts. In these circumstances the families concerned were either obliged to accept that their children should receive their education in Dutch and thus be brought up in a different language from their parents, or, if they wished their children to receive their education in the French language, they were obliged to send them to French-speaking schools some distance from their homes, which naturally caused considerable difficulties.

Six of these applications (brought by more than 400 families) were declared admissible in 1963 and 1964, in so far as they were based on an alleged violation of Article 2 of the Protocol, of Article 8 of the Convention (which protects everyone's right to respect for his family life) and of Article 14 of the Convention, which prohibits discrimination on any ground, including language, race or association with a national minority. After concluding its examination of the merits of these cases – which had been joined together, as they raised the same issues – the Commission adopted its report and referred the matter to the Court of Human Rights in June 1965.

By a judgement of 9 February 1967 the Court, rejecting a preliminary objection raised by the Belgian government, declared itself competent to examine the case. In its judgement on the merits of the case the Court held that there had been no violation of the Convention as regards five of the six points submitted to it, but that there was violation as regards the sixth point, which concerned the situation of certain children who were prevented, solely on the basis of the residence of their parents, from having access to the French-language schools in the six communes on the Brussels periphery which are subject to a special status as regards the use of languages, whereas a similar impediment would not have applied to Dutch-speaking children. The Court held that this constituted discriminatory treatment and therefore constituted a violation of Article 14 of the Convention read in conjunction with Article 2 of the Protocol.

One aspect of the judgement of particular importance for the future is its interpretation of Article 14 (the 'non-discrimination clause'), which has been quoted above in connection with that article. Another aspect concerns the very meaning of Article 2 of the Protocol, which, as we have seen, is couched in the negative form: 'No person shall be denied the right to education.' It was argued that this formulation did not confer any right which could be invoked by individual applicants in proceedings brought under the Convention. On this point the Court said: [137]

> In spite of its negative formulation, this provision uses the term 'right' and speaks of a 'right to education'. Likewise, the Preamble to the Protocol specifies that the object of the Protocol lies in the collective enforcement of 'rights and freedoms'. There is therefore no doubt that Article 2 does enshrine a right.
>
> The negative formulation indicates ... that the Contracting Parties do not recognise such a right to education as would require them to establish at their own expense, or to subsidise, education of any particular type or at any particular level. However, it cannot be concluded from this that the State has no positive obligation to ensure respect for such a right as is protected by Article 2 of

the Protocol. As a 'right' does exist, it is secured by Article 1 of the Convention to everyone within the jurisdiction of a Contracting State.

Three later cases raised the question of compatibility with Article 2 of the Protocol of a Danish law of 1970 on compulsory sex education in schools.[138]

THE RIGHT TO FREE ELECTIONS

This is one of the most important of all the rights guaranteed by the Convention and the Protocol. It is to be found in the Universal Declaration with the following formulation (Article 21, para. 3):

> The will of the people shall be the basis of the authority of government; this will shall be expressed in periodic and genuine elections which shall be by universal and equal suffrage and shall be held by secret vote or by equivalent free voting procedures.

The UN Covenant on Civil and Political Rights provides in its Article 25 that 'Every citizen shall have the right and the opportunity:

> (a) ...
> (b) To vote and to be elected at genuine periodic elections which shall be by universal and equal suffrage and shall he held by secret ballot, guaranteeing the free expression of the will of the electors.

The Consultative Assembly in August 1950 proposed the following text:[139]

> The High Contracting Parties undertake to respect the political liberty of their nationals and, in particular, with regard to their home territories, to hold free elections at reasonable intervals by secret ballot under conditions which will ensure that the government and legislature shall represent the opinion of the people.

When the governmental experts came to examine this text in 1951 they discovered certain difficulties. In the first place, what would be the meaning of the undertaking by the Contracting Parties 'to respect the political liberty of their nationals'? If it was intended to relate to such rights as freedom of assembly, freedom of expression and freedom of association it was unnecessary, because these rights were already covered by separate provisions in the Convention itself. If, on the other hand, it was intended to relate to other rights it was imprecise and its meaning obscure. In the second place, the experts considered the phrase 'with regard to their home territories' to be unnecessary, since the whole Protocol would apply only to the metropolitan territories of the Contracting Parties, in default of an express declaration extending its application to overseas territories. Thirdly, the expression 'under conditions which will ensure that the Government and legislature shall represent the opinion of the people' might be construed as a commitment to some form of proportional representation, which governments were unwilling to assume.

After a further exchange of drafts between the Committee of Ministers and the Legal Committee of the Assembly the definitive text was finally agreed as follows:

> The High Contracting Parties undertake to hold free elections at reasonable intervals by secret ballot, under conditions which will ensure the free expression of the opinion of the people in the choice of the legislature.

It will be observed that the formulation of this right is different from that of those which have been discussed above. The usual form is 'Everyone has the right...' or 'No one shall be held...', but in Article 3 of the Protocol 'The High Contracting Parties undertake to hold free elections ... etc'. There is no provision such as that in the UN Covenant that 'Every citizen has the right to vote'. In other words, there is an undertaking by governments to hold free elections but not a guarantee of the right to vote.

In a case where an applicant complained that, when in prison, he was not allowed to vote in the Saar plebiscite of October 1955 the Commission said: [140]

> Although, according to this article, the Contracting Parties undertake to hold free elections, it does not follow that they recognise the right to every individual to take part therein; in other words, an individual's right to vote is not guaranteed by Article 3.

A similar decision was taken in another case in which three Belgians who had long been resident in the Congo complained that they were not allowed to vote in elections in Belgium.[141] In a later case in which a convicted prisoner complained that he had not been allowed to vote in the *Land* elections in the Saar and in the German federal elections in 1965, the Commission considered whether the restrictions upon the right to vote of convicted prisoners affect 'the free expression of the opinion of the people in the choice of the legislature'. It answered that question in the negative.[142]

An unusual case concerning the right to vote (or not to vote) was brought in 1971, based on Article 9 of the Convention (freedom of conscience and belief) but also citing Article 3 of the First Protocol: *X* v. *Austria*. The applicant (himself a barrister) complained that under Austrian law he was obliged, under pain of a fine, to vote in the Austrian presidential election and was only given the choice of two candidates (Dr Jonas and Dr Waldheim), neither of whom he could support; if by law he was required to vote for one or the other, this violated his rights under Article 9. He argued that there were more than 200,000 Austrian citizens in the same situation. The Commission pointed out that he could, at the polls, hand in either a blank or a spoiled paper, and declared the application inadmissible.[143]

The holding of free elections was, of course, one of the issues raised in the *Greek case*. The Greek parliament had been dissolved on 4 April 1967, and elections were fixed for 28 May of that year but were cancelled by the military government after it seized power on 21 April 1967. The applicant governments stated that not only had political activities ceased and no elections been held; there was even no legal basis for holding elections and no indication that the respondent government contemplated elections in the near future. The Greek government replied that there was provision for elections in the new constitution of 1968, that implementing legislation was being drafted and that elections would be held when 'a normal state of affairs has been restored and appropriate conditions have been created'.

The Commission considered that there was a clear and persistent breach of Article 3 of the First Protocol, since the entry into force of the relevant provisions of the new constitution had been delayed, no electoral law had been promulgated, and the Greek people were thus prevented from expressing their political opinion by choosing a legislature in accordance with Article 3. The Commission observed that even if there were a 'public emergency threatening the life of the nation' in the sense of Article 15, that would not justify the suspension of parliamentary life; the parliament had continued to function in Greece during the civil war of 1946–49.[144] The Committee of Ministers decided that there was violation of Article 3 of the First Protocol.[145]

4. THE RIGHTS PROTECTED BY THE FOURTH PROTOCOL

As explained in Chapter I, section 3, the Fourth Protocol was the result of a proposal made by the Consultative Assembly in its *Recommendation 234 (1960)*, which asked the Committee of Ministers to draw up a further protocol to the Convention to protect certain additional rights not included in the Convention itself or in the First Protocol; in due course the text was drafted; the Fourth Protocol was signed on 16 September 1963; it entered into force on 2 May 1968, and by June 1975 had been ratified by ten Contracting Parties.[146]

The Fourth Protocol protects the following additional rights: freedom from imprisonment for civil debt; freedom of movement and of residence and freedom to leave any country, including one's own; freedom from exile and the right to enter the country of which one is a national; prohibition of the collective expulsion of aliens. The Assembly also proposed in Recommendation 234 (1960) the inclusion of two further rights included in the Universal Declaration (Articles 6 and 7) and in the Covenant on Civil and Political Rights (Articles 16 and 26): the right to recognition as a person before the law and the right to equality before the law. This proposal, however, was rejected.[147]

While the work on the Second Protocol proceeded, the Assembly made further proposals for the inclusion of additional rights therein. These were the rights of national minorities,[148] the right of asylum,[149] and the principle of local autonomy.[150] The Committee of Ministers was opposed to the inclusion of the principle of local autonomy, on the ground that this was not a fundamental human right; it agreed that the experts should study the Assembly's proposals relating to minorities and asylum. As regards minorities the result of the study was negative;[151] as regards asylum it led to the adoption by the Committee of Ministers in 1967 of its *Resolution (67) 14* on 'Asylum to persons in danger of persecution' but not to a provision in a protocol to the Convention.[152]

FREEDOM FROM IMPRISONMENT FOR CIVIL DEBT

Freedom from imprisonment on the ground of inability to fulfil a contractual obligation forms the subject of Article 11 of the Covenant on Civil and Political Rights. The Consultative Assembly proposed to take over the United Nations text without change; this would strengthen the existing provision of Article 5 of the Convention on the right to liberty and security of person. It would apply to contractual obligations of any kind, including non-delivery and non-performance, and not only money debts; at the same time, it would not apply to public obligations (fiscal or military), nor to civil obligations imposed by statute or by the order of a court, such as maintenance obligations or a judgement debt for damages. It is thus designed to prevent imprisonment for the sole reason that the individual has not the material means to fulfil his contractual obligations.

The Committee of Experts accepted the Assembly's proposal, but substituted 'No one shall be deprived of his liberty . . .' for 'No one shall be imprisoned . . .'. This modification is designed to secure a wider measure of protection and corresponds more closely to the wording of Article 5 of the Convention.

There is little case law relating to the Fourth Protocol, partly because it entered into force fifteen years later than the Convention and the First Protocol and partly because the rights protected by it are, in any event, less frequently invoked.

Article 1 of the Fourth Protocol was invoked by the Commission *ex officio* in the case of *X* v. *Federal Republic of Germany* (5025/71). The applicant complained of his detention, which was ordered by a county court (and confirmed on appeal) under Article 901 of the Code of Civil Procedure, which authorises detention of a debtor if, in certain circumstances, he fails to make an affidavit of his property at the request of his creditor. His allegation that his detention violated Article 5 was inadmissible because Article 5(1)(b) permits detention 'in order to secure the fulfilment of any obligation prescribed by law'. The Commission pointed out, however, that Article 1 of the Fourth Protocol 'could to some extent limit the scope of the conditions set out in Article 5 . . . justifying arrest and detention'. Nevertheless the application was declared inadmissible, because the detention of the applicant had been ordered in order to secure compliance with the obligation to swear an affidavit and not merely because he was unable to fulfil a contractual obligation.[153]

FREEDOM OF MOVEMENT AND OF RESIDENCE

The article on freedom of movement is based on paragraphs 1 and 2 of Article 12 of the Covenant on Civil and Political Rights. It provides that everyone lawfully within the territory of a State shall have the right to liberty of movement within that territory and freedom to choose his residence; also that 'Everyone shall be free to leave any country, including his own'.

A third paragraph in the article permits limitations on these rights provided they are in accordance with law and constitute

measures which are necessary in a democratic society in the interests
of national security, public safety, for the maintenance of *ordre
public* and so on. The limitations or restrictions on the right which
are permitted are broadly comparable to those included in Articles
8–11 of the Convention itself; the Committee of Experts gave much
attention to their drafting.[154]

In the case of *X* v. *Federal Republic of Germany* (3962/69) the
applicant complained that his detention in a labour institution (after
confinement in a hospital for inebriates and after detention for
vagrancy) prevented him from exercising his profession as a sailor,
since he was not allowed to leave the country, and thus violated
Article 2 of the Fourth Protocol. The Commission declared the
application inadmissible, since the detention came within the meaning of 'the maintenance of *ordre public*', which consitutes a limitation on the right to leave any country, including one's own, authorised
by paragraph 3 of Article 2.[155] A similar decision was taken in 1970
as regards a Pole condemned in Germany to four years' imprisonment for theft, who invoked Article 2 of the Fourth Protocol as a
reason for release and repatriation.[156]

FREEDOM FROM EXPULSION FROM, AND THE RIGHT TO ENTER THE
TERRITORY OF THE STATE OF WHICH ONE IS A NATIONAL

Essentially, Article 3 of the Fourth Protocol contains a guarantee
against exile: no one may be expelled from the territory of the
State of which he is a national, nor may he be refused the right to
enter that territory. Here the European text is more stringent than
the comparable UN text: first, paragraph 4 of Article 12 of the
Covenant on Civil and Political Rights provides that 'No one shall
be *arbitrarily* deprived of the right to enter his own country' (which
might permit refusal of entry in cases which the government considers justified and therefore not arbitrary); secondly, the UN text
does not contain any prohibition of exile as such.

In 1969 the Commission considered the applicability of Article
3 of the Fourth Protocol in a case, *X* v. *Sweden*, brought by an
applicant who was an Australian citizen of Greek extraction who
claimed also to possess Greek nationality. After being extradited
from Germany to Sweden he was convicted of fraud and sentenced
to six months' imprisonment to be followed by expulsion. He did
not contest the expulsion order, but requested expulsion to Greece
and not to Australia. Two police officers accompanied him to
Athens, where he was held in custody and incommunicado for

twenty-four hours then put forcibly aboard a plane for Australia. He then discovered that his ticket had been issued for the journey Stockholm–Athens–Sydney. He complained, *inter alia*, that he had been deprived of the right to enter the territory of the State of which he was a national. The Commission declared the application inadmissible, observing that the applicant's detention in Athens and the refusal to allow him to enter Greece were measures for which the Greek authorities were solely responsible; the case had not been brought against Greece, nor had Greece recognised the right of individual petition; consequently the Swedish authorities could not be held responsible for the act complained of.[157]

PROHIBITION OF THE COLLECTIVE EXPULSION OF ALIENS

Article 4 of the Fourth Protocol states succinctly, 'Collective expulsion of aliens is prohibited'. Article 13 of the Covenant on Civil and Political Rights deals with the individual expulsion of aliens and is intended to secure certain guarantees of due process of law: an alien may be expelled only in accordance with a decision reached in accordance with law, and has a right to submit reasons against his expulsion and to have his case reviewed by the proper authority. The Consultative Assembly, in *Recommendation 234 (1960)*, proposed certain similar but more effective guaranteees, including prohibition of the expulsion of an alien who has been resident in a country for ten years unless there are particularly serious reasons. The Committee of Experts on Human Rights decided not to include an article in the Protocol regarding the individual expulsion of aliens, principally because there is already a provision on the subject in Article 3 of the European Convention on Establishment of 13 December 1955.[158] As a result, Article 4 of the Fourth Protocol relates only to the collective expulsion of aliens – a measure which one may reasonably hope is unlikely to be adopted by a member State of the Council of Europe.[159]

NOTES

1 *Yearbook of the Convention*, I, p. 41.
2 Application 214/56, *Yearbook* II, p. 214, at p. 226.
3 For the facts of the case see Chapter II, under Article 5, pp. 51–3.
4 Report of the Commission in *Publications of the Court*, Series B, p. 15, at p. 67; judgement of the Court of 1 July 1961, *Yearbook* IV, p. 438, at p. 470.
5 Application 5451/72 of 6 March 1972, *Yearbook* XV, pp. 78–80, 228–40 and 254.
6 *Ibid.*, pp. 236, 240 and 254.

7 *Cf. Singh* v. *United Kingdom* (2992/66), *Yearbook* X, p. 478, at p. 486.

8 The proceedings of the Brussels colloquy are published in *Privacy and Human Rights*, Manchester, 1973; French edition, *Vie privée et droits de l'homme*, Brussels, 1973.

9 J. Velu, *ibid.*, pp. 12–95; T. Opsahl, *ibid.*, pp. 182–247.

10 *Op. cit.* n. 9, at pp. 12–25.

11 'The work of the Council of Europe for the promotion of human rights', *Human Rights Journal*, 1975, pp. 545–85, at pp. 554–8.

12 Application 104/55, *Yearbook* I, p. 228.

13 Application 1307/61, *Yearbook* V, p. 230.

14 *Ibid.*, pp. 234–6.

15 Scheichelbauer *v.* Austria, application 2645/65. Decision of the Commission on admissibility, *Yearbook* XII, p. 156.

16 *Yearbook* XIV, p. 902.

17 *Yearbook* XI, p. 76.

18 The proceedings of the Salzburg symposium were published by the Council of Europe as a separate booklet entitled *Symposium on Human Rights and Mass Communications*, Strasbourg, 1969.

19 *Yearbook* XIII, pp. 56–66.

20 The Committee of Ministers agreed in 1968 to include in the *Intergovernmental Work Programme of the Council of Europe* the following item: 'The right to privacy as affected by: (*a*) the press and other mass media; (*b*) modern scientific and technical devices.' For further developments see reference in n. 11 above.

21 This question of the effect of the Convention on third parties, generally known as the *Drittwirkung*, is discussed by Professor Jan de Meyer in his report to the Brussels colloquy, *op. cit.* n. 8, pp. 255–82.

22 Application 1855/63, *Yearbook* VIII, p. 200.

23 *H. Singh* v. *United Kingdom*, application 2992/66, *Yearbook* X, p. 478.

24 Application 3325/67, *Yearbook* X, p. 528.

25 *Yearbook* X, p. 478, at p. 502.

26 *Yearbook* XI, p. 788. The case is explained in more detail in Chapter IV, section 7.

27 *Yearbook* IV, p. 618. See, however, the decision of the Belgian *Cour de Cassation* of 21 September 1959, *Yearbook* III, p. 624.

28 *Yearbook* XIII, p. 928.

29 *Ibid.*, pp. 1002–6.

30 *Annual Review of the Commission*, 1974, p. 22.

31 Application 5961/72. Decision of the Commission on admissibility in *Collection of Decisions*, No. 44, p. 101, at p. 112. Friendly settlement in *Report of the Commission* of 19 July 1974. *Cf.* Chapter II, under Article 3.

32 Applications 1474/62, 1677/62, 1691/62 and 1769/63, which were joined. Decisions of the Commission on admissibility in *Yearbook* VI, p. 332, and *Yearbook* VII, p. 140. Judgements of the Court of 9 February 1967 (preliminary objection) and 23 July 1968 (merits) in *Yearbook* X, p. 596 and *Yearbook* XI, p. 832.

33 *Yearbook* XI, p. 870.

34 *Ibid.*, p. 884. See also at pp. 910, 942, 964 and 974. The case is recounted in greater detail below under Article 2 of the First Protocol.

35 *Yearbook* XII, *bis*, 'The Greek case', pp. 149–53, 511.

36 Application 2749/66, *Yearbook* X, p. 368.

37 Application 1983/63, *Yearbook* VIII, p. 228.

38 Report of the Commission on the 'Vagrancy' cases, para. 187.

39 Judgement of 18 June 1971, *Yearbook* XIV, p. 788, at p. 830.

40 Chapter II, *sub* Article 6. See reference in n. 41.

41 Judgement of 21 February 1975, pp. 20–2.

42 The text of the Agreement is given in *Yearbook* XII, p. 2.

43 Application 1769/62, *Inhabitants of Ghent* v. *Belgium, Yearbook* VI, p. 444, at p. 456.

44 Application 2299/64. Decision of the Commission on admissibility in *Yearbook* VIII, p. 324. Report of the Commission and decision of the Committee of Ministers, *Yearbook* X, p. 626. The facts of this case are given above in Chapter II, *sub* Article 4.

45 *Yearbook* X, p. 634.

46 *Ibid.*, p. 674. On the question of the right of conscientious objection see reference given in n. 11, at p. 553.

47 *Yearbook* IV, p. 630, at p. 640.

48 *Yearbook* XIV, p. 676. See also 'Stocktaking', October 1974, p. 32.

49 Application 5442/72, *Decisions and Reports*, No. 1, July 1975, p. 41.

50 *Cf. Symposium on Human Rights and Mass Communications*, published by the Council of Europe, 1969 (n. 18 above), particularly the reports of Professor Maarten Rooy and Dr Paul Hausner at pp. 41 and 61.

51 Application 214/56. Decision of the Commission on admissibility in *Yearbook* II, p. 214. Report of the Commission in *Publications of the Court*, Series B, 'De Becker case'. Judgement of the Court of 27 March 1962 in *Publications of the Court*, Series A, 'De Becker case', and in *Yearbook* V, p. 320. A more detailed summary of the case is given in the first edition of this book at pp. 63–8.

52 *Yearbook* V, p. 326.

53 *Ibid.*, p. 332.

54 Application 1747/62, *Yearbook* VI, p. 424, at p. 444.

55 Application 1167/61, *Yearbook* VI, p. 204, at p. 218.

56 Application 753/60, *Yearbook* III, p. 310, at p. 318.

57 Application 2690/65, *Yearbook* IX, p. 512.

58 Report of the Commission of 3 October 1968, *Yearbook* XI, p. 782.

59 Application 5178/71. *Annual Review*, 1973, p. 27; *ibid.*, 1974, p. 26; 'Stocktaking', October 1974, p. 56.

60 Application 5493/72. *Annual Review*, 1974, p. 26; 'Stocktaking', October 1974, pp. 57–8.

61 Application 6538/74, 'Stocktaking', October 1974, p. 58.

62 Council of Europe press communiqué C(75)12 of 7 April 1975.

63 Application 6452/74, 'Stocktaking', October 1974, p. 59.

64 *Annual Review*, 1974, p. 26.

65 Application 3071/67, *Yearbook* XI, p. 456, at p. 464.

66 Statement by the French Minister of Justice to the National Assembly on 17 November 1964. *Yearbook* VII, p. 454. *Cf.* C. Debbasch, 'La Convention et régime de l'ORTF', *Human Rights Journal*, Vol. III, 1970, pp. 638–47.

67 Council of Europe press communiqué F(74)27 of 3 May 1974.

68 Application 4464/70. Decisions of the Commission on admissibility in *Yearbook* XV, p. 288, at p. 308.

69 See reference in previous note.

70 The judgement of the Court of 27 October 1975 held unanimously that there had been no violation of Article 11 considered in isolation, and by ten votes to four that there was no violation of Article 11 considered in conjunction with Article 14. Four judges considered that Articles 11 and 14 taken together had been violated by reason of the refusal of the government to negotiate with the applicant union when it accepted to negotiate with other unions.

71 Application 4475/70. Decisions of the Commission on admissibility in *Yearbook* XIV, p. 496, and XV, p. 328. Summary in 'Stocktaking', October 1974, p. 44.

72 Application 5614/72. Decision of the Commission on admissibility in *Yearbook* XV, p. 594. Summary in 'Stocktaking', October 1974, p. 46.

73 *Annual Review*, 1974, p. 15.

74 Application 5589/72. Decision of the Commission on admissibility in *Yearbook* XV, p. 576. Summary in 'Stocktaking', October 1974, p. 47.

75 *Cf. Human Rights in the World*, pp. 93–4.

76 Application 892/60, *Yearbook* IV, p. 240.

77 Application 2535/65. *Collection of Decisions*, No. 17, p. 28. But contrast the decision of the Higher Administrative Court of Munster of 2 August 1960, based on Article 8 of the Convention; *Yearbook* IV, p. 618.

78 Application 6167/73, *Decisions and Reports*, No. 1, 1975, p. 64.

79 J. E. S. Fawcett, *The Application of the European Convention on Human Rights*, London, 1969, p. 229.

80 *Ibid.*

81 Consultative Assembly, *Official Reports*, August 1949, Vol. II, p. 404.

82 The Netherlands Supreme Court has held that Article 13 imposes on Contracting Parties the duty of ensuring that an effective remedy exists, but that it is not a provision that can be directly applied by national courts. (*Nederlandsie Jurisprudentie*, 1960, No. 483, p. 1121.)

83 Applications 3435–3438/67, by four young men who, at the ages of fifteen and sixteen, joined the army or the navy for a period of nine years and subsequently applied for discharge, which was refused. They alleged violation of Articles 4, 6 and 13. *Yearbook* XI, p. 562, at p. 606. See also *Yearbook* III, p. 212 and 286; X, p. 528; XII, pp. 288 and 306.

84 Application 5849/72, *Decisions and Reports*, No. 1, 1975, p. 46.

85 *Yearbook* XII *bis*, p. 174; *ibid.*, p. 512.

86 Cmnd. 6497 (1943), p. 8.

87 Application 86/55. *Yearbook* I, p. 198; application 436/58, *Yearbook* II, p. 386, at p. 390; application 3325/67, *Yearbook* X, p. 528.

88 Application 104/55, *Yearbook* I, p. 228; application 167/56, *ibid.*, p. 235.

89 The UN Covenants use 'distinction' in both the English and French texts.

90 *Yearbook* XI, p. 832, at p. 864.

91 *Ibid.*, p. 866.

92 Grandrath *v.* Federal Republic of Germany, *Yearbook* X, p. 626, at p. 680.

93 *Yearbook* XI, p. 832, at p. 864.

94 Reference n. 92, at p. 678.

95 *Yearbook* IV, p. 438, at pp. 472–4.

96 *Yearbook* XII *bis*, p. 72.

97 The report of the Commission on the *Cyprus* case has not been published, but its interpretation of Article 15 was discussed during the *Lawless case*. See particularly *Publications of the Court*, Series B, Lawless case, 1960–61, at pp. 74–81, 392–8 and 439 ff.

98 *Ibid.*, p. 408.

99 *Yearbook* IV, pp. 472–4.

100 *Ibid.*, pp. 474–80. The arguments relating to the application of Article 15 in the *Lawless case* are summarised more fully in the first edition of this book at pp. 130–8.

101 Reference n. 99, p. 486.

102 *Yearbook* XII *bis*, 'The Greek case', pp. 71–6.

103 *Ibid.*, p. 76. As regards the situation subsequent to 21 April 1967 see *ibid.*, p. 100.

104 *Ibid.*, p. 511.

105 Decision on admissibility of 1 October 1972 in *Yearbook* XV, pp. 80–258, As regards the enquiry carried out in this case, see Chapter IV, section 6.

106 *Ibid.*, p. 256.

107 *Ibid.*, p. 120.

108 *Ibid.*, p. 256.

109 *Yearbook* IV, pp. 482–6. By contrast, the UN Covenant on Civil and Political Rights requires in its Article 4 that a public emergency must be 'officially proclaimed' in order for the right of derogation to be exercised.

110 *Yearbook* XII *bis*, pp. 41–3.

111 For the circumstances leading up to the decision of the Committee of Ministers, arising from the non-communication to governments of a British derogation about Cyprus, see Chapter VI, section 1.

112 *Cf.* Chapter VII, under Article 64.

113 *Cf.* Nicole Questiaux; 'L'article 16 de la Constitution de 1958 devant la Convention', *Human Rights Journal*, Vol. III, p. 651.

114 Application 250/57, *Yearbook* I, pp. 222–5.

115 Application 712/60, *Collection of Decisions*, No. 8, June 1962, p. 29.

116 *Yearbook* IV, p. 438, at p. 452.

117 Application 4771/71. Decision of the Commission on admissibility in *Collection of Decisions*, No. 42, May 1973, p. 22. Report of the Commission and decision of the Committee of Ministers in separate booklet 'The Kamma case', Council of Europe, 15 April 1975.

118 See first reference in preceding note.

119 See second reference in n. 117, at pp. 10–13.

120 *Ibid.*, p. 61; 'Stocktaking', October 1975, p. 42.

121 Further details of the problems considered in drafting the Protocol may be found in the author's note 'The European Convention on Human Rights: recent developments', *British Yearbook of International Law*, 1951, pp. 359–65.

122 *Cf.* 'Annotations on the text of the draft International Covenants on Human Rights', UN Document A/2929, 1955, paras. 195–211 (pp. 65–7).

123 Application 511/59, *Yearbook* III, p. 394, at p. 424. See also application 1870/63, *Yearbook* VIII, p. 218.

124 X *v.* Federal Republic of Germany, application 551/59, *Yearbook* III, p. 244, at p. 250.

125 Gudmundsson *v.* Iceland, reference n. 123, at pp. 422–4.

126 Application 1497/62, *Yearbook* V, p. 286.

127 Application 2065/63, *Yearbook* VIII, p. 266.

128 Application 2248/64, *Yearbook* X, p. 170.

129 A, B, C and D *v.* United Kingdom, application 3039/67, *Yearbook* X, p. 506.

130 Application 5849/72, *Decisions and Reports*, No. 1, 1975, p. 46.

131 *Yearbook* XII *bis*, pp. 182–4, p. 512.

132 Council of Europe press communiqué C(75)19 of 30 May 1975.

133 Recommendation 24, *Texts adopted*, August 1950, p. 34.

134 See reference given in n. 121.

135 Greece, Sweden, Turkey and the United Kingdom. See *Yearbook* I, pp. 40–5.

136 Decisions of the Commission on admissibility in *Yearbook* VI, pp. 332 and 444; VII, pp. 140 and 252. Judgement of the Court on the preliminary objection of 9 February 1967, *Yearbook* X, p. 596; judgement on the merits of 23 July 1968, *Yearbook* XI, p. 832. See also *Inhabitants of Mol, Louvain and Vilvorde* v. *Belgium*, *Yearbook* VII, p. 252.

137 *Yearbook* XI, p. 832, at p. 858.

138 Kjeldsen *v.* Denmark, *Yearbook* XV, p. 428; Busk-Madsen *v.* Denmark, *Collection of Decisions*, No. 44, pp. 96–100; Pedersen *v.* Denmark, *ibid.* The three cases were joined. The Commission adopted its report in March 1975 and referred the cases to the Court in the following July.

139 Recommendation 24, *Texts adopted*, August 1950, p. 34.

140 X *v.* Federal Republic of Germany, application 530/59, *Yearbook* 111, 184 at p. 190.

141 X and others *v.* Belgium, application 1065/61, *Yearbook* IV, p. 260.

142 X *v.* Federal Republic of Germany, application 2728/66, *Yearbook* X, p. 336.

143. X *v.* Austria, application 4982/71, *Yearbook* XV, p. 468.

144 *Yearbook* XII *bis*, pp. 175–80.

145 *Ibid.*, p. 512.

146 For the proposal of the Legal Committee see Document 1057 of 17 November 1959; for Recommendation 234 (1960) see *Yearbook* II, p. 166, and III, p. 154; for the drafting see 'Explanatory reports on the Second to Fifth Protocols', Strasbourg, 1971, pp. 29–58. For the list of ratifications see Chapter I, n. 43. The text of the Fourth Protocol is given in Appendix 4.

147 'Explanatory reports on the Second to Fifth Protocols', pp. 52–3. The Committee of Experts considered that 'recognition as a person before the law' was unnecessary, as being already implied in other articles, while 'equality before the law' was a vague notion unsuitable for inclusion in a text which would have binding legal force. Does it mean equal rights for everyone or equality in the application of the law? If the former, it cannot be guaranteed; if the latter, it is largely covered already by Article 14.

148 Recommendation 285, *Texts adopted*, April 1961.

149 Recommendation 293, *Texts adopted*, September 1961.

150 Recommendation 295, *ibid.*

151 The prolonged discussions on the subject are summarised in A. H. Robertson, 'The promotion of human rights by the Council of Europe', *Human Rights Journal*, 1975, pp. 547–9.

152 *Ibid.*, pp. 549–52; Chapter VIII, section 1, *infra*, p. 281.

153 X *v*. Federal Republic of Germany, application 5025/71, *Yearbook* XIV, p. 692.

154 See explanatory report (reference n. 147), pp. 42–6.

155 X *v*. Federal Republic of Germany, application 3962/69, *Yearbook* XIII, p. 688.

156 X *v*. Federal Republic of Germany, application 4256/69, *Collection of Decisions*, No. 37, 1971, p. 67.

157 X *v*. Sweden, application 3916/69, *Collection of Decisions*, No. 32, 1970, p. 51.

158 European Treaty Series, No. 19, *European Conventions and Agreements*, Strasbourg, 1971, Vol. I, p. 115. Article 3 thereof prohibits the expulsion of nationals of the other Contracting Parties unless they endanger national security or offend against *ordre public* or morality; in addition, various procedural safeguards are provided.

159 The reasons for the decision of the Committee of Experts are given more fully in the explanatory report (see n. 147) at pp. 50–51.

CHAPTER IV

THE EUROPEAN COMMISSION OF HUMAN RIGHTS

Having defined the rights to be guaranteed, the Convention goes on to set up the international machinery which is to make the guarantee effective. The authors of the Convention did not consider that it was sufficient to have undertakings by the Contracting Parties to respect the different rights and freedoms: they required some measure of international control. In other words, national obligations were not enough: international machinery to reinforce them was also required. In this respect the Council of Europe followed the principle already established by the General Assembly of the United Nations in 1948, that is to say that the proclamation of the Universal Declaration would be followed by a covenant containing legal obligations and by another instrument providing for 'measures of implementation'.[1] This is made quite clear in Article 19 of the Convention, which provides that the Commission and Court are established 'to ensure the observance of the engagements undertaken by the High Contracting Parties'.

The member governments of the Council of Europe accepted the idea of the Assembly that a European Commission should be created for this purpose, as an impartial, international organ to which complaints could be made in the event of any member State failing to secure to anyone within its jurisdiction the rights and freedoms defined in the Convention. The principal function of the Commission is to investigate alleged breaches of the Convention; to secure, if possible, a friendly settlement of the matter; and, if this proves impossible, to draw up a report in which the Commission expresses an opinion as to whether a violation has occurred.

1. THE COMPOSITION AND ORGANISATION OF THE COMMISSION

The governments also accepted, in their general lines, the Assembly's proposals as regards the composition and functions of the Commission. The relevant provisions are contained in Section III of the Convention, which is constituted by Articles 20–37.

In accordance with Article 20 the Commission consists of a number of members equal to that of the High Contracting Parties. This meant that on 31 December 1974 the Commission had eighteen members, since all member States of the Council of Europe had by that date become Parties to the Convention. This provision is to be distinguished from the corresponding provision relating to membership of the Court; Article 38 provides that the number of judges shall be the same as the number of members of the Council of Europe; consequently for a number of years there were fewer members of the Commission than judges on the Court.

There is no provision in the Convention about the nationality of the members of the Commission, except the second sentence in Article 20 to the effect that no two members may be nationals of the same State. It would therefore be quite possible to elect persons who are not nationals of the member States, though this has not so far occurred and, while legally possible, seems politically improbable. Curiously enough, there is also no provision in the Convention about the qualifications of the members of the Commission. This fact caused some heart-searching when the first election took place, as will be recounted shortly.

In the election, both of the Commissioners and of the judges, account has been taken of the fact that the Council of Europe consists of two organs, a Committee of Ministers representing the governments and a Consultative Assemby representing the national parliaments; the procedure has been designed in such a way that the election is the result of the partnership of these two bodies. Under Article 21 of the Convention the members of the Commission are elected by the Committee of Ministers from a list of names drawn up by the Bureau of the Assembly, while Article 39 provides that the judges are elected by the Assembly from a list of persons nominated by the member governments.

For the election of the members of the Commission each national group of representatives in the Assembly puts forward three candidates, of whom at least two must be its own nationals. The Bureau of the Assembly then 'draws up' a list of names which is forwarded to the Committee of Ministers; the latter elects the members of the Commission by an absolute majority of votes. In practice the election takes place by secret ballot.

When the Bureau of the Assembly came to organise the first stage in the election procedure after the Convention had entered into force on 3 September 1953 a number of problems arose which appeared not to have been foreseen when the Convention was drafted. In the first place, how many States were to participate through their representatives in the procedure of proposing members of the Commission: should it be all States which had signed the Convention, i.e. all members of the Council of Europe, or only those which had ratified? Secondly, would membership of the Commission constitute a full-time occupation or would the members be required to sit only intermittently; in other words, would membership of the Commission be compatible with the exercise of other occupations or must a person elected give up all outside activity, like a member of the International Court of Justice, in which case the choice of candidates might be severely restricted? Thirdly, what role was to be played by the Bureau of the Assembly in 'drawing up' the list of candidates on the basis of the names put forward by the national groups of representatives in the Consultative Assembly; was it merely to have retyped and transmit to the Committee of Ministers the lists of candidates received from delegations, or did it involve powers of discretion and judgement in choosing between the candidates proposed, establishing a balanced list and perhaps even indicating preferences in one way or another? Fourthly, what qualifications should be required of candidates: should they be lawyers, officials, politicians or what? Were certain of these professions additional qualifications for membership of the Commission or, as was alleged in some cases, were they disqualifications?

In order to clarify these problems the Bureau asked the opinion of the Assembly's Committee on Legal and Administrative Questions, on receipt of which it exchanged correspondence with the Committee of Ministers and then proceeded to draw up the list of candidates. This was duly submitted to the Committee of Ministers in May 1954, and the first European Commission of Human Rights was then elected.[2]

As regards the number of States whose representatives should participate in the election procedure, Article 20 called for a Commission consisting of 'a number of members equal to that of the High Contracting Parties'. Clearly only those States which had ratified the Convention were 'High Contracting Parties'. It appeared, therefore, that a Commission of only ten members should be elected on the basis of names put forward by the representatives of the ten States which had ratified at that time. On the other hand, if this procedure were adopted the whole complicated machinery of election would have to be set in motion again each time an additional instrument of ratification was deposited, which would clearly be inconvenient and time-wasting. It was therefore decided that representatives of all signatories should present their lists of candidates and that the Committee of Ministers would elect fifteen persons to be members of the Commission but that, as regards those persons elected in respect of States which had not ratified, their election would not take effect until their respective countries had become Parties to the Convention by depositing their instruments of ratification. In this way eleven members of the Commission were effectively elected (Turkey having ratified in the meantime) and four others designated as members subject to the condition precedent of ratification. The Committee of Ministers, however, recommended to the Commission that the four persons thus designated should, pending the assumption of their full functions, be allowed to participate in a consultative capacity in the preparatory work of the Commission and in drawing up its rules of procedure.[3]

As regards the intermittent or permanent nature of the functions of members of the Commission, it was, of course, impossible to determine in advance what would be the volume of the Commission's work. Nevertheless it appeared unlikely that the Commission would have enough work to occupy all the time of its members, at least until it was empowered to entertain individual petitions; it was therefore agreed, subject to reconsideration of the matter whenever it should become necessary, to regard the duties of members of the Commission as intermittent and to fix their remuneration on a *per diem* basis.

The question of the qualifications required of candidates has provoked a good deal of discussion over the years. The Assembly Committee on Legal and Administrative Questions expressed the view in September 1953 that candidates should possess, in addition to the requisite moral qualities, either an extensive knowledge of international law or considerable experience of legal practice. Two years later the question was discussed whether membership of the Commission was compatible with a parliamentary mandate and with membership of the Assembly itself; this question was answered in the affirmative.[4]

A more difficult question was compatibility of membership of the Commission with holding a post as a national official; this arose at the first election in relation to a candidate who was legal adviser in his national Foreign Ministry. It was not then thought possible to lay down any rule on the subject, though it was agreed in the Committee of Ministers that this was an element for consideration when it came to voting. The candidate in question was in fact elected. The same question was discussed again several years later

and led to another study of the requisite qualifications for membership of the Commission by the Assembly's Committee on Legal
Affairs. The conclusion, which was submitted to, and approved by,
the Bureau of the Assembly, was that members of the Commission
should possess the following qualities: (1) high moral integrity;
(2) recognised competence in matters connected with human rights;
(3) substantial legal or judicial experience. The Bureau decided
to draw these requirements to the attention of national delegations
when requesting them to put forward their lists of candidates, and
also to draw their attention to 'the difficulties in which a member
of the Commission might find himself if he was at the same time
a member of a national public service, and to the doubts as to the
Commission's impartiality which might arise in such circumstances'.[5]
This decision has formed the basis of subsequent practice.

The first election took place on 18 May 1954.[6] In the event the
professions of the members elected were as follows: six judges or
former judges, six law professors, two practising lawyers and one
legal adviser. Three of the professors and the two practising lawyers
were also members of parliaments, one of them being an Under-
secretary for Foreign Affairs. Three of the original members of the
Commission were women.[7]

Though fifteen members had been elected, the Belgian, Dutch,
French and Italian members could not participate in the substantive
work of the Commission until their governments ratified the Convention; the Commission did, however, accept the recommendation
of the Committee of Ministers that they should be allowed to participate in a consultative capacity in the preparatory work, particularly
in drawing up the Rules of Procedure. The mandates of the Belgian,
Dutch and Italian members became effective in 1955, 1954 and 1955
respectively. The mandate of the French member lapsed.

The Commission held its first session in July 1954 and elected
Mr P. Faber of Luxembourg to act as its provisional President
during the first sessions, when the Rules of Procedure were drawn
up and adopted.[8] At its fourth session in December 1955 Sir
Humphrey Waldock and Professor C. Th. Eustathiades were
elected President and Vice-president respectively; in July 1957 and
again in June 1960 they were re-elected for another three years. On
the resignation of Sir Humphrey Waldock, M. Sture Petrén was
elected President of the Commission and held that office from
January 1962 until February 1967. He was succeeded by Professor
Max Soerensen (1967–72). After the denunciation of the Convention by Greece took effect in June 1970, Professor Eustathiades

ceased to be a member of the Commission and Mr J. E. S. Fawcett was elected Vice-president. He succeeded Professor Soerensen in the Presidency in 1972, when Professor G. Sperduti became Vice-president.

Under Article 22 of the Convention the members of the Commission hold office for six years and may be re-elected. However, the terms of office of seven of the original members, chosen by lot, expired at the end of three years. The intention was that there should be a renewal of approximately half the members of the Commission every three years. This objective, however, was only imperfectly achieved, on account of the number of occasional elections which became necessary in between the triennial dates on account of deaths, resignations and new ratifications of the Convention consequent on the admission of new members of the Council of Europe. The terms of office of the members elected as the result of new accessions ran for six years from the date of their election and thus did not fit into the triennial rhythm. In order to remedy this rather untidy situation the Fifth Protocol to the Convention, concluded on 20 January 1966,[9] added two new paragraphs to Article 22 of the Convention which authorise the Committee of Ministers, when proceeding to an 'occasional election', to fix the term of office of the new member for a period shorter or longer than six years – but not less than three nor more than nine years – in order that it should be coterminous with one of the two main groups and thus comply with the policy of ensuring that, as far as possible, one half of the membership of the Commission shall be renewed every three years.

As the result of deaths, resignations and the expiry of the terms of office of certain members who were not re-elected, the membership of the Commission has changed completely over a period of twenty years. Its composition on 30 June 1975 was as follows: J. E. S. Fawcett, President (British), G. Sperduti, Vice-president (Italian), F. Ermacora (Austrian), M. Triantafyllides (Cypriot), E. Busuttil (Maltese), L. Kellberg (Swedish), B. Daver (Turkish), T. Opsahl (Norwegian), J. Custers (Belgian), C. A. Nørgaard (Danish), C. H. F. Polak (Dutch), J. A. Frowein (German), G. Jörundsson (Icelandic), R. J. Dupuy (French), G. Tenekides (Greek), S. Trechsel (Swiss), B. Kiernan (Irish), N. Klecker (Luxembourg).

After dealing with the membership of the Commission and the method of election, the Convention continues in Article 23 with a provision which is important, though perhaps self-evident, that the members of the Commission 'shall sit in their individual capacity' and therefore not as representatives of their governments; consequently they may not receive instructions from their governments but must act in full freedom as dictated by their own conscience. They enjoy immunity from legal process in respect of all acts done by them in their official capacity by virtue of the Second Protocol to the General Agreement on Privileges and Immunities of the Council of Europe concluded on 15 December 1956.[10]

Articles 33–7 of the Convention contain other provisions relating to the functioning of the Commission which it will be convenient to consider at this stage.

Article 33 lays down that the Commission shall meet *in camera*. This is a wise provision, though it is sometimes criticised. It is wise for two reasons. First, because it permits a procedure of complete equality between the applicants, who are private citizens (not infrequently convicted criminals), and the respondent governments, which the latter would be most unlikely to accept in international proceedings if they were conducted in public. Secondly, it is wise because one of the functions of the Commission is (under Article 28) to seek a friendly settlement of a case on the basis of respect for human rights. Though, as we shall see below, the number of friendly settlements in the formal sense has been rather small, there have been a considerable number of informal settlements which have given satisfaction to an injured party – and, in a number of cases, will also benefit other persons who may in the future find themselves in the same predicament as the applicant. These settlements, whether formal or informal, result from discussions and negotiations with governments. Anyone with experience of such negotiations knows that they have a much greater chance of success if they are undertaken on a confidential basis and away from the glare of publicity.

Article 34 provides that the Commission shall take its decisions by a majority of the members present and voting. Rule 25 of the Rules of Procedure fixes the quorum (except for certain decisions on admissibility) at nine. The Commission meets 'as the circumstances require' (Article 35). In fact it holds about six sessions a year of one or two weeks each. In addition, until July 1973, the preliminary examination of the admissibility of individual applications was undertaken by a group of three members of the Commission, in accordance with Article 45 of the Rules of Procedure; the Annual Review of the work of the Commission for 1972 recorded thirty-two days on which such 'Groups of Three' met and considered nearly 400 applications as regards their admissibility. However, in July 1973 the system was changed with a view to accelerating the procedure, and the new text of Article 45 provides for preliminary examination by a single *rapporteur*; over 400 applications were dealt with in this way during 1974.[11] The work falling on the members of the Commission, however, is not limited to the above but also includes the participation of delegates in the work of the Court, in negotiations for friendly settlement and in the hearing of witnesses; it has been estimated that the sum total of these activities (and the preparatory paper work) occupies about half the total working time of the members.

The question has been raised from time to time whether membership of the Commission should not be considered (and remunerated) as a full-time occupation. There is indeed much to be said for this view. There would, however, be one serious disadvantage in such an arrangement: the majority of the members of the Commission have other professional occupations, mostly as professors of law, which they might well be unwilling to relinquish, so that a decision to treat membership as a full-time job would mean important changes in the membership of the Commission and would probably result in considerable difficulty in obtaining members with the requisite qualifications.

Finally, Article 36 of the Convention authorises the Commission to draw up its own Rules of Procedure,[12] while Article 37 provides that the secretariat of the Commission shall be provided by the Secretary General of the Council of Europe. The last point is carried further in the Rules of Procedure: rule 11 states that the Secretary General shall appoint the Secretary of the Commission, while the duties of the secretariat are to be laid down by the President in agreement with the Secretary General (rule 14). Certain functions of the Secretariat are specified in more detail (rules 12, 13 and 30A). The expenses of the Commission and of its secretariat are borne by the budget of the Council of Europe (Article 58).

This leads to consideration of the question whether the European Commission of Human Rights is an organ of the Council of Europe. A negative answer to this question is sometimes given, on the ground that the Statute of the Council of Europe of 5 May 1949 provides only for two organs of the Council: the Consultative Assembly and the Committee of Ministers. Therefore, it is argued, no other organ of the Council of Europe can exist unless the Statute is amended to say so. This answer, it is believed, is too legalistic. Of course the Commission of Human Rights is not mentioned in the Statute of the Council of Europe, because the Statute was concluded in 1949 and the Commission established as the result of the conclusion of the Convention on Human Rights in the following year. But it is necessary to consider the realities and not merely take a formalistic view of the texts. When the Commission is due to a Convention concluded in the framework of the Council of Europe, when its members are proposed by the Assembly and elected by the Committee of Ministers of the Council, when its secretariat is provided by the Secretary General of the Council, its expenses are paid by the budget of the Council and its accommodation is on the premises of the Council, then it would distort the normal meaning of the words to deny that it is an organ of the Council of Europe. Apart from these general considerations, the English Court of Appeal has held expressly that the Commission of Human Rights is an organ of the Council of Europe.[13]

The first Secretary of the European Commission of Human Rights was M. Polys Modinos, then Director of Human Rights in the secretariat of the Council of Europe and a former judge on the Mixed Courts in Egypt. The Deputy Secretary was Mr A. B. McNulty. After the establishment of the Court of Human Rights in 1959 M. Modinos was elected its first Registrar and Mr McNulty was appointed Secretary of the Commission – a post he was to hold for the next seventeen years. In 1961 M. M.-A. Eissen was appointed Deputy Secretary. His place was taken by Mr K. Rogge when M. Eissen was appointed Deputy Registrar of the Court in 1965.

2. INTER-STATE CASES

Articles 24 and 25 of the Convention deal with manner in which the Commission may be seized of a case. The first of these relates to inter-State action. 'Any High Contracting Party may refer to the Commission through the Secretary General of the Council of Europe any alleged breach of the provisions of the Convention by another High Contracting Party'. This is the procedure well known to international law whereby one State may arraign another before an international tribunal if the former believes that the latter has violated its international obligations. It will be observed, however, that this provision goes far beyond the classic doctrine of diplomatic protection of nationals abroad. In order to bring a case before the European Commission of Human Rights it is not necessary for the applicant State to allege that the rights of its own nationals have been violated by the respondent State; any violation of the rights guaranteeed by the Convention is a sufficient cause of action. In fact inter-State cases have related more frequently to situations in which the respondent State has allegedly violated the rights of its own citizens – situations in which no interference by the applicant State could be justified under the classic doctrine of diplomatic protection.

The procedure of inter-State complaints, however, has been rarely used during the first twenty years of the life of the Convention. Only eight such cases were registered by December 1974 and they constituted five groups:

1. Two cases brought by Greece against the United Kingdom in 1956 and 1957 (applications 176/56 and 299/57), relating to the situation in Cyprus at a time when the island was still a British colony.
2. A case brought by Austria against Italy in 1960 (application 788/60) relating to the trial of six young men who were members of the German-speaking minority in the South Tyrol.
3. Two cases brought by Denmark, Norway and Sweden against Greece in 1967 and 1970 (applications Nos. 3321–3/67, 3344/67 and 4448/70) (the Netherlands being a joint applicant in the first case), relating to the situation in Greece after the *coup d'état* of April 1967.
4. Two cases brought by Ireland against the United Kingdom in 1971 and 1972 (applications 5310/71 and 5451/72), relating to the situation in Northern Ireland.
5. A case brought by Cyprus against Turkey in 1974 (6780/74) relating to the Turkish intervention in Cyprus.

All these cases have been referred to in greater detail in Chapters III and IV above.

Though the English text of Article 24 permits a Contracting Party to refer to the Commission 'any alleged breach ... by another ... Contracting Party', this cannot be done unless the first Party is prepared to take the responsibility of making the allegations itself. It is not enough for State A to refer a matter to the Commission because, for example, an enquiry conducted by a non-governmental organisation has come to the conclusion that there is a systematic violation of human rights in State B. State A cannot, in such circumstances, merely ask the Commission to investigate. It must take upon itself the responsibility of bringing an accusation and producing evidence; it must itself make the allegations. This appears more clearly from the French text of the same article: 'Toute Partie Contractante peut saisir la Commission ... de tout manquement aux dispositions de la présente Convention qu'elle croira pouvoir être imputé à une autre Partie Contractante.' This point is emphasised because the wish has been expressed on occasion that a government should be able to draw a situation to the attention of the Commission (for example, the situation in Greece in the summer of 1967) and then leave it to the Commission to investigate. Such action, however, is not in conformity with Article 24.

3. THE RIGHT OF INDIVIDUAL PETITION

Several writers maintain that the Law of Nations guarantees to every individual at home and abroad the so-called rights of mankind without regarding whether an individual be stateless or not and whether he be a subject of a member State of the Family of Nations, or not. Such rights are said to comprise the right of existence, the right to protection of honour, life, health, liberty, and property, the right of practising any religion one likes, the right of emigration, and the like. But such rights do not in fact enjoy any guarantee whatever from the Law of Nations, and they cannot enjoy such guarantee, since the Law of Nations is a law between States, and since individuals cannot be subjects of this law.

So wrote Oppenheim in the first edition of his *Treatise on International Law* in 1905.[14] One of the achievements of the European Convention is that it demonstrates beyond any shadow of doubt that international law has developed from the position he stated so lucidly seventy years ago to a point where an individual not only has rights under international law but can himself bring a case before an international organ, even against his own government.[15] However, at the same time it must be recognised that this evolution has not been secured without difficulty and that not all European governments have so far been prepared to accept it.

Under Article 24 of the Convention, as already related, any High Contracting Party may refer to the Commission, through the Secretary General of the Council of Europe, any alleged breach of the provisions of the Convention by another High Contracting Party. The value of this provision, however, is limited. In international treaties which regulate the conduct of States *inter se* it is, of course, highly desirable to provide for a tribunal before which one State can arraign another for non-compliance with the terms of the treaty. However, when the object of the treaty is to protect not States but individuals, the real party in interest, if a breach occurs, is the individual whose rights have been denied. It is therefore this individual who stands in need of a remedy, and the remedy he needs is a right of appeal to an organ which is competent to call the offending party to account.

It may be argued – and was indeed argued when the Convention was being drafted – that only States are recognised as subjects of international law. The weakness of this argument in relation to human rights is to be found in practical considerations of common sense. The object of the Convention on Human Rights is to protect the rights of the individual citizen; if his rights are violated, this will in most cases be done by the authorities of his own State. Under the classic concept of international law this individual has no *locus standi*, on the theory that his rights will be championed by his government. But how can his government be his champion when it is *ex hypothesi* the offender? It may be argued that another government can take up the cudgels on his behalf and lodge a complaint against his government. This is possible. But few Foreign Offices have the inclination gratuitously to pick a quarrel with an ally over the treatment accorded by the latter to one of its own nationals; nor are they likely to have the information necessary to do so, even if they should have the inclination. Moreover, if it is necessary for the individual whose rights are denied to seek the help of a foreign government, this has the result of transforming the complaint of an individual into a dispute between States – which is obviously undesirable.

For these reasons the original proposals of the Consultative Assembly in August 1949 included an individual right of petition to the international Commission or, as the Legal Committee preferred to call it, 'a right of individuals to seek a remedy directly'. This right was made subject, of course, to the previous exhaustion of local remedies. During the negotiations, however, a difference of opinion arose as to the desirability of including the right of individual petition, the fear being expressed that this might easily lead to abuse, particularly in the interests of subversive propaganda. To guard against this danger two safeguards were introduced: a provision that 'nothing in this Convention may be interpreted as implying . . . any right to engage in any activity or perform any act aimed at the destruction of any of the rights and freedoms set forth herein . . .' (Article 17); and another provision to the effect that the Commission would not entertain petitions which were anonymous, manifestly ill founded, or an abuse of the right of petition (Article 27). Nevertheless the objections to the right of individual petition were maintained. As recounted in Chapter I, the Legal Committee of the Assembly stressed that in its view it was essential that this right of individuals to seek a direct remedy should be preserved, but the Committee of Ministers in August 1950 was unable to reach agreement in this sense and decided, as a compromise solution, to make the right optional, that is to say subject to an express declaration on the part of the government concerned that it recognises the competence of the Commission to receive petitions from individuals. It was, moreover, laid down that this procedure would come into effect only when six governments had made such declarations.

When the Assembly received the Ministers' draft Convention in August 1950 it was particularly concerned at this uncertain treatment of a right the maintenance of which it regarded as essential. In an endeavour to reinstate this provision, while taking account of the reluctance of some governments to accept it, the Assembly proposed that the procedure should be reversed and that the right of individual petition should obtain in all cases, unless the government concerned had made an express declaration to exclude it. The Ministers, however, found this amendment unacceptable and retained the formula which they had approved in August; the final text of Article 25 thus reads as follows:

(1) The Commission may receive petitions addressed to the Secretary-General of the Council of Europe from any person, non-governmental oganisation or group of individuals claiming to be the victim of a violation by one of the High Contracting Parties of the rights set forth in this Convention, provided that the High Contracting Party against which the complaint has been lodged has declared that it recognises the competence of the Commission to receive such petitions. Those of the High Contracting Parties who have made such a declaration undertake not to hinder in any way the effective exercise of this right.

(2) Such declarations may be made for a specific period.

(3) The declarations shall be deposited with the Secretary-General of the Council of Europe who shall transmit copies thereof to the High Contracting Parties and publish them.

(4) The Commission shall only exercise the powers provided for in this Article when at least six High Contracting Parties are bound by declarations made in accordance with the preceding paragraphs.

By 31 December 1974 the right of individual petition had been accepted by thirteen States, and this remedy was available to approximately 200 million persons within their jurisdiction. The States in question and the dates of their acceptance of the procedure were as follows: Austria (1958), Belgium (1955), Denmark (1953), the Federal Republic of Germany (1955), Iceland (1955), Ireland (1953), Italy (1973), Luxembourg (1958), the Netherlands (1960), Norway (1957), Sweden (1952), Switzerland (1974) and the United Kingdom (1966). The acceptances of Iceland, Ireland and Sweden were for an indefinite period; the others were for periods of two, three or five years, but had always been renewed when the time came.

The right of individual petition thus instituted has frequently been called the 'cornerstone' of the European system of protection. The comparative importance of the two procedures – inter-State complaints under Article 24 and individual petitions under Article 25 – is shown by the statistics of the Commission's work. By 31 December 1974 the Commission had been seized of eight inter-State cases and 6,847 individual applications. (On a question of terminology, it may be noted that the Convention itself uses, in its Articles 25, 27 and 28, the word 'petition'. The Commission, on the other hand, in its Rules of Procedure and other documents uses the term 'application' because 'petition' has other connotations, implying in certain countries action to seek a political remedy or a measure of grace. In French the same word, *requête*, is used both in the Convention and in the Rules of Procedure.)

The importance of the right of individual petition, however, is not merely based on statistics; it results rather from the consideration that without this right the Convention would lose most of its efficacy. Of course there is some value in having the normative provisions of the Convention incorporated into domestic law in countries which adopt this practice – clearly the first and most important means of protection is that established by the national law – but the whole *raison d'être* of the Convention is to furnish an international remedy when the national remedy is inadequate. This can be done effectively only when the right of individual petition is recognised.

It is axiomatic that there is no right without a remedy. This does not mean that, legally speaking, one cannot create a right without providing a remedy; what it means is that, practically speaking, the right has little or no value unless an effective remedy is available. The principal remedy instituted by the European Convention is the right of individual petition; in the countries which have not accepted this procedure the Convention is of comparatively little value. As stated by Senator Peridier in a report to the Assembly in September 1973,[16] 'It is undoubtedly the instauration of this procedure which makes the unique contribution of the Council of Europe to international law and means that our system of protection – whatever its faults – is the most effective yet devised by any international organisation.' The true value of the system was recognised by the Organisation of American States when drafting the American Convention on Human Rights, for they took the courageous step of including the right of individual petition not as an optional but as a mandatory provision in the American Convention.[17]

There are two further aspects of Article 25 which require comment, both arising out of its initial paragraph.

The first of these is that an applicant – whether a person, a non-governmental organisation or a goup of individuals – must, in order to succeed, claim to be the victim of a violation. It is not enough that a violation has occurred; the applicant must be directly affected by it or have a personal interest in it. He cannot complain of a violation to which he is a 'stranger'. On the other hand, if the direct victim is unable to act a near relative or someone else may act on his behalf.[18] The question has been asked, however, whether this provision is not too restrictive. Should it not be possible, for example, for a trade union to bring an application on behalf of one of its members, or for a civil rights society to do so in the general interest?[19] In the first case there would probably be no difficulty in fact, because the trade union could either assist its member in the presentation of his case or arrange to be appointed as his legal representative: in the latter case, however, the situation is more difficult. Unless the Convention is amended it would seem that a civil rights society could not bring a case in the general interest if it could not show that it was itself a victim of the violation complained of.

The remaining point to be noted is the final sentence of the first paragraph of Article 25 by which Contracting Parties which have accepted the right of individual petition 'undertake not to hinder in any way the effective exercise of this right'. Just what does this mean? Does it oveirule the normal regulations about the censorship of prisoners' mail and about receiving visits in prison? Does it confer on prisoners a right to leave their place of detention in order to attend the proceedings of the Commission? Does it confer on persons not under detention any rights which they would not have otherwise? These and many other questions arise which will be considered in the following section.

4. THE RIGHT OF FREE ACCESS TO THE COMMISSION

In the third section of Chapter I we gave an account of the origins and summarised the history of the *Agreement relating to Persons participating in Proceedings of the European Commission and Court of Human Rights*, signed on 6 May 1969.[20] It is now time to consider the substantive provisions of this agreement. As its title implies, it relates to the proceedings of the Court besides those of the Commission (and could also relate to the proceedings of the Committee of Ministers); it is also concerned with other matters in addition to the right of access to the Commission; but since its principal purpose is to facilitate access to that body it will be convenient to consider it at this stage.[21]

Article 1 of the Agreement defines the persons to whom it applies. In the first place this includes the agents, advisers and advocates of governments; secondly, persons taking part in proceedings instituted under Article 25 of the Convention, whether as individual applicants or as duly authorised representatives of non-governmental organisations or groups of individuals; thirdly, the lawyers acting for or assisting the applicants; finally, persons assisting delegates of the Commission and witnesses, experts and other persons called on to participate in the proceedings.

Article 2 of the Agreement grants immunity from legal process in respect of activities which form part of the proceedings: oral or written statements made and documents or other evidence submitted, which could include such forms of evidence as photographs or tape-recordings. The protection will continue after the termination of the proceedings. This is clearly necessary to permit the effective operation of the Commission and the Court. The immunity granted relates to all forms of civil and criminal process.

Several problems arose in this connection. The first related to the following question: if an applicant or a witness makes before the Commission statements which are slanderous or abusive of national authorities – e.g. as regards the judge before whom he was tried or the warders of the prison where he is detained – should he enjoy immunity for such statements? Some countries take a serious view of such conduct; others consider it unimportant if a convicted criminal is rude about the judge who sentenced him or about the gaoler who detains him. The suggestion was made that immunity might be limited to statements which are relevant to the application and not extend to what is slanderous or abusive; but the necessity for this limitation was questioned, the drafting would have been difficult, and the suggestion was not pressed. Immunity from legal process will therefore be absolute, as it is in many countries for statements made in court and for words spoken in parliament.

Another problem about the extent of immunity from legal process concerned official secrets. Governments which were prepared to be liberal in general in granting immunity for statements made before the Commission and the Court were not ready to accept a provision which would prevent them from taking action if an applicant or witness used the occasion to divulge official secrets and then claimed immunity on account of the forum in which the offence had occurred. This matter was dealt with not by altering the text of Article 2 of the Agreement but by inserting a new paragraph 3 in Article 5, which relates to waiver of immunity, the effect of which is that waiver will follow automatically if a government certifies that such action is necessary 'for the purpose of proceedings in respect of an offence against national security'.

A further problem which arose in relation to immunity concerned the repetition outside the Commission and the Court of statements made or evidence submitted to the Commission or the Court. Journalists may attend sessions of the Court, which are, of course, normally public; they can, and do, present themselves at the Palais des Droits de l'Homme in Strasbourg when the Commission is considering a case which has aroused public interest, such as the Greek case or the 'Belgian linguistic case'; they will naturally obtain such information as they can. When the Commission was hearing witnesses in the Greek case a number of them were literally besieged by journalists and interrogated about the statements they had made. An individual applicant who believes that his rights have been violated by his national authorities and has brought his case to Strasbourg may consider it quite natural to repeat to a journalist what he has already told the Commission. Yet governments which have accepted the right of individuals to bring their complaints before a Commission which sits *in camera* may be sensitive about the repetition of those complaints to the mass media.

It was thought that the governments had already made a considerable concession, in the interests of the proper conduct of the proceedings, in agreeing to grant immunity as regards statements made or evidence produced before the Commission and the Court; however, the same interests did not require that a similar immunity should be granted as regards subsequent repetition to the press, the radio and television. Consequently it was decided to add a second paragraph to Article 2 of the Agreement the effect of which is that the immunity will not apply to the communication outside the Commission or the Court of statements, documents or evidence submitted to those organs, or to any part thereof. There is thus imposed a definite limitation on the immunity which has been granted – but a limitation which, in all the circumstances, must be considered reasonable.

The third article of the Agreement establishes the right of freedom of correspondence of applicants, experts, witnesses and others with the Commission and the Court.

Doubt was felt at one stage as to whether this article was necessary at all. This was not because there was doubt as to whether the right should exist – that was readily accepted – but doubt whether any further provision was necessary to secure the right, since Article 8 of the Convention already protects in general terms the right of freedom of correspondence, while Article 25(1) *in fine*, as we have seen, provides that Contracting Parties which have accepted the right of individual petition undertake not to hinder in any way the effective exercise of this right. The reply to this line of argument was, in the first place, that the general provision of Article 8 was of little assistance in solving the problem of freedom of correspondence of applicants and witnesses with the Commission, because if a letter (e.g. from a prisoner) alleging violation of a particular right was stopped (e.g. by the prison authorities) it would be of little help to the author of the letter to know that he could then file a second application complaining of a violation of his freedom of correspondence, since several years might elapse before action was concluded on the second application (including exhaustion of domestic remedies), during which time action on the original application would be paralysed. If the intercepted letter came from a witness it was quite uncertain whether he would wish to file an application of his own based on Article 8. Secondly, experience had shown that the provision of Article 25(1) *in fine* was not sufficient; that was, indeed, the reason why the conclusion of the new instrument had been proposed. This was not an accusation of bad faith against governments which had accepted the right of individual petition; it meant simply that it was necessary to define more explicitly, in the light of experience gained from the practical operation of the Convention, what was the precise content of the rather general obligation contained in Article 25. Paragraph 1 of Article 3 therefore provides that the Contracting Parties shall respect the right of the persons to whom the Agreement applies to correspond freely with the Commission and the Court.

The second paragraph of this article deals with the particular problem of correspondence of persons under detention. The Commission of Human Rights has already had to consider a number of cases in which applicants have complained that their communications addressed to the Commission have been intercepted, censored, delayed or otherwise interfered with.[22] The Commission has recognised that national authorities should have the right, if they wish, to require that letters from prisoners to the Commission should be opened (or submitted unsealed) and read; but they should be forwarded uncensored and without undue delay. The Agreement accepts this view. The same paragraph provides that detained persons shall have the right to correspond with and consult (out of hearing of other persons) a lawyer about an application to the Commission or any consequential proceedings.

This text should go a long way towards establishing the necessary right of prisoners to correspond freely with the Commission – a right with which there have in the past been a number of interferences. It would indeed be better if all countries would accept the practice instituted in Belgium, whereby all letters of prisoners addressed to the Commission are forwarded immediately, unopened and by registered mail. Some governments, however, are not yet ready to follow this example. But the new Agreement should ensure that appropriate facilities for correspondence will be accorded by all Contracting Parties and not only by those which have made the optional declaration under Article 25.

Article 4 of the Agreement relates to freedom of movement in order to attend and return from the proceedings of the Commission and the Court of persons whose presence is required at those proceedings. It deals with four separate aspects of the matter: freedom to leave, freedom of transit, freedom to attend and freedom to return. This was perhaps the most difficult article to draft.

There was general agreement that, as a general rule, persons required to attend the proceedings should be allowed to do so and that no obstacles should be placed on their leaving their country of normal residence; but it was immediately apparent that a number of exceptions would have to be made if governments were to accept the general principle, in order to cover such cases as those of a person under detention, one whose departure would involve a security risk, someone performing his military service or a person subject to the order of a court limiting his freedom of movement, such as release on bail. The experts who drafted the Agreement therefore had recourse to a technique frequently used in the Convention itself: a first paragraph containing a general affirmation of a right followed by a second paragraph setting out the limitations which are permissible. These in fact are copied from the corresponding text of Article 2 of the Fourth Protocol to the Convention, which secures the right of freedom of movement within a country and freedom to leave any country, including one's own. These restrictions are very widely drawn, though it is only fair to observe that if a member government should consider it necessary to prevent an applicant or a witness from attending the proceedings of the Commission or the Court it would always be possible for the organ in question to send one or more of its members to hear the person concerned *in situ*.

The remaining provisions of the Agreement call for little comment. Article 5 deals with the question of waiver. After establishing the principle that immunities and facilities are accorded solely for the purpose of facilitating the proceedings of, and exercising rights before, the Commission and the Court, it goes on to provide that those two organs alone are competent to waive the immunity from legal process conferred by Article 2, and that they have the right and the duty to waive immunity if its maintenance would impede the course of justice and its waiver would not prejudice the proceedings.

The Agreement entered into force on 17 April 1971, after the deposit of the fifth instrument of ratification. By 30 June 1975 it had been ratified by ten States: Belgium, Cyprus, Ireland, Luxembourg, Malta, the Netherlands, Norway, Sweden, Switzerland and the United Kingdom. It should constitute a further useful step in rendering effective the remedies provided in the European Convention.

5. ADMISSIBILITY OF APPLICATIONS

The first task of the Commission, when it is seized of an application, is to decide whether it is 'admissible'. This notion is sometimes puzzling to English lawyers; certainly the term is not current in English legal procedure. The essence of the matter is whether or not the Commission is competent to deal with the matter and whether or not there is an appearance of violation of the Convention, or, in other terms, whether there is any *prima facie* violation or any case to answer.[23] The simplest and clearest example is that an application alleging the violation of a right which is not guaranteed by the Convention evidently cannot succeed and is therefore rejected at the outset as inadmissible. In such a clear case this will be done by the Commission *ex officio* without the necessity of inviting the respondent government to send its written observations or of holding a hearing of the parties. If there is doubt about the question of admissibility the government's observations may be sought, and oral hearings may take place; but they will, in principle, be limited to the question of admissibility and will constitute a separate and preliminary stage in the proceedings, before the Commission comes to examine the merits of the case. Exceptionally, if the problem of admissibility is a particularly difficult one, it may be joined to the examination of the merits of the case.

It is therefore necessary to distinguish clearly the two separate stages of the proceedings: the preliminary stage of examination of admissibility, and the second stage of examination of the merits. The first of these is the subject of this section.

The importance of this distinction is shown by the fact that more than 90 per cent of the applications filed with the Commission are rejected at the stage of admissibility. The Commission's *Annual Review for 1974* shows that by 31 December of that year the Commission had taken 5,975 decisions on individual applications; 5,598 had been declared inadmissible *de plano*, that is to say without even being communicated to the respondent government. A further 250 applications had been declared inadmissible after communication to the respondent government and consideration of its views; only 127 individual applications had been declared admissible.

The Commission has sometimes been criticised for rejecting as inadmissible such a large proportion of the applications filed. The answer to this criticism is that the rules set out in the Convention are strict and it is the Commission's duty to apply them. There are in fact, as we shall see shortly, seven separate grounds for declaring an application inadmissible – sometimes described as seven hurdles which the applicant has to jump; two are set out in Article 26 and five in Article 27. Though there may be a few cases in which there is room for legitimate difference of opinion, the Commission has loyally and conscientiously applied the rules established in the Convention – and indeed could not properly have done otherwise. If, therefore, anything requires to be changed it is the rules themselves rather than the Commission's application of them. Moreover if the proportion of applications rejected as inadmissible seems high it should not be forgotten that access to the Commission is very easy: there are no prescribed formalities, no fees and no requirement of submission of the case by a lawyer. In fact a large proportion of applicants have not taken legal advice: many appear not even to have read the Convention. Consequently it is not surprising if a high proportion of applications are doomed from the start.

It was thought for a number of years that the decisions of the Commission on the admissibility of applications were final and not subject to appeal. Indeed, neither the Convention nor the Rules of Procedure of the Commission or of the Court provide for the possibility of review of such decisions. However, in the 'Vagrancy' cases against Belgium the Court stated clearly in its judgement of 18 June 1971 that the decision of the Commission on admissibility was not binding on the Court,[24] while in its judgement on the Ringeisen case of 16 July 1971 it considered and rejected the arguments of the respondent government that the Commission's decision on admissibility was wrong.[25] One must conclude, therefore, that the Commission's decision that a case is inadmissible is final and not subject to review, but that a decision that a case is admissible could subsequently be reversed by the Court – and, theoretically, by the Committee of Ministers.

EXHAUSTION OF DOMESTIC REMEDIES

Article 26 of the European Convention reads as follows:

> The Commission may only deal with the matter after all domestic remedies have been exhausted, according to the generally recognised rules of international law, and within a period of six months from the date on which the final decision was taken.

The rule of exhaustion of domestic remedies is well known to international lawyers and is based on both justice and common sense.[26] It is based on justice, because it would be unjust that the international responsibility of a State should be engaged on account of the action of one of its agents or tribunals when a national means of redress is available but has not been used. Equally, the rule is based on common sense, because it is in the general interest (among other reasons, as being normally quicker, cheaper and more effective) than an aggrieved person should make use of domestic remedies, when they are available, to right a wrong, rather than address himself to an international organ – commission, court or other tribunal. Access to the international organ should be available, but only in the last resort, and after the domestic remedies have been exhausted. Normally this will mean that appeals against the acts of the executive branch of the government should be addressed to the national courts before being addressed to an international organ; equally, that appeals against decisions of inferior courts should be addressed to the higher courts and, if necessary and possible, to the Supreme Court, or Constitutional Court, before being addressed to an international organ. Not only are the domestic remedies, as indicated above, likely to be speedier and perhaps less expensive; in many cases they may be more effective, because a national court of appeal or Supreme Court can usually reverse the decision of a lower court, whereas the decision of an international organ does not have that effect, even though it will engage the international responsibility of the State concerned.[27]

The principle was stated clearly by the European Commission of Human Rights in the case of *Nielsen* v. *Denmark*:[28]

The rule requiring the exhaustion of domestic remedies as a condition of the presentation of an international claim is founded upon the principle that the Respondent State must first have an opportunity to redress by its own means within the framework of its own domestic legal system the wrong alleged to have been done to the individual (Interhandel case, *I.C.J. Reports*, 1959, p. 27); ... further, the Arbitrator in the Finnish Ships Arbitration (1934, *Reports of International Arbitral Awards,* Vol. III, p. 1501–2) and the Arbitral Tribunal in the Ambatielos Arbitration (1956, London, p. 27–8) seem clearly to have assumed that this principle implies that the Respondent State is entitled to insist upon the prior exhaustion of all those domestic remedies of a legal nature which appear to be capable of providing an effective and sufficient means of redress without differentiating between ordinary and extraordinary remedies; the Institute of International Law in its Resolution of 1954 also appears to have considered that in applying the local remedies rule the crucial question is not the ordinary or extraordinary character of a legal remedy but whether it gives the possibility of an effective and sufficient means of redress (*Annuaire*, 1956, Vol. 46, p. 364); moreover, in the Interhandel case mentioned above, although the United States Government had on several occasions expressed the opinion to the Swiss Government that the domestic remedies in the United States had been exhausted by the Swiss Company, the International Court of Justice upheld the objection to the admissibility of the claim on the ground that the Company had obtained a reopening of the proceedings in the United

States Courts by a writ of *certiorari* in the Supreme Court and that the reopened proceedings were still in progress;

Accordingly the rules governing the exhaustion of domestic remedies, as these are generally recognised today, in principle require that recourse should be had to all legal remedies available under the local law which are in principle capable of providing an effective and sufficient means of redressing the wrongs for which, on the international plane, the Respondent State is alleged to be responsible.

All this is on the assumption that domestic remedies are available and are effective. If no domestic remedies are available, then clearly there is no need to have recourse to them before the applicant can address himself to the competent international organ. Equally, if there are domestic remedies which are theoretically available but there is unreasonable delay on the part of national courts in granting a remedy, then the applicant should not be penalised as a result. International law has long recognised this limitation on the domestic remedies rule; it was to take account of it that the words 'according to the generally recognised rules of international law' were included in Article 26 of the European Convention.

A large number of applications addressed to the European Commission of Human Rights have been declared inadmissible for failure to comply with the rule of exhaustion of domestic remedies set out in Article 26, while in other cases objections raised by governments of non-exhaustion of domestic remedies have been rejected. It is now proposed to indicate some of the issues which have arisen in practice.

When an application has been declared inadmissible on this ground the Commission has stated that the applicant is not debarred from submitting a new application if he has in the meantime exhausted the domestic remedies, or can show that he is no longer required to do so according to the generally recognised rules of international law.[29] On the other hand, his ignorance of the existence of a remedy,[30] the fact that his means are insufficient to permit him to prosecute his case[31] or his personal opinion about the possible success of an appeal[32] do not discharge him from the obligation.

In some early decisions the Commission held that the burden of proof was on the applicant to show that he has exhausted his domestic remedies.[33] While this will still apply if the respondent government has alleged non-exhaustion, it will not be the case if the respondent government has manifestly declined to raise this issue when it was invited to express its opinion on the admissibility of an application.[34]

A difficult problem is raised by the necessity to determine, in particular cases, whether the domestic remedies which are alleged to be available are ineffectve or unduly delayed. The principle is recognised that the generally recognised rules of international law release an applicant from the obligation to exhaust domestic remedies if they are clearly ineffective;[35] one example of this would be a constant jurisprudence of domestic courts in a sense unfavourable to the applicant.[36] Other examples may arise in relation to particular procedures under different systems of national law.

In several cases the Commission has rejected for non-exhaustion of domestic remedies applications from applicants who had failed to address themselves to the Austrian Constitutional Court, which is competent to decide on appeals from decisions by the administrative authorities in regard to alleged violations of constitutional rights, including decisions about the legality of arrest and detention.[37] In Belgium an appeal to the *Cour de Cassation* was held to be not necessary when that court had no power to exempt the applicant from complying with a particular provision;[38] and an appeal for clemency ('recours en grâce') was not considered necessary under Article 26, because it is not a legal remedy.[39] In the Netherlands section 1401 of the Civil Code permits an action against the State for a wrongful act as a result of which damage has been inflicted on a person; consequently an applicant who complained of ten months' detention before deportation as an undesirable alien, but who had not brought such an action, was held not to have exhausted his domestic remedies.[40]

In the United Kingdom an applicant detained in prison who complained that he was not allowed under the prison regulations to send certain letters to the courts, but who had not applied to the Home Secretary for permission to do so (as he could have done under the regulations), was held not to have exhausted his domestic remedies.[41] On the other hand, in the case of *Alam and Khan* v. *the United Kingdom* (which finally resulted in a friendly settlement) the Commission held that 'it is incumbent upon the respondent Government, if they raise the objection of non-exhaustion, to prove the existence in their municipal legal system of a remedy which has not been exhausted'. Since it was not clear that there was a remedy against the refusal of the immigration authorities to allow the applicant to enter the United Kingdom, the objection of non-exhaustion was not sustained and this issue was joined to the merits of the case.[42]

The question whether an appeal to the Federal Constitutional

Court (*Bundesverfassungsgericht*) in Germany is a domestic remedy within the meaning of Article 26 has come up on a number of occasions. It is the more important because the Constitutional Court has the task of interpreting and applying the provisions of the German Basic Law (*Grundgesetz*) which contain constitutional guarantees of fundamental rights and freedoms, many of which are closely akin to those contained in the European Convention; moreover the normative provisions of the Convention have the force of rules of domestic law in the Federal Republic.

In several decisions the Commission has held that a constitutional appeal is a domestic remedy which is, in principle, covered by the provisions of Article 26 of the Convention.[43] This has applied, *inter alia*, to an applicant who complained that he had not been allowed to stand as a candidate in elections to the Federal parliament[44] and to another applicant who had been denied the right to vote.[45] Normally, therefore, the failure to appeal to the Constitutional Court will constitute a basis for rejection on the ground of non-exhaustion of domestic remedies.

A particularly difficult application of this rule occurred in the case of *Retimag* v. *Federal Republic of Germany*. Retimag was a Swiss company which owned property in Germany which the Federal Supreme Court ordered to be confiscated on the ground that it was in fact held and used for the Communist Party, which had been dissolved as an illegal organisation. Retimag filed an application with the European Commission of Human Rights. The German government objected, *inter alia*, that Retimag had not exhausted the remedy of constitutional appeal. It was not clear whether under German law a foreign company was entitled in such circumstances to lodge an appeal with the Constitutional Court. The Commission considered that this was a question of German constitutional law which could be decided only by the Constitutional Court itself, and on which the European Commission could not give a ruling. Since the applicants had not established that it was impossible for them to appeal to the Constitutional Court – which they could have done, if their argument was correct, by trying to appeal – the case was therefore declared inadmissible for failure to exhaust domestic remedies.[46] As Mr J. E. S. Fawcett, now President of the Commission, has written:[47]

> It may be inferred in general that, where there is a reasonable doubt as to whether a remedy is available under domestic law, an applicant cannot be regarded as having complied with the rule in

Article 26 unless he has taken proceedings in which that doubt can be resolved.

The second requirement of Article 26 of the Convention is that the application must be filed '... within a period of six months from the date on which the final decision was taken'. It will be observed that the six-months rule comes immediately after the local remedies rule and in the same article. The Commission has said, '... the two rules contained in Article 26 ... are closely interrelated, since not only are they combined in the same Article, but they are also expressed in a single sentence whose grammatical construction implies such correlation'.[48] At the same time it is necessary to distinguish between rejection under the six-months rule and a decision of inadmissibility *ratione temporis*. The latter occurs if the respondent government had not ratified the Convention, or not accepted the right of individual petition, at the relevant date; the six-months rule comes into play only when these other conditions are satisfied.

The effect of the six-months rule may be modified if the violation complained of is a continuing situation. This was so in the case of *De Becker* v. *Belgium*, in which the applicant suffered from a loss of his civic rights derived from legislation which had the effect of excluding any domestic remedy; the result was a continuing and permanent situation to which the six-months rule did not apply.[49]

If there is a difference in dates between the actual receipt of an application in the secretariat of the Council of Europe and its formal registration by the Secretary of the Commission, it is the date of actual receipt which counts for the application of the six-months rule.[50]

OTHER RULES ON ADMISSIBILITY

Article 27 of the European Convention on Human Rights sets out other conditions relating to the admissibility of individual applications, that is to say it enumerates various circumstances in which an individual application must be declared inadmissible. The article reads as follows:

1. The Commission shall not deal with any petition submitted under Article 25 which
   (a) is anonymous, or
   (b) is substantially the same as a matter which has already been examined by the Commission or has already been submitted

to another procedure of international investigation or settlement and if it contains no relevant new information.
2. The Commission shall consider inadmissible any petition submitted under Article 25 which it considers incompatible with the
provisions of the present Convention, manifestly ill-founded, or
an abuse of the right of petition.
3. The Commisson shall reject any petition referred to it which it
considers inadmissible under Article 26.

The first thing to be noted about Article 27 is that whereas
Article 26, which enunciates the rule of exhaustion of domestic
remedies, applies to *all* applications filed with the Commission
(whether inter-State complaints or individual applications), the
rules of admissibility contained in Article 27 apply only to 'any
petition submitted under Article 25', i.e. to individual applications.
It is not relevant, therefore, to cases brought by one State against
another State under Article 24 of the Convention, except for paragraph 3.

It will be noted that paragraphs 1 and 2 of Article 27 set out five
separate grounds of inadmissibility:

1. that the application is anonymous;
2. that it is substantially the same as a matter which has already
been examined by the Commission or has already been submitted to another procedure of international investigation or
settlement and contains no relevant new information;
3. that it is incompatible with the provisions of the Convention;
4. that it is manifestly ill founded;
5. that it is abusive.

It is obviously not possible to give here a complete synopsis of
the jurisprudence of the European Commission of Human Rights
relating to all five grounds of inadmissibility set out in Article 27
of the European Convention. This will be apparent from the fact
that, as stated above, of 5,975 individual applications considered
by the Commission by the end of 1974, 5,848 were declared
inadmissible by reason of the rules contained in Articles 26 and 27.
The most that we can do, therefore, is to consider some of the salient
features. More detailed information will be found in the *Digest of
Case Law*.[51]

Of the five grounds mentioned, the third and fourth are those
which have been most frequently applied and which have raised
the most interesting problems: 'incompatible with the provisions
of the Convention' and 'manifestly ill founded'.

First of all it is necessary to distinguish between the concepts of 'incompatible' and 'manifestly ill founded'. An application is 'incompatible' if there is no possibility that the Commission can consider the matter, for example because the right whose violation is alleged is not one of the rights protected by the Convention or because the State against which the case has been brought has not ratified the Convention or has not recognised the right of individual petition. In such a situation it is clear that the Commission is not competent to act, whatever the merits of the case and however clear the evidence. On the other hand a case may be 'manifestly ill founded' when all the formal conditions of competence are satisfied yet there is no evidence to support the applicant's allegations of fact or the Commission is satisfied that the act complained of falls within one of the limitations or restrictions on a right permitted by the Convention. A few examples will perhaps make this distinction clearer.

The Commission receives many complaints (perhaps from people who have never even read the Convention) of violation of a right or an alleged right which is not among those listed in section I of the Convention itself or in the First and Fourth Protocols. These are declared inadmissible *ratione materiae* as 'incompatible'. The *Digest of Case Law* lists thirty-six different examples of this, including the right to asylum, the right not to be extradited, the right to stand for election, the right to housing, the right to a nationality, the right to a pension, etc.[52]

Secondly, under general rules of international law, treaties and conventions are not retroactive in effect; consequently the Convention applies only, as regards each Contracting Party, to facts subsequent to the date of its entry into force in respect of that Party. Therefore, even though inadmissibility *ratione temporis* is not one of the grounds specifically mentioned in Articles 26 and 27, applications which do not respect this rule are declared inadmissible *ratione temporis* and are subsumed under the general concept of 'incompatible'.[53] The same applies to applications which are inadmissible *ratione loci* or on the other grounds *ratione materiae* (e.g. a request to prescribe interim measures).[54]

When we come, on the other hand, to decisions of inadmissibility on the ground that the application is 'manifestly ill-founded' other criteria apply. The reason for rejection of the application is not that the Commission is not competent to deal with the subject-matter, but rather that the evidence submitted does not show an appearance of a violation.

The Commission declares an application inadmissible as being manifestly ill founded only when an examination of the file, including an examination *ex officio*, does not disclose a *prima facie* violation of the rights and freedoms set out in the Convention.[55]

The general concept may be expressed in terms familiar to English lawyers as 'no *prima facie* case' or 'no case to answer'.[56] The clearest example of this occurs when the applicant fails to adduce any evidence in support of his claim. Other examples arise from the fact that many of the rights protected by the Convention are subject to limitations or restrictions which may be necessary in a democratic society in the interests of national security, public safety, for the prevention of disorder or crime, for the protection of the rights of others, and so on. If the facts complained of clearly fall within one of these limitations or restrictions, then the application is declared inadmissible as being 'manifestly ill founded'.

The difficulty which arises in some of these cases is the following. The Commission has no power to decide that an application is ill founded; it can express an opinion on the matter, if it has declared the case admissible, but the decision must be taken by the Committee of Ministers or the Court. On the other hand, it must reject the application as inadmissible if it is *manifestly* ill founded. The problem is to draw the line between what is ill founded – which can appear only from an examination of the merits – and what is so manifestly ill founded that it does not even deserve consideration on the merits.

The leading case on this subject is *Iversen* v. *Norway*, in which six members of the Commission out of ten considered (though on different grounds) that the application was manifestly ill founded, while four were of the contrary opinion. It is sometimes doubted whether the ill founded nature of the application was 'manifest' when four members of the Commission could not see it and it took the majority more than twenty pages of the decision to explain their reasons.[57] The decision of the Commission on the *Iversen case* in 1963 probably marks the high-water mark in what might be called its restrictive jurisprudence, i.e. an excessive tendency to declare 'manifestly ill founded' a case which may not be likely to succeed but which most people would consider to be at least deserving of examination on the merits. In later years the Commission has been less restrictive in its interpretation of 'manifestly ill founded', and the suggestion has been made by one authority that if one-third of the members of the Commission find the application not to be manifestly ill founded, then it should be admitted for examination of the merits.[58] It has also led in recent years to a certain tendency to join a decision on admissibility to the consideration of the merits of the case.

The second ground of inadmissibility envisages as one possibility that the matter is substantially the same as a matter already submitted to another procedure of international settlement. This has not often arisen in the past, but is likely to have increasing importance now that the United Nations Covenant on Civil and Political Rights and its Optional Protocol are in force. It may well happen that an individual applicant wishes to complain of the violation of a right which is protected both by the European Convention and by the United Nations Covenant. Assuming that the respondent government is party to both instruments and has accepted their optional provisions, can the applicant make use of both procedures – either simultaneously or consecutively – or is he limited to only one, and, if so, to which?

The member governments of the Council of Europe have considered this problem and have reached the conclusion that the applicant should have a free choice between the two procedures, but that he should not be allowed to use them both either simultaneously or successively. When he has once decided which procedure to use he should not (except in the case of an honest mistake) be allowed to go from one organ to the other and appear to appeal from the European Commission to the United Nations Committee, or vice versa. The principle of *ne bis in idem* should apply in favour of States as well as for the benefit of individuals.

It is here that the second ground of inadmissibility set out in Article 27 of the Convention comes into play. If a matter has already been submitted to the United Nations Human Rights Committee in New York, then Article 27 will oblige the European Commission to declare inadmissible another application based on the same facts and submitted in Strasbourg – unless it contains relevant new information. In the other direction, i.e. if the applicant tries first in Strasbourg and then in New York, Article 5, para. 2(a), of the Optional Protocol will render the application inadmissible in New York for as long as it is under examination in Strasbourg, but not thereafter. Consequently what would look like an 'appeal' from the European Commission to the United Nations committee would then become possible. In order to avoid this occurring the Committee of Ministers of the Council of Europe has suggested that European governments should make a reservation or declaration of interpretation at the time of ratifying the Optional Protocol, and several of them have in fact done so.[59]

The first and fifth grounds of inadmissibility set out in Article 27 – that the application is anonymous or abusive – have rarely arisen in practice and call for little comment. The fact that an application is partly inspired by political motives does not render it abusive.[60]

6. ESTABLISHING THE FACTS: INVESTIGATIONS

After the Commission has taken a decision on the admissibility of an application its second task is to establish the facts. This is provided for in Article 28 of the Convention, which reads in part as follows:

> In the event of the Commission accepting a petition referred to it:
> (a) it shall, with a view to ascertaining the facts, undertake together with the representatives of the parties an examination of the petition and, if need be, an investigation, for the effective conduct of which the States concerned shall furnish all necessary facilities, after an exchange of views with the Commission;
> (b) ...

There is, however, another problem which arises occasionally even before the Commission comes to establish the facts: the necessity for interim measures. There have been cases in which an applicant states that he is in immediate danger and asks the Commission to take action without delay to protect him from the measure with which he is threatened – for example, an order for expulsion. If such a case is dealt with in the ordinary way irremediable steps may have been taken before the Commission can even consider the case. (The question whether the Convention contains a protection against expulsion is considered above in Chapter II in relation to Article 3.)

In such a situation there is need for 'interim measures', that is to say measures which will protect the rights of the parties provisionally, on an interim basis, until such time as the Commission can act. Yet the Convention contains no provision authorising the Commission to order, or to request, interim measures. In these circumstances a practice has been worked out, on an unofficial basis, which is best described in the words of the Commission's Secretary:[61]

The common element in these cases is their urgency and it is the established practice of the Secretary, particularly when the Commission is not in session, to inform the Government immediately and unofficially of such a complaint, to ask it for any available information and to inform the Government when the case will be examined.

This practice, approved by the Commission and fully accepted by Governments, protects the applicant against any precipitate or unconsidered action and warns the Government of a complaint which may later, and then too late, show a violation of the Convention.

In nearly all such cases and often despite administrative difficulties, the Government concerned has arranged to postpone the applicant's extradition or expulsion until the Commission has had the possibility of examining the admissibility of the applicaton. Such cases are given priority by the Commission (Rule 38 of the Rules of Procedure) and often dealt with within a few weeks, or even days, of the original complaint.

Though such informal arrangements have worked satisfactorily on a number of occasions in the past, it may be thought preferable that the Commission – and eventually the Court and the Committee of Ministers – should be empowered officially to order, or at least to request, interim measures when the circumstances so require – a power which has been conferred on the International Court of Justice and on the Court of Justice of the European Communities.[62] This view was taken by the Legal Affairs Committee of the Consultative Assembly, which led the latter to adopt its *Recommendation 623 (1971)* proposing the conclusion of a protocol to the Convention for this purpose.[63] The Committee of Ministers referred this proposal to the Committee of Experts on Human Rights, which, however, took a rather negative view, principally on the ground that the informal system described above appeared to be working satisfactorily and might be prejudiced by any attempt to institute a more formal procedure. As a result the informal system continues to be used when necessary, and no legal power to order or request interim measures has been instituted.

As regards the function of 'ascertaining the facts', international law has long known the existence of commissions or other bodies entrusted with the task of fact-finding. The first step towards the settlement of an international (or any other) dispute is to establish the facts; consequently commissions of conciliation or arbitration necessarily have this function and must discharge it before they can undertake their principal task of proposing a solution to the problem of which they are seized.[64] As stated by Oppenheim,[65] 'one of the commonest obstacles preventing the successful settlement of a dispute by means of negotiation is the difficulty of ascertaining the precise facts which have given rise to the dispute. Herein lies the value of bodies such as the International Commission of Enquiry under the Hague Convention I,' that is the Hague Convention for the Pacific Settlement of International Disputes of 1899.

The first step towards establishing the facts relevant to any particular dispute is normally undertaken by obtaining the written submissions of the parties. Such written submissions or memorials (as they are usually called) will usually start by setting out the facts as they are known, or appear relevant, to each of the parties, and it frequently happens that an international commission entrusted with the task of conciliation or arbitration is able to draw up, on the basis of such submissions, an agreed statement of the facts which will be acceptable to both parties. The task of drawing legal conclusions will then begin.

It may happen, however, that it proves impossible to arrive at an agreed statement of the facts, or that the agreed statement is incomplete and further information is required. Evidence may then be obtained in a written form or by hearing witnesses, and in the latter case the evaluation of the evidence – particularly if it is conflicting – will depend to a considerable extent on the presentation and conduct of the individual witnesses, particularly under cross-examination. Hence the necessity – at the national level at least – for carefully defined rules of evidence and of procedure. In international proceedings the rules are usually less strict on account of the necessity to combine or harmonise the practice followed in different systems of law.

The various stages of an enquiry mentioned above can be undertaken by an international commission sitting at its normal place of business. But there are occasions when it is necessary to conduct an enquiry *in situ*. An obvious example is a boundary dispute. Various local factors – geographical, ethnological or other – may have to be taken into account; hence the need for enquiries or investigations on the spot. A slightly different example was the case of *Diversion of water from the River Meuse* (*Netherlands* v. *Belgium*), in which the Permanent Court of International Justice made an inspection on the spot on 13–15 May 1937, at the suggestion of the Belgian government, of the relevant works, canals and waterways in Belgium.[66] The same principle applies to other classes of dispute, and perhaps with particular force to allegations about the violation of human rights.

It is, of course, an accepted rule of international law, deriving from the principle of sovereignty, that an international commission of enquiry cannot enter the territory of a State without its consent. Well known examples of this are the failure of the UN *ad hoc* Working Group of Experts[67] to be admitted to South Africa and Namibia, and the inability of the Special Committee to examine Israeli practices affecting Human Rights in Occupied Territories[68] to obtain admission to Israel. In both these cases, however, the international body had been set up without the consent – and indeed in direct opposition to the wishes – of the government concerned. The latter's refusal of access to its territory was therefore hardly surprising. But if the international body or commission has been established under the terms of a treaty to which the government in question is a party the situation is different.

As regards the European Commission of Human Rights, it will be observed that Article 28 of the Convention, quoted above, imposes on the States concerned a clear obligation to furnish any necessary facilities for an investigation which the Commission may wish to undertake, which may, of course, include an investigation on the spot. The text stipulates that there shall be 'an exchange of views with the Commission', which implies a certain measure of consultation; but the consultation relates to the modalities of the investigation – the date, the place, the detailed arrangements – and not to the fundamental question whether or not the investigation shall be undertaken. In other words, it is not possible for the government, if it respects its obligations under the Convention, to refuse to allow the investigation to take place.

Is this inconsistent with the accepted rule of international law, stated above, that an international commission of enquiry cannot enter on the territory of a State without its consent? The answer to this question is in the negative, because the consent is given by the act of ratifying the treaty. But once the consent has been given in that way, it is of general application and it is no longer necessary for the Commission to ask for the consent of the government in each particular case. The situation whereby governments have given in advance a general consent to investigations on their territory is one of the features of the European Convention that are of particular importance.

In order to show how this has worked in practice it is proposed to give four examples of investigations carried out by the European Commission of Human Rights.

The first of these was in Cyprus in 1958. Two inter-State applications were dealt with by the Commission in 1957, 1958 and 1959. As explained in Chapter II (Article 3), they were both brought by Greece against the United Kingdom, and related to the situation in Cyprus while that island was still a British colony. In its first application of 7 May 1956 the Greek government alleged that the government of Cyprus had violated the Convention by introducing certain exceptional legislative and administrative measures in the island – even though the United Kingdom had, in accordance with Article 15 of the Convention, notified the Secretary General of a state of emergency, as a result of which it was temporarily suspending certain of the rights guaranteed. The application was declared admissible; a sub-commission was then appointed and held twelve sessions, including four hearings of the parties, and in January 1958 it carried out an investigation in Cyprus in order to judge on the spot as to the existence and extent of the state of emergency. On the basis of its findings the Commission submitted its report to the Committee of Ministers in October 1958.[69] However, before this report could be examined, the Zurich and London agreements settling the Cyprus question were concluded, so that on 20 April 1959 the Committee of Ministers, on the joint proposal of the Greek and United Kingdom governments, decided: 'In accordance with Article 32 of the European Convention for the Protection of Human Rights and Fundamental Freedoms, no further action is called for.'[70]

Though we now accept this procedure as normal under the terms of the Convention, it should be noticed how very much further it goes in the direction of international control than anything previously known under international law. The well known provisions of paragraph 7 of Article 2 of the United Nations Charter affirm the principle that 'Nothing contained in the present Charter shall authorise the United Nations to intervene in matters which are essentially within the domestic jurisdiction of any State . . .'. Nevertheless at a time when Cyprus was still a British colony the government afforded all necessary facilities for a sub-commission to visit the island to satisfy itself about the existence of an emergency within the meaning of Article 15 and examine the responsible officials on the spot. A special law was even enacted to grant diplomatic privileges and immunities to members of the Commission and their official staff when exercising their functions on the island.[71] The proceedings relating to the second application were terminated in the same way and raised no separate issues relevant to the present subject-matter.

Two individual applications brought against the Federal Republic and Austria respectively are good illustrations of the practice of the European Commission in conducting investigations on the spot. In the case of *Zeidler-Kornmann* v. *Federal Republic of Germany*[72] the applicant complained of ill treatment in the Tegel prison in Berlin, in violation of Article 3 of the European Convention, which prohibits 'torture or ... inhuman or degrading treatment or punishment'. The local remedies having been exhausted, the Commission declared the application admissible and, in accordance with Article 29 of the Convention, set up a sub-commission for the purpose of establishing the facts.[73]

The sub-commission first obtained the written observations of the applicant and of the government, and soon arrived at the conclusion that the issue depended entirely on the precise nature of the facts – which could be established only by interrogating the applicant, who was still detained in prison, and the prison officers concerned, and by visiting the prison where the events complained of took place. It therefore decided to take evidence in Berlin. The German authorities lent their full co-operation, and arrangements were made for the sub-commission to meet on the premises of the Supreme Restitution Court in that city and also to visit the Tegel prison. This was done from 23 to 26 April 1967.

On the basis of the report of the sub-commission the plenary Commission drew up its own report, which in due course was submitted to the Committee of Ministers of the Council of Europe in accordance with Article 31 of the Convention. The Commission had no difficulty in reaching the conclusion that the applicant had not been subjected to torture, and then went on to consider whether he had been subjected to 'inhuman or degrading treatment'. On the basis of the facts found by the sub-commission, including evidence taken from the prison governor, seven prison officers, another prisoner, the hospital officers and the prison doctor, the Commission did not find that the degree of force used was excessive in the circumstances and consequently it was of opinion that he was not subjected to 'inhuman or degrading treatment'. On the basis of this report the Committee of Ministers of the Council of Europe, acting in accordance with Article 32 of the Convention, decided on 26 June 1968 that there had been no violation of the Convention on Human Rights.[74]

Rather similar problems were raised in the case of *Simon-Herold* v. *Austria*.[75] The applicant, who was partly paralysed from poliomyelitis contracted in 1961, complained of the treatment he received when remanded in custody in Austrian prisons from 31 July 1969 to 23 January 1970. In particular he alleged that the general conditions under which he was detained, the lack of adequate medical care and his detention for fourteen days in a closed ward in the psychiatric section of a hospital in Linz amounted to 'inhuman or degrading treatment' in contravention of Article 3 of the Convention.

The Commission delegated three of its members to hear witnesses in Austria. The Wels Regional Court was put at their disposal by the Austrian authorities; seventeen witnesses were heard in Wels and Linz; the prison of the court and the psychiatric ward were visited; subsequently the applicant was heard by the Commission's delegates in Paris. After protracted negotiations a friendly settlement of the matter was reached in 1972; the Austrian authorities undertook not to prosecute for the alleged offence and the applicant agreed to withdraw his case before the Commission; at the same time the Austrian Minister of Justice issued new instructions about the treatment of sick or injured prisoners, stating that a prisoner must not be subjected to 'inhuman or degrading treatment' and that detention in the closed ward of a psychiatric hospital might constitute such treatment.[76]

The best known, and by far the most important, example of an investigation carried out by the European Commission of Human Rights was in the *Greek case*.[77] The substance of this case has been explained above;[78] in this chapter we shall limit ourselves to the manner in which the investigation was carried out on the spot.

The first question which the Commission had to examine in the Greek case was whether or not there existed in Greece in April 1957 an 'emergency threatening the life of the nation'. If so, the further questions would arise whether or not the measures taken by the Greek government were 'strictly required by the exigencies of the situation' and were 'not inconsistent with its other obligations under international law'. This involved not merely simple questions of fact but also matters of judgement, i.e. the conclusions to be drawn from the facts, which were of a complex and highly political nature. The Commission also had to examine the allegations of torture made by the applicant governments. Here it became necessary not only to 'establish the facts' in the ordinary sense of ascertaining whether torture had been practised but also to draw a conclusion as to whether or not the use of torture constituted an administrative practice authorised or tolerated by the respondent government. Other matters related to eleven other articles of the Convention whose violation was alleged by the applicant governments, which would become material to the case if it was held that the derogation under Article 15 was not justified.

An investigation into all these issues could be carried out effectively only on the spot. Consequently, after hearing about thirty witnesses in Strasbourg in November and December 1968, the sub-commission 'fixed 6 February 1969 as the opening date for its investigation in Greece'. In accordance with Article 28 of the Convention (quoted above) the Greek government was consulted about the arrangements, but not about the question whether the investigation should take place. At its request the date for the opening of the investigation was postponed until 10 March.

The sub-commission met in Athens on 9 March 1969 and began its investigation the following day. To a large extent the Greek government co-operated loyally with it and facilitated its task, and the sub-commission expressed its appreciation of this fact. Between 10 and 20 March it heard thirty-four witnesses as regards the allegations of torture and twenty witnesses about the existence of a state of emergency. In addition it visited the police stations of the Security Police in Athens and Piraeus and delegated one of its members to visit the Hagia Paraskevi detention camp. When the sub-commission wanted a medical opinion on the condition of certain witnesses who alleged that they had been physically tortured it summoned two forensic experts from the University of Geneva, who were accorded the necessary facilities. On the other hand the sub-commission was prevented by the government from hearing thirteen witnesses whom it wished to examine in connection with allegations of torture (including Alexander Panagoulis) and was also prevented from inspecting the detention camps on the island of Leros and from visiting the Averoff prison in Athens. Since it considered the reasons for these refusals unjustified, it terminated its visit on 19 March and reported the facts to the plenary Commission.[79]

Though some of the facilities it required were refused, the sub-commission did in fact accomplish a thorough investigation into the allegations of torture and about the existence of a state of emergency. This is illustrated by the facts that, in addition to hearing many witnesses on the torture issue, it visited, photographed and published the photographs of the famous (or infamous) Bouboulinas station of the Security Police in Athens; and during the hearings on the largely political question of the existence of a state of emergency threatening the life of the nation the witnesses included three former Prime Ministers (MM. Georgakopoulos, Stephanopoulos and Kanellopoulos), the Governor of the Bank of

Greece (M. Galanis), the chief of the armed forces (General Anghelis) and the Director General of Security at the Ministry of Public Order (M. Papaspyropoulos).

As is well-known, the European Commission of Human Rights, acting on the information obtained by the sub-commission in the course of its investigations (which included in the aggregate the hearing of more than eighty witnesses) reached the conclusions in its report of 18 November 1969 that there was not in Greece on 21 April 1967 (the date of the *coup d'état*) a public emergency threatening the life of the nation, as a consequence of which the Greek derogations were invalid; secondly, that there was a practice of torture and ill-treatment by the Athens Security Police, Bouboulinas Street, of persons arrested for political reasons; thirdly, that there was also violation of Articles 5, 6, 8, 9, 10, 11, 13 and 14 of the Convention on Human Rights and Article 3 of the First Protocol, but not of Article 7 of the Convention or Article 1 of the First Protocol. Its conclusions were endorsed by the Committee of Ministers – and thus became decisions of the Committee under Article 32 of the Convention – in its Resolution DH(70)1 of 15 April 1970.[80] In the meantime, when the Committee of Ministers was considering in December 1969 *Recommendation 547 (1969)* of the Consultative Assembly on the situation in Greece, the Greek Minister for Foreign Affairs announced the decision of his government to denounce the Statute and withdraw from the Council of Europe, and also to denounce the European Convention on Human Rights.[81]

The proceedings in this case have been described in some detail because they constitute the most striking example of the power of investigation of the European Commission of Human Rights; as already mentioned, they related not merely to the establishment of the facts but also to matters of political judgement, that is to say the determination by a government of the existence of an emergency threatening the life of the nation. The political importance of this power of the Commission – and, when appropriate, of the Court of Human Rights and of the Committee of Ministers of the Council of Europe – is seen from the fact that it may, and in the Greek case did, lead to the virtual expulsion of a State from membership of the Council of Europe.

One further illustration should be mentioned briefly, in conclusion, of the exercise by the European Commission of Human Rights of its powers of investigation. On 16 December 1971 the government of Ireland filed an inter-State application against the government of the United Kingdom relating to the situation in Northern Ireland.[82] On 1 October 1972 the Commission declared the application admissible, except as regards the allegations of violation of Article 2 (the right to life).[83] After an exchange of memorials and hearings on the merits in 1973, thirteen witnesses proposed by the Irish government were heard by three delegates of the Commission in November of that year. It then became necessary to hear a number of witnesses proposed by the British government, but the latter, in view of the exceptional situation in Northern Ireland and of the danger of retaliation against its witnesses by the Provisional IRA, was unwilling that the hearings should take place except under conditions of the greatest security, which would not obtain at the normal seat of the Commission, that is to say on the premises of the Council of Europe in Strasbourg. After protracted negotiations, arrangements were made for the hearings to take place in May 1974 at an airfield near Stavanger in Norway, guarded by members of the Norwegian army and security police; it was reported that members of the British security forces in Northern Ireland called as witnesses would not be identified and would be kept hidden behind screens.[84] Evidently this was a most unusual procedure, resulting from unusual and dangerous circumstances; indeed, it was probably unique in the annals of international investigation procedures.

Be that as it may, the power of investigation conferred by the European Convention on Human Rights – whether in matters of this importance or in other simpler situations such as those mentioned above concerning Austria and the Federal Republic – constitutes an indispensable part of the system of control instituted by the Convention and probably one of the most effective yet established under international law.

7. FRIENDLY SETTLEMENT AND SIMILAR MEASURES

After it has taken a decision on the admissibility of an application and established the facts, the third task of the Commission is to attempt to reach a friendly settlement. Paragraph (b) of Article 28 provides that the Commission

> ... shall place itself at the disposal of the parties concerned with a view to securing a friendly settlement of the matter on the basis of respect for Human Rights as defined in this Convention.

It will be observed that simple agreement between the individual applicant and the respondent government is not sufficient for the conclusion of a friendly settlement. The settlement must be approved by the Commission, and the latter will approve only if it is satisfied that the settlement is based on respect for human rights. Otherwise it might be possible for a government to put pressure on an applicant and induce him to agree to a settlement which did not adequately respect his rights. Moreover 'the function of the Commission is to be a medium or channel of negotiation, rather than to take the initiative by proposing terms for a friendly settlement'.[85]

In fact the number of friendly settlements achieved in accordance with the terms of Article 28 has been small; only nine by the end of 1974. A good example is afforded by the case of *Alam and Khan* v. *the United Kingdom*.[86] The first applicant was a Pakistani mill worker residing in Yorkshire, with two wives living in Pakistan. After a trip to that country he returned to England in 1965, accompanied by the second applicant, a boy of thirteen, who was his elder son by his second (polygamous) marriage. The father was admitted to the country, but the son was refused admission and sent back to Pakistan. A second attempt during the following year was equally unsuccessful. The application alleged violation of Article 6 of the Convention (right to a fair trial in the determination of one's civil rights and obligations), Article 8 (right to family life) and Article 13 (right to an effective remedy in the case of violation of one's rights). After the case had been declared admissible and written pleadings exchanged on the merits, a friendly settlement was achieved, on the basis of which the British government, while still maintaining its position on the question of violation, agreed to pay the cost of the boy's journey from Pakistan to London and to grant him an entry certificate; the Commission also took note of the government's intention to introduce a Bill – since incorporated into the Immigration Act, 1971 – granting to aliens a right of appeal to a court against decisions of immigration officers in respect of admission to and removal from the United Kingdom.[87]

Other cases of friendly settlement under Article 28 have been:
ʼ (a) *Boeckmans* v. *Belgium*, in which the applicant, who had been convicted of theft, complained of violation of the right to a fair trial on account of derogatory remarks made to him in court by the presiding judge during the trial. The basis of the settlement was that, while the validity of the sentence could not be questioned, it was recognised that 'the remarks made to the applicant ... were such as to disturb the serenity of the atmosphere during the proceed-

ings in a manner contrary to the Convention and may have caused the applicant a moral injury'; a payment was made to him of 65,000 Belgian francs, which 'would constitute adequate reparation for this injury'.[88]

(b) *Poershke* v. *Federal Republic of Germany*, in which the applicant, who had been convicted of attempted theft, complained of the length of his detention pending trial. Under the terms of the settlement he was granted conditional release on probation and agreed to withdraw his application to the Commission.[89]

○ (c) *Knechtl* v. *United Kingdom*. The applicant, while serving a prison sentence, had an operation for the amputation of his leg; he alleged that the necessity for the amputation was due to the negligence of the prison doctors and that he was not allowed to correspond with a solicitor with a view to instituting legal action against them, which violated his rights under Article 6 of the Convention. The settlement provided for an *ex gratia* payment to the applicant of £750 and the withdrawal of his application to the Commission, without prejudice to his right to continue action before the English courts; at the same time the British government laid before Parliament a white paper on 'Legal advice to prisoners' designed to liberalise the existing practice and grant greater latitude to prisoners when they wish to consult a solicitor.[90]

(d) *Sepp* v. *Federal Republic of Germany* involved the question of the excessive length of the criminal proceedings against the applicant. The proceedings lasted from July 1961 until August 1967 (when he was convicted of fraud and sentenced to twenty-three months' imprisonment), continuing until August 1968, when his appeal against this decision was rejected. Before serving his sentence the applicant left Germany for the Netherlands. The basis of the settlement was that the applicant would be granted, by way of a pardon, a suspension of the sentence (initially for two years, thereafter, subject to compliance with the conditions thereof, permanently), and that certain other measures would be taken in his favour, while he undertook not to pursue the case further either before a German court or before the Commission.[91]

(e) *Simon-Herold* v. *Austria*. This case has been summarised in the preceding section as an illustration of the Commission's power of investigation *in situ*.[92] It also illustrates (like the case of *Knechtl* v. *United Kingdom*) the point that the measures taken as part of a friendly settlement were of general application and likely to benefit not only the applicant concerned in this case but also other detained persons who might in the future find themselves in a similar situation.

(f) *Mellin* v. *Federal Republic of Germany* was another case involving excessive delay in criminal proceedings. They were begun in February 1961, and ten years later the applicant was convicted on a charge of embezzlement and sentenced to three years' imprisonment and a fine. The basis of the settlement was a remission of sentence and an undertaking by the applicant not to take further proceedings either before a German court or before the Commission. The latter also took note of various measures introduced in the Federal Republic to accelerate criminal proceedings, including the abolition of the preliminary judicial enquiry and the suspension of proceedings when twice the prescription period has elapsed.[93]

(g) *Amekrane* v. *United Kingdom*;[94] and (h) *Gussenbauer* v. *Austria*.[95]

The original text of Article 29 of the Convention provided that the functions of the Commission in establishing the facts of a case (including, if necessary, an investigation) and in endeavouring to reach a friendly settlement should be performed by means of a sub-commission of seven members of the Commission, of which two would be appointed by the parties to the case and the remainder chosen by lot. In practice this was not found satisfactory, principally because it might happen that, when the case came back before the plenary Commission, matters discussed at length in the sub-commission would have to be reopened and discussed again by those members who had not participated in the sub-commission's work. This was evidently time-wasting. Accordingly, as explained in Chapter I, section 3, the Commission itself proposed in 1961 that the system of sub-commissions should be abolished. The Committee of Ministers referred those proposals to the Committee of Experts on Human Rights, which agreed to the proposal and proceeded to draft the Third Protocol to the Convention. Article 1, paragraph 1, of the Third Protocol thus simply deletes Article 29 of the original text of the Convention.[96]

It may nevertheless happen that the Commission requires some task to be undertaken, such as hearing witnesses or conducting an investigation, which can be done more efficiently by a few members rather than by the plenary Commission. Some examples of this were given in the previous section of this chapter. It is provided for in Rule 51(1) of the Rules of Procedure:

> The Commission may charge one or more of its members to carry out an enquiry or any other form of investigation or to perform any other task necessary for the proper execution of its functions

under Article 28 of the Convention. Such member or members shall report to the Commission.

When the Commission succeeds in effecting a friendly settlement, it is required by Article 30 of the Convention to draw up a report containing a brief statement of the facts and of the solution reached; this is sent to 'the States concerned' (in practice, so far, only one State has been concerned in each of the friendly settlements reached), to the Committee of Ministers of the Council of Europe, and to the Secretary General for publication. Communication of the report to the Committee of Ministers necessarily involves transmission to all member States of the Council of Europe and thus to all Contracting Parties to the Convention. The practice has been developed that the Committee of Ministers formally takes note of the report, in order to have it on the record that the requirements of the Convention have been complied with.

As we have seen in the previous section, the examination of the application with a view to ascertaining the facts is undertaken 'together with the representatives of the parties'. Evidently the same is true *a fortiori* of attempts to achieve a friendly settlement. At this stage of the proceedings it is practically indispensable for an individual applicant to have legal assistance. For this purpose the Commission proposed that a system of legal aid for those who have insufficient means should be instituted and charged to the budget of the Council of Europe. The Committee of Ministers agreed to this proposal. The relevant provisions are set out in an addendum to the Commission's Rules of Procedure; the system does not apply at the initial stages of examination of admissibility but can apply when the Commission has communicated an application to the respondent government for its observations on admissibility or when the application has been declared admissible.[97]

Though the number of friendly settlements within the meaning of Article 28 of the Convention was limited to nine during the first twenty-one years after its entry into force, there has been a larger number of cases which have been withdrawn by the applicant and struck off the list as a result of some sort of unofficial arrangement with the government concerned. Some examples are the following cases: *Angelika Kurtz* v. *Federal Republic of Germany*, which concerned a family dispute about the custody of a child involving the question whether she should be taken, against the will of her father, to live with her mother in the Democratic Republic;[98] *NV Televizier* v. *the Netherlands*, in which a company forbidden to publish television programmes by reason of the Dutch copyright Act alleged that this prohibition constituted an infringement of the right to freedom of expression;[99] *Rebitzer* v. *Austria,* which concerned compensation for a prisoner convicted of murder and sentenced to imprisonment for life, whose conviction was quashed on a retrial after he had spent seventeen years in prison;[100] and *Karnell and Hardt* v. *Sweden,* which related to compulsory religious education in schools.[101] These four cases are samples taken from among a larger number which illustrate a developing practice whereby the satisfaction accorded to an applicant under national law (in the *Rebitzer case* the applicant received one million schillings as compensation) leads to the termination of the proceedings in a manner which is analogous to a friendly settlement, even though not expressly concluded under the terms of Article 28 of the Convention.[102]

8. THE CONCLUSIONS OF THE COMMISSION

The fourth task of the Commission (after the decision on admissibility, the establishment of the facts and the attempt to reach a friendly settlement) is to formulate its conclusions. Article 31, paragraph 1, of the Convention reads:

> If a solution is not reached, the Commission shall draw up a report on the facts and state its opinion as to whether the facts found disclose a breach by the State concerned of its obligations under the Convention. The opinions of all members of the Commission on this point may be stated in the Report.

It will be observed that the function of the Commission is limited to stating an *opinion.* It does not have the power to take a decision on the question of violation. As we shall see in later chapters, it is only the Court or the Committee of Ministers that can take such a decision. The theory on which the Convention was based by its authors in 1950 was that the Commission had functions of screening (to throw out undeserving applications) and of conciliation, but not of decision.

In the light of experience this may seem surprising. In fact the majority of cases have gone in the past to the Committee of Ministers for final decision and a smaller number to the Court, but in recent years the number referred to the latter body has increased markedly. However, the Committee of Ministers rarely gives any detailed statement of its reasons for a decision, usually limiting itself

to confirming the opinion of the Commission. It is therefore important that the Commission should give a detailed statement of its
reasons. This it has always done.

In the great majority of cases decided by the Committee of
Ministers the decisions are taken not by the Ministers themselves
but by their Permanent Representatives, who are diplomats authorised to take decisions as the Ministers' Deputies in the name of, and
on behalf of, the Ministers.[103] The reason why this system is surprising is that the Permanent Representatives, however highly
qualified as diplomats, do not have the training or the experience
to exercise judicial or quasi-judicial functions; nor do they have
the time (among the dozens of other questions with which they have
to deal) to examine in detail the complicated legal issues which
are usually involved in a case of this sort.

These considerations led the Commission to propose in 1961 that
its powers should be increased to the modest extent of allowing it
to take a decision that no violation had occurred if its members
were unanimously of that opinion.[104] This proposal was also inspired by the thought that the Commission would more easily
declare that a case was admissible if it had the power subsequently
to decide that there was no violation – i.e. if it could take the second
decision itself with the minimum of formality and without the
necessity of engaging the procedure before the Committee of
Ministers or the Court. However, the Committee of Experts on
Human Rights (to which the proposal was referred by the Committee of Ministers) again took a cautious view, and opposed any
change in the division of powers instituted by the Convention; it
was unwilling to grant to the Commission the power of taking
decisions on a question of violation.[105] It then elaborated a rather
unsatisfactory compromise which would allow the Commission, after
declaring an application admissible, subsequently, if it is unanimous,
'to reject the petition if, in the course of its examination, it finds
that the existence of one of the grounds for non-acceptance provided
for in Article 27 has been established'. The Third Protocol to the
Convention has now had the effect of inserting this provision as
a new Article 29 of the Convention in place of the original Article
29 which instituted the system of sub-commissions.[106]

The new text of Article 29 has been described as 'a rather unsatisfactory compromise' because what it means, in effect, is that
the Commission may decide that a case is admissible and proceed
to examine the merits thereof, and then come back again on its
original decision and decide that it is inadmissible after all – pro-

vided that there is unanimity for the second decision. Clearly this is unlikely to occur very often;[107] consequently the new text of Article 29 can hardly be considered a significant improvement of the procedure instituted by the Convention.

The last sentence of paragraph 1 of Article 31 (quoted above) permits all members of the Commission to formulate individual opinions. This is quite frequently done in important cases, as regards both concurring and dissenting opinions.

Paragraph 2 of Article 31 provides:

> The Report shall be transmitted to the Committee of Ministers. It shall also be transmitted to the States concerned, who shall not be at liberty to publish it.

The confidential nature of the report at this stage of the proceedings has been reaffirmed on various occasions. In the *Lawless case* the Irish government asked the Committee of Ministers to publish the Commission's conclusions (at a time when the case was not yet before the Court), but this request was refused because the report was still confidential.[108] On 12 June 1974, after the report of the Commission on the *Case of the East African Asians* had been transmitted to the Committee of Ministers, a question about it was asked in the House of Commons and the Minister of State replied, quite rightly, that the report was confidential and its contents could not be divulged.[109] A similar answer was given in the Swedish parliament in 1972 in reply to a question about the contents of the government's memorial submitted to the Commission in a case then under examination.[110] Indeed, there is good reason for keeping the report confidential at this stage, because there is always the possibility that the Committee of Ministers, at the political level, may be able to arrange a friendly settlement of a case, and the chances of success are greater if the discussions are conducted on a confidential basis and away from the glare of publicity. It is for the same reason that, when the Committee of Ministers has taken its decision on a case and decided to publish the report of the Commission (which is the usual practice, though exceptions are sometimes made), the chapter in the report about the attempt to reach a friendly settlement is not published but remains confidential.

A separate question is whether the confidential nature of the report of the Commission means that it cannot be communicated to the individual applicant to whose case it relates. This was the central issue in the Irish government's preliminary objections in the *Lawless case*, and will be considered in the following chapter.

The final paragraph in Article 31 of the Convention provides that:

In transmitting the Report to the Committee of Ministers, the Commission may make such proposals as it thinks fit.

This would appear to envisage proposals for possible remedial measures in a case of a violation, or perhaps proposals for a friendly settlement which the Commission might wish to submit to the Committee of Ministers for discussion at the inter-governmental level.

In practice this faculty is seldom used. A notable exception was in the *Greek case*, when the Commission took much care in formulating proposals for the gradual restoration of democratic freedoms in Greece. These proposals were submitted to the Committee of Ministers in November 1969 in accordance with Article 31, paragraph 3, and subsequently annexed by the committee to its resolution of 15 April 1970, which decided that the military government then in power had violated ten separate articles of the Convention and urged it to restore human rights and fundamental freedoms in Greece, taking into account the Commission's proposals.[111]

A different but related question arose in connection with the case of *Austria* v. *Italy*.[112] The Commission in its report expressed the opinion that there had been no violation of the Convention; at the same time it expressed the view that it was 'desirable for humanitarian reasons, among which may be counted the youth of the prisoners, that measures of clemency be taken in their favour'.[113] This view was not formulated as a 'proposal' under paragraph 3 of Article 31; it was rather a wish or recommendation resulting from the Commission's study of the case and of the surrounding circumstances.

This raised the question of the scope of the Commission's power to make proposals and recommendations. The view was expressed that paragraph 3 of Article 31 was intended to permit the Commission to make proposals if it considered that a violation had occurred; in such a case it was reasonable that it should make proposals about the remedial action to be taken; but if it had already arrived at the conclusion that there was no violation, then, it was argued, there was no need for it to make any proposals or recommendations at all, and an attempt to do so would be *ultra vires*.

The Ministers instructed the Committee of Experts on Human Rights to examine this question – together with a number of other questions relating to the exercise by the Committee of Ministers of its functions under Article 32 of the Convention. The study which ensued, and the conclusions to which it gave rise, are discussed below in Chapter VI. As regards the particular point with which we are now concerned, the Experts arrived at the conclusion that 'the Commission is not entitled to make proposals under Article 31(3) of the Convention in cases where it considers that there has not been a violation of the Convention'. The Committee of Ministers approved this conclusion and included it as Rule 6 in the *Rules for the Application of Article 32 of the Convention on Human Rights*.[114]

As we have seen, the report of the Commission expressing an opinion on the question of violation is transmitted to the Committee of Ministers, and therefore to all member governments of the Council of Europe. The case may be referred to the Court of Human Rights, if the respondent government has accepted its jurisdiction; otherwise it is for the Committee of Ministers to take a decision. These two possibilities will be examined in the two following chapters.

NOTES

1 *Cf. Human Rights in the World*, pp. 28–30; Sohn and Buergenthal, *International Protection of Human Rights*, pp. 514–39.

2 Fifth report of the Committee of Ministers to the Assembly, *Documents of the Assembly*, 1954, Document 237, paras. 47–8.

3 *Ibid.*, para. 49.

4 *Documents*, 1955, Document 439; Resolution 96, *Texts adopted*, April 1956.

5 Progress report of the Bureau and Standing Committee, 18 September 1970, *Documents*, 1970, Document 2825, para. IX.

6 The following were elected members of the Commission: M. Akbay (Turkish), L. J. C. Beaufort (Dutch), P. Berg (Norwegian), W. Black (Irish), E. M. Dominedo (Italian), C. T. Eustathiades (Greek), P. Faber (Luxembourg), Mme I. Fuest (Saar), Mme I. Hansen (Danish), Mme G. Janssen-Pevtschin (Belgian), I. Jonasson (Icelandic), G. Pernot (French), S. Petrén (Swedish), A. Suesterhenn (German), C. H. M. Waldock (British).

7 All three women members had ceased to hold office, for various reasons, by May 1966, since when the members of the Commission have all been men. It is surprising, when the Convention is designed to secure the protection of human rights for all without discrimination, *inter alia* on grounds of sex, that this has not occasioned protests. The remedy lies in the hands of the parliamentary representatives who draw up the lists of candidates.

8 At its first session in July 1954 the Commission entrusted the task of drafting its Rules of Procedure to a sub-committee of five members. The rules were then adopted pursuant to Article 36 of the Convention, during the Commission's second session on 2 April 1955. After certain subsequent amendments had been made, the Commission adopted revised Rules of Procedure during its twenty-fourth session from 1 to 5 August 1960. Further amendments have been made from time to time. The current rules are to be found in *European Convention on Human Rights: Collected Texts*, published periodically by the Council of Europe (tenth edition, August 1975).

9 The amended text of Article 22 is given in Appendix 1.

10 *Yearbook* I, 1955–57, p. 86.

11 *Annual Review*, 1974, pp. 5–6.

12 *Cf.* n. 8 above.

13 *Zoernsch* v. *Waldock and McNulty*, 1964. All E.R., p. 256. Willmer, L. J., said 'the Commission is so related to, and so bound up with the Council that it cannot properly be described as anything other than an organ of the Council'.

14 Oppenheim, *International Law*, 1905, Vol. I, *Peace*, p. 346. Later editions of Oppenheim by Sir Hersch Lauterpacht, however, have considerably modified this view. Sohn and Buergenthal's *International Protection of Human Rights* (Indianapolis, 1973), pp. 1–8, juxtaposes Oppenheim's views in 1912, including the extract quoted in the text, with Lauterpacht's revised version contained in the eighth edition of this work, published in 1955. The relevant text concludes as follows: 'It is probable that the Charter of the United Nations, with its repeated recognition of "human rights and fundamental freedoms", has inaugurated a new and decisive departure with regard to this abiding problem of law and government. In some instances – as, for example, in the European Convention on Human Rights – that development has assumed the complexion of explicit rules legally binding upon States.'

15 For the development of international law in relation to slavery, humanitarian law and the protection of minorities see *Human Rights in the World*, pp. 15–22.

16 Report on the twenty-fifth anniversary of the Universal Declaration and the twentieth anniversary of the European Convention on Human Rights, *Documents of the Assembly*, 1973, Document 3334, para. 37.

17 *Human Rights in the World*, pp. 128–9.

18 *Digest of Case Law*, pp. 256–60; J. E. S. Fawcett, *The Application of the European Convention on Human Rights*, Oxford, 1969, pp. 282–5.

19 *Cf.* report of Professor Christian Dominice at the Parliamentary Conference on Human Rights, Vienna, 1971. *Report of the Conference*, pp. 64–7.

20 See pp. 19–21 above. The text of the Agreement is given in *Yearbook* XII, p. 2.

21 The text of this section is based on an article contributed to the *Miscellanea W. J. Ganshof van der Meersch*, Brussels, 1972, Vol. I, p. 545, which discusses the issues involved in greater detail.

22 See Jacques Velu, 'The right to respect for private life, the home and communications', in *Privacy and Human Rights*, Manchester, 1973, at pp. 81–5.

23 *Cf.* Fawcett, *op. cit.*, p. 313.

24 *Yearbook* XIV, p. 788, at p. 798

25 *Yearbook* XIV, p. 838, at p. 844.

26 Article 2 of the Optional Protocol to the UN Covenant on Civil and Political Rights and Article 46 of the American Convention on Human Rights contain similar requirements of exhaustion of domestic remedies.

27 Article 26 of the Convention is discussed fully by Fawcett, *op. cit.*, pp. 288–309.

28 Application 343/57, Nielsen *v.* Denmark, *Yearbook* II, p. 412.

29 Application 347/58, *Yearbook* II, p. 406.

30 Applications 1211/62 and 1918/63, *Yearbook* V, p. 224.

31 Application 181/56, *Yearbook* I, p. 139.

32 Application 289/57, *Yearbook* I, p. 148.

33 Applications 188/56 and 232/56, *Yearbook* I, pp. 174, 143.

34 Application 1994/63, *Yearbook* VII, p. 252.

35 Applications 332/57 and 434/58, *Yearbook* II, pp. 308, 354.

36 Applications 222/56 and 514/58, *Yearbook* II, p. 343, and III, p. 196; Application 1936/63, *Yearbook* VII, p. 224.

37 Applications 2547/65 and 2742/66, *Yearbook* IX, p. 458, and X, p. 342.

38 Application 214/56, De Becker *v.* Belgium, *Yearbook* II, p. 214.

39 Application 458/59, *Yearbook* III, p. 222.
40 Application 1983/63, *Yearbook* IX, p. 286.
41 Application 2749/66, *Yearbook* X, p. 368.
42 Application 2991/66, Alam and Khan *v.* UK, *Yearbook* X, p. 478. See further in section 7 of this chapter.
43 Applications 27/55, *Yearbook* I, p. 138; 222/56, *Yearbook* II, p. 343; 254/57, *Yearbook* I, p. 150; 261/57, *Yearbook* I, p. 255; 603/59, *Yearbook* III, p. 296; 1086/61, *Yearbook* V, p. 148.
44 Application 2366/64, *Yearbook* X, p. 208.
45 Application 2728/66, *Yearbook* X, p. 336.
46 Application 712/60, Retimag *v.* Federal Republic of Germany, *Yearbook* IV, p. 384.
47 Fawcett, *op. cit.*, p. 299.
48 Application 214/56, De Becker *v.* Belgium, *Yearbook* II, p. 214. See also application 343/5, Nielsen *v.* Denmark, *Yearbook* II, p. 412.
49 Application 214/56, De Becker *v.* Belgium, *Yearbook* II, p. 214. Contrast application 1029/61, *Yearbook* IV, p. 214.
50 *Digest of Case Law relating to the European Convention on Human Rights, 1955–67*, Heule, 1970, p. 304.
51 See previous note. Cases relating to Article 26 are given at pp. 266–304; those relating to Article 27 at pp. 306–40.
52 *Ibid.*, pp. 314–20.
53 *Ibid.*, pp. 322–6.
54 *Ibid.*, pp. 328–34.
55 *Ibid.*, p. 334.
56 Fawcett, *op. cit.*, p. 313.
57 Application 1468/62, Iversen *v.* Norway, *Yearbook* VI, p. 278. The case is discussed above in Chapter II under Article 4.
58 Fawcett, *op. cit.*, p. 314.
59 *Yearbook* XIII, 1970, p. 76. The problems arising from the 'coexistence' of the European Convention and the United Nations Covenants are discussed more fully in A. H. Robertson, *Human Rights in the World*, Chapter 4.
60 Iversen *v.* Norway, *Yearbook* VI, p. 278, at p. 326. For other decisions on 'abusive' applications see *Digest*, pp. 338–40.
61 'Notes on the results achieved under the European Convention on Human Rights' by A. B. McNulty, Secretary of the Commission, Document B(74)7, p. 52.
62 Article 41 of the Statute of the International Court of Justice and Article 61 of the Rules of Court; Articles 185 and 186 of the EEC treaty.
63 *Texts adopted*, January 1971; *Yearbook* XIV, p. 68.
64 This section is largely based on an article, 'Enquêtes en matière de droits de l'homme', published in *L'Inspection internationale*, ed. G. Fischer and D. Vignes, Paris, 1975.
65 *Oppenheim's International Law*, ed. Lauterpacht, seventh edition, 1952, Vol. II, p. 7.
66 *PCIJ*, Series A/B, No. 70, p. 9 (1937); Hudson, *World Court Reports*, Vol. IV (1936–42), pp. 177–82.
67 Established by Resolution 2 (XXIII) of the Commission on Human Rights of 6 March 1967 to survey developments concerning the policies of *apartheid* and racial discrimination in southern Africa.
68 Established by General Assembly Resolution 2851 (XXVI) of 20 December 1971.
69 The proceedings are summarised in *Yearbook of the Convention on Human Rights*, Vol. II, 1958–59, pp. 174–8.
70 Resolution (59)12 of the Committee of Ministers, *ibid.*, p. 186.
71 Statute law of 8 January 1958, *ibid.*, p. 198.
72 Application 2686/65, *Yearbook* XI, 1968, p. 1020.
73 The system of sub-commissions was subsequently abolished when the Third

Protocol to the Convention entered into force on 21 September 1970. But the Commission may, under Rule 51 of its Rules of Procedure, 'charge one or more of its members to carry out an enquiry or any other form of investigation or to perform any other task necessary for the proper execution of its functions under Article 28 of the Convention'.

74 See reference given in n. 72 at p. 1028.

75 Application 4340/69, *Yearbook* XIV, p. 352.

76 Report of the Commission of 19 December 1972 on the friendly settlement reached in this case, ('Stocktaking', October 1975, pp. 23–5.)

77 The report of the Commission and the resolution of the Committee of Ministers on the Greek case constitute a special volume of the *Yearbook of the Convention on Human Rights*, Vol. XII, Part II (or XII *bis*), published 1972.

78 In Chapter II, under Article 3, pp. 39–41.

79 Council of Europe press release C(69)11 of 24 March 1969.

80 *Yearbook* XII *bis* (the Greek case), at pp. 511–15. The Commission's conclusions on Article 15 are given *ibid.*, pp. 73–6; on Article 3 at pp. 503–5. The application of Article 15 is discussed further in Chapter III under Article 15.

81 *Yearbook* XII, 1969, pp. 78–82 and 130–2. The action of the Committee of Ministers on this case is recounted in Chapter VI, section 3.

82 Application 5310/71, *Yearbook* XIV, p. 100.

83 *Yearbook* XV, pp. 76–258. The case is recounted in greater detail in Chapter II under Article 3.

84 *The Times*, 1, 2 and 3 May 1974.

85 Fawcett, *op. cit.*, p. 316.

86 Application 2991/66. Decision on admissibility in *Yearbook* X, p. 478; friendly settlement in *Yearbook* XI, p. 788.

87 See previous note.

88 Application 1727/62, *Yearbook* VI, p. 370 (admissibility); VIII, p. 410 (friendly settlement).

89 Application 2120/64, *Yearbook* IX, p. 328 (admissibility); IX, p. 632 (friendly settlement).

90 Application 4115/69, *Yearbook* XIII, p. 730 (admissiiblity); 'Stocktaking', October 1975, p. 21 (friendly settlement).

91 Application 3897/68, *Yearbook* XIII, p. 626 and p. 640 (admissibility); 'Stocktaking', October 1975, pp. 22–3 (friendly settlement).

92 For the facts of the case see 'Stocktaking', October 1975, pp. 23–4.

93 Application 5765/72, 'Stocktaking', October 1975, p. 25.

94 This case is recounted above in Chapter II, under Article 3.

95 Application 5219/71, *Yearbook* XV, p. 558. This application raised the question whether the appointment by the Court of a barrister as counsel for the defence in a criminal case without a fee violated Article 4 of the Convention, 'Stocktaking', October 1975, p. 27.

96 For the history of the Protocol see 'Explanatory reports on the Second to Fifth Protocols', published by the Council of Europe, 1971, pp. 23–8.

97 *Collected Texts*, tenth edition, 1975, p. 315.

98 Application 2707/66, *Yearbook* X, p. 320.

99 Application 2690/65, *Yearbook* IX, p. 512, and XI, p. 782.

100 Application 3245/67, *Yearbook* XII, p. 206.

101 Application 4733/71, *Yearbook* XIV, pp. 664 and 676.

102 More detailed information about the four cases mentioned and about eight other cases of 'unofficial arrangements' are given in 'Stocktaking on the European Convention', published by the Secretary of the Commission, October 1975 (Document DH(75)4) at pp. 28–35. The case of *Gericke* v. *Federal Republic of Germany* concerned a period of three years' detention awaiting trial. The applicant, who was an accomplice of Wemhoff, was pardoned and released on probation before he had served two-thirds of his sentence, and the case was then struck off the list. (*Yearbook* VII, p. 348; 'Stocktaking', 1975, p. 28.)

103 See A. H. Robertson, *The Council of Europe*, second edition, London, 1961, pp. 33–4.

104 *Yearbook* IV, 1961, p. 106.

105 'Explanatory report on the Third Protocol' (*cf.* n. 96 above), p. 26.

106 See Article 29 (amended) of the Convention in Appendix 1.

107 Two cases in which it has occurred are Swedish Pilots' Association *v.* Sweden (*Yearbook* XV, p. 328) and Raupp *v.* Federal Republic of Germany (*Collection of Decisions*, No. 42, p. 85).

108 See the first edition of this book, at p. 119.

109 Hansard, 12 June 1974.

110 *Yearbook* XIV, p. 912.

111 Resolution DH(70)1 and appendix. *Yearbook* XII *bis*, 'The Greek case', pp. 511–15.

112 Application 788/60, *Yearbook* IV, p. 116 (admissibility); VI, p. 742 (report of the Commission). The case is summarised above in Chapter II under Article 6.

113 *Ibid.*, p. 800.

114 *Yearbook* XII, p. 12. *cf. infra*, pp. 247–9.

CHAPTER V

THE EUROPEAN COURT OF HUMAN RIGHTS

The report of the Commission drawn up in accordance with Article 31 of the Convention is transmitted to the Committee of Ministers of the Council of Europe. If the matter is not referred to the Court of Human Rights within a period of three months the Committee of Ministers is called upon, under Article 32 of the Convention, to take a decision on the question whether there has been a violation of the Convention. The functions and procedure of the Committee of Ministers are discussed in the following chapter; this chapter will be devoted to the functions and procedure of the Court.

It is appropriate, in the first place, to recall the history of the establishment of the Court, which was summarised briefly in Chapter I.

1. THE HISTORY OF THE COURT

The first draft of the Convention prepared by the International Juridical Section of the European Movement[1] envisaged the creation of both a Commission and a Court of Human Rights, but with rather different functions from those conferred on the two organs that were finally established. Both States and individuals were to have the right to petition the Council of Europe in respect of any infringement of the rights guaranteed by the Convention; these petitions were to be dealt with by the Commission, which could decide by a two-thirds majority to conduct, if necessary, an enquiry on the territory of the State concerned. If the Commission decided that the Convention had been violated it was to make a recommendation to the State in question with a view to obtaining redress. A case could be referred to the Court by the Commission, or by a State or (with the authorisation of the Commission) by the individual party 'for the purpose of determining any relevant question of fact or point of law coming within the jurisdiction of the Court'. The Court was to consist of nine judges, elected by the Committee of Ministers and the Consultative Assembly of the Council of Europe (by a procedure rather similar to that for the election of the members of the International Court of Justice) from a list of names put forward by the Contracting Parties to the Convention. The Court was to have extensive powers:

> The Court may either prescribe measures of reparation or it may require that the State concerned shall take penal or administrative action in regard to the persons responsible for the infringement, or it may demand the repeal, cancellation or amendment of the act.

If a State failed to comply with a judgement of the Court the matter was to be 'referred to the Council of Europe for appropriate action'.

It is interesting to compare these original proposals with the provisions that were finally adopted; in doing so one notes inevitably how the powers which were to be conferred on the international organs (the Commission and the Court) were gradually watered down and the traditional rights of sovereign States asserted. The result, of course, was to make the Convention a less effective instrument than had been originally envisaged. The rights of individuals to petition the Commission was made subject to an express declaration of the governments that they accepted this procedure; the right of individuals to bring a case before the Court was suppressed entirely; the power of the Commission to 'make recommendations to the State concerned, with a view to obtaining redress' was reduced to 'placing itself at the disposal of the parties concerned with a view to securing a friendly settlement', and, if that failed, expressing an opinion to the Committee of Ministers. Finally, the powers of the Court (ordering reparation, cancellation of the act, and punishment of the offender) were reduced to 'affording just satisfaction to the injured party', while its very existence was made conditional on the deposit by eight States of a declaration recognising the jurisdiction of the Court as compulsory.

The Assembly's proposals of September 1949 were already – as a result of discussions in the Legal Committee – somewhat less bold than the original plan of the European Movement. They included the creation of both a Commission and a Court of Human Rights; the Commission was to be open both to States and to individuals; but only States and the Commission itself might refer matters to the Court. Moreover the function of the Commission was clearly stated as one of conciliation and that of the Court as 'judicial decision', but there was no provision that the Court could require States to take remedial action or demand the repeal or cancellation of their acts. As regards membership, the Assembly proposed a

Court of nine judges (there being at the time twelve members of the Council of Europe), the intention being apparently to show clearly that its members were independent judges and in no way representatives of the member States. A provision was also inserted to the effect that the parties could refer a matter to the International Court of Justice at The Hague instead of the Court of Human Rights if they preferred.[2]

As explained in Chapter I, a serious difference of opinion arose during the negotiations on the fundamental question whether a European Court of Human Rights should be created at all. Since the proposal to create a court with compulsory jurisdiction did not receive the support of the majority, it was not included in the draft Convention. A compromise solution was then sought, which would involve an optional provision whereby the Court would have jurisdiction only in respect of those states which expressly accepted it by making a declaration to that effect. As regards its composition, it was decided to set up a European Court with as many judges as the number of member States, which would all participate in the election of the judges and in the expenditure involved. Moreover, since a Court consisting of twelve to fifteen judges would be inconveniently large (by the summer of 1950 the number of member States had increased to fifteen), it was decided that cases should be heard by chambers of the Court consisting of seven judges.

The decision to make the Court an organ of all member States but with optional jurisdiction led to the need for specifying the minimum number whose acceptance of the jurisdiction would be required to make it effective, since it would obviously be absurd to set up a European Court in whose establishment fifteen States would participate if its jurisdiction were to be accepted only by two or three. Considerable discussion took place as to the minimum number required, and in August 1950 the Committee of Ministers fixed on the figure of nine.[3] The Assembly asked, however, that the number required should be reduced from nine to eight, which would represent a simple majority of the fifteen member States.[4] This proposal was accepted by the Committee of Ministers and incorporated in the final text of Article 46 of the Convention as signed on 4 November 1950.

On the date of entry into force of the Convention (3 September 1953) only three States had accepted the right of individual petition (Denmark, Ireland and Sweden) and two the compulsory jurisdiction of the Court (Denmark and Ireland). By 5 July 1955, when the right of individual petition became effective, five States had made declaration under Article 46 of the Convention: Belgium, Denmark, the Federal Republic of Germany, Ireland and the Netherlands; it was only in 1958 that three further acceptances were received, those of Luxembourg, Austria and Iceland.

Once the eight acceptances of the compulsory jurisdiction of the Court had been received, the procedure for the election of the judges was put in motion. Under Article 39 of the Convention the judges are elected by the Consultative Assembly of the Council of Europe from lists of persons nominated by the member States; each member is required to nominate three candidates, of whom two at least must be its nationals. (This repeats in reverse the procedure for the election of the members of the Commission of Human Rights, who, under Article 21, are elected by the Committee of Ministers from a list of names drawn up by the Bureau of the Consultative Assembly on the basis of lists proposed by the national delegations, each of which puts forward three candidates. The participation of both organs of the Council of Europe is thus secured in the election of both the Commission and the Court.)

On 17 October 1958 the Consultative Assembly in its *Recommendation 183* asked the Committee of Ministers that the list of candidates required under Article 39 of the Convention should be submitted by the member States without delay, and in its Order 129 decided to place the question of the election of the members of the Court on the agenda of its next part-session. The Committee of Ministers approved the list of candidates at its twenty-third session in December,[5] and the election was set down on the Assembly's order of business for 21 January 1959.

Before the election could take place, however, a question of procedure had to be settled. Article 39 of the Convention provides that the members of the Court shall be elected by the Consultative Assembly *by a majority of the votes cast*. Does this mean an absolute or a simple majority? Mr Lannung of Denmark, chairman of the Assembly's Legal Committee, argued that the Assembly should, in the absence of any clear provision in the Convention, apply its ordinary rule of procedure relating to elections (Rule 35(b)), which requires an absolute majority of the votes cast at the first ballot and a relative majority at the second ballot. Mr Lynch of Ireland, a Vice-president of the Assembly, on the other hand, argued that only one ballot should be held, at which a simple majority would suffice for election; he based this contention on the fact that Article 21 of the Convention states explicitly that an 'absolute majority' is required for the election of the members of the Commission and that Article 10 of the Statute of the International Court explicitly requires an 'absolute majority' for the election of the judges. Since Article 39 of the Human Rights Convention speaks only of 'a majority of the votes cast', it must, he argued, be supposed that its authors had deliberately omitted the word 'absolute' and therefore intended that a relative or simple majority should suffice. The Assembly first voted on this procedural question and decided to apply its normal rule, requiring an absolute majority at the first ballot and a relative majority at the second.[6]

The judges were then elected. In fact fifteen candidates obtained an absolute majority on the first ballot, so that the Court was thus complete and no second ballot was required. The judges elected were[7] Professor Herman Mosler (Federal Republic of Germany), Professor Alf Ross (Denmark), Professor Kemal Arik (Turkey), Professor Alfred Verdross (Austria), M. René Cassin (France), Judge Terje Wold (Norway), Mr Richard McGonigal, s.c. (Ireland), Professor Ake Holmbäck (Sweden), Lord McNair (United Kingdom), Professor Georges Maridakis (Greece), Professor Giorgio Balladore Pallieri (Italy), Professor Frederick van Asbeck (Netherlands), Judge Eugène Rodenbourg (Luxembourg), Judge Einar Arnalds (Iceland) and Professor Henri Rolin (Belgium).

2. THE COMPOSITION AND ORGANISATION OF THE COURT

With the passage of time the membership of the Court has changed considerably on account of deaths, resignations, new elections and the admission of new members of the Council of Europe. On 30 June 1975 the membership of the Court was as follows (in order of precedence): MM. G. Balladore Pallieri, President (Italian), Hermann Mosler, Vice-president (German), René Cassin (French), A. Verdross (Austrian), E. Rodenbourg (Luxembourg), M. Zekia (Cypriot), J. Cremona (Maltese), G. J. Wiarda (Netherlands), P. P. O'Donoghue (Irish), Mme H. Pedersen (Danish), MM. T. H. Vilhjalmsson (Icelandic), S. Petrén (Swedish), R. Ryssdal (Norwegian), A. Bozer (Turkish), W. J. Ganshof van der Meersch (Belgian), Sir Gerald Fitzmaurice (British), Mme D. Bindschedler-Robert (Swiss), M. D. Evrigenis (Greek).

Paragraph 2 of Article 39 (which was added by the legal advisers in Rome on the eve of the signature of the Convention)[8] provides that the same procedure for the election of the judges – i.e. election by the Assembly from lists submitted by member governments –

shall be followed, as far as applicable, in the event of the admission of new members of the Council of Europe and in filling casual vacancies. One practical problem has arisen in the application of this provision. It could be construed to mean – for example, on the occasion of the admission of a new member State – that only the government concerned should put forward a list of candidates; but it could also be construed to mean that *all* member governments should put forward lists of candidates whenever there is a vacancy. The second interpretation can be supported by the argument that all member governments are interested in the composition of the Court and that the independent character of the functions of a judge would be better secured if he did not owe his election solely to the proposal of the State of which he is a national. In practice, however, the Committee of Ministers has adopted the former interpretation, and only the government of the new member State has put forward candidates in such circumstances. The same applies in the case of casual vacancies due to the death or resignation of a judge; only the government of the State of which the outgoing judge was a national has proposed candidates for the succession. This solution corresponds to the requirements of common sense when it is expected – even though it is not required – that each member State will have one of its nationals serving as a judge on the Court.[9]

Paragraph 3 of Article 39 of the Convention relates to the qualifications of the judges. It provides that they shall be of high moral character and 'must either possess the qualifications required for appointment to high judicial office or be jurisconsults of recognised competence'. This reproduces almost textually the qualifications required of the judges of the International Court of Justice under Article 2 of its Statute, though it omits the final words in the phrase 'jurisconsults of recognised competence *in international law*'. A comparable requirement exists as regards the Court of Justice of the European Communities, whose judges are similarly required to 'fulfil the conditions required for holding the highest judicial office in their respective countries or be jurists of recognised competence' (Article 167 of the EEC treaty).

A point of some importance that was discussed informally before the judges were elected was that of compatibility of the office of judge with certain other functions. Article 16 of the Statute of the International Court provides explicitly that 'no member of the Court may exercise any political or administrative function, or engage in any other occupation of a professional nature'. A similar rule applies to the judges of the Court of the European Communities; Article 4 of the Protocol to the Rome Treaty containing the Statute of the Court of Justice provides: 'The judges may not hold any political or administrative office. They may not engage in any paid or unpaid professional activities, except by special exemption granted by the Council.' This could not apply, however, to the members of the Court of Human Rights, because it is not in continuous session and, under Article 42 of the Convention, the judges are remunerated only on a daily basis when actually engaged on the business of the Court. Since they must, therefore, engage in other activities – at least in the majority of cases – it became necessary to consider what other activities were permissible.

There were five types of other activity which the candidates for election were considered likely to exercise: those of judge, practising lawyer, professor of law, official, or member of parliament. The prevailing view was that there was no incompatibility between the first three professions and the function of judge; on the other hand it seemed to be the prevailing view that the occupation of a national official (for example, that of legal adviser in a government department) was incompatible with the independence required of a member of the Court. The same would apply to holding a diplomatic appointment. The case of a member of parliament was more difficult. On the one hand it could be argued that he might be required, as part of his parliamentary duties, to take sides on a question which might subsequently come before the Court and that the two functions were therefore incompatible; on the other hand the likelihood of this happening was small, and if an individual was otherwise a suitable candidate it might be unwise to exclude him for purely hypothetical considerations.[10] It was, moreover, evident that a member of the Court could not also be a member of the Commission, since the latter may refer to the Court a case which it has already examined itself.

These questions were discussed informally before the election took place but no decisions taken or formal rules laid down. Indeed, the Assembly and its organs had no power to take decisions on matters arising out of, but not settled by, the Convention. It was therefore left for individual representatives to consider the compatibility or otherwise of the office of judge with the exercise of other professions when they came to decide for which candidate they would vote.

The question of incompatibility was subsequently considered

by the Court itself when it came to settle its rules of procedure. Rule 4 reads as follows:

> A judge may not exercise his functions while he is a member of a Government or while he holds a post or exercises a profession which is likely to affect confidence in his independence.
> In case of need the Court shall decide.

It goes without saying that the judges exercise their functions in complete independence and are in no way representatives of the States of which they are nationals or of particular parties to a dispute. Rule 3 of the Rules of Court contains the following provision:

> 1. Before taking up his duties, each elected judge shall, at the first sitting of the Court at which he is present after his election, take the following oath or make the following solemn declaration: 'I swear' – or 'I solemnly declare' – 'that I will exercise my functions as a judge honourably, independently and impartially and that I will keep secret all deliberations.'
> 2. This act shall be recorded in the minutes.

In accordance with this rule the first judges took the oath or made the solemn declaration at the ceremonial sitting of the Consultative Assembly held on 20 April 1959 to commemorate the tenth anniversary of the Council of Europe, in the presence of the Speakers or Presidents of the national parliaments, the Foreign Ministers of the member States, and the French Prime Minister.[11]

Another question relating to the qualifications of the judges was raised in 1973; it concerned their age. The view was expressed in the Legal Affairs Committee of the Assembly that a man who had already reached the age at which a judge is required to retire in his own country should not be elected to the European Court, particularly as the term of office is for nine years; the same rules, it was argued, should apply in this respect both nationally and internationally. Once more the Assembly had no power to take a decision which would constitute a rule binding for the future, but these views were communicated to the Bureau of the Assembly, which authorised the President to approach the Committee of Ministers 'with a view to ensuring that in future the age of candidates is taken into account when nominations are being considered'.[12] The matter was thus drawn to the attention of member governments.

It is believed that the Assembly's view in this matter was short-sighted and that the comparison with national practice is misleading. It is reasonable to impose an age limit for the work of a national judge, which is continuous and arduous; but the same argument does not apply to the work of the European Court of Human Rights, which is intermittent, at long intervals, and for short periods – the Court sits only for a few days each year. The European Court should therefore be glad to profit, at its infrequent sessions, from the knowledge and experience of distinguished jurists who may have reached the retiring age for national judges; the value of so doing is shown by the fact that some of the most eminent members of the European Court have made a distinguished contribution to its work when they were more than seventy-five – and, in some cases, more than eighty – years old.

Article 40 of the Convention deals with the term of office of the judges. They are elected for a period of nine years, but in order to secure a certain rotation without changing the whole court at one time it was provided that, after the first election, the terms of office of four judges would expire at the end of three years and those of four more at the end of six years. The intention was thus to renew one-third of the membership of the Court every three years. However, the same problem arose for the Court as that described above (Chapter IV, section 1) in relation to the Commission: with the passage of time a number of other elections became necessary on account of deaths, resignations, or the admission of new members. The judges elected as the result of the admission of new members of the Council of Europe held office for nine years from the date of their election; the pattern of elections every four years was thus only partially observed. To remedy this rather untidy situation a new paragraph 3 was added to Article 40 of the Convention by the Fifth Protocol of 20 January 1966, the effect of which is that the term of office of a judge may be fixed for a period other than nine years (but not more than twelve nor less than six years) in order that it should be coterminus with one of the main groups. This was done 'in order to ensure that, as far as possible, one third of the membership of the Court shall be renewed every three years'.[13]

The judges enjoy, while exercising their functions, certain privileges and immunities, including immunity from legal process of every kind in respect of words spoken or written and all acts done by them in their official capacity. This is the result not of the Convention but of the *Fourth Protocol to the General Agreement on Privileges and Immunities of the Council of Europe* of 16 December 1961.[14] It is perhaps regrettable that, by the terms of Article 2 of this Protocol, the immunity is conferred on the judges 'while exercising their functions and during journeys made in the exercise of their functions', because the immunity attaching to a judge in respect of the words he has spoken or written while discharging his judicial functions should not cease when he retires from the Court. This question of the duration of the immunity of the judges was discussed when the American Convention on Human Rights was being drafted in Costa Rica in 1969, and as a result of an intervention by M. Balladore Pallieri, a judge on the European Court (and later its President), a sentence was added to Article 70 of the American Convention reading: [15] 'At no time shall the judges of the Court or the members of the Commission be held liable for any decision or opinions issued in the exercise of their functions.' It may be hoped that the European text will be interpreted in the same way should the need arise.[16]

Article 41 of the Convention provides that the Court shall elect its President and Vice-president for a period of three years. They may be re-elected. The Presidents have been Lord McNair (1959–65), M. René Cassin (1965–68), M. Henri Rolin (1968–71), Sir Humphrey Waldock (1971–74) and Professor Balladore Pallieri, elected on 7 May 1974. The Vice-presidents have been M. René Cassin (1959–65), M. Henri Rolin (1965–68), Sir Humphrey Waldock (1968–71), Professor Balladore Pallieri (1971–74) and Dr Hermann Mosler, elected on 7 May 1974.

The intermittent nature of the functions of the judges, already referred to, is recognised by Article 42 of the Convention, according to which their remuneration (called 'compensation' – perhaps because an important part of it is an allowance for expenses) is fixed on a daily basis at a rate determined by the Committee of Ministers.

Article 43 deals with the question of chambers of the Court. Since a court of fifteen or more judges is inconveniently large for most purposes, it is provided that 'for the consideration of each case brought before it the Court shall consist of a Chamber composed of seven judges'. The judge who is a national of any State party to the case shall be a member of the chamber *ex officio*; if there is none the State concerned has the right to designate a person of its choice to sit as judge. The other members of the chamber are chosen by lot by the President of the Court.

These provisions seem quite reasonable. At the present stage of international development it is probably necessary to retain the system of the 'national judge' – i.e. that the chamber should include *ex officio* a judge who is the national of a State party to the case[17] – as is done in Article 31 of the Statute of the International Court of Justice. Two problems, however, have arisen in practice, and Rule 21 of the Rules of Court, relating to the constitution of chambers, has been amended no fewer than five times.

The first problem is that when the members of the chamber are simply selected by lot it may happen that certain judges never sit at all. Lord McNair was President of the Court for six years from 1959 to 1965, when indeed the Court was seized of but few cases; he was never once called on to hear a case. To remedy this situation paragraph 3 of Rule 21 was amended so as to provide that the President, or, failing him, the Vice-president, should sit in any chamber *ex officio*.

The second problem was concerned with the possibility of conflicts of jurisprudence between different chambers, which led to the conclusion that it would be desirable that cases which might involve such a conflict, and also other particularly important cases, should be heard by the plenary Court instead of by a chamber of seven judges. A new Rule 48 was therefore adopted, the first paragraph of which reads as follows:

> Where a case pending before a Chamber raises a serious question affecting the interpretation of the Convention, the Chamber may, at any time, relinquish jurisdiction in favour of the plenary Court. The relinquishment of jurisdiction shall be obligatory where the resolution of such question might have a result inconsistent with a judgment previously delivered by a Chamber or by the plenary Court. Reasons need not be given for the decision to relinquish jurisdiction.

It is not clear that this provision is altogether consistent with Article 43 of the Convention, but there are evident advantages in its adoption, and its validity has not been questioned. It was first applied in the 'Belgian linguistic case' in 1966.[18]

3. THE JURISDICTION AND PROCEDURE OF THE COURT

Under Article 45 of the Convention 'the jurisdiction of the Court shall extend to all cases concerning the interpretation and application of the present Convention which the High Contracting Parties or the Commission shall refer to it in accordance with Article 48'. 'In the event of a dispute as to whether the Court has jurisdiction, the matter shall be settled by the decision of the Court' (Article 49).

It will be observed that an individual applicant who has brought a case before the Commission does not have the right to refer it to the Court; only the High Contracting Parties and the Commission have that right, as is stated explicitly in Article 44. The extent to which the individual applicant has the possibility of making his views known to the Court will be considered in the following section of this chapter.

A case may be referred to the Court, however, only (a) if the Commission has acknowledged the failure of efforts for a friendly settlement (Article 47); (b) within a period of three months after the transmission of the report of the Commission to the Committee of Ministers (Articles 32 and 47); (c) if the Party or Parties concerned have accepted the jurisdiction of the Court (Articles 46 and 48). Such acceptance may be as the result of a declaration made under Article 46 accepting the jurisdiction of the Court as compulsory or may be *ad hoc* for the particular case (Article 48).

Declarations under Article 46 recognising the jurisdiction of the Court as compulsory *ipso facto* (in French, 'obligatoire de plein droit') may be made unconditionally or on condition of reciprocity or for a specified period. At 31 December 1974 fourteen Contracting Parties had made such declarations: only Ireland and Switzerland had done so for an indefinite period of time, the other declarations being for periods which varied from two to five years.[19] Eleven Parties imposed the condition of reciprocity:[20] Austria, Denmark, France, the Federal Republic of Germany, Italy, Luxembourg, the Netherlands, Norway, Sweden, Switzerland and the United Kingdom. Three Parties did not impose this condition: Belgium, Iceland and Ireland. The Contracting Parties which had not recognised the compulsory jurisdiction of the Court were Cyprus, Greece, Malta and Turkey.

Provided that the jurisdiction of the Court has been accepted by the Party or Parties concerned, the following, according to Article 48, have the right to refer a case to the Court: the Commission; a Party whose national is alleged to be a victim; a Party which referred the case to the Commission; a Party against which the complaint has been lodged. In fact the majority of cases of which the Court has been seized have been referred to it by the Commission. In some cases the respondent government has referred a case to the Court,[21] but such cases are likely to be the exception, for the simple reason that a government is less likely to lose a case when it is decided by the Committee of Ministers than when it is decided by the Court. In the former event it will lose its case only if the representatives of twelve governments vote against it, whereas if the case is decided by the Court the unfavourable opinion of four judges will suffice for an adverse decision. The second and third possibilities mentioned in Article 48 have not yet been realised in practice.

It is thus the Commission which is the principal source of the business of the Court, as the result of decisions by the Commission to refer a case to the Court rather than leave it with the Committee of Ministers for a determination on the question of violation. What are the criteria that apply to such decisions?

There is nothing in the Convention or in the Rules of Procedure which affords guidance on this subject. There are, however, certain indications or tendencies (one cannot say more) which appear to result from past practice.[22]

The first of these concerns the substance of the issue involved in the case. It may concern difficult legal problems, as in the 'Belgian linguistic case'; in that event the Court is a more appropriate body to take a final decision than the Committee of Ministers and there is a tendency to refer such issues to the Court. Another illustration of the same principle is the need for an authoritative interpretation of provisions of the Convention which are frequently invoked and difficult to apply, such as the notion of 'reasonable time' in Articles 5(3) and 6(1) which arose in a series of cases referred to the Court (*Wemhoff, Neumeister, Matznetter, Stögmuller, Ringeisen*) or the concept of 'civil rights and obligations' in Article 6(1) (discussed by the Court in several cases, including *Ringeisen*). On the other hand, if the issue is essentially one of fact (as, for example, the degree of force used to prevent insubordination in a prison – in the case of *Zeidler-Kornmann* v. *Federal Republic of Germany*), then, once the Commission has carried out an investigation and established the facts, there is little point in referring the case to the Court for a repetition of this exercise, which is most unlikely to produce a different result.

A second consideration is the attitude which has been adopted by the members of the Commission themselves. If they are unanimous, or nearly unanimous, in expressing the opinion that there has been no violation of the Convention, then there seems little point in setting in motion the fairly elaborate and protracted procedure of a hearing by the Court (which is likely to last a year and may last considerably longer) when the result is almost a foregone conclusion; then it seems reasonable to leave it to the Committee of Ministers to endorse the opinion of the Commission, as, in such circumstances, it probably will do. If, on the other hand, the Commission is narrowly divided on the question of violation (as in the *Lawless case*), then there is a stronger argument for referring the case to the Court.

A third consideration is of a different nature. If a case has important political implications – possibly so important that it may lead to the virtual expulsion of a State from the Council of Europe, as in the *Greek case* – then there is a different reason for leaving it with the Committee of Ministers rather than referring it to the Court, namely that the decision of a committee of eighteen Foreign Ministers is likely to carry more weight – and perhaps to lead to remedial action – than a judgement of the Court. In the *Greek case* itself there was not a choice, because Greece had not accepted the jurisdiction of the Court; but should such a situation arise again in relation to a State which has accepted the Court's jurisdiction there may still be valid reasons for leaving the case with the Committee of Ministers, that is to say the greater political weight attaching to decisions of that body.

When the Court has been duly seized of a case it then examines the matter in accordance with the procedure set out in the Rules of Court. Article 55 authorises the Court to draw up its own rules and to determine its own procedure; its first task, therefore, after it had been constituted in January 1959 was to do so. A series of meetings was held for the purpose during the spring and summer of that year; the rules were adopted in September 1959.[23]

The Rules of Court contain two separate parts or titles. Title I deals with the 'Organisation and working of the Court'. It deals with such questions as the oath of office and incompatibility of function, the functions of the President and Vice-president, the election and duties of the Registrar and his staff,[24] publicity of hearings, secrecy of deliberations, and so on. The seat of the Court is at the seat of the Council of Europe in Strasbourg; the quorum is nine judges; decisions are taken by a majority of the judges present, and, if the voting is equal, the President has a second and casting vote. Chapter V of Title I (Rules 21–5) provides for the constitution of the chambers of seven judges, and closely follows Article 43 of the Convention. There are appropriate provisions relating to the appoint of substitute judges (to serve in place of a judge chosen by lot who is unable to sit or has withdrawn) and *ad hoc* judges, who will sit in a chamber if the Court does not include a judge having the nationality of one of the parties or if the judge called upon to sit in that capacity is unable to sit or withdraws. In such a case the party concerned may appoint either another elected judge or some other person of its choice who has the qualifications laid down in the Convention.

Title II of the rules deals with the procedure of the Court. The official languages are English and French; there are appropriate provisions for interpretation and translation; judgements will be given in both languages and the Court will indicate which text is authoritative. The parties to a case will be represented by agents, who may be assisted by advocates or advisers, as in the International Court. There are the necessary rules about filing and notification of cases, exchange of written pleadings, hearings or oral pleadings, and the summoning and hearing of witnesses and experts. There are three rules of particular interest in this title. The first of these, Rule 48 (already referred to), provides that a chamber may refer a case to the plenary Court if it raises a serious question of interpretation of the Convention; indeed, it is obliged to do so in cases where the resolution of the question might have a result inconsistent with a judgement previously delivered by a chamber or by the plenary Court. Once it is seized of such a case the plenary Court may either continue to deal with the matter itself or refer it back to the chamber once it has decided the question of interpretation. The second point is that Rule 53 contains a provision, broadly comparable to that in Article 79 of the rules of the International Court, authorising a party or the Commission to request the interpretation of a judgement already rendered, provided this is done within a period of three years. In such cases the matter is to be dealt with so far as possible by the chamber which pronounced the judgement in the first case, even if this means calling back judges who have retired. Rule 54 also contains provisions for the revision of judgements broadly comparable to Article 61 of the Statute of the Hague court.

By far the most interesting provision, however, is that on relations between the Commission and the Court. Since a case can come before the Court only after it has been considered by the Commission, it is obviously of importance to decide what the relations between the two organs will be. The Convention is silent on this point. Article 47 (as we have seen) provides that the Court may consider a case only after the Commission has failed to bring about a friendly settlement, in which eventuality the Commission's report is to be sent to the Committee of Ministers and to the States concerned but is not to be published (Article 31). Nothing is said about its communication to the Court. Is the Court to be allowed to see it? And is the Court to have the benefit of other knowledge of the proceedings before the Commission, for example by receiving a copy of the record, or by hearing oral statements from the Commission?

The Court, being aware of this problem, adopted a rule designed to meet it. Rule 29 reads as follows:

1. The Commission shall delegate one or more of its members to take part in the consideration of a case before the Court. The delegates may, if they so desire, have the assistance of any person of their choice.
2. The Court shall, whether a case is referred to it by a Contracting Party or by the Commission, take into consideration the report of the latter.

It will be observed that this text is in terms which are very general and leave plenty of room for manoeuvre. In fact the procedural problems arising out of the relations between the Commission and the Court were examined at length in the *Lawless case*, and are discussed in the following section of this chapter.

From the purely formal point of view the judgements of the Court are dealt with in Rule 50, which sets out what shall be their contents: they are to include statements of the proceedings and of the facts of the case, the reasons on points of law, the operative provisions of the judgement, and so on. This is partly based on Article 51 of the Convention, which requires that reasons shall be given for the judgement of the Court and permits any judge to deliver a separate opinion. Paragraph 2 of Rule 50 makes this more explicit by providing that any judge who has taken part in the consideration of the case shall be entitled to annex to the judgement 'either a separate opinion, concurring or dissenting with that judgement, or a bare statement of dissent'.

What is more interesting to international lawyers, however, is the effect of the judgement. In the first place it must be remembered that the Court of Human Rights is not a *quatrième instance* to which appeal lies from the highest courts of the Parties who have accepted its jurisdiction. It cannot, therefore, upset the judgement of a national court; it is in no sense a *cour de cassation*. It cannot say that a national decision was wrong; but it can, and if the case arises it must, say that a national decision was in violation of the Convention.

It is curious that the Convention does not anywhere state explicitly what the Court is to decide. It is, however, clear from the whole tenor of the Convention and is stated indirectly in Article 50 that the function of the Court is to decide whether: 'a decision or measure taken by a legal authority or any other authority of a High Contracting Party is completely or partially in conflict with the obligations arising from the present Convention...' In other words, it is clearly the function of the Court to decide whether or not there has been a violation of the Convention. But, as we have seen at the beginning of this chapter, the Court does not have the power, if it decides that there is a violation, to prescribe what remedial measures should be taken. In this respect its powers are more limited than those of the proposed Inter-American Court of Human Rights, which is empowered by Article 63 of the American Convention to 'rule that the injured party be ensured the enjoyment of his right or freedom that was violated' and, if appropriate, 'that the consequences of the measure or situation that constituted the breach of such right or freedom be remedied and that fair compensation be paid to the injured party'.[25]

The philosophy or basic conception of the European Convention is rather that, if the Court decides that a violation has occurred, it is left to the government concerned to draw the necessary conclusions and decide what remedial action is necessary. (This is also the case, as we shall see in the following chapter, when the Committee of Ministers has decided that a violation has occurred.) It is implicit in Article 53 of the Convention, which provides: 'The High Contracting Parties undertake to abide by the decision of the Court in any case to which they are parties.'

The European Court does, however, have power to award damages in certain circumstances. Article 50 of the Convention reads as follows:

> If the Court finds that a decision or a measure taken by a legal authority or any other authority of a High Contracting Party is completely or partially in conflict with the obligations arising from the present Convention, and if the internal law of the said Party allows only partial reparation to be made for the consequences of this decision or measure, the decision of the Court shall, if necessary, afford just satisfaction to the injured party.

It is certainly a cause for satisfaction that the Court has the power to 'award just satisfaction to the injured party'. But the text of Article 50 is not altogether satisfactory. It is apparently based on an arbitration treaty between Germany and Switzerland.[26] What is curious is that this text specifically empowers the Court to 'afford just satisfaction to the injured party' if the internal law allows only partial reparation, but is silent as to the position if the internal law allows complete reparation – or none at all. It may be argued that in such cases the Court has *a fortiori* the power to 'afford satisfaction'. But the *argumentum a contrario* is also possible. It could be argued that any provisions of the Convention which appear to limit the sovereignty of States should be construed restrictively and that therefore the Court – like the Committee of Ministers – has power to decide whether a State has violated the Convention but that thereafter it is for the State concerned – and not for the Court – to decide what 'just satisfaction' should be awarded to the injured party, except in the specific and limited circumstances covered by Article 50.[27] It is, of course, for the Court to interpret Article 50. In its judgement on the merits of 16 July 1971 in the *Ringeisen case* it held that the detention of the applicant on remand had exceeded the limits of a 'reasonable time' in violation of Article 5(3) of the Convention and reserved for him the right to apply for just satisfaction.[28] The applicant duly addressed such a request to the Commission, which submitted it to the Court. In a second judgement of 22 June 1972 the Court awarded Ringeisen as compensation the sum of DM20,000.[29]

In the *Vagrancy case* the Belgian government argued that the applicants' request for 'just satisfaction' under Article 50 was inadmissible because they had not exhausted their domestic remedies. The government contended that Article 26 of the Convention applied not only to the original application under Article 25 but also to a claim for compensation after the Court's decision that there had been a violation. Secondly, the government argued that since the applicants had not exhausted domestic remedies in a claim for compensation before the national courts they had not established that Belgian internal law 'allows only partial reparation to be made for the consequences' of the violation. The Court rejected both arguments. It said:[30]

> If the draftsmen of the Convention had meant to make the admissibility of claims for 'just satisfaction' subordinate to the prior exercise of domestic remedies they would have taken care to specify this in Article 50 as they did in Article 26, combined with Article 27(3), in respect of petitions addressed to the Commission. In the absence of such an explicit indication of their intention, the Court cannot take the view that Article 50 enunciates in substance the same rule as Article 26.

The *Ringeisen case* also afforded the first example of the application of Rule 53 of the Rules of Court, which provides for the possibility of the interpretation of a judgement already delivered. After the award to Ringeisen of compensation in the sum of DM20,000 the question arose whether this money should be paid to him direct without attachment or whether it should be included among his assets in the bankruptcy proceedings instituted against him in Austria and thus become available for distribution to his creditors. The Austrian government considered that it was for the Austrian courts to decide this question and therefore paid the money into court. Ringeisen thereupon asked the Commission to seek an interpretation of the judgement of 22 June 1972 in order that the European Court should indicate what were its intentions when it delivered that judgement. The Commission submitted the matter to the Court, which rendered a third judgement on 23 June 1973 in which it stated that the compensation should be paid to Ringeisen personally, free from attachment.[31] This was duly done.

Article 53 of the Convention provides, as already mentioned: 'The High Contracting Parties undertake to abide by the decision of the Court in any case to which they are parties', while Article 54 continues:

> The judgement of the Court shall be transmitted to the Committee of Ministers, which shall supervise its execution.

It is therefore for the Party (or Parties) concerned to give effect to the judgement, and should they fail to do so it would be for the Committee of Ministers to decide what action should be taken. The role of the committee in this respect will be considered in the following chapter.

These provisions seem reasonable in the circumstances and what might be expected in a treaty between States that are partners in an organisation like the Council of Europe, which is based on the principle of intergovernmental co-operation. It is, however, interesting to contrast the provisions of the treaties setting up the European Communities. The Court of Justice of the Communities renders judgements which are, in their own right, executory in the territory of the member States; they may be put into forced execution under the legal procedure in effect in each State; a Minister of the national government is responsible for signing the necessary papers after satisfying himself as to the authenticity of the decision, but he may not question its substance.[32] A desirable improvement in the system established by the European Convention would be a similar provision to the effect that the decisions of the Court of Human Rights are directly enforceable in the member States; a further protocol to the Convention could be concluded for this purpose. This was one of the proposals made by the Consultative Assembly in its *Recommendation 683* of 23 October 1973 on 'Action to be taken on the Conclusions of the Parliamentary Conference on Human Rights'.[33] When nine of the Contracting Parties have accepted the provisions of the Rome treaty to the effect that the decisions of the Luxembourg court are executory, there is no reason of principle why they should not do the same for the Court in Strasbourg.

4. THE POSITION OF THE APPLICANT BEFORE THE COURT

As we have seen, Article 44 of the Convention is quite categorical in stating that 'Only the High Contracting Parties and the Commission shall have the right to bring a case before the Court'. (The French text is not quite the same: 'Seules les Hautes Parties Contractantes et la Commission ont qualité pour se présenter devant la Cour.' Both texts are based on Article 34 of the Statute of the International Court of Justice.[34] It is therefore quite clear that if the Commission or a Contracting Party refers to the Court a case which originated in an individual application brought before the Commission under the terms of Article 25 of the Convention, then the individual applicant does not himself have the right to refer his case to the Court (this also follows from Article 48); equally he does not have the right to appear as a party to the proceedings before the Court. But does this mean that he has no access to the Court at all?

The question was considered by the Court in the first case of which it was seized, the *Lawless case* in 1960. Consideration of this problem also involved the further question: what is the role of the delegates of the Commission in proceedings before the Court? Those two matters will be discussed in the present section.

The Commission adopted its report on the *Lawless case* on 1 February 1960. In its report it expressed the opinion, by a narrow majority, that there had been no violation of the Convention by the Republic of Ireland. (The substance of the case is discussed above in connection with Articles 5 and 15 of the Convention.[35]) On 12 April 1960 the Commission decided to refer the case to the Court for final decision.

The reference of the case by the Commission to the Court raised for the first time the problem of the role of the Commission in such circumstances. Was the Commission to appear as a party to the proceedings before the Court? If so, was the Commission to act as the advocate of the individual applicant, since he himself could not be heard, though justice required that his case should be stated? Was the Court to re-examine all the facts of the case or would it accept the findings of fact of the Commission? Was the Commission authorised to transmit to the Court its report, which had been drawn up for the Committee of Ministers, when there was no provision to that effect in the Convention and this was bound to have the result of destroying, in whole or part, its confidential character? If the Commission was not to act as the advocate of the applicant, how, if at all, was his point of view to be brought to the Court's attention?

To deal with the simpler problems first, that of transmission of the Commission's report to the Court was settled quite simply on a basis of common sense. It would obviously facilitate the proceedings that the report should be available to the Court, and the latter clearly expected it, since – as mentioned in the preceding section – paragraph 2 of Rule 29 of the Rules of Court reads as follows: 'The Court shall, whether a case is referred to it by a Contracting Party or by the Commission, take into consideration the report of the latter.' The Commission thus transmitted its report to the Court, and the correctness of this procedure has never been questioned.

As regards the right of the Commission to take part in the proceedings before the Court, the latter evidently considered this question when drawing up its rules. Paragraph 1 of Rule 29 (also mentioned above) reads as follows:

> The Commission shall delegate one or more of its members to take part in the consideration of a case before the Court. The delegates may, if they so desire, have the assistance of any person of their choice.

Rule 21 of the Commission's Rules of Procedure contains a corresponding provision. In accordance with these texts, then, the Commission, when referring the Lawless case to the Court on 12 April 1960, appointed Professor C. H. M. Waldock, its President, as its principal delegate and M. C.-Th. Eustathiades and Mr S. Petrén as assistant delegates. The nature of their role before the Court was thus described by Professor Waldock in his opening address: [36]

> The fact that in every case the Commission has to conduct an objective and impartial investigation into the facts and the law,

and has confidentially to place itself at the disposal of the Parties for the purpose of seeking a friendly settlement of the case, makes it impossible for the Commission, when the case comes before the Court, to depart from its objectivity and impartiality, and impossible for it to identify itself either with the Government or with the individual.

This is not to say, Mr President, that being objective and impartial is inconsistent with the Commission's having to express its opinion on the case. On the contrary, the Convention requires the Commission to state its opinion in its Report, and in the present case the Commission has given its opinion. But for the Commission to express its opinion on a case is one thing, and for it to take up the case of one side and to contend for the success of that case before the Court is quite another thing.

It is thus clearly established that the Commission does not consider that it should discharge the role of advocate for the individual applicant in the proceedings before the Court. The problem how the individual's case is to be presented to the Court thus still subsists.

The Commission in fact had carefully considered this problem. On 30 March 1960 the Commission adopted a new Rule 76 of its Rules of Procedure, reading as follows:

When a case brought before the Commission in pursuance of Article 25 of the Convention is subsequently referred to the Court, the Secretary of the Commission shall immediately notify the Applicant. Unless the Commission shall otherwise decide, the Secretary shall also in due course communicate to him the Commission's Report, informing him that he may, within a time limit fixed by the President, submit to the Commission his written observations on the said Report. The Commission shall decide what action, if any, shall be taken in respect of these observations.

In accordance with this provision the Commission transmitted its report to Mr Lawless on 13 April 1960 – that is, after referring the case to the Court – and invited him to submit his observations to the Commission. At the same time the Commission pointed out that the document must be kept secret and that the applicant was not entitled to publish it. The government of Ireland raised a preliminary objection to this communication of the report to the applicant.[37]

The government's argument may be summarised as follows. The Convention (as mentioned above) provides in its Article 31 that the Commission's report shall be transmitted to the Committee of

Ministers and to the governments concerned, which shall not be at liberty to publish it. It is therefore clearly the intention that the report shall be kept secret and not open to publication; and the absence of any provision in the Convention authorising its transmission to an individual was no mere accident. Furthermore, it was argued, the government continued to be bound by the obligation of secrecy even after the case had been referred to the Court; it was inconceivable that a State should be in a position of inferiority to the Commission as regards the obligation of secrecy. In the course of the oral hearings the Attorney General of Ireland even disclosed that the government had asked the Committee of Ministers to publish the Commission's conclusion that no violation of the Convention had occurred, but this request was refused.[38] Since the Commission had no means of compelling the applicant to respect the obligation of secrecy, this meant that the government was even in a position of inferiority by comparison with him. The government therefore asked the Court to hold that the publication of the report by the Commission was in contravention of the Convention and that Rule 76 was *ultra vires*.

The Commission's point of view on this preliminary objection was to recognise that Article 31 of the Convention imposed an obligation of secrecy as regards the publication of the report but to maintain that this was limited in two respects. First, it related to publication to the press or to third parties, but not to communication to a party to the proceedings; 'obvious considerations of equity militate in favour of a party to the proceedings before the Commission being informed of the Commission's conclusions concerning his own case'. Secondly, the obligation to secrecy, it was argued, related to the Commission's report once it had been transmitted to the Committee of Ministers and *while the case was pending before the Committee of Ministers*. The report should then be kept secret in order to make possible a last attempt at conciliation, in confidential discussions, before the Committee of Ministers was called on to decide whether a breach had occurred. The President of the Commission was able to quote from the *travaux préparatoires* to show that this was the intention of the authors of the Convention in inserting the stipulation of secrecy. However, once the matter was referred to the Court of Human Rights the provisions of secrecy which relate to the proceedings before the Committee of Ministers would no longer apply and the problem should then be viewed in quite a new light, as the proceedings before the Court are public. It is to be observed, moreover, that the Commission's Rule 76 permits communication of the report to the individual applicant only *after* the case has been referred to the Court. At that stage, the President of the Commission stated, the Commission considers that 'it is free, if it thinks fit, to publish or to communicate to any person the contents of its report in connection with proceedings before the Court'.

In accordance with its Rule 76 the Commission not only communicated the report to the individual applicant but also invited his written observations. This was done with a view to transmitting them in due course, if thought appropriate, to the Court. This was the way in which the Commission sought to make it possible for the individual's point of view to be communicated to the Court even though he had no *locus standi* as a party to the proceedings. In its Memorial the Commission specifically asked the Court:

(1) to give leave for the Commission to submit to the Court the applicant's comments on the Commission's Report as one of Commission's documents in the case; and

(2) in general, to give directions as to the right of the Commission to communicate to the Court the comments of the Applicant in regard to matters arising in the proceedings.

The Irish government took strong exception to this procedure. It pointed out that in the course of the *travaux préparatoires* the Committee of Senior Officials which undertook the final drafting of the Convention had 'thought it necessary to point out clearly that only the High Contracting Parties and the Commission and not private individuals shall have the right to bring a case before the Court'. This indeed is stated *expressis verbis* in Article 44 of the Convention. The government's Counter-memorial continued: [39]

> The Commission in its present Memorial recognises this as being the position, but it attempts by a subterfuge to bestow on the individual the quality of a party before the Court, by enabling the individual to make submissions to the Court in the form of a document which the Commission wishes to annex to its Memorial, and further by seeking directions as to the communication to the Court of the comments of the applicant in regard to matters arising in the present proceedings. If this were permitted, the Applicant would be enabled to play an active part in the proceedings before the Court in much the same way as if he were a party.
>
> The Commission is in this way attempting to modify the Convention by an oblique procedure and without the approval of the High Contracting Parties who are the authors of the Convention.

The President of the Commission, however, adduced during the oral hearings some powerful arguments in support of the latter's position. He pointed out, in the first place, that the Convention was quite silent as to the position of the individual in the proceedings before the Court but that the Commission 'found it difficult to attribute to the authors of the Convention an intention to place an impenetrable curtain between the individual and an organ specifically set up as a judicial tribunal to make a judicial determination of his case'. The Commission agreed with the government that Article 44 of the Convention clearly prevented an individual from appearing before the Court as a party to the proceedings, but it could not accept that this article was intended to prevent him from having any contact at all with the proceedings before the Court. The individual and the government were on a footing of equality before the Commission; the Commission's report was a new factor in the case now before the Court; the government would have every opportunity of challenging the contents of this report in the proceedings before the Court; the individual must be given, by some means or other, a similar opportunity.

In support of this view the President of the Commission cited the opinion of the International Court of Justice in the case of the judgements of the Administrative Tribunal of the International Labour Organisation.[40] This concerned an appeal by UNESCO to the International Court against judgements of the Administrative Tribunal in favour of four individuals; under Article 66 of the Statute of the Court only States and International organisations have access to the Court; the latter nevertheless held that: 'the judicial character of the Court requires that both sides directly affected by these proceedings should be in a position to submit their views and their arguments to the Court', and arrangements were made that UNESCO would transmit to the Court the observations in writing of the individuals concerned. In replying to this point, however, the Irish Attorney General distinguished the UNESCO case on the ground that the procedure then followed was adopted after discussion, and by agreement with the Organisation; in the present case he objected to the action of the Commission, which had been taken without consulting, and contrary to the wishes of, the Irish government. He recognised that the acceptance of his view would place the individual in a certain position of inequality, but he thought this was 'more fanciful than real', and continued: [41]

The inequality, such as it is, is, in my submission, deliberate, not in the sense of States wishing to place individual citizens at a disadvantage, but because in agreeing to the limited, I concede very limited, jurisdiction of the Court created by the Convention, States went as far as it appeared to them that they would be warranted in doing at present in recognising, for individuals, a status of any kind in international law.

The Commission had also noticed that the Court itself had not apparently intended to shut itself off from any contact with the individual applicant. Rule 29 of the Rules of Court provides that the delegates of the Commission in the proceedings before the Court 'may, if they so desire, have the assistance of any person of their choice'; this certainly seemed to authorise the delegates to consult the applicant himself if they wished. The Commission therefore sought the directions of the Court as to the way in which the applicant's comments on the Commission's report or on any new points arising in the course of the proceedings should be brought to the Court's attention. In conclusion the President of the Commission pointed out that, in raising this point, the Commission was thinking not only of the particular individual whose case was under examination but of all the individuals whose cases might come before the Court for final decision in the years to come.

The Court delivered its judgement on the preliminary objections and questions of procedure on 14 November 1960.[42] It considered first of all the question 'Is Rule 76 of the Rules of Procedure of the Commission in general contrary to the terms of the Convention?' The Court was here rather cautious as to its own competence in the matter. It pointed out that the Commission and the Court were independent organs set up by the Convention, each with its own functions and responsibilities; and that the Court had no general power to interpret the Convention in an abstract manner but only to decide particular cases referred to it in accordance with Articles 45 and 47. From these considerations it concluded that:

> the Court is not competent to take decisions such as that to delete a rule from the Commission's Rules of Procedure – a step which would affect all Parties to the Convention – since this would amount to having power to make rulings on matters of procedure or to render advisory opinions; that, accordingly, the Court has no power to consider the point raised in a general manner by the Commission and the Irish Government.

The Court then turned from the general to the particular, namely to the communication of the Commission's report in this case to

Mr Lawless. It recognised the need for secrecy in the proceedings before the Commission and the Committee of Ministers; but it reaffirmed the public character of the hearings before the Court. After pointing out that this public character attached only to the oral proceedings and the judgement, but not to the documents in the case (except when authorised by the Court), it went on to distinguish between publication in general and communication to the person directly concerned subject to injunctions of secrecy. This distinction led to the conclusion that:

> the Court is of the opinion that the Commission is enabled under the Convention to communicate to the Applicant, with the proviso that it must not be published, the whole or part of its Report or a summary thereof, whenever such communication seems appropriate; therefore, in the present case, the Commission, in communicating its Report to G. R. Lawless, the Applicant, did not exceed its powers . . .

Finally the Court considered the Commission's request for leave to communicate to the Court the applicant's observations on its own report and on other points which might arise during the proceedings. After reviewing the arguments on both sides, it drew attention to the fact that 'it is in the interests of the proper administration of justice that the Court should have knowledge of and, if need be, take into consideration the applicant's point of view'. It went on to point out that there already existed three ways in which this could be done: in the Commission's report, in the statements of the delegates of the Commission before the Court and by hearing the applicant as a witness. Its conclusion, then, was that, having been unable as yet to examine the merits of the case, it was not in a position to reach a decision on the Commission's request and reserved its right to do so at a later date, i.e. in connection with the examination of the merits of the case.

While the Court considered that it was outside its competence to give a ruling on the general question whether Article 76 of the Commission's Rules of Procedure was in conformity with the Convention, it implicitly validated the rule, since the rule exists and is applied, and the only body that could conceivably have invalidated it has declined to do so. Moreover the Court held that, in this particular case, the communication of the report to Mr Lawless, with the proviso that he should not publish it, was in order; this would therefore seem to be a clear precedent for the future.

The communication to the applicant, however, was only a first step. The main point of such communication is to permit the applicant to submit his observations on the report to the Commission and to enable the latter, if it considers appropriate, to forward them to the Court. It is the legality of this procedure which is the more important issue. On this point the Court postponed its decision on the Commission's request for authorisation to submit a memorandum containing the applicant's observations, but it did state that 'it is in the interests of the proper administration of justice that the Court should have knowledge of and, if need be, take into consideration, the applicant's point of view'; moreover, the Court continued, it has at its disposal for this purpose '. . . the written and oral observations of the delegates and counsel of the Commission, which, as the defender of the public interest, *is entitled of its own accord to make known the applicant's views to the Court*, even if it does not share them, as a means of throwing light on the points at issue'. This dictum was taken by the Commission as a guide for its future conduct, and formed the object of further interpretation by the Court a few months later.

After the judgement on the preliminary objections (14 November 1960) further written pleadings were exchanged. The Commission, in preparing its statement, considered that it was entitled to submit to the Court the written observations of the applicant on its own earlier report – this evidently in reliance on the Court's decision that 'the Commission was entitled of its own accord . . . to make known the applicant's views to the Court . . .'. Accordingly it included in its statement a lengthy passage of nearly twenty pages of the applicant's views; its impartiality in doing so was shown by the fact that these views were in some respects sharply critical of the Commission's own findings and of the reasoning of some of its members. The government again objected that this was improper. The Court, in a separate decision of 7 April 1961,[43] ruled that the passage in the Commission's statement reproducing the applicant's views was not, at that stage, to be considered as part of the proceedings in the case; nevertheless the Commission could itself 'take account of' the applicant's views and, implicitly, make use of them in the oral hearings. The Court thus gave a rather restrictive interpretation of its own earlier judgement on the preliminary objections; the conclusion would appear to be that the Commission may 'take account of' (in French, 'faire état') of the applicant's views and summarise or quote them in the oral hearings, but not merely reproduce them in its written pleadings. In other words, the Court's decision would appear to mean that it is unwilling to allow the Commission simply to reproduce and submit to it extensive extracts from the applicant's own statement – in which case the role of the Commission is no more than that of a postbox; the Commission may, however, make use of the applicant's views (even though it does not agree with them) in presenting relevant arguments to the Court – in which case it plays an active role on its own responsibility, even though with the assistance of the individual applicant.[44]

This question has been dealt with in some detail and at some length because the Court's decisions on the preliminary objections in the *Lawless case* constitute important precedents for the future, which have already been followed in a number of cases and which relate to the most fundamental feature of the European Convention, namely the right of access of the individual applicant to the Commission and Court of Human Rights. The matter was taken one stage further in the *First vagrancy case*.[45] During the oral hearings of this case in November 1970 the principal delegate of the Commission informed the Court that the delegates intended to be assisted by the applicant's lawyer, whom they wished to address the Court, in accordance with Rule 29(1) of the Rules of Court, which provides that the delegates may have the assistance of any person of their choice. The agent of the Belgian government having expressed objections, the Court in a judgement of 18 November 1970 approved the action proposed by the delegates.[46]

5. ADVISORY OPINIONS OF THE COURT

The European Convention on Human Rights does not itself contain any provision which empowers the Court to give advisory opinions. There is nothing comparable to Article 96 of the Charter of the United Nations, which confers such power on the International Court of Justice. Competence to give advisory opinions was, however, conferred on the Court of Human Rights by the Second Protocol to the Convention of 6 May 1963,[47] which entered into force on 21 September 1970 and constitutes the subject of this section.[48]

The conclusion of this Protocol was the result of a proposal of the Consultative Assembly,[49] whose Legal Committee had become aware of a number of provisions of uncertain interpretation contained in the Convention. One of these related to the effect of declarations accepting the jurisdiction of the Court as compulsory on condition of reciprocity; another to the procedure for the election of new judges in the event of casual vacancies; a third to the procedure of the Committee of Ministers under Article 32; a fourth to the effect of decisions of the Court under Article 50; another to the exercise of the powers of the Secretary General under Article 57. The Legal Committee considered whether some suitable measures could not be adopted in order to make it possible to obtain authoritative interpretations of provisions of the Convention with regard to which such uncertainties arose. Of course, under the terms of Article 45 the jurisdiction of the Court extends 'to all cases concerning the interpretation and application of the . . . Convention which the High Contracting Parties or the Commission . . . refer to it in accordance with Article 48'. But this provision permits the Court to interpret the Convention only when a case has been brought before it alleging a violation of one of the rights guaranteed. The provisions mentioned above, with regard to which there are uncertainties of meaning, are not among the articles securing substantive rights but are rather provisions of a procedural or similar nature; while questions relating to their interpretation might conceivably arise in the course of proceedings relating to an alleged violation, they raise problems which it is preferable to settle on their own merits and in isolation, independently of contentious proceedings.

These considerations had led the Legal Committee to suggest that it would be appropriate that the Court of Human Rights should be given the competence to render advisory opinions on questions such as those which have been mentioned. The point of departure for its study of the problem was a motion tabled on 22 October 1957 by Professor Wahl (of the University of Heidelberg and a member of the Bundestag) and others for the creation of a European Supreme Court.[50] The basic argument which he put forward was that the task of the Council of Europe of achieving greater unity between its members in, *inter alia*, the legal field had led to the conclusion of a number of European conventions designed to secure harmonisation or uniformity of law. But, as shown by the French jurist Bartin at the end of the last century, the adoption of uniform rules will not be effective if they are interpreted in divergent ways by national courts. Hence the need for an international body capable of giving authoritative interpretations of such texts.

The motion was referred by the Assembly for consideration to the Legal Committee, which appointed Professor Wahl as its *rapporteur*. While he was working on his report three things occurred which influenced later developments. First, the eighth acceptance of the compulsory jurisdiction of the European Court of Human Rights was received, which made it possible for the Court to be constituted. This made the *rapporteur* modify his original proposal. Why set up a separate European Court to interpret other European conventions when one was about to be created to interpret the Convention on Human Rights? Rather, it would be natural to confer additional functions on the Court whose members were now to be elected. Secondly, the *rapporteur's* attention was drawn to the desirability of instituting a procedure to interpret the provisions of the Convention on Human Rights with respect to matters which were not covered by its Article 45. Thirdly, the treaty instituting the European Economic Community entered into force with its well known Article 177 empowering the Court of Justice to give preliminary rulings in certain circumstances at the request of national courts. This shed a new light on the problem of uniform interpretation of European treaties.

After these matters had been studied in a sub-committee set up for the purpose, Professor Wahl drew up two separate reports. The first of these[51] related to the interpretation of the Convention on Human Rights. The Assembly debated this report on 22 January 1960 and adopted its *Recommendation 232*, in which its proposed that the Committee of Ministers should convene a Committee of Experts with instructions to conclude an agreement that would confer on the Court, in addition to its existing competence defined in Article 45 of the Convention, the competence to interpret the Convention when a doubt has arisen of a legal character, even though no case of a contentious nature had been brought in accordance with the existing procedures.

The second report, presented at the same time,[52] was also discussed by the Assembly on 22 January 1960 and led to the adoption of *Recommendation 231*. This proposed the preparation of a multilateral agreement conferring on the European Court of Human Rights the competence to interpret any convention concluded under the auspices of the Council of Europe, or any other international treaty concluded between two or more member States, in so far as the provisions of these conventions or treaties are applicable by national courts. A draft agreement for this purpose was attached to the recommendation, which was intended to be the basis for the intergovernmental negotiations which should follow; this was inspired by the provisions of Article 177 of the EEC treaty.

When the Committee of Ministers came to examine these proposals it showed little enthusiasm for the recommendation on uniform interpretation of European treaties. In effect it rejected *Recommendation 231*, and informed the Assembly as follows: [53]

> The Member Governments of the Council of Europe have been invited to answer the question whether the proposals of the Recommendation are compatible with the Constitutions of their respective countries.
>
> Since most Governments were not inclined to accept the proposals contained in the said Recommendation, the Committee of Ministers feel unable to accede to the Assembly's request ...
>
> Some Governments have expressed doubts as to the advisability of extending the competence of the European Court, in view of the fact that the Court was set up to decide matters arising from the application of the Convention for the Protection of Human Rights and Fundamental Freedoms. Moreover, since many European countries have recognised the competence of other international courts to render advisory opinions, there seems to be a danger that interpretations by the European Court might conflict with those of other international courts.

The weakness of these arguments is immediately apparent.

Recommendation 232 met with a less negative reception. It was referred to the Committee of Experts on Human Rights, which had recently been appointed and was engaged in drafting the Fourth Protocol to the Convention on Human Rights, guaranteeing certain additional rights not provided for in the Convention itself or in the First Protocol. The Experts examined the general principle raised by the proposal and reported favourably thereon to the Committee of Ministers in April 1961. They considered that it was desirable to confer on the Court the competence to give advisory opinions, provided that this would not interfere with the essential function of the Court, i.e. its judicial function. 'It would be of advantage,' said the Experts, 'that the bodies envisaged by the Convention for the Protection of Human Rights should have the benefit of the Court's expert opinion on the meaning of the Convention and of any text supplementary thereto, in so far as they define the functions of those bodies and the relationship between them.'

In this respect the point of view of the Experts was generally similar to that of the Assembly's Legal Committee, though perhaps more precise or explicit. In another respect the attitude of the Experts was more restrictive than that of the committee; whereas the latter had proposed that advisory opinions might be requested by the Committee of Ministers, the Consultative Assembly and the Secretary General – and possibly also by a Contracting Party, within certain limits – the Committee of Experts proposed that the right should be granted to the Committee of Ministers alone.[54]

In July 1961 the Ministers approved the conclusions of the Committee of Experts and instructed them to draft an agreement for the purpose. This task was discharged within the following twelve months and the Experts submitted their text to the Ministers in June 1962. This draft defined the proposed new competence of the Court in the following terms:

(1) The Court may, at the request of the Committee of Ministers, give advisory opinions on legal questions concerning the interpretation of the Convention and the Protocols thereto.

(2) Such opinions shall not deal with any question relating to the content or scope of the rights or freedoms defined in Section 1 of the Convention and in the Protocols thereto, or with any other question which the Commission, the Court or the Committee of Ministers might have to consider in consequence of any such proceedings as could be instituted in accordance with the Convention.

In their commentary the Experts explained that it was their intention to exclude not only questions regarding the content or scope of the rights and freedoms defined in Section 1 of the Convention and its Protocols but also any other question which might arise in the course of contentious proceedings. This would embrace 'all questions of substance which, while they do not concern the content of the rights and freedoms, involve obligations on the Contracting Parties'. Examples given of such obligations were the undertaking in Article 25(1) *in fine* not to hinder in any way the effective exercise of the right of individual petition, and the obligation of Contracting Parties under Article 57 to furnish, on the request of the Secretary General, explanations of the way in which their internal law ensures the effective implementation of the rights guaranteed; questions regarding the conditions of admissibility of applications defined in Articles 26 and 27 of the Convention would equally be excluded from the consultative competence of the Court.

While it is not difficult to understand the principle that matters which might come before the Court for determination in contentious proceedings relating to an alleged violation should not form the subject of an advisory opinion, the competence of the Court has been so restrictively defined by the Committee of Experts that there would seem to be very few matters arising out of the Convention which would not be excluded from its consultative competence.

The Court of Human Rights itself, of course, was keenly interested in these developments. While the discussions were continuing it submitted to the Committee of Ministers certain proposals for the amendment of other provisions of the Convention. Two of these were for the amendment of Article 40 (relating to the procedure for the election of the judges) and Article 43 (relating to the system of chambers). The Court's proposals as regards Article 40 were accepted by the governments and incorporated in the Fifth Protocol, signed on 20 January 1966; the suggestion that the system of chambers should be abolished and all cases heard by the plenary Court was not accepted, however. The Court also proposed that the scope of the Second Protocol should be widened so as to authorise it to give preliminary rulings at the request of certain national courts on any question of interpretation of the Convention which might arise in proceedings before such courts; the fate of this proposal is discussed in the following section.

The Commission of Human Rights also followed closely the negotiations for the Second Protocol, and in 1962 proposed that this Protocol should be so drafted as to authorise the Commission (as well as the Committee of Ministers) to request advisory opinions from the Court.[55] This proposal was also referred to the Committee of Experts on Human Rights, but was rejected; the majority of the Experts considered it desirable that all requests for advisory opinions should be channelled through the Committee of Ministers, which 'as a body representing the governments, was the one best qualified to appreciate the advisability of asking the Court for an advisory opinion'.[56]

The Second Protocol was therefore completed without the additions proposed either by the Commission or by the Court. It required ratification by all Contracting Parties before it would enter into force; this condition having been realised, it entered into force on 21 September 1970. The text is given in Appendix 3.

6. PRELIMINARY RULINGS OF THE COURT

As explained in the previous section, the Assembly's *Recommendation 231* contained a far-reaching proposal that the Court of Human Rights should be given competence to interpret any convention concluded under the auspices of the Council of Europe or any other international treaty concluded between two or more member States, in so far as the provisions of these conventions or treaties are applicable by national courts. This proposal, however, was rejected by the Committee of Ministers.

A more limited proposal was made by the Court of Human Rights itself while the Second Protocol was being drafted. This was to include in a protocol an article conferring on the Court the competence to give preliminary rulings at the request of certain national courts on any question of interpretation of the Convention arising before such courts; also to include another article giving the Court power to render an advisory opinion at the request of governments on any question of interpretation of the Convention arising in connection with a draft regulation, decree, Bill or projected Bill under examination by their competent authorities.[57]

The Court's proposals for extending its own competence in these two respects were referred by the Committee of Ministers to the Committee of Experts on Human Rights, and their examination began in October 1962. By June 1964 the Committee of Experts had submitted its report to the Ministers. This revealed that the Court had withdrawn the first of its proposals about competence to interpret the Convention at the request of certain national courts; while the Experts had, by a majority, advised against the acceptance of the second proposal about giving advisory opinions at the request of the government of a Contracting Party.[58]

The published documents do not reveal the reasons why the Court of Human Rights had withdrawn the first proposal; it may be assumed, however, that this was due to opposition expressed in certain quarters, on the ground that such a procedure would tend to 'short-circuit' the system of control established by the Convention. It may be argued that if a question of interpretation of the Convention has to be considered by a national court in a country where the provisions of the Convention have the force of internal law, then any dispute about the correctness of the interpretation given by the national court should be brought before the Commission of Human Rights in the first place, in accordance with the procedure set out in Article 25 of the Convention – assuming, of course, that the State in question has accepted the competence of the Commission to entertain individual applications. On this view, a system which would permit the national court to request the opinion of the Court of Human Rights direct would be instituting a new procedure different from that intended by the authors of the Convention, which would exclude the Commission and prevent it from exercising its proper role. Whatever the reasons, the Court of

Human Rights appears to have considered that the chances of acceptance of its proposal were slender, and therefore withdrew it.

The question of the desirability of conferring on the Court of Human Rights the competence to give 'preliminary rulings' on the interpretation of the Convention at the request of national courts has subsequently been raised again on several occasions. At the *Second International Colloquy about the Convention on Human Rights*, held in Vienna in October 1965, Professor Ermacora, a member of the Commission, drew attention to the problem of uniform interpretation of the Convention and to the fact that, in the absence of any procedure designed to secure such interpretation, national courts are left to make their own individual and frequently divergent interpretations. This was, he said, the reason for the proposal that the European Court should be empowered to give authoritative interpretations by means of advisory opinions; as a result of its rejection 'the Convention continues to lead an independent existence in the individual legal systems of the Contracting States, which is by no means a satisfactory situation'.[59] Subsequently, during the same colloquy, Professor Thomas Buergenthal, in comparing the jurisprudence of national courts with that of the Convention organs as regards the rights of the individual in court proceedings, drew attention to a number of divergences between the interpretation of national courts with that of the Convention organs,[60] while Professor Scheuner, in making a similar comparison of other rights, drew attention to the need for uniform interpretation of the Convention.[61]

The question was raised again at the *Parliamentary Conference on Human Rights* in Vienna in 1971, by Professor Christian Dominice of the University of Geneva.[62] This led to its inclusion by the Consultative Assembly in its 'Proposals for a short and medium-term programme for the Council of Europe in the general field of human rights' annexed to its *Recommendation 683 (1972)* on 'Action to be taken on the Conclusions of the Parliamentary Conference on Human Rights'.[63]

The question arises whether it would not be appropriate to relaunch the idea of what (for sake of brevity) we may call the 'preliminary competence' of the Court. In considering this question it is as well to examine rather more closely the reasons for the inclusion of Article 177 in the Rome treaty and the way it has been applied.

Article 177 reads as follows:

The Court of Justice shall have jurisdiction to give preliminary rulings concerning:

(a) the interpretation of this Treaty;
(b) the validity and interpretation of acts of the institutions of the Community;
(c) the interpretation of the statutes of bodies established by an act of the Council, where those statutes so provide.

Where such a question is raised before any court or tribunal of a Member State, that court or tribunal may, if it considers that a decision on the question is necessary to enable it to give judgment, request the Court of Justice to give a ruling thereon.

Where any such question is raised in a case pending before a court or tribunal of a Member State against whose decisions there is no judicial remedy under national law, that court or tribunal shall bring the matter before the Court of Justice.

The existence of this provision derives from the very nature of Community law as it results from the application of the treaty. Community law is neither national law nor international law, though it comprises elements of both. Nor is it the constitutional law of the Communities, though that also forms part of it. Again, it cannot be simply defined as the law applied by the Court of Justice of the Communities, because other institutions, particularly the Commission and the Council of Ministers, contribute both to its formulation and to its implementation; moreover national courts in the member States are called on to apply it with increasing frequency. Community law not only creates obligations for member States which are enforceable by Communty institutions but also establishes rules which are directly enforceable by and against individuals, enterprises and government agencies in national courts. It might perhaps be defined as the complex of legal rights and obligations created directly or indirectly by the Treaty of Paris and the two Treaties of Rome, whether enforced by the Community institutions themselves or by the national legal systems.

When Community law is something as complex as this it is clearly a question of major importance that its development and application should be effected systematically and harmoniously. Consequently the Court of Justice of the Communities not only has the general task set out in Article 164 of the treaty to 'ensure the observance of law and justice in the interpretation and application of the Treaty'; it also has the more specific function of securing uniform interpretation by national courts by means of the procedure of 'preliminary interpretation'. 'There are various indications of the growing penetration of domestic legal systems by Community law and of the steadily improving comprehension of the new situation by those working in this field,' said the Commission in its 'First General Report on the Activities of the Communities in 1967', after the merger of the Executives.[64] By the end of 1973 448 decisions of national courts concerning Community law had been recorded, of which 234 were in the Federal Republic of Germany and sixty-three in France.[65] Requests for preliminary rulings accounted for more than half the cases filed with the Court in 1973.[66] At the special sitting of the Court held on 23 October 1968 to mark its tenth anniversary the President, Judge Lecourt, was able to record that 'collaboration between the Court of Justice of the Communities and national courts has been established in practice on a broad basis by the references made over a period of ten years at different levels of the judicial hierarchy' and to cite references made by the *Cours de Cassation* in Belgium, France and Luxembourg and the *Conseils d'Etat* or supreme administrative courts in Germany, Belgium and the Netherlands.[67]

We observe, then, a system of Community law in full evolution, which is applied both by national courts and by the Court of Justice of the Communities, in which the latter is the keystone of the whole system and the guarantor of uniform interpretation. How far, if at all, does the system instituted by the European Convention on Human Rights correspond to this?

In many respects it clearly does so. It is not claimed, of course, that 'Convention law' is necessarily binding with the force of internal law for all Contracting Parties. But, as is now well known, this is the case, with local variations, in a number of countries, including Austria, Belgium, France, Germany, Italy, Luxembourg and the Netherlands. Convention law – like Community law, even though to a lesser extent – does indeed transcend the traditional boundaries between international law and national law. More than four hundred decisions of national courts directly referring to the provisions of the Convention, and in some cases consciously applying them, have now been collected.[68] These provisions thus form part not only of the international legal order but also of the national legal systems and thus (like the rules of Community law) create rights and obligations for individuals.

Another aspect of the matter which merits our attention – and will do so increasingly in the years to come – is that there is a growing body of opinion, and some jurisprudence, in support of the view that the rules of the Convention are matters of *ordre public* in national law, and that they must therefore be applied by national judges even if they are not invoked by the parties to a case.[69] If this view is accepted, then it is evident that the effect of the Convention on national law will become increasingly important in the years to come.

To sum up, it may be stated that the law of the Convention (like Community law) is neither national law nor international law, but has elements of both. It is not simply the law applied by the Commission and Court of Human Rights, because, on the one hand, the Committee of Ministers of the Council of Europe also applies it, and, on the other hand, national courts do so as well. It creates not only obligations for States but also rights which are enforceable by individuals; it establishes, in the field of civil liberties, a new legal order designed to substitute for the particular systems of individual States a common European system.[70]

If this is so, what should be our attitude to the idea of granting 'preliminary competence' to the Court? Surely the same reasons which made this necessary for Community law make it also desirable for Convention law. Otherwise we shall have a legal system which is applied both nationally and internationally but without a keystone to the arch and without any guarantee of uniform interpretation.

What, then, of the objection that this would institute a new procedure different from that intended by the authors of the Convention and that it would, to some extent, 'short-circuit' the Commission of Human Rights?

There are, it is submitted, two answers to this objection. The first is that, while it may be true that to confer a 'preliminary competence' on the European Court would institute a new procedure different from that intended by the authors of the Convention, it should be remembered that the whole problem of the direct application of the Convention in internal law was (so far as one can tell) not considered at all by those who drafted it in 1950. The countries which have been most concerned with this problem are Germany and Austria; neither was a member of the Council of Europe in the spring of 1950. The amendment of the constitution of the Netherlands (Articles 65–7) dates only from 1956. There is no evidence that any serious thought was given to this matter by the authors of the Convention. If, therefore, a procedure is now proposed which is different from that which they instituted, this is because a problem has arisen which did not arise and which was not foreseen in 1950.

What of the second objection, that the proposed procedure would 'short-circuit' the Commission? At first sight this seems a more serious objection; but, on closer analysis, it is not really so. The main purpose of the Convention is the protection of the rights of the individual. Perhaps this should be the only object; in any event, it is the overriding objective. Consequently other considerations are of relatively minor importance and should be outweighed by that of rendering more effective the system of protection.

Now the purpose of 'preliminary rulings' is to enable a national court to obtain an authoritative interpretation on a point of law when applying the Convention or considering the compatibility of national law with the Convention. In both cases it will be, in all probability, dealing with a case which involves the rights of an individual. Anything possible should therefore be done to enable it to discharge its functions in the best possible manner. And if the utilisation of the procedure of 'preliminary consultation' would permit it to do so more effectively, that should be the overriding consideration. Moreover, if the result would be to settle in this way a problem of interpretation without the necessity for instituting contentious proceedings before the Commission, it is surely preferable, in the general interest, that the rights of the individual should be protected effectively at the national level by the national courts and the necessity for international proceedings thus avoided. Moreover it should not be difficult to find some way of associating the Commission in a consultative capacity or as *amicus curiae* with the work of the Court when the latter is called upon to give a 'preliminary ruling'.

Our conclusion, therefore, is that a strong case can be made out for granting to the Court of Human Rights the competence to interpret the Convention by a preliminary ruling given at the request of a national court, and that the time is now ripe for a reconsideration of this proposal. The experience of the Court of Justice of the Communities supports this view; so does the evolution of the notion of 'Convention law', interpenetrating and transcending both national law and international law, which has developed considerably during the fifteen years since the proposal was first made. The institution of such a procedure could only strengthen the effectiveness of the Convention and therefore the authority of the organs it has created. It may be hoped, therefore, that some suitable occasion will be found to reopen this question before long. As Professor Max Sørensen, later President of the Commission and now a judge on the Court of Justice of the Communities, said at the Vienna colloquy in 1965:[71]

Today we are half-way between the point of departure and the goal. The new principles, established by the European Communities, point the way. Present-day needs, arising out of European co-operation even outside the framework of the Six, encourage us to go ahead. In the end there will be no half measures. No doubt national tradition and the well known conservatism of lawyers will slow down our progress, but the integration of national legal systems into a coherent European system is the only practical way of achieving the aims of the great European Conventions.

NOTES

1 See Chapter I, section 2, n. 9.

2 This was inserted at the request of Professor Henri Rolin, who wished 'to maintain a monopoly of competence for the Hague Court'. See the speech of M. P.-H. Teitgen in *Official Report*, 8 September 1949, p. 1282.

3 The draft Convention proposed by the Committee of Ministers in August 1950 is to be found in *Documents of the Assembly*, 1950, Document 11, Appendix A.

4 The Assembly committee's opinion is to be found in Document 93 of 24 August 1950, and in Recommendation 24, *Texts adopted*, 1950.

5 *Documents of the Assembly*, 1959, Document 918. On the role of the Committee of Ministers in approving the list of candidates see Chapter VI, section 1.

6 *Official Report*, 21 January 1959.

7 The names are given in the order of the number of votes cast for the different candidates.

8 See Chapter I, n. 28.

9 In 1960 the Assembly recommended that a special agreement should be concluded to ask the opinion of the Court on this question of procedure. (Recommendation 235, 1960; *Yearbook* III, 1960, p. 156.) In 1965 the Committee of Ministers decided that 'the practice adopted over the last five years, whereby Governments other than those directly concerned do not put forward candidates, should be followed in the future'. (*Yearbook* VIII, 1965, p. 62.)

10 In the 'Belgian linguistic case' M. Henri Rolin stood down from his position as judge because he had previously, as a member of the Belgian Senate, voted in favour of the legislation which was attacked in the case before the Court. (*Yearbook* X, 1967, p. 19.)

11 The speech of Lord McNair, President of the Court, on this occasion is reproduced in *Yearbook* II, 1958–59, at pp. 154–6.

12 Progress report of the Bureau and Standing Committee of 14 May 1973, *Documents of the Assembly*, 1973, Document 3292, p. 9.

13 See Article 40 (amended) of the Convention (Appendix 1), and 'Explanatory report on the Second to Fifth Protocols', pp. 67–9.

14 *European Treaty Series*, No. 36; European Convention on Human Rights, *Collected Texts*, tenth edition, 1975, p. 807; *European Conventions and Agreements*, Vol. II, p. 9.

15 See *Human Rights in the World*, pp. 136 and 270.

16 The English Court of Appeal has held that the immunity of the President of the Commission continues after the expiry of his term of office: *Zoernsch* v. *Waldock and McNulty* (Chapter IV, n. 13).

17 For an attempt to abandon this system and provide that the judge who is the national of a State Party should be required to stand down, see the account of the negotiation of the American Convention in *Human Rights in the World*, Chapter V, at p. 133.

18 *Yearbook* IX, 1966, p. 652. A later example was the Golder case in 1974 *Publications of the Court*, Series A, Vol. 18, p. 3).

19 Two years: Belgium, Italy, the United Kingdom. Three years: Austria, France. Five years: Denmark, the Federal Republic, Iceland, Luxembourg, the Netherlands, Norway, Sweden.

20 Acceptance subject to reciprocity gives rise to the following questions. If a Contracting Party has accepted the compulsory jurisdiction of the Court on condition of reciprocity, can the Commission then refer a case brought against that Party to the Court? This question was discussed at some length by the Committee of Legal Experts which undertook the final revision of the text on the eve of the signature of the Convention in 1950. (*Cf.* Chapter I, n. 28.) On the one hand it was argued that in the case of the Commission no reciprocity exists and that therefore, since this condition is unfulfilled, no jurisdiction lies. On the other hand it was asserted that the condition of reciprocity relates only to cases brought by other High Contracting Parties, and does not affect the ability of the Commission to bring a case before the Court, since the Commisssion is *sui generis*, and the right of the Commission to refer cases to the Court is an essential part of the procedure established by the Convention (e.g. in Article 48) which cannot be excluded in default of a clear intention to do so. In practice cases have been referred to the Court by the Commission when the respondent government had accepted its jurisdiction on condition of reciprocity (Austria and the Federal Republic) but no objections to the jurisdiction were raised on that score.

21 E.g. Austria as regards the cases of Neumeister, Stögmüller and Matznetter; Belgium as regards the Vagrancy cases; the United Kingdom as regards the Golder case.

22. On this subject see S. Petrén, 'La saisine de la Cour européenne par la Commission européenne des Droits de l'homme', in *Mélanges Modinos*, Paris, 1968, pp. 233–44.

23 The Rules of Court may be found in *European Convention on Human Rights: Collected Texts* (tenth edition, July 1975), Section IV, pp. 401–44, and in a separate booklet, *Rules of Court*, published by the registry of the Court (revised edition, May 1973). For an account of the rules as originally drafted see M.-A. Eissen, 'La Cour Européenne des Droits de l'Homme – de la Convention au Règlement', *Annuaire Français de Droit International*, 1959, pp. 21–39. For subsequent amendments see H. Petzold, 'Le règlement de la Cour européenne des Droits de l'homme', *Annales de Droit*, Vol. XXXIV, 1974, pp. 165–87.

24 The Court elected as Registrar on 16 September 1959 M. Polys Modinos, then Director of Human Rights in the Secretariat General of the Council of Europe. In 1960 Dr H. Golsong was elected Deputy Registrar. After M. Modinos was elected Deputy Secretary General of the Council of Europe in 1962 Dr Golsong was elected Registrar of the Court and M. M.-A. Eissen Deputy Registrar. After Dr Golsong was appointed Director of Legal Affairs in the Secretariat General M. Eissen was elected Registrar of the Court in 1968 and Mr John Smyth Deputy Registrar. In 1975 M. Eissen was re-elected as Registrar and (Mr Smyth not seeking re-election) Mr H. Petzold was elected as Deputy Registrar.

25 *Human Rights in the World*, pp. 135 and 268.

26 German–Swiss Treaty on Arbitration and Conciliation, 1921, Article 10. *Cf.* Geneva General Act for the Pacific Settlement of International Disputes, 1928, Article 32.

27 See also on this subject William Vis, 'La reparation des violations de la

Convention', in *La Protection internationale des Droits de l'homme dans le cadre européen*, 1961, p. 279.

28 *Yearbook* XIV, 1971, p. 838, at p. 864. On 8 November 1972 the Court added paragraphs 3 and 4 to Rule 50 of the Rules of Court. The effect of paragraph 3 is to require a chamber, when it has decided that there is a breach of the Convention, to reserve the possibility of an award of damages under Article 50 if the question has not already been raised or is not ready for decision.

29 *Yearbook* XV, 1972, p. 678, at p. 692.

30 *Yearbook* XV, 1972, pp. 670–2.

31 *Yearbook* XVI, 1973, p. 468.

32 See Articles 44 and 92 of the ECSC treaty; Articles 187 and 192 of the EEC treaty; and Articles 159 and 164 of the Euratom treaty.

33 *Texts adopted*, October 1972, Recommendation 683, para. C(2), *Yearbook* XV, p. 58.

34 It is curious that the French text of Article 44 uses exactly the same words as Article 34 of the Statute of the ICJ – 'ont qualité pour se présenter devant la Cour' – while the English texts differ. Article 34 of the Statute uses the words may be parties in cases before the Court', while Article 44 of the Convention says 'shall have the right to bring a case before the Court'.

35 *Supra*, Chapter II, under Article 5, and Chapter III, under Article 15. A separate chapter was devoted to the Lawless case in the first edition of this book.

36 'The Lawless case: pleadings, oral arguments and documents, *Publications of the Court*, Series B, 1960–61, p. 234.

37 The Irish government also objected to the jurisdiction on the ground that the Commission had adopted its report on 19 December 1959 but had transmitted it to the Committee of Ministers and the Government only on 1 February 1960. This meant that the decision to refer the case to the Court, taken on 1 April 1960, was within three months of the date of actual transmission of the report but not within three months of the data at which the report should, in the government's view, have been transmitted. This objection was, however, withdrawn during the course of the oral hearings.

38 See reference n. 36, at p. 282.

39 See reference n. 36, at pp. 217 and 298.

40 *ICJ Reports*, 1956, p. 57, at p. 86.

41 See reference n. 36, at p. 298.

42 *Yearbook* III, 1960, p. 492.

43 *Yearbook* IV, 1961, p. 444.

44 The apparent difference between the Court's more liberal attitude in November 1960 and the more restrictive interpretation in April 1961 appears to be due, at least in part, to a difficulty of translation. The earlier judgement, in French, said that 'la Commission a le droit . . . *de faire état* devant la Cour sous sa propre responsabilité des considérations du requérant . . .'. This was translated on the earlier occasion, as 'The Commission . . . is entitled of its own accord . . . *to make known* the applicant's views to the Court . . .'. In the judgement of 7 April 1961 the Court still held that the Court was entitled 'de faire état' of the applican't views, but this was translated as 'to take [them] into account'. 'Faire état' is indeed an imprecise expression. But the Court was careful to point out that only the French text was authentic.

45 Applications 2832/66, 2835/66 and 2899/66, De Wilde, Ooms and Versyp *v.* Belgium, *Yearbook* X, 1967, p. 420; XIV, 1971, p. 788.

46 *Yearbook* XIV, 1971, at p. 792. On 28 October 1975, in the case of *Five Dutch soldiers* v. *the Netherlands*, the applicants' lawyer addressed the Court, theoretically to assist the delegates of the Commission but, practically speaking, to elaborate the point of view of the applicants on their case.

47 The text is given in Appendix 3.

48 This and the following sections are based on an article entitled 'Advisory

opinions of the Court' published in a volume of *mélanges* in honour of M. René Cassin, *R. Cassin Amicorum Discipulorumque Liber*, 1970, Vol. I, pp. 225–40.

49 *Recommendation 232* of 22 January 1960.

50 *Documents of the Assembly*, 1957, Document 737.

51 *Ibid.*, Document 1061 of 24 November 1959.

52 *Ibid.*, Document 1062 of 24 November 1959.

53 Twelfth report of the Committee of Ministers, *Documents of the Assembly*, 1961, Document 1257, paras. 239–40.

54 It is interesting to compare the competence of the Inter-American Court of Human Rights in this respect. Under Article 64 of the American Convention the Court may give advisory opinions relating not only to that Convention but also to other treaties protecting human rights in the American States and also to the compatibility of domestic laws in any state member of the OAS with the provisions of the American Convention. (*Human Rights in the World*, pp. 135–6.)

55 Fourteenth report of the Committee of Ministers, *Documents of the Assembly*, 1963, Document 1564, para. 243.

56 Report of the Committee of Experts on the drafting of the Second Protocol, in *Explanatory Reports on the Second to Fifth Protocols*, Strasbourg, 1971, p. 16.

57 Fourteenth report of the Committee of Ministers, *Documents of the Assembly*, 1963, Document 1564, para. 253.

58 Sixteenth report of the Committee of Ministers, 1965, Document 1897, para. 303. *Cf.* n. 56 above.

59 *Human Rights in National and International Law* (proceedings of the Vienna colloquy), 1968, p. 44 (English edition); p. 75 (French edition); p. 39 (German edition).

60 *Ibid.*, pp. 151–200 (English edition); pp. 263–325 (French edition); pp. 141–83 (German edition).

61 *Ibid.*, pp. 223 (English edition); p. 357 (French edition); p. 202 (German edition).

62 *Parliamentary Conference on Human Rights*, Strasbourg, 1972, pp. 70–1.

63 *Texts adopted by the Assembly*, October 1972, Recommendation 683, appendix, para. C(4); *Yearbook XV*, p. 58.

64 At p. 463.

65 *Seventh General Report on the Activities of the European Community*, 1973, p. 483, table 18.

66 *Ibid.*, p. 481, table 16.

67 *Second General Report*, 1968, p. 469, para. 637.

68 *Collection of Decisions of National Courts*, published by the Directorate of Human Rights of the Council of Europe, 1972.

69 See W. J. Ganshof van der Meersch, 'La Convention a-t-elle, dans le cadre du droit interne, une valeur d'ordre public?', *Proceedings of the Vienna Colloquy*, pp. 155–251 (French edition); pp. 97–143 (English edition); pp. 93–134 (German edition).

70 *Cf.* the statement of the Commission in the case of *Austria* v. *Italy*, quoted in Chapter II, Section 1(b), at p. 32.

71 *Human Rights in National and International Law* (proceedings of the Vienna colloquy), 1968, p. 31 (English edition); p. 61 (French edition); p. 32 (German edition).

CHAPTER VI

THE COMMITTEE OF MINISTERS

The Committee of Ministers of the Council of Europe was established by the Statute of the Council of Europe, signed on 5 May 1949. Its existence therefore antedates the Convention on Human Rights of 4 November 1950 and is quite distinct from that of the organs of the Convention, the major part of its activities being extraneous to the Convention, and not directly related to human rights. The Committee is, however, relevant to the subject-matter of this work because the Convention on Human Rights conferred certain additional functions on an existing organ, as a result of which the Committee of Ministers assumed an important role as part of the European system for the protection of human rights. The nature of that role and the way in which it is discharged form the subject of this chapter.

The Committee of Ministers is the executive organ of the Council of Europe. This results from Article 13 of the Statute, which describes the Committee as 'the organ which acts on behalf of the Council of Europe'. The Consultative Assembly, as a parliamentary body, is the 'deliberative organ' of the Council which presents its conclusions, in the form of recommendations, to the Committee of Ministers (Article 22 of the Statute). The Committee of Ministers decides, on the recommendation of the Assembly or on its own initiative, what action shall be taken 'to further the aim of the Council of Europe', which, under Article 1 of the Statute, is 'to achieve a greater unity between its Members, for the purpose of safeguarding and realising the ideals and principles which are their common heritage, and facilitating their economic and social progress'. Article 1 continues by providing in its second paragraph that 'this aim shall be pursued . . . by agreements and common action in economic, social, cultural, scientific, legal and administrative matters *and in the maintenance and further realisation of human rights and fundamental freedoms*'.[1]

The action to be taken in pursuance of the aim of the Council of Europe may, under Article 15 of the Statute, include 'the con-

clusion of conventions or agreements and the adoption by governments of a common policy with regard to particular matters'. The
first convention so concluded was, as related in Chapter I, the
Convention on Human Rights. Subsequently more than eighty other
conventions and agreements have been concluded, providing for
measures of European co-operation in other fields within the competence of the organisation.[2]

The members of the Committee of Ministers are, under Article
14 of the Statute, the Ministers for Foreign Affairs of the member
States. Nevertheless, when unable to be present a Minister may be
replaced by an alternate, who should in principle be another
Minister; in fact for the greater part of their business the Ministers
are replaced by officials of the Foreign Ministries known as the
Ministers' Deputies. Under Article 20 of the Statute various decisions of the Committee of Ministers on procedural, administrative
and financial matters can be taken by a majority vote; but their
more important decisions, including recommendations to the
member governments, require unanimity.

The first role of the Committee of Ministers in relation to the
Convention on Human Rights was, as recounted in Chapter I, that
it approved the Assembly's proposals for the conclusion of the
Convention, instituted the intergovernmental negotiations and finally
approved the text and decided to open it for signature. Secondly,
the Committee of Ministers is vested with certain specific functions
by the Convention and has its own role to play in ensuring the
proper functioning of the machinery established thereby. Thirdly,
the protection of human rights is not considered by the organs of
the Council of Europe as something which has been effectively
accomplished and therefore requires no further action; on the contrary, the Assembly is constantly making new proposals to improve
the machinery already established or to secure the protection of
additional rights; certain such proposals have also been made by
the Commission and the Court. It is then for the Committee of
Ministers – as the executive organ of the Council – to decide what
action shall be taken on these proposals; further information on
this subject is given in Chapter VIII below.

The functions specifically conferred on the Committee of
Ministers by the Convention on Human Rights fall into three
categories: administrative functions, judicial or quasi-judicial
functions and supervisory functions. These will be considered
separately in the following sections.

1. ADMINISTRATIVE FUNCTIONS OF THE COMMITTEE OF MINISTERS

The first administrative function of the Committee of Ministers is in relation to the election of the members of the Commission. Article 21 of the Convention provides that they shall be elected by an absolute majority of votes from a list of names drawn up by the Bureau of the Consultative Assembly. The role of the Bureau in establishing this list has been discussed above.[3] On receipt of this list, the Committee of Ministers proceeds to the election. The voting is by secret ballot. The results are published in communications of the Committee of Ministers to the Assembly and, when considered necessary, in press communiqués.

The second administrative function of the Committee of Ministers is in relation to the election of the members of the Court. Article 39 of the Convention provides that they shall be elected by the Consultative Assembly from a list of persons nominated by the members of the Council of Europe. The procedure for election in the Assembly has been discussed above.[4] It is to be observed that Article 39 of the Convention does not confer any function on the Committee of Ministers as such in the election procedure; it provides for nominations by the 'Members of the Council of Europe'. However, since it is in the Committee of Ministers that the representatives of the member States meet for the purpose of transacting business relating to the Council of Europe, it is in fact in the Committee of Ministers that the nominations are made, and it is the Committee of Ministers which draws up the list for transmission to the Assembly. Indeed, in its communication to the Assembly of 15 December 1958 transmitting the first list of candidates for election to the Court the Committee of Ministers deliberately and consciously intervened in the procedure, as evidenced by the following extract from their letter:[5]

... Although the Convention makes no express stipulation to that effect, the Committee of Ministers has itself decided to combine into a single list, as specified in the aforesaid Article 39, the fifteen lists submitted by the Governments of Member States.

The Committee of Ministers has unanimously recognised that the judges will sit in a purely individual capacity and will enjoy, in the exercise of their high office, the complete independence implied by the Convention. It considers that in this respect the candidates presented offer the fullest possible guarantees, together with all the qualifications required by Article 39, paragraph 3.

I

For subsequent elections the lists of candidates have been transmitted to the Assembly by the Committee of Ministers and not by the governments individually.

The last point illustrates the fact that the Committee of Ministers provides a forum in which all the High Contracting Parties are represented and in which they can conveniently examine matters arising out of the Convention which are not within the competence of the Commission or the Court. The Committee of Ministers may thus discuss questions of uncertain interpretation of the treaty – other than those, of course, which arise during proceedings before the other two organs. An example of this occurred in 1956 in relation to Article 15.

After providing for the possibility of derogation in time of war or other public emergency threatening the life of the nation, Article 15 provides in its paragraph 3:

> Any High Contracting Party availing itself of this right of derogation shall keep the Secretary-General of the Council of Europe fully informed of the measures which it has taken and the reasons therefor. It shall also inform the Secretary-General of the Council of Europe when such measures have ceased to operate and the provisions of the Convention are again being fully executed.

The first such derogations were made by the United Kingdom in May 1954, when the British government reported to the Secretary General that a state of emergency had been proclaimed in the Federation of Malaya and Singapore, in Kenya and in British Guiana.[6] This was followed in October 1955 and April 1956 by two similar communications relating to Cyprus.[7] On 7 May 1956 the Greek government brought its first case against the United Kingdom relating to the emergency measures in Cyprus, and did so in ignorance of the fact that the United Kingdom had made two derogations under Article 15. The question then arose whether the Secretary General should have communicated to all Contracting Parties the notices of derogation which had been deposited by the British government.

On the one hand it could be argued that all Contracting Parties should be informed when a derogation has been made, since it modifies to some extent their mutual obligations. On the other hand it was pointed out that Article 15 does not expressly impose a duty on the Secretary General to notify the Contracting Parties of communications made to him, whereas Articles 25 (on the right of individual petition), 46 (on the compulsory jurisdiction of the Court) and 66 (on ratification) specifically provided for such notification; it was argued that this difference in drafting must be supposed to be intentional, in which case there was no duty on the Secretary General to notify to other Parties communications received under Article 15. The Secretary General referred this question to the Committee of Ministers for a decision, and the latter, in September 1956, adopted its *Resolution (56) 16* to the effect that 'any information transmitted to the Secretary General by a Contracting Party in pursuance of Article 15, paragraph 3, of the Convention must be communicated by him as soon as possible to the other Contracting Parties and the European Commission of Human Rights'.[8] Subsequently the Consultative Assembly asked the Committee of Ministers to decide that the Secretary General should also communicate such information to the chairman of the Committee of Ministers and the President of the Assembly.[9] The Committee of Ministers replied in the following February that there was nothing to prevent his doing so, but the Committee was not prepared to take a formal decision that he must, since the Convention said nothing about communicating other declarations, notifications, etc, to those officers; consequently a decision relating to Article 15, paragraph 3, 'might either appear to create a precedent or else give rise to arguments *a contrario*'.[10]

Another administrative function of the Committee of Ministers in relation to the Convention concerns the secretariat. Article 37 of the Convention provides that 'the Secretariat of the Commission shall be provided by the Secretary General of the Council of Europe'. Since, under Articles 37 and 38 of the Statute of the Council, the Secretary General is responsible to the Committee of Ministers and has to submit to the Committee his budgetary requirements, this means that it is the Committee of Ministers which votes the credits for – and thus determines the size of – the secretariat of the Commission.[11]

The position is generally similar, though slightly different, for the Court. The Convention itself makes no provision for the secretariat or registry of the Court. The Rules of Court (Rules 11 and 12) provide that the Court shall elect its Registrar and Deputy Registrar 'after the President has in this respect obtained the opinion of the Secretary General of the Council of Europe'. Rule 13 continues, 'the President or the Registrar on his behalf, shall request the Secretary General of the Council of Europe to provide the Registrar with the staff, permanent or temporary, equipment and facilities necessary for the Court'. It provides in addition that the officials of the registry (other than the Registrar and Deputy Registrar) shall be appointed by the Secretary General, with the agreement of the President or the Registrar.

This means, generally speaking, that all members of the secretariat of the Commission and of the registry of the Court are officials of the Council of Europe, subject to its administrative and financial regulations as determined by the Committee of Ministers, except as regards the method of appointment of the Registrar and Deputy Registrar and the definition of functions by the two Presidents. When it is remembered that both organs also depend on the Council of Europe for their premises and for all their general services (documentation, translation, interpretation, etc) the intimate nature of their links with the Council is apparent.[12] They are therefore *pro tanto* subject, in the last resort, to the decisions of the Committe of Ministers.

2. JUDICIAL OR QUASI-JUDICIAL FUNCTIONS OF THE COMMITTEE OF MINISTERS

The most important function of the Committee in relation to the Convention is under Article 32. This deals with the situation where the Commission has drawn up a report stating its opinions whether the facts in a particular case disclose a breach by the State concerned of its obligations under the Convention. Article 32 then provides as follows:

(1) If the question is not referred to the Court in accordance with Article 48 of this Convention within a period of three months from the date of the transmission of the Report to the Committee of Ministers, the Committee of Ministers shall decide by a majority of two-thirds of the members entitled to sit on the Committee whether there has been a violation of the Convention.

(2) In the affirmative case the Committee of Ministers shall prescribe a period during which the High Contracting Party concerned must take the measures required by the decision of the Committee of Ministers.

(3) If the High Contracting Party concerned has not taken satisfactory measures within the prescribed period, the Committee of Ministers shall decide by the majority provided for in paragraph (1) above what effect shall be given to its original decision and shall publish the Report.

(4) The High Contracting Parties undertake to regard as binding on them any decision which the Committee of Ministers may take in application of the preceding paragraphs.

In such circumstances, therefore, the Committee of Ministers has a judicial or quasi-judicial function, for it has to 'decide . . . whether there has been a violation of the Convention'. This will only arise, however, if the matter has not been referred to the Court in accordance with Article 48, that is to say by the Commission itself or by a High Contracting Party concerned in the case, which can occur only if the Party against which the complaint has been made has accepted the jurisdiction of the Court – either by a general declaration under Article 46 or in the particular case.

It will be observed that the Committee of Ministers can take decisions under Article 32 of the Convention *by a two-thirds majority* of the members entitled to sit on the Committee, whereas its more important decisions under the Statute of the Council of Europe, as mentioned above, require unanimity. This provision permitting decisions by a two-thirds majority was of course necessary because otherwise a State against which a complaint has been lodged would be in a position to block a decision unfavourable to itself in the Committee of Ministers.[13]

It will also be observed that the Committee, like the Court, has no power to invalidate or overrule a national decision; nor does it have power to prescribe what remedial measures should be taken in case of a violation. It is clear from paragraph (2) of Article 32 that it is for the government concerned to decide what measures are required, and to take them; the Committee of Ministers, at this stage, must limit itself to prescribing a period within which the necessary measures must be taken.

What sanction is possessed by the Committee of Ministers if the government does not respect its decision? The only sanction specifically provided for in the Convention is that mentioned in paragraph (3) of Article 32, namely publication of the report of the Commission. This is perhaps a more powerful sanction than is generally believed, because no responsible government can view with complacency the prospect of the publication by the Foreign Ministers of eighteen States of a report indicating that it has violated its international obligations regarding respect for human rights. Moreover in a democratic country – and all Contracting Parties are democratic States *ex hypothesei* – the publication of such a report would put powerful ammunition in the hands of a parliamentary opposition. But the possible sanctions are in fact much more drastic, even though not mentioned in the Convention, because Article 8 of the Statute of the Council of Europe empowers the Committee of Ministers to suspend or expel from membership any State which has seriously violated Article 3 of the Statute – the article which makes respect for the rule of law and for 'the enjoyment by all persons within its jurisdiction of human rights and fundamental freedoms' a condition of membership of the organisation. The ultimate sanction, therefore, is expulsion. It may be hoped, of course, that the necessity to resort to this sanction will rarely, if ever, arise. The only case to date in which the possibility of its utilisation has arisen was the *Greek case*. But then, from the formal point of view, the Committee of Ministers in December 1969 was acting on a recommendation of the Consultative Assembly and not on the report of the Commission; moreover the action of the Greek government in withdrawing from the Council of Europe and denouncing the Convention forestalled the impending decision of expulsion.

It is in many ways surprising that a judicial role should be conferred on an organ which is essentially political in character. As explained in Chapter I and Chapter V, the original proposals for the European Convention on Human Rights submitted to the Council of Europe by the European Movement in July 1949 did not envisage any such role for the Committee of Ministers. Nor did the proposals of the Consultative Assembly, made to the Committee of Ministers in September 1949 in *Recommendation 38*. However, when the detailed drafting work was undertaken several governments let it be known that they were not prepared to accept the jurisdiction of a European Court; it therefore became necessary to confer the power for taking decisions about reports of the Commission on some other body. It was then decided to use the Committee of Ministers of the Council of Europe for this purpose.

What is the dominant factor when a political organ is required to settle a legal dispute? Does law take precedence over political considerations, or vice versa? An answer to this question may be found in the *Advisory opinion of the International Court of Justice* of 28 May 1948 on the conditions for the admission of a State to membership of the United Nations (Article 4 of the Charter). The Court stated:

> ... The political character of an organ cannot release it from the observance of the treaty provisions established by the Charter when they constitute limitations on its powers or criteria for its judgment.

The General Assembly of the United Nations had put to the Court the question whether a member of the United Nations, when voting on the admission of a new member, was juridically entitled to make its consent to such admission dependent on conditions not expressly provided for in paragraph 1 of Article 4 of the Charter. The Court replied that a member State is not juridically entitled to make its consent conditional in this way; if a State recognised that the conditions set out in Article 4 were fulfilled by the candidate State, it could not subject its affirmative vote to other considerations not provided for in the Charter. This therefore indicated a clear duty for a political organ – either the Security Council or the General Assembly – to observe strictly the provisions of the relevant treaty and not introduce other considerations of a political character. The same is true by analogy of the Committee of Ministers of the Council of Europe when it discharges it functions under the Convention on Human Rights; though a political organ, it is bound by the conditions of the treaty and cannot take account of considerations of political expediency not set out therein. It is not exempt from following the law and is not free to take decisions on grounds of its own choosing. Its action must be taken within the limits of Article 32 of the Convention.

3. PROCEDURE OF THE COMMITTEE OF MINISTERS

After the Convention on Human Rights entered into force in 1953 more than five years were to elapse before the Committee of Ministers was called upon to exercise its powers under Article 32 of the Convention. This was in connection with the case of *Greece against the United Kingdom*, brought in 1956, alleging violation of the Convention by the latter in the island of Cyprus. After declaring the case admissible and proceeding to an investigation of the facts the Commission attempted – but failed – to secure a friendly settlement. On 2 October 1958 the Commission sent its report to the Committee of Ministers, setting out its opinion on the question of violation. It then became necessary for the Committee to take a number of decisions about the procdure which it would follow in dealing with this case – and also in dealing with other cases in the future. This led to the first attempt to draw up Rules of Procedure for the Committee of Ministers when exercising its functions under Article 32 of the Convention.

The Directorate of Human Rights in the secretariat of the Council of Europe, which had at an earlier stage assisted the Commission of Human Rights in drawing up its Rules of Procedure and later assisted the Court in a similar task, submitted a set of fairly detailed draft Rules of Procedure to the Committee of Ministers. The latter, however, was unwilling to be bound by a set of detailed rules, which the Committee considered would limit its freedom of action unduly. It wished to reserve the greatest possible degree of flexibility in its procedure and therefore decided that it 'should, in the matter of enquiries into cases, act as appeared to it most appropriate in each particular instance'.

Nevertheless it was clear that certain basic questions needed to be decided and incorporated into a few simple rules. The first of these was the question whether a State or States which were parties to a case would have the right to vote when the Committee of Ministers was called upon to take a decision under Article 32 of the Convention. The same question applied in relation to a State which was a member of the Council of Europe but had not ratified the European Convention on Human Rights. (In fact France was the only member which had not ratified the Convention at that time.) The answer to these two questions was fortunately simple, because Article 32 of the Convention provides that the decision on the question of violation shall be taken by the Committee of Ministers ... 'by a majority of two-thirds of the members entitled sit on the Committee ...'. This clearly meant that all members are entitled to take part in the decision, whether or not they are parties to the particular case in question and whether or not they have ratified the Convention.

At the same time it was recognised that if the chairmanship of the Committee of Ministers (which rotates between the members in alphabetical order) is held by a State which is party to a dispute that comes up for consideration by the Committee, the chairman should stand down and pass on the chairmanship to the representative of the next State which is not a party to the dispute.

Three simple rules were therefore drafted to cover these three points and approved by the Committee of Ministers in 1959.[14]

The next event of significance in this connection was the case brought by *Austria against Italy* in 1960, which was referred to the Committee of Ministers in 1963. The Commission, after declaring the case admissible, established the facts of the case, attempted unsuccessfully to reach a friendly settlement and then submitted its report to the Committee of Ministers early in 1963.[15]

The Commission expressed the opinion that there had been no violation of the Convention on Human Rights in this case. At the same time the Commission considered it desirable for humanitarian reasons, among which it counted the youth of the prisoners, that measures of clemency should be taken in their favour. The Committee of Ministers considered the report of the Commission in the autumn of 1963, and then realised that certain further problems of procedure had arisen.

As we have seen in Chapter IV, Article 31 of the Convention provides in paragraph 3: 'In transmitting the report to the Committee of Ministers, the Commission may make such proposals as it thinks fit.' However, in the case of *Austria against Italy* the wish that clemency should be shown to the prisoners was not put to the Committee of Ministers as a 'proposal' under the terms of Article 31, paragraph 3. The Ministers therefore limited themselves to informing the governments concerned that they had taken note of the wish expressed by the Commission.[16] At the same time they decided to have a study made of the procedural problems which had arisen.

The first related to the extent of the Commission's power to make proposals or suggestions when adopting its report and to the procedure of the Committee of Ministers when considering such proposals or suggestions; the second question was wider in scope and concerned the powers of the Committee of Ministers to undertake an examination of the substance of a case when it is considering the report of the Commission.

As regards the power of the Commission to make proposals or suggestions, there was no doubt that such a power existed, since it is specifically provided for in paragraph 3 of Article 31. However, it was asserted that this power was intended to be used in cases when the Commission was of opinion that a violation had occurred; it would then be only natural that the Commission, having examined the case in detail, should make proposals as to the best way of remedying the violation. If, on the other hand, the Commission reached the conclusion that there was no violation, then, it was argued, it was quite unnecessary for it to make any proposals at all, and an attempt to do so might even be considered *ultra vires*.

The wider question concerning the powers of the Committee of Ministers was the following. If the Committee has the duty, under Article 32 of the Convention, of deciding whether a violation has occurred, and if (as is the case) the Committee can act only after it has received the report of the Commission, should its consideration be limited to the matters dealt with in the Commission's report or can the Committee of Ministers hear further arguments, and possibly take evidence itself? In support of the former view it can be argued that once the Commission has established the facts of the case and heard the arguments of the parties it should not be necessary for the Committee of Ministers to go through this procedure all over again; moreover the Committee is not a suitable body to interrogate witnesses and weigh up conflicting arguments, because its members do not have legal or judicial experience. On the other hand, it can be claimed that when the Committee of Ministers has the responsibility of deciding whether a government is responsible for violation of the Convention on Human Rights the Committee should be at liberty to hear any evidence or consider any arguments it believes to be relevant.

In June 1964 the Committee of Ministers asked the Committee of Experts on Human Rights to study these and certain other questions relating to the procedure to be followed under Article 32 of the Convention. The Experts did so, and reported back to the Ministers early in the following year. The Ministers accepted their advice and adopted certain additional rules in the spring of 1966.

On the first question the Experts took a rather conservative view. They considered that it was necessary to look at Article 31 of the Convention in the context of the other articles relating to the powers of the Commission. Article 28 deals with the procedure for friendly settlement and Article 31 with the procedure to be followed if no friendly settlement is achieved. Consequently the Commission is no longer engaged in conciliatory functions at this stage. The Experts were therefore of opinion that it was not the intention of the authors of the Convention to empower the Commission to make proposals concerning the conduct of a State when there has been no violation of the Convention. Moreover proposals made by the Commission in the absence of a violation might constitute criticism of the legislation or administration of a State which had in fact fulfilled its obligations under the Convention. If such a power were to exist, it would have to be conferred explicitly; the principle of restrictive interpretation of treaties should apply.

The Experts then considered what action the Committee of Ministers is empowered to take in cases where it has decided that there is a violation of the Convention. As we have seen above, paragraph 2 of Article 32 empowers the Committee of Ministers to 'prescribe a period during which the High Contracting Party concerned must take the measures required by the decision of the Committee of Ministers' but does not authorise the Committee of Ministers to prescribe what measures must be taken; it is rather for the government concerned to draw its own conclusions. Nevertheless the Experts were of opinion – and the Ministers agreed – that the Committee of Ministers may 'give advice or make suggestions or recommendations to the State concerned, provided that these are closely related to the violation'. Such advice, suggestions or recommendations, however, would not be binding on the government to which they are addressed, because they would not be 'decisions' within the meaning of Article 32, paragraph 4, of the Convention.

The Experts then came to the wider question whether the Committee of Ministers can reopen the discussion on the substance of a case or whether it should confine itself to approving or rejecting the opinion expressed by the Commission in its report. Here the Experts were assisted by the *travaux préparatoires*. At the Conference of Senior Officals held in June 1950 the Luxembourg delegate proposed that the Committee of Ministers should be bound by the Commission's opinion in the sense that it can only reject or adopt it as a whole, without amendment. The Luxembourg delegate's proposal was not adopted by the conference, 'which considered that the Committee of Ministers must be left entire freedom of decision'. The Committee of Ministers therefore has the power to confirm, amend or reverse the opinion of the Commission as it may consider appropriate.

This then led to the further question whether the Committee of Ministers can consider memorials and counter-memorials submitted by governments (for example, in an inter-State case) and whether it can go further and hear witnesses and consider other forms of evidence. It followed necessarily that the Committee must have all the necessary powers to reach a decision. On the other hand, as pointed out above, the members of the Committee of Ministers are not well qualified to undertake this sort of work. The Experts therefore expressed the view that, since the Commission is, in its nature, better equipped to take evidence, etc, the Committee of Ministers ought not normally to undertake such tasks; the Experts were of opinion that the Committee of Ministers should invite the Commission to undertake these tasks on its behalf, unless in exceptional circumstances it appeared essential that the Committee of Ministers should do so itself.

These various decisions were incorporated in further rules approved by the Committee of Ministers in the spring of 1966.[17]

One would have thought that by the summer of 1966, when the matters related above had been under discussion for nearly eight years, the situation would have become quite clear and any necessary rules would have been exhaustively discussed and finally adopted. This, however, was far from the case. In the autumn of 1966 the Committee of Ministers discovered that there were further problems not adequately covered by the rules which they had already adopted, and consequently they instructed the Committee of Experts on Human Rights to study these problems and draft further proposals.[18]

Some of the problems raised at this stage related to finer points of drafting – and sometimes led to minor revisions of the rules previously adopted. But three of them raised questions of principle.

The first of these was whether a government which is not a party to the proceedings before the Commission may intervene in the proceedings before the Committee of Ministers. A typical case where this might arise is when an individual (X) who is a national of one State (A) resides in another State (B) and brings a case before the Commission against his State of residence. It is quite likely that State A will have no knowledge of the proceedings – until the report of the Commission comes before the Committee of Ministers. However, at that stage the government of A, perhaps acting on the principle of protecting the interests of its own nationals abroad or perhaps for other reasons, may wish to champion the cause of X before the Committee of Ministers. Has it the right to do so, even though it was not a party to the proceedings before the Commission?

The Experts were of opinion – which was shared by the Committee of Ministers – that each representative on the Committee has an intrinsic right to make submissions and deposit documents relating to any case under consideration. Consequently the question whether a State was or was not a party to the proceedings before the Commission does not affect its rights in the proceedings before the Committee of Ministers. The Committee added a rider, however, to this decision as regards the possibility that a State might make a formal request to the Committee of Ministers which had not been made before the Commission – for example, a request for damages. The Committee of Ministers reserved its position as regards such a possibility. The necessity for such a reservation, however, is hard to understand, since neither the Commission nor the Committee of Ministers has any power to award damages to the victim of a violation.

The second question of principle raised at this stage of the discussions concerned the relationship of the individual applicant to proceedings before the Committee of Ministers. Now it is clear from the terms of the Convention that an individual applicant is not a party to the proceedings before the Committee of Ministers, but does it necessarily follow that he should be totally excluded from the proceedings in which he is the person most directly concerned?

A similar problem arose as regards the position of the individual applicant in relation to the proceedings of the Court in the *Lawless case*, as explained in Chapter V. There too the individual applicant has no right to be heard by the Court and is not a party to the proceedings before the Court. Nevertheless in the Lawless case the Court pointed out that: [19]

> the Applicant, although he is not entitled to bring the case before the Court, to appear before the Court or even to make submissions through a representative appointed by him, is nevertheless directly concerned in the proceedings before the Court; it must be borne in mind that the Applicant instituted the proceedings before the Commission and that, if the Court found that his complaints were justified, he would be directly affected by any decision, in accordance with Article 50 of the Convention, on the substance of the case.

In fact the applicant received a copy of the Commission's report and was invited to send his observations on it to the Commission. Subsequently the Court held that the Commission 'is entitled of its own accord to make known the applicant's views to the Court, even if it does not share them, as a means of throwing light on the points at issue'.[20]

It was therefore proposed that a somewhat similar procedure should be established permitting the communication to the individual applicant of the report of the Commission when a case is before the Committee of Ministers – as was done in the Nielsen case by an *ad hoc* decision[21] – and subsequently the communication to the Committee of Ministers directly or indirectly of the applicant's observations thereon. In the procedure worked out in the Lawless case the Commission had the responsibility for communicating the report to the individual applicant and obtaining his observations thereon; in a certain sense it acted as a screen and exercised its own judgement in deciding what observations it was appropriate to submit to the Court. A similar function, it was argued, could be discharged by the Secretary General in the course of proceedings before the Committee of Ministers.

Once again the Committee of Experts was rather cautious in its approach to the problem submitted for its consideration. It considered that the communication to an individual applicant of the complete text or extracts from the report of the Commission should take place only as an exceptional measure (e.g. where the Committee of Ministers wishes to obtain the observations of the applicant), only on a strictly confidential basis, and only with the consent of the State again which the application was lodged. Consequently, the Experts were of opinion that it was not necessary to establish a procedure for communicating the observations of the applicant to the Committee of Ministers, since the communication of the report to the applicant will take place only as an exceptional measure. At a later date an even more negative decision was taken about communications addressed to the Committee of Ministers by an individual applicant. Though the applicant is not allowed to see the report of the Commission on his case, he is informed that it has been transmitted to the Committee of Ministers and that the latter will in due course take a decision thereon (if the case is not referred to the Court). It may then happen – and in fact it has happened – that the applicant sends to the Council of Europe a statement of his views which he asks should be communicated to the Committee of Ministers when it is considering his case. The Committee has decided that such statements from an individual applicant may not be communicated to the Committee of Ministers – unless, as an exceptional measure, they have been specifically requested.

The third question of principle examined during the discussions in 1966 and 1967 was raised by the European Commission of Human Rights.

As explained above, the Committee of Ministers decided in 1966 that, since the Commission is in its nature better equipped to take evidence than is the Committee of Ministers, the latter should not normally undertake such tasks but, if the need arises, should ask the Commission to do so on its behalf. However, in October 1967 the Committee of Ministers was informed that the Commission considered that it would not be able to undertake this task, since at the time when the case is before the Committee of Ministers the Commission has already transmitted its report under Article 31 of the Convention and is therefore *functus officio.* How, then, was the Committee of Ministers to proceed if it became necessary for it to examine a case in detail by considering memorials and perhaps by hearing witnesses? By the end of 1967 this had ceased to be an academic question, because the governments of Denmark, Norway, Sweden and the Netherlands had brought a case against the government of Greece which was then under examination by the Commission and was likely to come before the Committee of Ministers in due course.

In these circumstances the Committee of Experts suggested to the Committee of Ministers that there were the following possibilities: (a) to conclude a protocol to the Convention conferring on the Commission the power to undertake such tasks on behalf of the Committee of Ministers; (b) the Committee of Ministers could take evidence, etc, in plenary session (possibly with alternate members) or appoint a sub-committee for the purpose; (c) under Article 17 of the Statute the Committee of Ministers may set up advisory and technical committees for specific purposes; it could therefore take advantage of this provision when exercising its functions under the Convention on Human Rights.

The Ministers examined these suggestions in October 1967. They decided not to adopt the first of the three possibilities but to leave the choice between the other two open for a decision *ad hoc* should the need arise.

The decisions of the Committee of Ministers on the three questions of principle explained above were incorporated in the rules at the end of 1967.[22] Since by this time the rules had been discussed and adopted at five separate meetings of the Committee of Ministers over a period of years running from 1959 to 1967, with the result that there was little logical arrangement and certain minor inconsistencies, a restatement was produced in a more logical form, with a commentary set out in an appendix. This revised version, which was approved in June 1969, is known as 'the Rules of the Committee of Ministers for the application of Article 32 of the European Convention on Human Rights'.[23]

How has the system thus established worked in practice? When one comes to answer this question one finds that the Committee of Ministers has, in the great majority of cases with which it has had to deal, been singularly fortunate in having its task facilitated by the preliminary work of the Commission and, in some cases, by other circumstances.

By the end of 1974 the Committee of Ministers had taken seventeen decisions under Article 32 of the Convention. These decisions may be grouped into four categories.

In nine cases the Committee of Ministers was able simply to endorse the opinion of the Commission that no violation had occurred.[24]

A second group is constituted by cases in which there was a violation at the time when the application was filed but action had been taken to remedy the violation before the date at which the Committee of Ministers was called upon to take its decision. The best known examples are *Pataki and Dunshirn* v. *Austria, Glaser*

et al. v. *Austria* and *Plischke* v. *Austria,* which related to the
Austrian Code of Criminal Procedure and have been summarised
above.[25] Since Austria had not only amended the Code of Criminal
Procedure but also granted the right to a new hearing to persons
whose appeals had been rejected under the procedure previously in
force and whose applications had been declared admissible by the
European Commission, the Committee of Ministers was able to
decide that there had been a violation of the Convention but that
the necessary steps had been taken to remedy it; the Committee
went on to express its satisfaction that Austria had thus put its
legislation into conformity with the requirements of the Convention.[26]

In those cases the remedial action had been taken while they
were still before the Commission. In the *Second vagrancy case
against Belgium* the Commission was of opinion that the detention
of four vagrants had constituted a violation of Article 5(4) of the
Convention in that they had no right of appeal against the order for
their detention. (The same question arose in the *First vagrancy case*
which had been referred to the Court.[27]) After the Commission had
transmitted its report to the Committee of Ministers the Belgian
law was amended in August 1971 and the Committee of Ministers
was able in October 1972 to express its satisfaction that the necessary remedial action had been taken.[28] A broadly similar situation
arose in one of the 'Belgian linguistic cases': *Inhabitants of Les
Fourons* v. *Belgium.*[29]

The third group was constituted by the two cases brought by
Greece v. *the United Kingdom* in 1956 and 1957 relating to the
situation in Cyprus while that island was still a British colony.
They have been summarised above in Chapter IV, section 6.[30] What
is relevant in the present context is that after the report of the
Commission on the first case (application 176/56) had been transmitted to the Committee of Ministers a political settlement of the
Cyprus problem was reached (even if it was not to prove permanent)
by the agreements concluded in Zurich and London in 1959, with
the result that the Greek and United Kingdom governments jointly
proposed to the Committee of Ministers that no further action was
called for. The Committee of Ministers took a formal decision in
this sense on 20 April 1959.[31] As regards the second case (application
299/57), a similar request was made to the Commission after it
had declared the application partially admissible and while it was
engaged on the procedure of establishing the facts. The Commission
was careful to point out that the withdrawal of an application con-

cerned the Commission as well as the parties, and it required to be satisfied 'that the termination of the proceedings was calculated to serve, and not to defeat, the purposes of the Convention'. Having satisfied itself on this point, the Commission decided to terminate the proceedings on this application without judging the merits, and so reported to the Committee of Ministers on 16 July 1959. On 14 December 1959 the Committee of Ministers, having considered this report, decided that no further action was called for.[32]

In both these cases, therefore one may say that there was in effect a friendly settlement – even though it was not a friendly settlement within the meaning of Article 28 of the Convention – and the Committee of Ministers was spared the awkward task of taking a decision on the merits.

The fourth type of situation is illustrated by the only case in which the Committee of Ministers, by the end of 1974, was called upon to take a decision to the effect that a Contracting Party was guilty of violating the Convention. This was the *Greek case*, the substance of which has also been explained above.[33]

Consideration of the *Greek case* was complicated by the fact that two parallel procedures had been pursued in the Council of Europe at the same time. On the one hand there was the case brought before the Commission of Human Rights under Article 24 of the Convention; on the other, the Consultative Assembly of the Council of Europe, basing itself on certain articles of the Statute, had recommended that the Committee of Ministers should expel the Greek government from the organisation. The relevant provisions were Article 3, which requires that every member must respect the rule of law and ensure the observance of human rights and fundamental freedoms, and Article 8, the sense of which is that a State which has seriously violated Article 3 may be suspended from membership. While the proceedings under Article 24 of the Convention were continuing before the Commission – and quite understandably they took some time, slightly more than two years – the Assembly considered that, irrespective of the result of those proceedings, there was a strong case for holding that the Greek government had violated Article 3 of the Statute and that the Committee of Ministers should therefore act under Article 8 without waiting for the result of the proceedings before the Commission of Human Rights. A recommendation was addressed to the Committee of Ministers in this sense in January 1969.[34] When the Ministers met in London for their forty-fourth session in May 1969 strong pressure was put upon them both by parliamentarians and by several governments to the effect that they should act accordingly. Knowing that the report of the Commission was nearly ready, they promised the decision at their next session.[35]

This was held in Paris on 12 December 1969. The Commission's report had been sent to governments on 18 November; its contents were therefore known to the Ministers – the Report expressed the opinion that the Greek government had violated ten articles of the Convention – even though it was not formally on the agenda of the meeting, because Article 32 of the Convention provides that a period of three months shall elapse, during which the case may be referred to the Court, before the Ministers take a decision on the case.

In accordance with the promise made in the previous May the Ministers in December 1969 discussed the situation in Greece and the question whether that country could remain a member of the organisation. At a dramatic meeting, during which a draft resolution for the suspension of Greece circulated among the delegations and received a wide measure of support, the Greek Foreign Minister announced the decision of his government to withdraw from the Council of Europe and to denounce the Convention on Human Rights.[36] However, the denunciation of the Convention would take effect only after the expiry of a period of six months and the denunciation of the Statute at the end of the following year; moreover, as regards the Convention on Human Rights, Article 65(2) makes it quite clear that denunciation does not affect any duties or obligations arising out of events which may have occurred before the denunciation becomes effective. At the same session in December the Committee of Ministers adopted a resolution in which they took note of the Greek declarations and drew the conclusion that Greece would cease to participate in the work of the Council of Europe immediately.

However, the Committee of Ministers was still required by Article 32 of the Convention on Human Rights to take a decision on the report of the Commission on the case brought by the three Scandinavian governments and the Netherlands. This they proceeded to do at their next session in April 1970. They endorsed the opinion of the Commission and decided that Greece had violated ten articles of the Convention on Human Rights; at the same time they expressed the hope that democratic liberties would be restored in Greece in the near future, that she would then resume her membership of the Council of Europe, and they decided to 'follow developments in Greece in this respect'.[37]

There was one procedural problem that arose during these discussions which is relevant to the subject matter of this chapter. The question was this: did the Greek government have the right to take part in the deliberations of the Committee of Ministers during the early months of 1970, when the Committee would discuss the report of the Commission of Human Rights on the Greek case? Normally there would have been no doubt that the government did have this right, because the notice of denunciation of the Convention deposited in December 1969 took effect only in June 1970. However, the terms of that notice and of the denunciation of the Statute were such as to indicate that the Greek government did not wish to play any further part in the work of the Council of Europe, and in January 1970 the Committee of Ministers reached the conclusion that there had been a *de facto* suspension of Greece from the Council of Europe.[38] In these circumstances the Ministers concluded that Greece no longer had the right to participate in the deliberations of the Committee of Ministers.[39] Whether this decision of the Committee of Ministers was justified is very doubtful. Politically convenient it may have been, but it cannot be supported as legally correct. The basis for continuing the proceedings against the Greek government after it had denounced the Convention was Article 65, the tenor of which has been already cited. The effect of this article is that a Contracting Party is still subject to the obligations which it has accepted under the Convention as regards events which occurred before the date when its notice of denunciation takes effect. But the Convention accords rights as well as imposing obligations; and one of those rights is that of taking part in the proceedings of the Committee of Ministers when it takes a decision in accordance with the provisions of Article 32. This right is accorded even to States which are members of the Council of Europe but which have not ratified the Convention, because Rule 2 of the rules adopted by the Committee of Ministers for the application of Article 32 of the Convention states:

> The representative of any Member State on the Committee of Ministers shall be fully qualified to take part in exercisng the functions and powers set forth in Article 32 of the Convention, even if that State has not yet ratified the Convention.

A fortiori a State which has ratified the Convention and is still subject to the obligations resulting therefrom, even though it has given a notice of denunciation which has not yet taken effect, is 'fully qualified to take part in exercising the functions and powers set forth in Article 32 of the Convention'. The decision to the contrary taken in the early months of 1970 in relation to Greece had no practical effect, because the Greeks themselves refused to take part in the proceedings; but it may be hoped that the decision will not be invoked as a precedent in the future.

We can thus conclude this section by recognising that much effort has been expended on working out a number of Rules of Procedure to guide the Committee of Ministers of the Council of Europe when it is called upon to discharge its functions under Article 32 of the Convention. These rules, though less detailed than the secretariat of the Council of Europe had suggested, are likely to prove adequate to cover the greater number of situations which are likely to arise. It must be recognised, however, that they are restrictive – some would say unduly restrictive – as regards the possibility of obtaining the views of an individual applicant on the report of the Commission when his case is under examination by the Committee of Ministers – a situation for which, *mutatis mutandis*, the Commission and the Court have worked out a more satisfactory procedure to be followed when a case is referred to the Court. Secondly it must be observed that no rules have been settled to regulate the procedure to be followed if it becomes necessary to take evidence during the consideration of a case by the Committee of Ministers.

To summarise, during a period of twenty years the Committee was called upon to exercise its powers under Article 32 of the Convention in relation to thirty cases, fourteen of which had been joined together as one. On only one occasion – the *Greek case* – was the Committee led to decide that a government was responsible for a continuing violation; and that government had already announced its intention of leaving the organisation and had denounced the Convention. In several cases – those involving the Austrian Code of Criminal Procedure and the second Belgian 'Vagrancy case' – there had been a violation but the government concerned had taken the necessary remedial measures before the Committee of Ministers was seized of the matter. In the majority of cases referred to the Ministers they were able simply to endorse the opinion of the Commission that no violation had occurred.

4. SUPERVISORY FUNCTIONS OF THE COMMITTEE OF MINISTERS

As explained at the end of Chapter V, section 3, the Committee of

Ministers also has the task of supervising the execution of the judgements of the Court. This results from Article 54 of the Convention:

> The judgement of the Court shall be transmitted to the Committee of Ministers which shall supervise its execution.

which follows immediately after the undertaking contained in Article 53:

> The High Contracting Parties undertake to abide by the decision of the Court in any case to which they are parties.

Moreover, as we have seen in section 3 of Chapter V, the Court not only pronounces judgement on the substance of a case submitted to it but may also, in certain circumstances, 'afford just satisfaction to the injured party'. The duty of supervision therefore relates both to judgements on the merits and to awards of damages.

The provisions of Articles 53 and 54 of the European Convention recall those of Article 94 of the UN Charter. In paragraph 1 of Article 94 each member 'undertakes to comply with the decision of the International Court of Justice in any case to which it is a party'; while the second paragraph permits one party to have recourse to the Security Council if the other party fails to comply with the judgement – as the United Kingdom did in the Corfu Channel case. The Security Council 'may, if it deems necessary, make recommendations or *decide upon measures to be taken* to give effect to the judgment'.

The American Convention on Human Rights adopts yet a different procedure. Article 65 of the convention requires the court to submit to the General Assembly of the Organisation of American States an annual report on its work during the previous year. This article continues that the report 'shall specify, in particular, the cases in which a State has not complied with its judgments and make the pertinent recommendations'.[40]

Once more, therefore, it appears that the necessary provisions have been written into the European Convention to give the needed authority to the judgements of the Court, even though Article 54 of the Convention is less far-reaching than Article 94 of the Charter, and there is nothing comparable to Article 187 of the EEC treaty which makes the judgements of the Court of Justice directly enforceable.

Again, one is led to ask: how has this system worked in practice? In fact the number of judgements of which the Committee of Ministers has been called upon to supervise the execution is rather small.

The first of these was the judgement of the Court in the *Case relating to certain aspects of the laws on the use of languages in education in Belgium* of 23 July 1968. This decision was immediately transmitted to the Committee of Ministers. It was only in October 1972 that the action taken by the Committee of Ministers was published. This was to the effect that the 'Committee, in virtue of its obligations under Article 54 of the European Convention on Human Rights, took note of the measures taken by Belgium, in accordance with Article 53, in the context of its constitutional reform, which were carried into effect in the new legislation introduced in Belgium'.[41] It will be observed that this decision does not record any expression of opinion by the Committee of Ministers on the substance of the issue (i.e. whether the new legislation effectively remedied the violation). The Committee merely 'took note' of the measures taken by Belgium.

In 1968 and 1969 four judgements of the Court were transmitted to the Committee of Ministers relating to cases about prolonged detention on remand. In the *Neumeister case* against Austria the Court decided on 27 June 1968 that there had been a violation of the Convention,[42] and the judgement was transmitted to the Committee of Ministers with a view to the application of Article 54. Nothing further was published to show what action the Committee of Ministers took thereon. However, in 1972 Neumeister made a further application to the Commission asking that the Court should award 'just satisfaction' under Article 50 of the Convention, and in May 1974 the Court awarded his costs in the case. These were duly paid and the matter was thus closed.

As regards the *Stögmüller case*, also against Austria, the Court held in November 1969 that there was a violation of the Covention by Austria,[43] and the judgement was duly transmitted to the Committee of Ministers. No information has been published about any action taken by the Committee of Ministers on this judgement.

Two other judgements of the Court given at about the same time and also relating to the question of detention on remand raised no problems. These were the judgements in the *Wemhoff case* against the Federal Republic of Germany[44] and the *Matznetter case* against Austria.[45] In both cases the Court held that there had been no violation of the Convention, so that no action was called for on the part of the Committee of Ministers.

Another case which posed no problem for the Committee was the *First vagrancy case* against Belgium.[46] This raised the same problem concerning the right to appeal against an order for detention which arose in the *Second vagrancy case* mentioned in the previous section; the difference was that the first case was referred to the Court for decision, so that the task of the Committee was to supervise the execution of the judgement of the Court under Article 54, instead of taking a decision itself under Article 32. In fact, since Belgium had already amended the law which the Court had held to be in violation of the Convention, the Committee of Ministers took note of the new law and expressed satisfaction at the action taken by Belgium to put its law into conformity with the Convention.[47]

Similarly the Committee of Ministers had no difficulty with the *Delcourt case*, also against Belgium. The judgement of the Court of 17 January 1970 having held that there was no violation,[48] no action on the part of the Committee of Ministers was called for.

The *Ringeisen case* was more difficult. In its judgement of 16 July 1971 the Court held that there had been a violation of the Convention by Austria by reason of the prolonged detention of the applicant pending trial; at the same time the Court reserved for Mr Ringeisen the right to apply for 'just satisfaction' under Article 50.[49] Such an application was in fact made, so that no action by the Committee of Ministers was required as regards the first judgement.

In a second judgement of 22 June 1972 the Court awarded to the applicant 'compensation in the sum of 20,000 German marks to be paid by the Republic of Austria';[50] it also transmitted this judgement to the Committee of Ministers. At the same time the Court recognised that a problem might arise by reason of the bankruptcy proceedings against Ringeisen in Austria. Should the money be paid directly to Ringeisen, who was now living in Germany, or could it be claimed by the trusteee in bankruptcy for the purpose of making an additional payment to the creditors? The Court considered that it could leave this point 'à la sagesse des autorités autrichiennes'. The Austrian government in fact deposited the sum of money with the Regional Court in Vienna, since several of the creditors laid claim to it, and left it to the Austrian courts to decide on the priorities. The Committee of Ministers was therefore confronted with a difficult task in 'supervising the execution of the judgement of the Court'. It decided to advise Ringeisen to make an application to the Regional Court in Vienna.

This Ringeisen refused to do, arguing that the European Court had intended that the money should be paid to him personally, without attachment, but that his rights to it would be foreclosed if he submitted to the jurisdiction of the Regional Court and the decision went against him. He therefore asked the Commission to request the interpretation of the judgement, in accordance with Rule 53 of the Rules of Court. The Committee of Ministers therefore again postponed action pending the outcome of this new *démarche*.

The Commission complied with Ringeisen's request in December 1972, and the Court in a further judgement of 23 June 1973 interpreted its earlier decision of the previous year in the sense claimed by Ringeisen, that is to say that the sum of DM20,000 awarded to him as 'just satisfaction' under Article 50 of the Convention should be paid to him personally, in Germany, free from attachment.[51] When the Committee of Ministers came to consider the matter under Article 54 of the Convention in October of the same year it was informed that the money had been paid to Ringeisen and its mission was thus accomplished.

A problem of procedure arose during the Ringeisen case when the applicant sent a communication to the Committee of Ministers about the non-payment of the damages which had been awarded to him. As explained in the previous section, the Committee of Ministers has decided that, when it is exercising its functions under Article 32 of the Convention unsolicited communications from an individual applicant may not be distributed to the Committee of Ministers. By contrast, during the consideration of the Ringeisen case it decided that such communications may be distributed and considered by the Committee when it is exercising its functions of supervision under Article 54 of the Convention in relation to a judgement of the Court awarding damages under Article 50.[52] This decision is to be welcomed as a modest step in the right direction.

The action taken by the Committee of Ministers in application of Article 54 of the Convention down to the end of 1974 may therefore be summarised as follows:

1. In three cases (*Wemhoff*, *Matznetter*, *Delcourt*) the Committee of Ministers was able simply to take note of the judgements of the Court to the effect that there was no violation.[53]

2. In the *First vagrancy case* the Court had held that there was a violation of the Convention, but the law in question was changed before the Committee of Ministers was called upon to act under Article 54, and the Committee was therefore able to 'express its satisfaction' at the action taken by Belgium to put its law into conformity with the Convention.

3. In the *Belgian linguistic case* four years elapsed before the law

was changed, and the Committee of Ministers simply 'took note' of the measures taken by Belgium without expressing any opinion on the substance of the matter.

4. In the *Ringeisen case* the Committee of Ministers was able finally to take note that the Austrian government had complied with the judgement of the Court awarding damages to the applicant after the interpretation of that judgement on 23 June 1973.

5. There are two cases – *Neumeister* and *Stögmüller* – where action by the Committee of Ministers appears to have been in suspense for several years, though the Neumeister case was finally settled by the Court's award of costs in May 1974.

It appears, therefore, that when the Committee of Ministers has undertaken the task of supervising the execution of the judgements of the Court there have been only three cases when the Committee was confronted with a judgement clearly holding that there was a violation with regard to which no remedial action had been taken. In the *Belgian linguistic case* the matter was postponed for four years, until action to amend the legislation in question was finally taken. In the two Austrian cases about detention on remand the postponement of any action for several years without explanation inevitably raises the question whether the system is functioning satisfactorily.

There are two separate observations to be made in this connection, and perhaps two lessons to be learnt from this experience. The first is that the obligation imposed on the Committee of Ministers by Article 54 is in some circumstances extremely difficult and delicate to discharge. If the Court holds in its judgement that a certain provision of national legislation is not in conformity with the Convention, and if the legislation in question is then changed, it may be quite simple to decide that the violation has been remedied (as in the *First vagrancy case*) but it may be far from simple, and may involve difficult legal issues. Opinion may be divided among lawyers in the country concerned as to whether the new law brings the national legislation into conformity with the Convention and effectively remedies the violation which the Court has found. How is the Committee of Ministers to judge such a difficult legal problem?

The answer, of course, is that the Committee of Ministers is not well qualified to do so. If in the course of exercising its functions under Article 54 the Committee has to decide a difficult legal issue it should be able to obtain an opinion from a qualified legal body. One possibility, in theory, would be to ask for the opinion of the

Court; but the terms of the Second Protocol are not such as to apply in the circumstances under consideration. We therefore find ourselves confronted with another *lacuna* in the Convention: the Committee of Ministers needs an expert legal opinion, but no provision has been made to permit it to obtain one. Consideration should therefore be given to the idea of instituting a procedure – perhaps by the conclusion of a further protocol to the Convention – which would permit the Committee of Ministers to ask the opinion of the Court on any problem of a legal character which the Committee needs to decide when it is exercising its functions under Article 54 of the Convention.

The second observation is of a different nature and relates to a situation where the Court has found a violation of the Convention but has not made an award of damages under Article 50. The argument is sometimes advanced that in such cases the only further action which may reasonably be expected is a request for 'just satisfaction' under Article 50, and that if the applicant does not make such a request no further action is necessary on the part of the Committee of Ministers. It was perhaps with this argument in mind that the Court on 8 November 1972 added a new paragraph 3 to Rule 50 of the Rules of Court, to the effect that a chamber, if it finds that there is a breach of the Convention, shall either give in the same judgement a decision on the application of Article 50 or reserve that question for later determination if it is not yet ready for decision.

Acceptance of this argument, it is believed, would have the result of further weakening the system of international control which has already shown itself to be less effective in practice than the authors of the Convention no doubt intended. If a violation occurs, the award of damages by the Court is not the only possible form of 'satisfaction' for the injured party. Reparation may be made by the national authorities – for example, in appropriate cases, by the reduction of a prison sentence, by an *ex gratia* payment or even by a pardon. Other remedial measures may be called for, such as increasing the number of examining magistrates (if undue delay in bringing an accused person to trial is due to insufficiency of available staff) or the transfer to another post or dismissal of an incompetent official. Many other hypotheses can be evisaged. The basic point is that if the Court has held that a violation has occurred it is necessary that the government concerned should take whatever remedial measures are necessary or make whatever reparation is possible – independently of the question whether or not the applicant applies for damages under Article 50 of the Convention. It is the function of the Committee of Ministers to see that this is done; it is before the Committee of Ministers that the respondent government should explain how it has fulfilled its obligation under Article 53 of the Convention 'to abide by the decision of the Court'. An effective system of implementation therefore requires positive action by the Committee of Ministers under Article 54 whenever a decision of violation of the Court is communicated to the Committee for supervision of its execution, whether or not that judgement contains an order for the payment of compensation.

The Statute of the Council of Europe has placed in the hands of the Committee of Ministers a powerful sanction in the form of suspension from membership (Article 8). We may hope that it will never be necessary for the Committee to use it. But so long as this sanction exists it is the ultimate basis of the Committee's powers both under Article 32 and under Article 54 of the Convention. To date the Committee has been very prudent in the exercise of those powers; for the future we must hope that it will use them more effectively and thus come up to the expectations of the authors both of the Convention and of the Statute.

As indicated at the beginning of this chapter, the Committee of Ministers also has an important role to play under the Statute of the Council of Europe in the 'promotion' or 'further realisation' of human rights and fundamental freedoms – quite apart from the specific functions conferred on it by the Convention on Human Rights which have been examined in the present chapter. This further role will be discussed in Chapter VIII below.

NOTES

1 For the structure and functions of the Committee of Ministers under the Statute of the Council of Europe see A. H. Robertson, *The Council of Europe*, second edition, 1961, pp. 24–40, and *Manual of the Council of Europe*, 1970, Chapter III.

2 Nos. 1–72 may be found in *European Conventions and Agreements*, two volumes, published by the Council of Europe in 1971 and 1972. A list as at 31 December 1969 is given in *Manual of the Council of Europe*, pp. 313–5.

3 Chapter IV, section 1.

4 Chapter V, section 1.

5 Letter from the chairman of the Committee of Ministers to the President of the Assembly of 15 December 1958, *Documents of the Assembly*, 1958, Document 918.

6 *Yearbook of the Convention*, Vol. I, pp. 48–9.

7 *Ibid.*, pp. 49–50.

8 *Resolution (56)16* of the Committee of Ministers, Supplementary report of

the Committee of Ministers, *Documents of the Assembly*, 1957, Document 624.
9 Resolution 103, *Texts adopted by the Assembly*, October 1956.
10 *Documents of the Assembly*, 1957, Document 624.
11 Rule 14 of the Commission's Rules of Procedure provide that the duties of the secretariat of the Commission shall be laid down by the President in agreement with the Secretary General. See further Chapter IV, section 1.
12 For consideration of the question whether the Commission is an 'organ of the Council of Europe' see Chapter IV, section 1, *in fine*.
13 The provision in Article 32(1) that the Committee of Ministers 'shall decide by a majority of two-thirds of the members entitled to sit on the Committee' means that twelve votes are required (out of eighteen) for a valid decision. But what is the position if there is not a two-thirds majority? It may happen that the voting in the Committee of Ministers gives the result of, for example, ten votes to eight or ten to five with three abstentions. If the report of the Commission expresses the opinion that there has been a violation, and a simple majority of the Committee of Ministers takes the same view, it cannot be said that the Committee has decided that there was a violation, because there is not a two-thirds majority as required by the Convention. But equally, it is unrealistic to say that the Committee has decided that there is no violation when the majority of the members think that there is. Should this situation arise in practice, it would seem that the only possible conclusion (regrettable as it may be) is that the Committee of Ministers has failed to act as required by the Convention.
14 *Yearbook* IV, 1961, p. 14.
15 *Yearbook* VI, 1963, p. 742.
16 *Ibid.*, p. 800.
17 *Yearbook* VIII, 1965, p. 8.
18 *Yearbook* IX, 1966, p. 72.
19 Judgement of the Court of 14 November 1960 on the preliminary objections and questions of procedure, p. 14. *Yearbook* III, 1960, p. 492, at p. 512.
20 This question is discussed in greater detail in Chapter V, section 3.
21 Nielsen *v.* Denmark, *Yearbook* IV, 1961, p. 590.
22 *Yearbook* X, 1967, p. 4.
23 *Yearbook* XII, 1969, pp. 12–18.
24 Nielsen *v.* Denmark (343/57), *Yearbook* IV, p. 590; Ofner and Hopfinger *v.* Austria (524/59 and 617/59), *Yearbook* VI, p. 708; Austria *v.* Italy (788/60), *Yearbook* VI, p. 796; Grandrath *v.* Federal Republic of Germany (2299/64), *Yearbook* X, p. 694; Zeidler-Kornmann *v.* Federal Republic of Germany (2686/65), *Yearbook* XI, p. 1020; Köplinger *v.* Austria (1850/63), *Yearbook* XII, p. 438; Soltikow *v.* Federal Republic of Germany (2257/64), *Yearbook* XIV, p. 868; Jentzsch *v.* Federal Republic of Germany (2604/65), *Yearbook* XIV, p. 876; Scheichelbauer *v.* Austria (2645/65), *Yearbook* XIV, p. 902. A similar situation arose in *Kamma* v. *the Netherlands*, discussed in Chapter III, under Article 18.
25 In Chapter II, *sub* Article 6.
26 *Yearbook* VI, p. 736; VII, p. 434; VIII, p. 464.
27 *Yearbook* XIV, p. 788.
28 Decision of 16 October 1972, *Yearbook* XV, p. 694.
29 Resolution DH(74)1, 'Stocktaking', October 1975, p. 14.
30 *Supra*, pp. 173–4.
31 *Yearbook* II, 1958–59, pp. 174–8 and 186.
32 *Ibid.*, pp. 178–80 and 196.
33 See Chapter II, *sub* Article 3, and Chapter IV, section 6. The proceedings in the Greek case are contained in a separate volume, XII *bis*, of the *Yearbook of the Convention*.
34 Recommendation 547, *Texts adopted*, January 1969, *Yearbook* XII, 1969, p. 126; see also Recommendation 569, *Texts adopted*, October 1969, *ibid.*, p. 128.
35 Resolution (69)18 of the Committee of Ministers, *Yearbook* XII, p. 130.

36 *Ibid.*, pp. 78–84.
37 Resolution DH(70)1, *Yearbook* XII, Part 2 (XII *bis*), pp. 511–14. In November 1974 the committee decided (Resolution DH(74)2 that no further action was necessary in this respect, as Greece had been readmitted as a member of the Council of Europe.
38 Communication of the Committee of Ministers to the Assembly, 2 April 1970, Document 2735, p. 1.
39 Reply by the chairman of the Committee of Ministers to a question by Mr Max van der Stoel, *Official Report*, 29 January 1970, item 4, p. 1051.
40 *Human Rights in the World*, pp. 135 and 269. This section is partly based on a paper presented at a colloquy organised by the Faculty of Law of the University of Grenoble in January 1973 on 'L'efficacité des mécanismes juridictionnels de protection des personnes privées dans le cadre européen'. The proceedings are published in *Human Rights Journal*, Vol. VI, 1973, pp. 603 ff.
41 Communication of the Committee of Ministers to the Consultative Assembly of 3 October 1972, *Documents of the Assembly*, 1972, Document 3170; *Yearbook* XV, pp. 62–4.
42 *Yearbook* XI, 1968, p. 812.
43 *Yearbook* XII, 1969, p. 364.
44 Judgement of 27 June 1968, *Yearbook* XI, p. 796.
45 Judgement of 1 November 1969, *Yearbook* XII, p. 406.
46 Judgement of 18 June 1971, *Yearbook* XIV, p. 788.
47 Communication of the Committee of Ministers to the Consultative Assembly, *Documents of the Assembly*, January 1972, Document 3067 Add.; *Yearbook* XV, 1972, p. 62.
48 Judgement of 17 January 1972, *Yearbook* XIII, p. 1100.
49 *Yearbook* XIV, 1971, p. 838, at p. 864.
50 *Yearbook* XV, 1972, p. 678.
51 *Publications of the Court*, Series A, judgement of 23 June 1973; *Yearbook* XVI, p. 468.
52 *Yearbook* XV, p. 64.
53 It does not appear that the judgements of the Court in the Lawless case (1961) and the De Becker case (1962) were ever officially communicated to the Committee of Ministers. In fact no action by the Committee was called for in those cases.

CHAPTER VII

THE GENERAL PROVISIONS OF THE CONVENTION

Section V of the Convention consists of Articles 57 to 66, which constitute the general provisions; some of them are of greater interest than is often the case in the concluding articles to a treaty.

Article 57 is of particular importance. It provides that 'on receipt of a request from the Secretary General of the Council of Europe, any High Contracting Party shall furnish an explanation of the manner in which its internal law ensures the effective implementation of any of the provisions of this Convention'. This places in the hands of the Secretary General a powerful instrument, namely the right to ask for explanations from a High Contracting Party as to the way it implements the Convention; not only does the Secretary General have the right to enquire, but also the State concerned has the obligation to 'furnish an explanation'.

Under the Statute of the Council of Europe the powers of the Secretary General are rather limited. The Charter of the United Nations confers on the secretariat the status of one of the principal organs of the United Nations.[1] Its European counterpart has a more humble position; under Articles 36 and 37 of the Statute the Secretary General appoints the members of the secretariat, furnishes such secretariat services as may be required and 'is responsible to the Committee of Ministers for the work of the Secretariat.' The Consultative Assembly, in one of its many attempts to strengthen the machinery of the Council of Europe, has recommended that the Secretary General should be recognised as an 'organ of the Council', but this the Committee of Ministers has refused.[2] In reply to the question which pinpoints the issue so nicely – 'Is the Secretary General a Secretary or a General?'[3] it must be admitted that the powers conferred by the Statute place him much nearer to the first category than to the second.[4] It is therefore only the more surprising that the Convention on Human Rights should confer on him this power of calling on governments to furnish explanations as to the way in which they comply with their international obligations.

It appears from the *travaux préparatoires*[5] that at one stage during the negotiation of the treaty in 1950 a proposal was made not to create a Commission and Court of Human Rights (as the Assembly had proposed) but to limit the 'measures of implementation' to a right of enquiry by the Secretary General. The first part of this proposal was rejected, but the second was retained and resulted in Article 57. While this does place in the hands of the Secretary General a potentially powerful weapon, it also places him in a delicate situation. The Convention is silent as to the circumstances in which he should exercise this power, and he may find himself in something of a dilemma: if he makes an enquiry when he has no reason to suppose that the internal law of a Contracting Party is deficient in securing the effective implementation of human rights, then the operation may be pointless; on the other hand, if he makes an enquiry when there is reason to suspect that the internal law is deficient in this respect, then he risks accusations of an unfriendly action, possibly amounting to interference, from one (or more) of the governments before which he is responsible.

For more than ten years after the entry into force of the Convention the Secretary General's powers under Article 57 were never exercised. In 1964 the fourth Secretary General, Mr Peter Smithers, decided to use them for the first time. In doing so, and in order to avoid any impression that his action was directed against any particular member State, he asked *all* Contracting Parties to explain how their internal law ensured the effective implementation of *all* the normative provisions of the Convention and the First Protocol. The results of this enquiry were extremely interesting – and remarkably varied. All Contracting Parties replied in due course, and their replies varied from a few lines stating that the rights and freedoms set out in the Convention and First Protocol were protected by the national constitution (Iceland) to a fifty-page memorandum (United Kingdom) explaining the relevant provisions of the common law and of statute law, to which were annexed several dozen statutes, including Magna Carta and others in force for more than three centuries. The replies were communicated to the Commission and Court of Human Rights and substantial extracts were transmitted for information to the Consultative Assembly.[6] After the matter had been discussed in the Legal Affairs Committee, the Assembly adopted its *Resolution 367 (1968)* expressing its satisfaction at the action taken by the Secretary General and the hope that further and more detailed use would be made in future of the Article 57 procedure.[7]

A second enquiry was made by the fifth Secretary General, Mr Lujo Toncic, in 1972. This related to a much more specific point, namely the way in which the internal law of the Contracting Parties complies with the requirement of Article 5(5) of the Convention that 'everyone who has been the victim of arrest or detention in contravention of the provisions of this article shall have an enforceable right to compensation'. Once again the replies were communicated to the Commission and Court of Human Rights and, for information, to the Consultative Assembly, which did not consider the replies altogether satisfactory.[8] It appeared from this exercise that, if there is a certain value in the use of the powers conferred on the Secretary General by Article 57, the procedure needs to be amplified in certain respects. Certainly it is useful to obtain information about the manner in which national law ensures the implementation of human rights; but it would be more useful to institute a procedure whereby a critical examination can be effected of the information furnished by the governments and any necessary recommendations made to them if the provisions of national law are not effective or do not altogether correspond to the requirements of the Convention. Its absence constitutes a lacuna which needs to be filled.

Article 58 of the Convention provides that the expenses of the Commission and the Court shall be borne by the Council of Europe. This means in practice that they are determined by the Committee of Ministers, as explained in Chapter VI, section 1.

Article 59 deals with the privileges and immunities to which the members of the Commission and the Court shall be entitled for the unhampered discharge of their functions; it provides that they shall be entitled to the privileges and immunities provided for in Article 40 of the Statute of the Council of Europe and in the agreements made thereunder. Article 40 of the Statute contains general provisions relating to the officials of the organisation; it was supplemented by the *General Agreement on Privileges and Immunities of the Council of Europe*, signed in Paris on 2 September 1949.[9] A separate protocol to this agreement was concluded on 15 December 1956 relating to the privileges and immunities of members of the Commission;[10] another on 16 December 1961 for the Court.[11] A further protocol relating to immunities of agents, counsel and witnesses was under discussion at one time, but, as explained in Chapter I, section 3, it was finally decided to deal with this matter in a separate *Agreement relating to Persons participating in Proceedings of the European Commission and Court of Human Rights*, the substance of which is discussed in section 4 of Chapter IV.

Article 60 of the Convention then provides that its provisions shall not be construed in any way as limiting, or derogating from, any of the rights and freedoms which may be ensured under the national law of any Contracting Party or under any other international agreement to which it is a party. The first part of this provision contains the answer to persons who have sometimes criticised the Convention or even (as in France) opposed ratification on the ground that some of its provisions were less favourable to the individual than existing rules of national law. In cases where this is true (and there are some) the more favourable provisions will still apply. The second part of this article is relevant to the question of 'coexistence' between the European Convention and the United Nations Covenant on Civil and Political Rights. If certain provisions of the Covenant are more favourable to the individual, for example in utilising more liberal definitions of the rights and freedoms guaranteed, then any more restrictive definitions in the European Convention will not limit those other more favourable provisions.[12]

Article 61 is to the effect that nothing in the Convention shall prejudice the powers conferred on the Committee of Ministers by the Statute of the Council of Europe. This is perhaps a statement of the obvious; in any event, it is hard to see how the Convention, which confers additional functions on the Committee of Ministers, could be construed as limiting the statutory powers of the Committee in any way.

Article 62 then states that the Parties will not, except by special agreement, submit a dispute arising under the Convention to a means of settlement other than those provided for therein. It is believed that this article was inserted in the Convention in 1950 in order to preserve intact the European system of protection created thereby and prohibit reference of disputes arising thereunder to the International Court of Justice at The Hague; this was necessary because the Assembly had proposed in 1949 that reference to the International Court should be available as an alternative remedy.[13] Article 62 has perhaps now an added significance. Should it be taken to exclude the possibility of reference of a dispute arising under the European Convention to the Human Rights Committee which will be set up under the terms of the UN Covenant on Civil and Political Rights? This would seem consistent with the intention of Article 62. At the same time, it is not clear that this is its meaning, because the article provides that Parties 'will not avail themselves of treaties, conventions or declarations *in force between*

K

them', which would seem to mean 'in force between them' at the time of signature of the European Convention, i.e. in 1950. The relevance of Article 62 to the problem of 'coexistence' is therefore not clearly established.[14]

Article 63 is of particular interest; it is sometimes known as 'the colonial clause'. One of the contentious issues which arose during the course of the negotiations in 1950 was the question whether the Convention should apply to the overseas and colonial territories of the High Contracting Parties. One view held was that it should be so drafted as to apply automatically to such territories unless they were specifically excluded; the other view was that it should apply in the first place only to the metropolitan territories but be capable of extension to overseas territories by express declaration. The protagonists of the first view were anxious to secure as extensive an application of the Convention as possible, and felt that the governments were less likely to exclude the colonial territories if such exclusion involved a public declaration. The advocates of the second view maintained that certain countries, particularly the United Kingdom, could not constitutionally apply the Convention to their colonial territories without first consulting the colonial legislatures. Therefore, if extension to the colonies were automatic, it would not be possible for the governments of these countries to ratify the Convention before consulting a large number of separate legislatures to obtain their approval. Consequently the practical result of the formula proposed would be to delay the ratification of the Convention by some of the principal signatories for such period as would be necessary for these consultations to take place – which might mean a very considerable delay. Belgium, France, the Netherlands and the United Kingdom were all directly interested in this question, which, of course, had important political aspects.

The problem was referred for decision to the Committee of Ministers, which in August 1950 decided in favour of an article requiring express declarations by the High Contracting Parties before the Convention would extend to their colonial territories. This text provoked a lively discussion in the Assembly during the course of its examination of the draft Convention later in the same month, and a strong feeling was expressed by some members in favour of the prinicple of automatic extension. The Assembly inserted in its *Recommendation 24 (1950)* a paragraph calling on the Ministers to delete the 'colonial clause' which they had incorporated in their draft, which would have the effect that the Convention would apply automatically to overseas territories.[15] This question was then reconsidered by the Committee of Ministers in November, but the Assembly's proposal was not found acceptable, with the result that Article 63 remained in the final text as approved by the Ministers in August; that is to say that any State may at the time of ratification or subsequently declare that the Convention shall extend to all or any of the territories for whose international relations it is responsible.

In accordance with this provision the Danish government, in April 1953, extended the application of the Convention to Greenland, the Netherlands government in November 1955 to Surinam and the Netherlands West Indies, and the British government in October 1953 to forty-one overseas territories.[16] With the passage of time many of these overseas countries attained their independence; by 1969 a declaration by the government of the United Kingdom attached a revised list of eighteen overseas territories to which the Convention still applied.[17] Moreover the Netherlands has also extended the right of individual petition to Surinam[18] and the United Kingdom to the overseas territories to which the Convention has been extended.[19]

It was, of course, all to the good that the provisions of the European Convention should apply to nearly fifty overseas territories in various parts of the world, but it raised the problem of what would happen when those territories became independent. The metropolitan countries then cease to be responsible for their international relations and the provisions of the Convention will thus automatically cease to apply.[20] It would, however, be highly regrettable if one of the results of independence was a diminution in the protection afforded to human rights in the newly independent country. Some other means of ensuring their protection must therefore be found; and this is precisely what has happened.

Nigeria affords an interesting example. It was one of the British colonies to which the Convention applied by virtue of the declaration made on 23 October 1953. When the decision was taken to grant Nigeria independence it became necessary to ensure that human rights would continue to be protected, all the more so as one of the major problems that arose in determining its future political structure was that of the status of important minorities in the country. In 1957 the government of the United Kingdom convened a constitutional conference for Nigeria which set up a Minorities Commission to 'ascertain the facts about the fears of minorities in any part of Nigeria and to propose means of allaying these fears whether well – or ill founded'. The Minorities Commission recommended in its report that comprehensive provisions, based primarily on the European Convention, should be included in the constitution for this purpose. The conference accepted this recommendation and adopted a chapter on Fundamental Rights, which in many cases reproduced the exact text of the European Convention, and which was included in the new constitution which entered into force when Nigeria attained independence on 1 October 1960.[21]

Another case is that of *Sierra Leone*. A constitutional conference for Sierra Leone was held in April and May 1960, and agreed that fundamental rights should be included in the Constitution to be adopted on independence and that the relevant provisions should be based on those adopted by the Nigerian conference. A list of human rights and freedoms was annexed to the conference report, and again followed closely the text of the corresponding provisions of the European Convention. It was finally incorporated in the new constitution of Sierra Leone as Chapter II: Protection of the Fundamental Rights and Freedoms of the Individual.[22]

It is beyond the scope of this book to follow this matter further in any detail; it will suffice to say that the influence of the European Convention may be traced, to a greater or lesser degree, in the constitutions of Kenya, Uganda, Zambia, Mauritius, Trinidad and Tobago, Jamaica and Guyana. The same may be said of the constitution of Cyprus of 1960,[23] though the subsequent history of that island – and of some of the other countries mentioned above – has shown that the existence of liberal constitutional provisions is no guarantee against civil strife.[24]

Article 64 of the Convention deals with reservations. They are permitted, but only 'in respect of any particular provision of the Convention, to the extent that any law in force ... is not in conformity with the provision'. In that case the reservation must contain a brief statement of the law concerned. Reservations of a general character are not permitted.

A number of reservations have in fact been made. Article 2 of the First Protocol on the right of education has given rise to the largest number: five reservations, by the Federal Republic, Greece, Sweden, Turkey and the United Kingdom.[25] The most interesting reservation is perhaps that of Norway in relation to Article 9 of the Convention on freedom of thought, conscience and religion. Article 2 of the Norwegian constitution of 17 May 1814 contained an absolute ban on Jesuits, and Norway therefore only ratified the Convention subject to this limitation on the application of Article 9. A few years later the Norwegian constitution was amended in this respect, and on 4 December 1956 the reservation was withdrawn,[26] thus affording an interesting illustration of the way in which the European Convention can influence even the constitutions of the member States.

The French ratification of the Convention, deposited on 3 May 1974, was accompanied by two reservations and one declaration of interpretation. The first reservation related to Articles 5 and 6 and reserved the right to apply the existing French law concerning military discipline and military justice. The second reservation related to Article 15 of the Convention and concerned Article 16 of the French constitution of 1958, which permits the President of the Republic in certain circumstances to proclaim a state of emergency; the effect of the reservation is that if the President makes such a proclamation, then the conditions for a derogation under Article 15 of the Convention shall be considered as fulfilled. This means, in effect, that a decision by the President of the Republic cannot subsequently be questioned by the organs of the Convention. The French declaration of interpretation concerns Article 10 of the Convention on freedom of expression; it interprets this article as consistent with the French law of 10 July 1972 which grants a monopoly to the Radio-diffusion Télévision Française.[27]

Article 65 of the Convention provides for the possibility of denunciation, which may only take place five years after a State has become a Party and after six months' notice. Denunciation will not affect the obligations of the denouncing State arising out of acts performed before the denunciation becomes effective. A State which ceases to be a member of the Council of Europe will automatically cease to be a Party to the Convention.

It was in conformity with Article 65 that the Greek goverment denounced the Convention on 12 December 1969[28] – an act which was happily revoked in November 1974, after a democratic regime had been restored in Greece, and that country resumed its membership in the Council of Europe and ratified the Convention again.

Article 66 contains the arrangements about signature and ratification. Ten ratifications were necessary for the Convention to enter into force; this was achieved on 3 September 1953. It is to be noted that the Convention is only open to signature by members of the Council of Europe; in this respect it differs from the usual practice established in the conventions and agreements subsequently concluded by the members of the Council, which usually contain a clause providing that the Committee of Ministers may invite non-member States to accede. In 1962 the Consultative Assembly proposed that the Convention on Human Rights should be amended so as to permit accession in this way,[29] but the Committee of Ministers did not consider it necessary to make such an amendment.[30]

NOTES

1 Article 7 of the Charter.

2 Opinion 14/14, paragraph 39, in *Texts adopted by the Assembly*, July 1955. Communication of the Committee of Ministers of 3 April 1956, *Documents of the Assembly*, Document 48 (1956).

3 See S. M. Schwebel, *The Secretary General of the United Nations*, Cambridge, Mass., 1952.

4 There have, however, been certain developments in later years. See A. H. Robertson, *The Council of Europe*, second edition, 1961, pp. 71-3.

5 See Chapter I, n. 24.

6 Document H(67)2 of 10 January 1967.

7 *Yearbook* XI, 1968, p. 82. The resolution expressed the hope that future enquiries would be made 'on precise questions of a more limited and detailed nature, with the object of ascertaining what is the judicial or administrative practice . . . as regards the implementation of specific provisions of the Convention'.

8 The Assembly's comments were contained in *Resolution 596 (1975)*. The report of the Legal Affairs Committee (Document 3618 of 1 July 1975) showed that in six cases the national law corresponded closely to the requirements of the Convention, in six other cases this was not so, and in three cases further information was required. In the meantime the sixth Secretary General had made a further enquiry under Article 57 relating to Articles 8, 9, 10 and 11 of the Convention.

9 *European Treaty Series*, No. 2. See A. H. Robertson, *The Council of Europe*, second edition, 1961, pp. 76-8.

10 *Yearbook* I, 1955-57, p. 86. For the case of *Zoernsch* v. *Waldock and McNulty* see Chapter IV, n. 13.

11 *Yearbook* IV, 1961, p. 16. See also Chapter V, section 2.

12 On the question of 'coexistence' between the European Convention and the UN Covenant see below, Chapter VIII, section 1, and the references there given.

13 See Chapter I, section 2.

14 See reference given in n. 12, and Resolution (70)17 of the Committee of Ministers. *Yearbook* XIII, 1970, p. 72.

15 This paragraph was not the result of a proposal by the Legal Committee, whose chairman opposed it during the debate. It was adopted by a narrow majority of forty-six votes to thirty-seven. (Paragraph VII of Recommendation 24 of 25 August 1950.)

16 The list is given in *Yearbook* I, 1955-57, pp. 46-7.

17 *Yearbook* XII, 1969, p. 76.

18 *Ibid.*, p. 24.

19 *Ibid.*, pp. 26-8.

20 *Cf.* M.-A. Eissen, 'The independence of Malta and the European Convention', *British Yearbook of International Law*, 1965-66, p. 401; and 'Malawi and the European Convention', *ibid.*, 1968-9, p. 190.

21 *Yearbook* III, 1960, pp. 706–24.

22 *Yearbook* IV, 1961, p. 656.

23 *Yearbook* III, 1960, pp. 678–704.

24 On the whole question of constitutional development in the former British colonies see F. A. de Smith, *The New Commonwealth and its Constitutions*, London, 1964.

25 The texts of the reservations are published in the volume of the *Yearbook of the Convention* corresponding to the year when they were made. They may be found conveniently grouped together in the *Collected Texts* (published periodically by the Directorate of Human Rights), tenth edition, 1975, pp. 605–8.

26 *Yearbook* I, 1955–57, p. 42.

27 Council of Europe press communiqué F(74)27 of 4 May 1974. As regards the reservation relating to Article 15 see above, Chapter III, *sub* Article 15.

28 *Yearbook* XII, 1969, p. 78.

29 Recommendation 316, *Yearbook* V, 1962, p. 42.

30 *Yearbook* VI, 1963, p. 74.

CHAPTER VIII

CONCLUSIONS

On 6 May 1974 the Council of Europe celebrated its twenty-fifth anniversary. At a special ceremony to mark this occasion the Foreign Minister of Belgium, speaking as chairman of the Committee of Ministers, said: [1]

> Without any doubt there is one field of activity where the work of the Council has been most significant: I mean all that has been undertaken under the sign of human rights and fundamental freedoms. It is there that the Council of Europe has established its distinctive image.

Many other statements could be quoted to the same effect, and not only by Europeans. U Thant, speaking as Secretary General of the United Nations, said of the human rights work of the Council of Europe, in a speech to the Assembly on 3 May 1966,[2] 'You have given a most significant lead to other regions of the world, and have built on the broad initiatives of the United Nations.'

This is no reason, however, for smug complacency. While there can be no doubt that its work for human rights is the most important achievement of the Council of Europe, legitimate pride should not degenerate into self-satisfaction. If the European system for the protection of human rights is the best yet established by any international organisation, it is by no means perfect and is certainly capable of improvement. (A number of suggestions for that purpose have been made in earlier chapters of this book.) It is therefore necessary to realise that the task of the Council of Europe in the field of human rights was not finished by the conclusion of the European Convention; indeed, it never will be finished in that or any other way. This is because it is simply not possible in this imperfect world to devise any system which will be perfect and complete. Gaps will be found in any arrangements that have been established; new needs will arise as new developments occur in the organisation of society, particularly in an era of technological and political change; new measures will therefore be necessary from time to time in order to complete and perfect any system that has been instituted.[3]

1. THE PROMOTION OF HUMAN RIGHTS

This necessity for evolution was recognised when the Council of Europe was established in 1949 and when the European Convention on Human Rights was concluded in the following year. The Statute of the Council of Europe provides in its first article that the aim of achieving a greater unity between its members shall be pursued in a number of different fields (economic, social, cultural, scientific, legal and administrative) and also in the maintenance *and further realisation* of human rights and fundamental freedoms. In other words the Council is required to work not only for the protection of such rights and freedoms as they already exist (or as they existed in 1949) but also for their further development and for the realisation of further rights.[4] This was also recognised by the authors of the Convention. The Teitgen report quoted in Chapter I[5] proposed that the Convention should protect 'those rights and freedoms [which] are the common denominator of our political institutions' and that other rights 'must also, in the future, be defined and protected'. In 1950 the governments added a preamble to the Convention indicating that, in concluding this treaty, they were taking 'the first steps for the collective enforcement of certain of the rights stated in the Universal Declaration'. Clearly this implied that further steps were to follow. In the terminology currently in use in international organisations, the work of 'further realisation' or protection of additional rights is usually known as 'promotion of human rights', which requires intergovernmental action designed to secure agreement on new measures to be taken, whereas 'protection of human rights' involves judicial or quasi-judicial measures of application of standards which have already been agreed. The United Nations Commission on Human Rights is thus essentially an organ of promotion, whereas the European Commission and Court of Human Rights, since they are concerned with the application of an existing treaty, are organs of protection.[6] In the framework of the Council of Europe it has been necessary to establish another organ with the promotional function, since that is not within the competence of the Commission and the Court. They are not legislative bodies, and indeed the doctrine of separation of powers known in all democratic States would militate against their assuming legislative functions. Other machinery is therefore necessary for this purpose.

At the national level, legislation is the function of parliaments, acting whenever possible in agreement with the governments, and very often on the proposal of the governments. The Council of Europe has developed its own version of the international legislative process. Both the parliamentary and the governmental organs participate therein, but in a different way from that which obtains nationally. The proposals for new legislation usually emanate from the Consultative Assembly, having been prepared by its Legal Affairs Committee, and are then realised – or transformed into action – by the Committee of Ministers, assisted by committees of governmental experts. It has thus worked out a regular procedure by which a parliamentary committee studies what further action is required for the promotion of human rights and submits its conclusions to the Assembly; the latter addresses recommendations to the Committee of Ministers; the Ministers, if they accept the principle involved – as they have done in the past in the majority of cases – then instruct the Committee of Experts on Human Rights to draft the necessary legal texts, which then come back to the Ministers for final approval and signature. If this point is stressed in this context, it is because credit is given, quite rightly, to the Commission and Court of Human Rights for their judicial work, but insufficient credit has been given to the parliamentary committee in the Assembly and to the governmental Committee of Experts on Human Rights for the great volume of legislative work which they have done for the promotion of human rights.[7]

By making use of the procedures just described the Council of Europe has been able over the years to take a series of measures which have extended its human rights programme far beyond the 'first steps' represented by the conclusion of the Convention in 1950. Some of these measures (summarised in Chapter I, section 3) concerned the conclusion of the five Protocols to the Convention, of which the First and Fourth added seven further rights and freedoms to the original list of twelve, while the second conferred on the Court the competence to give advisory opinions and the Third and Fifth Protocols amended or completed certain provisions of the Convention of a procedural nature. Quite a separate exercise was the conclusion of the European Social Charter.[8] But that is not all. Many other proposals have been made for the 'further realisation' of human rights and fundamental freedoms, which we will attempt to summarise briefly.

These proposals have related principally to the inclusion in the system of protection of additional rights which are not included in the Convention itself or in its First or Fourth Protocols; sometimes the attempt has been made to protect additional rights by

the conclusion of further protocols and sometimes by the preparation of separate conventions or agreements or simply by the adoption
of resolutions by the Committee of Ministers. These attempts have
been sometimes, but not always, successful.

THE RIGHTS OF MINORITIES. The negative aspect of prohibiting
discrimination against minorities in the exercise of the rights
guaranteed in the Convention and its Protocols was covered by
Article 14 of the Convention, the 'non-discrimination clause'. In
1961 the Assembly sought to go further by tackling the 'positive
aspect', that is to say by ensuring to minorities the special rights
or advantages which are necessary to conserve their existing
character, such as the use of their own language, the practice of
their religion and the development of their own culture. In *Recommendation 285 (1961)* the Assembly proposed the inclusion in a
protocol to the Convention of a text based on Article 27 of the UN
Covenant on Civil and Political Rights,[9] but the Committee of
Ministers rejected the proposal.

THE RIGHT OF ASYLUM. During the same year the Assembly proposed the inclusion in a protocol of the right of asylum, which is
included in the Universal Declaration of Human Rights as Article
14 and in the constitutions of several member States. After much
discussion this led to the adoption by the Committee of Ministers
of its *Resolution (67) 14 on Asylum to Persons in danger of Persecution*,[10] which is broadly similar to Resolution 2312 (XXII) of
the General Assembly of the United Nations, adopted in December
1967. The Consultative Assembly renewed its proposal for a
protocol on this subject in 1972.

THE RIGHT OF CONSCIENTIOUS OBJECTION. The Assembly adopted
in January 1967 its *Resolution 337* containing a *Declaration on the
Right of Conscientious Objection*, and its *Recommendation 478*
asking the Committee of Ministers to incorporate the principles set
out in the declaration in a convention or in a recommendation to
governments.[11] The committee, however, decided not to act on
this proposal, apparently on the ground that a number of member
States already recognised the right of conscientious objection and
that the others were not prepared to change their legislation in this
respect.[12]. The Assembly, however, renewed its proposal in 1972.[13]

THE RIGHT OF PRIVACY. The Council of Europe has done much

work aimed at securing a better protection of the right of privacy. This includes two recommendations of the Consultative Assembly relating respectively to human rights and modern scientific and technical developments[14] and to mass communication media and human rights;[15] the organisation of a Symposium on Human Rights and Mass Communications Media at Salzbourg in 1968;[16] discussion by the sixth conference of European Ministers of Justice and at the Third International Colloquy about the European Convention on Human Rights in Brussels in 1970;[17] and several years' work by the Committee of Experts on Human Rights and by a special committee on computers and privacy. It is impossible to give an adequate summary of the results of all this,[18] but mention may be made of proposals to protect the individual against interference with his privacy resulting from modern technical devices,[19] recommendations to governments relating to the use of computers in the private and public sectors,[20] proposals to ensure the protection of privacy against interference by the mass media,[21] the organisation of a Round Table on Press Councils in Stockholm in September 1974, and a recommendation to governments on the right of reply.[22]

NE BIS IN IDEM. In 1964 the Commission of Human Rights proposed that the principle of protection against double jeopardy should be included in a protocol to the Convention;[23] their request was partly satisfied when the rule *ne bis in idem* was included in Articles 53 to 55 of the European Convention on the International Validity of Criminal Judgements.[24]

PROTECTION AGAINST DISCRIMINATION. The Council of Europe has taken several initiatives to support the work of the United Nations in this field, with particular reference to the *Convention on the Elimination of all Forms of Racial Discrimination* of 21 December 1965. The Committee of Ministers' *Resolution (68) 30* of 31 October 1968 recommended various steps which European governments should take for this purpose.[25] Other measures were adopted in support of the International Year to Combat Racism and Racial Discrimination in 1971.[26] But the Assembly's proposal for a protocol to the Convention to secure equal treatment in the enforcement of the law and prohibit discrimination as regards voting rights, access to employment, housing and access to the public service[27] was not accepted by the Committee of Ministers.[28]

THE UNITED NATIONS COVENANTS ON HUMAN RIGHTS. Another matter of common interest to the Council of Europe and the United Nations is the entry into force of the two United Nations Covenants on Economic, Social and Cultural Rights, and on Civil and Political Rights respectively, which were approved by the General Assembly on 16 December 1966. This in turn has led to a comparison of the second Covenant and its Optional Protocol with the provisions of the European Convention, and a study of the problems which may arise if the member States of the Council of Europe become parties to both instruments.

Relations between the Council of Europe and the United Nations in the field of human rights have developed significantly in recent years. In 1966 the Council was officially invited to attend sessions of the UN Commission on Human Rights and of its Sub-commission on the Prevention of Discrimination and the Protection of Minorities[29] – which it has done regularly ever since; the Council was represented at, and presented an important report to, the Teheran conference which celebrated International Human Rights Year, 1968;[30] the Assembly organised a special sitting on 26 September 1968 as its own contribution to International Human Rights Year;[31] and in 1973 it held a debate on the subject of the twenty-fifth anniversary of the Universal Declaration and the twentieth anniversary of the entry into force of the European Convention.[32] On several occasions the Assembly has called on member governments to ratify the UN Covenants and the Optional Protocols thereto.[33]

The Committee of Experts on Human Rights produced two important reports on the problems arising from the 'coexistence' of the European Convention and the UN Covenant on Civil and Political Rights and its Optional Protocol: the first in 1968 on the two systems of control,[34] and the second in 1970 on the differences in the enumeration and definition of the rights.[35] It was hoped that the conclusion of these studies would open the way for ratification of the UN Covenant and its Optional Protocol by the member States of the Council of Europe. By the end of 1974 five of them had ratified both Covenants: Cyprus, Denmark, Norway, Sweden and the Federal Republic of Germany, of which the three Scandinavian countries had also ratified the Optional Protocol.

HUMANITARIAN LAW. Another subject in which the Council of Europe has interested itself latterly is the development of humanitarian law. After the two meetings of government experts in Geneva in 1971 and 1972, which prepared two draft protocols to the Geneva Conventions of 1949, the Legal Affairs Committee studied these developments with the assistance of the International Institute of Humanitarian Law in San Remo and of representatives of the International Committee of the Red Cross; in September 1973 it presented a comprehensive report to the Assembly,[36] on the basis of which the latter made various recommendations to the governments with a view to the attitude they should adopt at the diplomatic conference to be held in the following year.[37]

The last matter to be recounted in this section relates to the establishment of a *new Human Rights Programme*. In 1970 the Assembly and its Legal Affairs Committee took the initiative of proposing a general review of the human rights work of the Council of Europe. The basic idea which underlay this proposal was that the Convention on Human Rights was concluded in 1950 in the light of the sad experiences to which Europe had been subjected during the previous decade; twenty years later it was desirable to consider whether the Convention corresponded to the needs of the 1970s and 1980s; in an age of future planning it was appropriate to draw up a new programme for developing the protection of human rights in Europe in the light of new needs. Moreover, as the original proposal for the conclusion of the European Convention had emanated from the Consultative Assembly in 1949,[38] it was for that same body to undertake the proposed review some twenty years later.[39] For this purpose the Assembly decided in January 1971 to convene a Parliamentary Conference on Human Rights 'to define the basic choices to be made in the matter and thus determine the essential items of an "outline programme" for the years ahead.'[40]

The *Parliamentary Conference on Human Rights* was held in Vienna, in the Austrian parliament, from 18 to 20 October 1971, under the presidency of Mr Max van der Stoel, later Foreign Minister of the Netherlands. The participants included over eighty members of parliament from the member States of the Council of Europe, representatives of the Committee of Ministers, of the Commission and Court of Human Rights and of the governmental Committee of Experts; also several national Ombudsmen and representatives of international and non-governmental organisations. Four main subjects were discussed: what rights should be protected; whose rights should be protected; how the existing protection of human rights could be strengthened; and how to prevent abuse of the system of protection.[41] The conference did not question – indeed, it paid tribute to – the work of the Commission and Court under the Convention of 1950; but it did not consider whether the existing system could be strengthened or extended in new directions in the light of new developments.

At the final sitting of the conference certain conclusions were drawn by Senator Marcel Prélot, chairman of the Legal Affairs Committee,[42] while Professor René-Jean Dupuy of the University of Nice (and subsequently a member of the European Commission of Human Rights) presented, as a result of the discussions, proposals for a new short-term and medium-term programme of the Council of Europe in the field of human rights.[43] All the material was then submitted to the Legal Affairs Committee of the Consultative Assembly, which produced in due course three texts: a 'Final Resolution of the Conference';[44] *Resolution 505 (1972)* of the Assembly, which invited national parliaments to give effect to certain proposals of the conference aimed at strengthening the protection of human rights in the national legal systems;[45] and *Recommendation 683 (1972)*, addressed to the Committee of Ministers, containing 'Proposals for a short-term and medium-term programme for the Council of Europe in the general field of human rights'.[46]

These proposals related naturally to the matters discussed at the conference and mentioned above. The Assembly asked the Ministers to institute (by various procedures) further studies relating to the following additional rights and freedoms (a number of which had already been considered previously): asylum, conscientious objection, the right to life (its beginning and its end), environmental rights, protection against discrimination as regards access to employment and allocation of housing, equality in the enforcement of the law, the rights of women and children, the specific needs of prisoners (particularly political prisoners), freedom of information and of the press. Eight separate proposals were then made as regards the machinery for the protection of human rights:

1. The establishment of national bureaux or departments responsible for co-ordinating activities at the national level.
2. The conclusion of an agreement rendering decisions of the Court of Human Rights enforceable in national law.
3. Incorporation of the normative provisions of the Convention into national law where this is not already the case.
4. Conferring upon the Court of Human Rights competence to give preliminary rulings at the request of a national court.
5. Facilitating access to the Commission of Human Rights by the physically and mentally handicapped.

6. Consideration of possible conflicts of jurisdiction between the new UN procedure under ECOSCC Resolution 1503 (XLVIII) and the European system.
7. Reinforcing of human rights against interference by private persons and agencies.

Finally the Assembly proposed that a study should be made of the duties of man and of the possibility of preparing a European text aimed at preventing abuses.

All this, it is apparent, constituted an ambitious programme which would require much work and study. Early in 1973 the Committee of Ministers instructed the Committee of Experts on Human Rights to examine these proposals in consultation with the Commission and Court of Human Rights – and, where appropriate, with other Council of Europe committees. The results of these studies will be reflected in the Programme of Work of the Council of Europe during the years to come.

2. HUMAN RIGHTS AND COMMUNITY LAW

Something has been said above about the question of 'coexistence' between the European Convention on Human Rights and the UN Covenant on Civil and Political Rights; a different but related problem concerns the relationship between the European Convention and the legal system resulting from the Treaty of Rome establishing the European Economic Community. From 1958 to 1972 five of the six Parties to the Rome treaty were also parties to the European Convention; from 1 January 1973 this applied to eight out of nine members; since the French ratification of the European Convention in 1974 all nine Parties to the Treaty of Rome are also Parties to the Convention on Human Rights. What, if any, is the relationship between the two treaties of 1950 and 1957? Do the rules set out in the Convention on Human Rights apply to the institutions of the Community? Should they be applied not only by the Strasbourg organs but also by the Luxembourg Court? Could an application be brought before the European Commission of Human Rights on account of an alleged violation by one of the Community institutions?

These interesting questions have received a good deal of attention from jurists,[47] but it cannot be claimed that all the answers have been found. It would seem that an application to the European

Commission of Human Rights relating to an act of one of the Community institutions could not be admitted unless (as was once suggested) the Convention was amended to permit accession by the Community as such and such accession in fact took place. But this is most unlikely. On the other hand, respect for the fundamental principles of human rights law has begun to find its way into Community law as interpreted by the Court of Justice in Luxembourg.

In the *International Handelsgesellschaft case* in 1970 the Court of Justice was seized of a request by the Administrative Court of Frankfurt-am-Main to give a preliminary ruling in a case which disputed the compatibility of certain Community farming regulations (requiring a deposit on exports of grain) with Articles 2 and 14 of the German Basic Law. In its judgement of 17 December 1970 the Court of Justice emphasised the autonomy of Community law, which could not be invalidated by provisions of national law even of a constitutional character; but it went on to say[48] 'that, in fact, respect for basic rights forms an integral part of the general principles of law whose observation is ensured by the Court of Justice'; and 'that the protection of these rights, consonant with the constitutional traditions common to member States, must be assured within the context and aims of the Community'.

Matters were taken a stage further with the case of *J. Nold Kohlen und Baustoffgrosshandlung* v. *the Commission* in May 1974. This raised the question of freedom to pursue a commercial activity, the refusal of which was alleged to involve violation of the right of property – a right which is guaranteed by the Basic Law of the Federal Republic and by the constitutions of other member States and also by the First Protocol to the European Convention on Human Rights. In its judgement of 14 May 1974 the court devoted a separate section to 'the alleged violation of fundamental rights'; it reaffirmed that *fundamental rights are an integral part of the general principles of law the observation of which it ensures.* The court continued by stating that in ensuring the protection of these rights it must be guided by the constitutional traditions common to member States and that international treaties for the protection of human rights in which member States have collaborated or of which they are signatories can also furnish guidelines of which account should be taken in the framework of Community law.[49]

We thus find the Court of Justice firmly committed to the principle that fundamental rights constitute an integral part of the general principles of Community law; but it is principally 'the constitutional traditions of member States' that will indicate what those rights are. The reference to international instruments concerning the protection of human rights occupies a secondary position – the European Convention is not even mentioned specifically at this stage; those instruments 'can furnish guidelines of which account should be taken' – but not rules which should be applied. We are a long way from seeing the provisions of the European Convention incorporated by reference into Community law as an agreed statement of 'the constitutional traditions common to member States', which it might reasonably be considered to represent when all nine of them have ratified it and the majority of them give to its normative provisions the force of internal law.

As a result, the notion of 'fundamental rights as an integral part of the general principles of Community law' is valuable but very general. Indeed, one cannot be surprised at this, because it was not necessary either in the Handelsgesellschaft case or the Nold case to be more specific; in both cases the Court held that the acts complained of did not violate the fundamental rights the observance of which it is required to ensure.

The very general nature of the notion of 'fundamental rights as an integral part of the general principles of Community law' was emphasised in a decision of the German Federal Constitutional Court of 29 May 1974. The Frankfurt Administrative Court, which had asked the Luxembourg Court for a preliminary ruling on the problem raised in the *International Handelsgesellschaft case* subsequently referred to the Constitutional Court the question whether the EEC requirement for a deposit on grain exports was consistent with the German Basic Law. This raised the wider issue whether a provision of Community law might be held by the Constitutional Court to be inconsistent with the Basic Law, and therefore unenforceable in the German courts, even though it had been held by the Luxembourg court to be not inconsistent with the fundamental rights which are part of the general principles of Community law. It was argued that the finding of the Luxembourg court was conclusive and could not be questioned by the German Constitutional Court. The latter, however, rejected this view by a majority of five to three. While recognising the autonomous nature of Community law, which the Luxembourg court is competent to interpret, the Constitutional Court stated that it is itself the sole judge of the constitutional rights of German citizens; the Community cannot lessen those rights and cannot be harmed by the action of a national court in protecting them. In case of conflict, therefore, it would be the duty of the Constitutional Court to up-hold the constitutional rights of German citizens even against provisions of Community law. In coming to this conclusion the Constitutional Court was careful to point out that it was necessary to take account of the present state of development of the European Community: it does not yet have a directly elected democratic legislature nor a constitutional instrument setting out a catalogue of basic rights of its own. It was this absence of a detailed statement of basic rights in Community law which would make it necessary, in the event of conflict, to rely on detailed provisions of the national constitutions.[50]

This decision has been much discussed and is likely to lead to further consideration of the question of relations between con-stitutional guarantees of fundamental rights in the nine member States and the notion of 'fundamental rights as an integral part of the general principles of Community law'. Any examination of this problem cannot ignore the European Convention, more parti-cularly as it can be considered to constitute an expression of the 'constitutional traditions which are common to the member States' (in the words of the Luxembourg court in the *Nold case*) and because its provisions already have the force of domestic law in the majority of the member States.

During 1975 the matter was taken a stage further in the following way. At the 'summit meeting' in Paris in October 1972 the Heads of State and of Government of the Nine stated their objective 'of transforming, before the end of the present decade and with the fullest respect for the treaties already signed, the whole complex of the relations of member States into a European union'.[51] This objective was reaffirmed at the Paris 'summit' in December 1974; it was then decided that the time had come for the Nine to agree as soon as possible on a common conception of European union. The Commission, the Court of Justice and the Assembly were all invited to put forward their proposals, and M. Tindemans, the Belgian Prime Minister, was requested to prepare for the end of the year 1975 a report in which he would synthesise the various suggestions made and the results of different consultations which he was asked to undertake.

Any 'common conception of European union' must envisage that it would be based on respect for human rights and fundamental freedoms. Indeed, the draft treaty for a European Community prepared by the '*Ad hoc* Assembly' in 1953 made a cardinal point of this.[52] The Commission in its 'Report on European Union' of 26 June 1975 stated:[53]

> The democratic nature of the European Union, which should be explicitly stated in the Treaty of Union, means that the protection of human rights is a fundamental element in the new political edifice and in the operation of its institutions.

It went on to consider ways in which this objective could be achieved. The Commission thought the most suitable approach would be to incorporate a list of specified rights in the basic Act on which the Union would rest, which could include not only civil and political but also economic and social rights; other possibilities would be simply to include in the Act a general obligation to respect human rights and fundamental freedoms or to incorporate by reference the provisions of the European Convention.

By the summer of 1975 the question was thus posed but a good deal of further discussion was necessary before the situation would be clarified.[54] One important consideration to be borne in mind was the following: when eight out of nine member States already had chapters on basic rights in their national constitutions, when all of them were Parties to the European Convention and the majority of them gave effect to its normative provisions as rules of internal law, and when two of them were already Parties to the UN Covenants (and others likely to become Parties in the future), the greatest care should be taken to avoid possible conflicts between existing obligations (both national and international) and any new provisions that might be included in a new Treaty of European Union. Otherwise, the problems of 'coexistence' might be impossible to solve. There is a strong case for incorporating by reference the rights and freedoms already set out in the European Convention and its Protocols – and possibly also those set out in the European Social Charter of 1961; if this were done it would follow the precedents of the French constitutions of 1946 and 1958, which included by reference the provisions of the French Declaration of the Rights of Man and of the Citizen of 1789; also the precedents of a number of newly independent countries which have included by reference in their new constitutions the Universal Declaration of Human Rights of 1948 – as, for example, the constitution of Senegal of 7 March 1963.

The first edition of this book recounted some of the attempts which were made during the early years of the life of the Council of Europe to secure the establishment of a European Court of

Justice which would have wider competence than the European Court of Human Rights and might conceivably have taken over the functions of the Court of Justice of the Communities.[55] It is clearly not practical politics at the present time to suggest a merger of the European Court of Human Rights and the Luxembourg court, but the idea has been kept alive as a long-term objective[56] and is not without sense when one remembers that nine of the Contracting Parties to the European Convention constitute the total membership of the Communities and that most of the others are associated with them in one way or another. Professor Max Sørensen, a former President of the European Commission of Human Rights and now a judge on the Luxembourg Court, wrote in 1972: [57]

> Plans for a 'Grand Design' with a view to the reorganisation and amalgamation of European institutions have been conceived, but never realised. The rational urge of the human mind and the hard realities of governing Europe will some day breathe new life into these plans and overcome the political obstacles of various kinds which have delayed their realisation.
>
> One element in such a 'Grand Design' might very well be an amalgamation of existing judicial bodies on the European level and a corresponding extension of the jurisdiction of a new European Court of Justice to all subject-matters and all persons covered by the separate judicial bodies existing at present. Unity of jurisdiction is to some extent an important element of a fair and adequate administration of justice, and the very ideal of human rights may in this way be harnessed to future moves for the reform of European institutions.

The current discussions aimed at 'agreeing, as soon as possible, on a common conception of European union' might afford the occasion which is required for far-reaching decisions which would make respect for human rights and fundamental freedoms the cornerstone of a new political edifice, and thus the distinctive image of the European Union, for the establishment of which so many have laboured with such ardour for the last thirty years.

NOTES

1 *Official Report of Debates*, 1974–5, Vol. I, p. 27 (unofficial translation).
2 *Ibid.*, 1966–67, Vol. I, p. 48.
3 The following pages are taken or summarised from an article entitled 'The promotion of human rights by the Council of Europe', published in *Human Rights Journal*, 1975, pp. 545–85, which was originally written as a separate chapter for this book but omitted for reasons of space.
4 *Cf.* 'Report on the twenty-fifth anniversary of the Universal Declaration of

Human Rights and the twentieth anniversary of the European Convention . . .'
(Peridier report), *Documents of the Assembly*, 1973, Document 3334, paras. 49–50.

5 *Documents of the Assembly*, 1949, Document 77.

6 *Cf.* K. Vasak, 'Institutions . . . for the promotion and protection of human
rights', *Human Rights Journal*, Vol. I, 1968, pp. 164–79.

7 The Committee of Experts on Human Rights was established by Resolution
(60)6 of the Committee of Ministers of 22 March 1960. The chairmen of the
Committee of Experts have been M. Ugo Caldarera (Italy), 1960–63; Sir Samuel
Hoare (United Kingdom), 1963–72; M. Willibald Pahr (Austria), 1972–74;
M. Claudio Zanghi (Italy), 1974–75.

8 *Cf.* first edition of this book, Chapter VIII; Fadil Sur, 'La Charte Sociale,
européenne – dix années d'application', *European Yearbook*, Vol. XXII; H.
Wiebringhaus, 'La Convention européenne . . . et la Charte Sociale européenne'.
Human Rights Journal, Vol. VIII, p. 527.

9 *Texts adopted by the Assembly*, January 1961. The Assembly also proposed
to include the right of minorities to establish their own schools and receive
teaching in the language of their choice.

10 *Yearbook of the Convention*, Vol. X, p. 104.

11 *Yearbook* X, p. 90.

12 Assembly Document 2280 of 23 September 1967, p. 12.

13 Recommendation 683 (1972), para. A(1), *Yearbook* XV, p. 54.

14 Recommendation 509 (1968), *Yearbook* XI, p. 76.

15 Recommendation 582 (1970), *Yearbook* XIII, 56.

16 The proceedings are published in *Human Rights and Mass Communications*,
Strasbourg, 1969.

17 The proceedings are published in *Privacy and Human Rights*, Manchester,
1973.

18 For a fuller account see the article referred to in n. 3, at pp. 200–11.

19 *Yearbook* XIII, pp. 84–6.

20 Resolutions (73)22 and (74)29 of the Committee of Ministers, *European
Yearbook*, Vol. XXI, p. 361, and Vol. XXII, p. 405.

21 UN Document E/CN. 4/1 63 of 27 November 1974, p. 12.

22 UN Resolution (74)26 of the Committee of Ministers, *European Yearbook*,
Vol. XXII, p. 399. See also James Reston *et al.*, 'Freedom of the press',
Human Rights Journal, Vol. VII, 1974, pp. 593–638.

23 *Yearbook* VII, p. 76.

24 *European Conventions and Agreements*, Vol. II, 1972, p. 427, at p. 444.

25 *Yearbook* XI, p. 94.

26 *Yearbook* XIV, p. 70.

27 *Yearbook* XIII, p. 66.

28 *Yearbook* XV, p. 66.

29 ECOSOC Resolution 1159(XLI) of 5 August 1966.

30 Teheran conference document A/Conf. 32/L. 9.

31 *Yearbook* XI, pp. 108–54.

32 *Official Report of Debates*, 27 September 1973; report of the Committee
on Legal Affairs (Peridier report), Document 3334 of 13 September 1973, which
discusses these questions in greater detail. See also article cited in n. 3, at pp.
213–17.

33 Recommendation 548, *Yearbook* XII, 120; Recommendation 642, *Yearbook* XIV, p. 74; Resolution 552, *Texts adopted*, September 1973.

34 The decisions taken by the Committee of Ministers on the basis of this
report are published in *Yearbook* XIII, pp. 70–6.

35 This report has been published *in extenso* by the Council of Europe as
Document H(70)7, September 1970. The problems of 'coexistence' are discussed
more fully in *Human Rights in the World*, Manchester, 1972, Chapter IV.

36 The 'Alber report', Document 3336, September 1973.

37 Recommendation 714, *Yearbook* XVI, p. 68. See also article cited in n. 3, at pp. 217–23.

38 The 'Teitgen report' of 5 September 1949; *cf.* n. 5.

39 *Documents of the Assembly*, 1971, Document 2894.

40 Resolution 467, *Yearbook* XIV, p. 68.

41 The proceedings of the conference are to be found in a separate booklet, *Parliamentary Conference on Human Rights*, published by the Council of Europe in 1972.

42 *Ibid.*, pp. 104–10.

43 *Ibid.*, p. 110.

44 *Ibid*, p. 112.

45 *Ibid*, p. 125; *Yearbook* XV, p. 54.

46 *Yearbook* XV, pp. 54–60.

47 H. Golsong, 'Interférences entre les obligations incombant à un état en vertu de la Convention européenne des droits de l'homme et d'autres Accords internationaux', *La Protection internationale des droits de l'homme dans le cadre européen* (Strasbourg colloquy), Paris, 1961, pp. 253–9; F. Capotorti, 'Possibilities of conflict in national legal systems between the European Convention and other international agreements', *Human Rights in National and International Law* (Vienna colloquy), Manchester, 1968, p. 72, at p. 92; M. Waelbroeck, 'Is the European Convention ... binding on the Communities?', *ibid.*, p. 94; P. Pescatore, written communications at the Vienna *Parliamentary Conference on Human Rights*, Strasbourg, 1972, p. 74; G. Cohen-Jonathan, 'Droits de l'homme et pluralité des systèmes européens de protection internationale,' *Human Rights Journal*, Vol. V, 1973, pp. 615–49, and 'Les droits de l'homme dans les Communautés européennes', *Mélanges Eisenmann*, Paris, 1974, pp. 398–418. See also P. Pescatore, 'Les droits de l'homme et l'integration européenne', *Cahiers de droit européen*, 1968, p. 629; and references given in nn. 56 and 57.

48 Judgement of 17 December 1970, *Collection of Jurisprudence of the Court*, XVI, 1970, p. 1125. See also the *Stauder case*, judgement of 12 November 1969, *ibid.*, XV, 1969, p. 425.

49 Judgement of 14 May 1974, *Collection of Jurisprudence of the Court*, 1974, p. 491, at p. 508.

50 The decision of the Federal Constitutional Court is summarised in *ICLQ*, Vol. 24, 1975, p. 143.

51 *European Yearbook*, Vol. XV, p. 485.

52 A. H. Robertson, 'The European political community', *British Yearbook of International Law*, 1952, pp. 383–401.

53 'Report on European union' by the Commission of the European Communities, *Bulletin of the European Communities*, Supplement 5/75, July 1975.

54 The Centre Universitaire d'Études des Communautés Européennes of the University of Paris I, organised a colloquy on the subject in Paris in April 1975.

55 *Human Rights in Europe*, first edition, pp. 166–71.

56 Hermod Lannung, 'Human rights and the multiplicity of European systems for international protection', *Human Rights Journal*, Vol. V, 1973, p. 651, at pp. 660–1.

57 Max Sørensen, 'The enlargement of the European Communities and the protection of human rights', *European Yearbook*, Vol. XIX, pp. 3–17.

CONVENTION FOR THE PROTECTION OF HUMAN RIGHTS AND FUNDAMENTAL FREEDOMS[1]

The Governments signatory hereto, being Members of the Council of Europe,

Considering the Universal Declaration of Human Rights proclaimed by the General Assembly of the United Nations on 10 December 1948;

Considering that this Declaration aims at securing the universal and effective recognition and observance of the Rights therein declared;

Considering that the aim of the Council of Europe is the achievement of greater unity between its Members and that one of the methods by which that aim is to be pursued is the maintenance and further realisation of Human Rights and Fundamental Freedoms;

Reaffirming their profound belief in those Fundamental Freedoms which are the foundation of justice and peace in the world and are best maintained on the one hand by an effective political democracy and on the other by a common understanding and observance of the Human Rights upon which they depend;

Being resolved, as the Governments of European countries which are likeminded and have a common heritage of political traditions, ideals, freedom and the rule of law to take the first steps for the collective enforcement of certain of the Rights stated in the Universal Declaration,

Have agreed as follows:

ARTICLE 1

The High Contracting Parties shall secure to everyone within their jurisdiction the rights and freedoms defined in Section I of this Convention.

SECTION I

ARTICLE 2

1. Everyone's right to life shall be protected by law. No one shall be deprived of his life intentionally save in the execution of a sentence of a court following his conviction of a crime for which this penalty is provided by law.

2. Deprivation of life shall not be regarded as inflicted in contraven-

tion of this Article when it results from the use of force which is no more than absolutely necessary:

(*a*) in defence of any person from unlawful violence;

(*b*) in order to effect a lawful arrest or to prevent the escape of a person lawfully detained;

(*c*) in action lawfully taken for the purpose of quelling a riot or insurrection.

ARTICLE 3

No one shall be subjected to torture or to inhuman or degrading treatment or punishment.

ARTICLE 4

1. No one shall be held in slavery or servitude.

2. No one shall be required to perform forced or compulsory labour.

3. For the purpose of this Article the term 'forced or compulsory labour' shall not include:

(*a*) any work required to be done in the ordinary course of detention imposed according to the provisions of Article 5 of this Convention or during conditional release from such detention;

(*b*) any service of a military character or, in case of conscientious objectors in countries where they are recognised, service exacted instead of compulsory military service;

(*c*) any service exacted in case of an emergency or calamity threatening the life or well-being of the community;

(*d*) any work or service which forms part of normal civic obligations.

ARTICLE 5

1. Everyone has the right to liberty and security of person.

No one shall be deprived of his liberty save in the following cases and in accordance with a procedure prescribed by law;

(*a*) the lawful detention of a person after conviction by a competent court;

(*b*) the lawful arrest or detention of a person for non-compliance with the lawful order of a court or in order to secure the fulfilment of any obligation prescribed by law;

(*c*) the lawful arrest or detention of a person effected for the purpose of bringing him before the competent legal authority on reasonable suspicion of having committed an offence or when it is reasonably considered necessary to prevent his committing an offence or fleeing after having done so;

(*d*) the detention of a minor by lawful order for the purpose of educational supervision or his lawful detention for the purpose of bringing him before the competent legal authority;

(e) the lawful detention of persons for the prevention of the spreading of infectious diseases, of persons of unsound mind, alcoholics or drug addicts or vagrants;

(f) the lawful arrest or detention of a person to prevent his effecting an unauthorised entry into the country or of a person against whom action is being taken with a view to deportation or extradition.

2. Everyone who is arrested shall be informed promptly, in a language which he understands, of the reasons for his arrest and of any charge against him.

3. Everyone arrested or detained in accordance with the provisions of paragraph 1(c) of this Article shall be brought promptly before a judge or other officer authorised by law to exercise judicial power and shall be entitled to trial within a reasonable time or to release pending trial. Release may be conditioned by guarantees to appear for trial.

4. Everyone who is deprived of his liberty by arrest or detention shall be entitled to take proceedings by which the lawfulness of his detention shall be decided speedily by a court and his release ordered if the detention is not lawful.

5. Everyone who has been the victim of arrest or detention in contravention of the provisions of this Article shall have an enforceable right to compensation.

ARTICLE 6

1. In the determination of his civil rights and obligations or of any criminal charge against him, everyone is entitled to a fair and public hearing within a reasonable time by an independent and impartial tribunal established by law. Judgment shall be pronounced publicly but the press and public may be excluded from all or part of the trial in the interest of morals, public order or national security in a democratic society, where the interests of juveniles or the protection of the private life of the parties so require, or to the extent strictly necessary in the opinion of the court in special circumstances where publicity would prejudice the interests of justice.

2. Everyone charged with a criminal offence shall be presumed innocent until proved guilty according to law.

3. Everyone charged with a criminal offence has the following minimum rights:

(a) to be informed promptly, in a language which he understands and in detail, of the nature and cause of the accusation against him;

(b) to have adequate time and facilities for the preparation of his defence;

(c) to defend himself in person or through legal assistance of his own choosing or, if he has not sufficient means to pay for legal assistance, to be given it free when the interests of justice so require;

(*d*) to examine or have examined witnesses against him and to obtain the attendance and examination of witnesses on his behalf under the same conditions as witnesses against him;

(*e*) to have the free assistance of an interpreter if he cannot understand or speak the language used in court.

ARTICLE 7

1. No one shall be held guilty of any criminal offence on account of any act or omission which did not constitute a criminal offence under national or international law at the time when it was committed. Nor shall a heavier penalty be imposed than the one that was applicable at the time the criminal offence was committed.

2. This Article shall not prejudice the trial and punishment of any person for any act or omission which, at the time when it was committed, was criminal according to the general principles of law recognised by civilised nations.

ARTICLE 8

1. Everyone has the right to respect for his private and family life, his home and his correspondence.

2. There shall be no interference by a public authority with the exercise of this right except such as is in accordance with the law and is necessary in a democratic society in the interests of national security, public safety or the economic well-being of the country, for the prevention of disorder or crime, for the protection of health or morals, or for the protection of the rights and freedoms of others.

ARTICLE 9

1. Everyone has the right to freedom of thought, conscience and religion; this right includes freedom to change his religion or belief and freedom, either alone or in community with others and in public or private, to manifest his religion or belief, in worship, teaching, practice and observance.

2. Freedom to manifest one's religion or beliefs shall be subject only to such limitations as are prescribed by law and are necessary in a democratic society in the interests of public safety, for the protection of public order, health or morals, or for the protection of the rights and freedoms of others.

ARTICLE 10

1. Everyone has the right to freedom of expression. This right shall

include freedom to hold opinions and to receive and impart information and ideas without interference by public authority and regardless of frontiers. This Article shall not prevent States from requiring the licensing of broadcasting, television or cinema enterprises.

2. The exercise of these freedoms, since it carries with it duties and responsibilities, may be subject to such formalities, conditions, restrictions or penalties as are prescribed by law and are necessary in a democratic society, in the interests of national security, territorial integrity or public safety, for the prevention of disorder or crime, for the protection of health or morals, for the protection of the reputation or rights of others, for preventing the disclosure of information received in confidence, or for maintaining the authority and impartiality of the judiciary.

ARTICLE 11

1. Everyone has the right to freedom of peaceful assembly and to freedom of association with others, including the right to form and to join trade unions for the protection of his interests.

2. No restrictions shall be placed on the exercise of these rights other than such as are prescribed by law and are necessary in a democratic society in the interests of national security or public safety, for the prevention of disorder or crime, for the protection of health or morals or for the protection of the rights and freedoms of others. This Article shall not prevent the imposition of lawful restrictions on the exercise of these rights by members of the armed forces, of the police or of the administration of the State.

ARTICLE 12

Men and women of marriageable age have the right to marry and to found a family, according to the national laws governing the exercise of this right.

ARTICLE 13

Everyone whose rights and freedoms as set forth in this Convention are violated shall have an effective remedy before a national authority notwithstanding that the violation has been committed by persons acting in an official capacity.

ARTICLE 14

The enjoyment of the rights and freedoms set forth in this Convention shall be secured without discrimination on any ground such as sex, race, colour, language, religion, political or other opinion, national or social origin, association with a national minority, property, birth or other status.

ARTICLE 15

1. In time of war or other public emergency threatening the life of the nation any High Contracting Party may take measures derogating from its obligations under this Convention to the extent strictly required by the exigencies of the situation, provided that such measures are not inconsistent with its other obligations under international law.

2. No derogation from Article 2, except in respect of deaths resulting from lawful acts of war, or from Articles 3, 4 (paragraph 1) and 7 shall be made under this provision.

3. Any High Contracting Party availing itself of this right of derogation shall keep the Secretary General of the Council of Europe fully informed of the measures which it has taken and the reasons therefor. It shall also inform the Secretary General of the Council of Europe when such measures have ceased to operate and the provisions of the Convention are again being fully executed.

ARTICLE 16

Nothing in Articles 10, 11 and 14 shall be regarded as preventing the High Contracting Parties from imposing restrictions on the political activity of aliens.

ARTICLE 17

Nothing in this Convention may be interpreted as implying for any State, group or person any right to engage in any activity or perform any act aimed at the destruction of any of the rights and freedoms set forth herein or at their limitation to a greater extent than is provided for in the Convention.

ARTICLE 18

The restrictions permitted under this Convention to the said rights and freedoms shall not be applied for any purpose other than those for which they have been prescribed.

SECTION II

ARTICLE 19

To ensure the observance of the engagements undertaken by the High Contracting Parties in the present Convention, there shall be set up:

1. A European Commission of Human Rights hereinafter referred to as 'the Commission';

2. A European Court of Human Rights, hereinafter referred to as 'the Court'.

SECTION III

ARTICLE 20

The Commission shall consist of a number of members equal to that of the High Contracting Parties. No two members of the Commission may be nationals of the same State.

ARTICLE 21

1. The members of the Commission shall be elected by the Committee of Ministers by an absolute majority of votes, from a list of names drawn up by the Bureau of the Consultative Assembly; each group of the Representatives of the High Contracting Parties in the Consultative Assembly shall put forward three candidates, of whom two at least shall be its nationals.

2. As far as applicable, the same procedure shall be followed to complete the Commission in the event of other States subsequently becoming Parties to this Convention, and in filling casual vacancies.

ARTICLE 22[2]

1. The members of the Commission shall be elected for a period of six years. They may be re-elected. However, of the members elected at the first election, the terms of seven members shall expire at the end of three years.

2. The members whose terms are to expire at the end of the initial period of three years shall be chosen by lot by the Secretary General of the Council of Europe immediately after the first election has been completed.

3. In order to ensure that, as far as possible, one half of the membership of the Commission shall be renewed every three years, the Committee of Ministers may decide, before proceeding to any subsequent election, that the term or terms of office of one or more members to be elected shall be for a period other than six years but not more than nine and not less than three years.

4. In cases where more than one term of office is involved and the Committee of Ministers applies the preceding paragraph, the allocation of the terms of office shall be effected by the drawing of lots by the Secretary General, immediately after the election.

5. A member of the Commission elected to replace a member whose term of office has not expired shall hold office for the remainder of his predecessor's term.

6. The members of the Commission shall hold office until replaced. After having been replaced, they shall continue to deal with such cases as they already have under consideration.

ARTICLE 23

The members of the Commission shall sit on the Commission in their individual capacity.

ARTICLE 24

Any High Contracting Party may refer to the Commission, through the Secretary General of the Council of Europe, any alleged breach of the provisions of the Convention by another High Contracting Party.

ARTICLE 25

1. The Commission may receive petitions addressed to the Secretary General of the Council of Europe from any person, non-governmental organisation or group of individuals claiming to be the victim of a violation by one of the High Contracting Parties of the rights set forth in this Convention, provided that the High Contracting Party against which the complaint has been lodged has declared that it recognises the competence of the Commission to receive such petitions. Those of the High Contracting Parties who have made such a declaration undertake not to hinder in any way the effective exercise of this right.

2. Such declarations may be made for a specific period.

3. The declarations shall be deposited with the Secretary General of the Council of Europe who shall transmit copies thereof to the High Contracting Parties and publish them.

4. The Commission shall only exercise the powers provided for in this Article when at least six High Contracting Parties are bound by declarations made in accordance with the preceding paragraphs.

ARTICLE 26

The Commission may only deal with the matter after all domestic remedies have been exhausted, according to the generally recognised rules of international law, and within a period of six months from the date on which the final decision was taken.

ARTICLE 27

1. The Commission shall not deal with any petition submitted under Article 25 which

(a) is anonymous, or

(b) is substantially the same as a matter which has already been examined by the Commission or has already been submitted to another procedure of international investigation or settlement and if it contains no relevant new information.

2. The Commission shall consider inadmissible any petition submitted under Article 25 which it considers incompatible with the provisions of the present Convention, manifestly ill-founded, or an abuse of the right of petition.

3. The Commission shall reject any petition referred to it which it considers inadmissible under Article 26.

ARTICLE 28

In the event of the Commission accepting a petition referred to it:

(*a*) it shall, with a view to ascertaining the facts, undertake together with the representatives of the parties an examination of the petition and, if need be, an investigation, for the effective conduct of which the States concerned shall furnish all necessary facilities, after an exchange of views with the Commission;

(*b*) it shall place itself at the disposal of the parties concerned with a view to securing a friendly settlement of the matter on the basis of respect for Human Rights as defined in this Convention.

ARTICLE 29[3]

After it has accepted a petition submitted under Article 25, the Commission may nevertheless decide unanimously to reject the petition if, in the course of its examination, it finds that the existence of one of the grounds for non-acceptance provided for in Article 27 has been established.

In such a case, the decision shall be communicated to the parties.

ARTICLE 30[3]

If the Commission succeeds in effecting a friendly settlement in accordance with Article 28, it shall draw up a Report which shall be sent to the States concerned, to the Committee of Ministers and to the Secretary General of the Council of Europe for publication. This Report shall be confined to a brief statement of the facts and of the solution reached.

ARTICLE 31 (part b)

1. If a solution is not reached, the Commission shall draw up a Report on the facts and state its opinion as to whether the facts found disclose a breach by the State concerned of its obligations under the

Convention. The opinions of all the members of the Commission on this point may be stated in the Report.

2. The Report shall be transmitted to the Committee of Ministers. It shall also be transmitted to the States concerned, who shall not be at liberty to publish it.

3. In transmitting the Report to the Committee of Ministers the Commission may make such proposals as it thinks fit.

ARTICLE 32

1. If the question is not referred to the Court in accordance with Article 48 of this Convention within a period of three months from the date of the transmission of the Report to the Committee of Ministers, the Committee of Ministers shall decide by a majority of two-thirds of the members entitled to sit on the Committee whether there has been a violation of the Convention.

2. In the affirmative case the Committee of Ministers shall prescribe a period during which the Contracting Party concerned must take the measures required by the decision of the Committee of Ministers.

3. If the High Contracting Party concerned has not taken satisfactory measures within the prescribed period, the Committee of Ministers shall decide by the majority provided for in paragraph 1 above what effect shall be given to its original decision and shall publish the Report.

4. The High Contracting Parties undertake to regard as binding on them any decision which the Committee of Ministers may take in application of the preceding paragraphs.

ARTICLE 33

The Commission shall meet *in camera.*

ARTICLE 34[4]
29(3)

Subject to the provisions of Article 29, the Commission shall take its decisions by a majority of the members present and voting.

ARTICLE 35

The Commission shall meet as the circumstances require. The meetings shall be convened by the Secretary General of the Council of Europe.

ARTICLE 36

The Commission shall draw up its own rules of procedure.

L

ARTICLE 37

The secretariat of the Commission shall be provided by the Secretary General of the Council of Europe.

SECTION IV

ARTICLE 38

The European Court of Human Rights shall consist of a number of judges equal to that of the Members of the Council of Europe. No two judges may be nationals of the same State.

ARTICLE 39

1. The members of the Court shall be elected by the Consultative Assembly by a majority of the votes cast from a list of persons nominated by the Members of the Council of Europe; each Member shall nominate three candidates, of whom two at least shall be its nationals.

2. As far as applicable, the same procedure shall be followed to complete the Court in the event of the admission of new Members of the Council of Europe, and in filling casual vacancies.

3. The candidates shall be of high moral character and must either possess the qualifications required for appointment to high judicial office or be jurisconsults of recognised competence.

ARTICLE 40[5]

1. The members of the Court shall be elected for a period of nine years. They may be re-elected. However, of the members elected at the first election the terms of four members shall expire at the end of three years, and the terms of four more members shall expire at the end of six years.

2. The members whose terms are to expire at the end of the initial periods of three and six years shall be chosen by lot by the Secretary General immediately after the first election has been completed.

3. In order to ensure that, as far as possible, one third of the membership of the Court shall be renewed every three years, the Consultative Assembly may decide, before proceeding to any subsequent election, that the term or terms of office of one or more members to be elected shall be for a period other than nine years but not more than twelve and not less than six years.

4. In cases where more than one term of office is involved and the Consultative Assembly applies the preceding paragraph, the allocation of the terms of office shall be effected by the drawing of lots by the Secretary General immediately after the election.

5. A member of the Court elected to replace a member whose term of office has not expired shall hold office for the remainder of his predecessor's term.

6. The members of the Court shall hold office until replaced. After having been replaced, they shall continue to deal with such cases as they already have under consideration.

ARTICLE 41

The Court shall elect its President and Vice-President for a period of three years. They may be re-elected.

ARTICLE 42

The members of the Court shall receive for each day of duty a compensation to be determined by the Committee of Ministers.

ARTICLE 43

For the consideration of each case brought before it the Court shall consist of a Chamber composed of seven judges. There shall sit as an *ex officio* member of the Chamber the judge who is a national of any State party concerned, or, if there is none, a person of its choice who shall sit in the capacity of judge; the names of the other judges shall be chosen by lot by the President before the opening of the case.

ARTICLE 44

Only the High Contracting Parties and the Commission shall have the right to bring a case before the Court.

ARTICLE 45

The jurisdiction of the Court shall extend to all cases concerning the interpretation and application of the present Convention which the High Contracting Parties or the Commission shall refer to it in accordance with Article 48.

ARTICLE 46

1. Any of the High Contracting Parties may at any time declare that it recognises as compulsory *ipso facto* and without special agreement the jurisdiction of the Court in all matters concerning the interpretation and application of the present Convention.

2. The declarations referred to above may be made unconditionally

or on condition of reciprocity on the part of several or certain other High Contracting Parties or for a specified period.

3. These declarations shall be deposited with the Secretary General of the Council of Europe who shall transmit copies thereof to the High Contracting Parties.

ARTICLE 47

The Court may only deal with a case after the Commission has acknowledged the failure of efforts for a friendly settlement and within the period of three months provided for in Article 32.

ARTICLE 48

The following may bring a case before the Court, provided that the High Contracting Party concerned, if there is only one, or the High Contracting Parties concerned, if there is more than one, are subject to the compulsory jurisdiction of the Court or, failing that, with the consent of the High Contracting Party concerned, if there is only one, or of the High Contracting Parties concerned if there is more than one:

(*a*) the Commission;

(*b*) a High Contracting Party whose national is alleged to be a victim;

(*c*) a High Contracting Party which referred the case to the Commission;

(*d*) a High Contracting Party against which the complaint has been lodged.

ARTICLE 49

In the event of dispute as to whether the Court has jurisdiction, the matter shall be settled by the decision of the Court.

ARTICLE 50

If the Court finds that a decision or a measure taken by a legal authority or any other authority of a High Contracting Party is completely or partially in conflict with the obligations arising from the present Convention, and if the internal law of the said Party allows only partial reparation to be made for the consequences of this decision or measure, the decision of the Court shall, if necessary, afford just satisfaction to the injured party.

ARTICLE 51

1. Reasons shall be given for the judgment of the Court.

2. If the judgment does not represent in whole or in part the

unanimous opinion of the judges, any judge shall be entitled to deliver a separate opinion.

ARTICLE 52

The judgment of the Court shall be final.

ARTICLE 53

The High Contracting Parties undertake to abide by the decision of the Court in any case to which they are parties.

ARTICLE 54

The judgment of the Court shall be transmitted to the Committee of Ministers which shall supervise its execution.

ARTICLE 55

The Court shall draw up its own rules and shall determine its own procedure.

ARTICLE 56

1. The first election of the members of the Court shall take place after the declarations by the High Contracting Parties mentioned in Article 46 have reached a total of eight.

2. No case can be brought before the Court before this election.

SECTION V

ARTICLE 57

On receipt of a request from the Secretary General of the Council of Europe any High Contracting Party shall furnish an explanation of the manner in which its internal law ensures the effective implementation of any of the provisions of this Convention.

ARTICLE 58

The expenses of the Commission and the Court shall be borne by the Council of Europe.

ARTICLE 59

The members of the Commission and of the Court shall be entitled, during the discharge of their functions, to the privileges and immunities provided for in Article 40 of the Statute of the Council of Europe and in the agreements made thereunder.

ARTICLE 60

Nothing in this Convention shall be construed as limiting or derogating from any of the human rights and fundamental freedoms which may be ensured under the laws of any High Contracting Party or under any other agreement to which it is a Party.

ARTICLE 61

Nothing in this Convention shall prejudice the powers conferred on the Committee of Ministers by the Statute of the Council of Europe.

ARTICLE 62

The High Contracting Parties agree that, except by special agreement, they will not avail themselves of treaties, conventions or declarations in force between them for the purpose of submitting, by way of petition, a dispute arising out of the interpretation or application of this Convention to a means of settlement other than those provided for in this Convention.

ARTICLE 63

1. Any State may at the time of its ratification or at any time thereafter declare by notification addressed to the Secretary General of the Council of Europe that the present Convention shall extend to all or any of the territories for whose international relations it is responsible.

2. The Convention shall extend to the territory or territories named in the notification as from the thirtieth day after the receipt of this notification by the Secretary General of the Council of Europe.

3. The provisions of this Convention shall be applied in such territories with due regard, however, to local requirements.

4. Any State which has made a declaration in accordance with paragraph 1 of this Article may at any time thereafter declare on behalf of one or more of the territories to which the declaration relates that it accepts the competence of the Commission to receive petitions from individuals, non-governmental organisations or groups of individuals in accordance with Article 25 of the present Convention.

ARTICLE 64

1. Any State may, when signing this Convention or when depositing

its instrument of ratification, make a reservation in respect of any particular provision of the Convention to the extent that any law then in force in its territory is not in conformity with the provision. Reservations of a general character shall not be permitted under this Article.

2. Any reservation made under this Article shall contain a brief statement of the law concerned.

ARTICLE 65

1. A High Contracting Party may denounce the present Convention only after the expiry of five years from the date on which it became a Party to it and after six months' notice contained in a notification addressed to the Secretary General of the Council of Europe, who shall inform the other High Contracting Parties.

2. Such a denunciation shall not have the effect of releasing the High Contracting Party concerned from its obligations under this Convention in respect of any act which, being capable of constituting a violation of such obligations, may have been performed by it before the date at which the denunciation became effective.

3. Any High Contracting Party which shall cease to be a Member of the Council of Europe shall cease to be a Party to this Convention under the same conditions.

4. The Convention may be denounced in accordance with the provisions of the preceding paragraphs in respect of any territory to which it has been declared to extend under the terms of Article 63.

ARTICLE 66

1. This convention shall be open to the signature of the Members of the Council of Europe. It shall be ratified. Ratifications shall be deposited with the Secretary General of the Council of Europe.

2. The present Convention shall come into force after the deposit of ten instruments of ratification.

3. As regards any signatory ratifying subsequently, the Convention shall come into force at the date of the deposit of its instrument of ratification.

4. The Secretary General of the Council of Europe shall notify all the Members of the Council of Europe of the entry into force of the Convention, the names of the High Contracting Parties who have ratified it, and the deposit of all instruments of ratification which may be effected subsequently.

Done at Rome this 4th day of November 1950, in English and French, both texts being equally authentic, in a single copy which shall remain deposited in the archives of the Council of Europe. The Secretary General shall transmit certified copies to each of the signatories.

RATIFICATIONS

Austria: 3 September 1958
Belgium: 14 June 1955
Cyprus: 6 October 1962
Denmark: 13 April 1953
France: 3 May 1974
Federal Republic of Germany: 5 December 1952
Greece:[6] 28 March 1953
Iceland: 29 June 1953
Ireland: 25 February 1953
Italy: 26 October 1955
Luxembourg: 3 September 1953
Malta: 23 January 1967
Netherlands: 31 August 1954
Norway: 15 January 1952
Sweden: 4 February 1952
Switzerland: 28 November 1974
Turkey: 18 May 1954
United Kingdom: 8 March 1951

Entry into force: 3 September 1953

NOTES

1 As amended by Protocols Nos. 3 and 5, which entered into force on 21 September 1970 and 20 December 1971 respectively.

2 As amended by Protocol No. 5, which entered into force on 20 December 1971.

3 As amended by Protocol No. 3, which entered into force on 21 September 1970.

4 As amended by Protocol No. 3, which entered into force on 21 September 1970.

5 As amended by Protocol No. 5, which entered into force on 20 December 1971.

6 Greece denounced the Convention on 12 December 1969 but ratified again on 28 November 1974.

FIRST PROTOCOL TO THE CONVENTION

The Governments signatory hereto, being Members of the Council of Europe,

Being resolved to take steps to ensure the collective enforcement of certain rights and freedoms other than those already included in Section I of the Convention for the Protection of Human Rights and Fundamental Freedoms signed at Rome on 4 November 1950 (hereinafter referred to as 'the Convention'),

Have agreed as follows:

ARTICLE 1

Every natural or legal person is entitled to the peaceful enjoyment of his possessions. No one shall be deprived of his possessions except in the public interest and subject to the conditions provided for by law and by the general principles of international law.

The preceding provisions shall not, however, in any way impair the right of a State to enforce such laws as it deems necessary to control the use of property in accordance with the general interest or to secure the payment of taxes or other contributions or penalties.

ARTICLE 2

No person shall be denied the right to education. In the exercise of any functions which it assumes in relation to education and to teaching, the State shall respect the right of parents to ensure such education and teaching in conformity with their own religious and philosophical convictions.

ARTICLE 3

The High Contracting Parties undertake to hold free elections at reasonable intervals by secret ballot, under conditions which will ensure the free expression of the opinion of the people in the choice of the legislature.

ARTICLE 4

Any High Contracting Party may at the time of signature or ratification or at any time thereafter communicate to the Secretary General of the Council of Europe a declaration stating the extent to which it undertakes that the provisions of the present Protocol shall apply to such of the territories for the international relations of which it is responsible as are named therein.

Any High Contracting Party which has communicated a declaration in virtue of the preceding paragraph may from time to time communicate a further declaration modifying the terms of any former declaration or terminating the application of the provisions of this Protocol in respect of any territory.

A declaration made in accordance with this Article shall be deemed to have been made in accordance with Paragraph (1) of Article 63 of the Convention.

ARTICLE 5

As between the High Contracting Parties the provisions of Articles 1, 2, 3 and 4 of this Protocol shall be regarded as additional Articles to the Convention and all the provisions of the Convention shall apply accordingly.

ARTICLE 6

This Protocol shall be open for signature by the Members of the Council of Europe, who are the signatories of the Convention; it shall be ratified at the same time as or after the ratification of the Convention. It shall enter into force after the deposit of ten instruments of ratification. As regards any signatory ratifying subsequently, the Protocol shall enter into force at the date of the deposit of its instrument of ratification.

The instruments of ratification shall be deposited with the Secretary General of the Council of Europe, who will notify all Members of the names of those who have ratified.

Done at Paris on the 20th day of March 1952, in English and French, both texts being equally authentic, in a single copy which shall remain deposited in the archives of the Council of Europe. The Secretary General shall transmit certified copies to each of the signatory Governments.

RATIFICATIONS

Austria: 3 September 1958
Belgium: 14 June 1955
Cyprus: 6 October 1962
Denmark: 13 April 1953
France: 3 May 1974
Federal Republic of Germany: 13 February 1957
Greece: 28 November 1974
Iceland: 29 June 1953

Ireland: 25 February 1953
Italy: 26 October 1955
Luxembourg: 3 September 1953
Malta: 23 January 1967
Netherlands: 31 August 1954
Norway: 18 December 1952
Sweden: 22 June 1953
Switzerland: [not ratified]
Turkey: 18 May 1954
United Kingdom: 3 November 1952

Entry into force: 18 May 1954

SECOND PROTOCOL CONFERRING UPON THE EUROPEAN COURT OF HUMAN RIGHTS COMPETENCE TO GIVE ADVISORY OPINIONS

The member States of the Council of Europe signatory hereto:

Having regard to the provisions of the Convention for the Protection of Human Rights and Fundamental Freedoms signed at Rome on 4 November 1950 (hereinafter referred to as 'the Convention') and, in particular, Article 19 instituting, among other bodies, a European Court of Human Rights (hereinafter referred to as 'the Court');

Considering that it is expedient to confer upon the Court competence to give advisory opinions subject to certain conditions,

Have agreed as follows:

ARTICLE 1

1. The Court may, at the request of the Committee of Ministers, give advisory opinions on legal questions concerning the interpretation of the Convention and the Protocols thereto.

2. Such opinions shall not deal with any question relating to the content or scope of the rights or freedoms defined in Section I of the Convention and in the Protocols thereto, or with any other question which the Commission, the Court or the Committee of Ministers might have to consider in consequence of any such proceedings as could be instituted in accordance with the Convention.

3. Decisions of the Committee of Ministers to request an advisory opinion of the Court shall require a two-thirds majority vote of the representatives entitled to sit on the Committee.

ARTICLE 2

The Court shall decide whether a request for an advisory opinion submitted by the Committee of Ministers is within its consultative competence as defined in Article 1 of this Protocol.

ARTICLE 3

1. For the consideration of requests for an advisory opinion, the Court shall sit in plenary session.

2. Reasons shall be given for advisory opinions of the Court.

3. If the advisory opinion does not represent in whole or in part the unanimous opinion of the judges, any judge shall be entitled to deliver a separate opinion.

4. Advisory opinions of the Court shall be communicated to the Committee of Ministers.

ARTICLE 4

The powers of the Court under Article 55 of the Convention shall extend to the drawing up of such rules and the determination of such procedure as the Court may think necessary for the purposes of this Protocol.

ARTICLE 5

1. This Protocol shall be open to signature by member States of the Council of Europe, signatories to the Convention, who may become Parties to it by:

(a) signature without reservation in respect of ratification or aceptance;

(b) signature with reservation in respect of ratification or acceptance, followed by ratification or acceptance.

Instruments of ratification or acceptance shall be deposited with the Secretary General of the Council of Europe.

2. This Protocol shall enter into force as soon as all States Parties to the Convention shall become Parties to the Protocol, in accordance with the provisions of paragraph 1 of this Article.

3. From the date of the entry into force of this Protocol, Articles 1 to 4 shall be considered an intergral part of the Convention.

4. The Secretary General of the Council of Europe shall notify the member States of the Council of:

(a) any signature without reservation in respect of ratification or acceptance;

(b) any signature with reservation in respect of ratification or acceptance;

(c) the deposit of any instrument of ratification or acceptance;

(d) the date of entry into force of this Protocol in accordance with paragraph 2 of this Article.

In witness whereof, the undersigned, being duly authorised thereto, have signed this Protocol.

Done at Strasbourg, this 6th day of May 1963, in English and in French, both texts being equally authoritative, in a single copy which shall remain deposited in the archives of the Council of Europe. The Secretary General shall transmit certified copies to each of the signatory States.

RATIFICATIONS

Austria: 29 May 1967
Belgium: 21 September 1970
Cyprus: 22 January 1969
Denmark: 6 May 1963
France: [not ratified]
Federal Republic of Germany: 3 January 1969
Greece: 8 January 1975
Iceland: 16 November 1967
Ireland: 12 September 1963
Italy: 3 April 1967
Luxembourg: 27 October 1965
Malta: 23 January 1967
Netherlands: 11 October 1966
Norway: 12 June 1964
Sweden: 13 June 1964
Switzerland: 28 November 1974
Turkey: 25 March 1968
United Kingdom: 6 May 1963

Entry into force: 21 September 1970

FOURTH PROTOCOL

SECURING CERTAIN RIGHTS AND FREEDOMS OTHER THAN THOSE ALREADY INCLUDED IN THE CONVENTION AND IN THE FIRST PROTOCOL THERETO

The Governments signatory hereto, being Members of the Council of Europe;

Being resolved to take steps to ensure the collective enforcement of certain rights and freedoms other than those already included in Section I of the Convention for the Protection of Human Rights and Fundamental Freedoms signed at Rome on 4 November 1950 (hereinafter referred to as 'the Convention') and in Articles 1 to 3 of the First Protocol to the Convention, signed at Paris on 20 March 1952,

Have agreed as follows:

ARTICLE 1

No one shall be deprived of his liberty merely on the ground of inability to fulfil a contractual obligation.

ARTICLE 2

1. Everyone lawfully within the territory of a State shall, within that territory, have the right to liberty of movement and freedom to choose his residence.

2. Everyone shall be free to leave any country, including his own.

3. No restrictions shall be placed on the exercise of these rights other than such as are in accordance with law and are necessary in a democratic society in the interests of national security or public safety, for the maintenance of *ordre public*, for the prevention of crime, for the protection of health or morals, or for the protection of the rights and freedoms of others.

4. The rights set forth in paragraph 1 may also be subject, in particular areas, to restrictions imposed in accordance with law and justified by the public interest in a democratic society.

ARTICLE 3

1. No one shall be expelled, by means either of an individual or of

a collective measure, from the territory of the State of which he is a national.

2. No one shall be deprived of the right to enter the territory of the State of which he is a national.

ARTICLE 4

Collective expulsion of aliens is prohibited.

ARTICLE 5

1. Any High Contracting Party may, at the time of signature or ratification of this Protocol, or at any time thereafter, communicate to the Secretary General of the Council of Europe a declaration stating the extent to which it undertakes that the provisions of this Protocol shall apply to such of the territories for the international relations of which it is responsible as are named therein.

2. Any High Contracting Party which has communicated a declaration in virtue of the preceding paragraph may, from time to time, communicate a further declaration modifying the terms of any former declaration or terminating the application of the provisions of this Protocol in respect of any territory.

3. A declaration made in accordance with this Article shall be deemed to have been made in accordance with paragraph 1 of Article 63 of the Convention.

4. The territory of any State to which this Protocol applies by virtue of ratification or acceptance by that State, and each territory to which this Protocol is applied by virtue of a declaration by that State under this Article, shall be treated as separate territories for the purpose of the references in Articles 2 and 3 to the territory of a State.

ARTICLE 6

1. As between the High Contracting Parties the provisions of Articles 1 to 5 of this Protocol shall be regarded as additional Articles to the Convention, and all the provisions of the Convention shall apply accordingly.

2. Nevertheless, the right of individual recourse recognised by a declaration made under Article 25 of the Convention, or the acceptance of the compulsory jurisdiction of the Court by a declaration made under Article 46 of the Convention, shall not be effective in relation to this Protocol unless the High Contracting Party concerned has made a statement recognising such right, or accepting such jurisdiction, in respect of all or any of Articles 1 to 4 of the Protocol.

1. This Protocol shall be open for signature by the Members of the Council of Europe who are the signatories of the Convention; it shall be ratified at the same time as or after the ratification of the Convention. It shall enter into force after the deposit of five instruments of ratification. As regards any signatory ratifying subsequently, the Protocol shall enter into force at the date of the deposit of its instrument of ratification.

2. The instruments of ratification shall be deposited with the Secretary General of the Council of Europe, who will notify all Members of the names of those who have ratified.

In witness whereof, the undersigned, being duly authorised thereto, have signed this Protocol.

Done at Strasbourg, this 16th day of September 1963, in English and in French, both texts being equally authoritative, in a single copy which shall remain deposited in the archives of the Council of Europe. The Secretary General shall transmit certified copies to each of the signatory States.

RATIFICATIONS

Austria: 18 September 1969
Belgium: 21 September 1970
Denmark: 30 September 1964
France: 3 May 1974
Federal Republic of Germany: 1 June 1968
Iceland: 16 November 1967
Ireland: 29 October 1968
Luxembourg: 2 May 1968
Norway: 12 June 1964
Sweden: 13 June 1964

Entry into force: 2 May 1968

BIBLIOGRAPHY

The quantity of literature – both books and articles – about the European Convention on Human Rights is very considerable. In November 1973 the Directorate of Human Rights of the Council of Europe published a 'Bibliography relating to the European Convention on Human Rights' (Document H(73)13) running to more than a hundred pages.

For the official publications which constitute source materials the reader is referred to the 'Note on sources' at the beginning of this volume.

The following are the principal books about the Convention:

ANTONOPOULOS, N., *La Jurisprudence des organes de la Convention européenne des Droits de l'Homme, Aspects européens*, Série E, No. 5, Leyden: Sijthoff, 1967.

CASTBERG, S., *The European Convention on Human Rights*, Leyden: Sijthoff, 1974.

ERMACORA, F., *Handbuch der Grundfreiheiten und der Menschenrechte*, Vienna: Verlag Manz, 1963.

FAWCETT, J. E. S., *The Application of the European Convention on Human Rights*, Oxford: Clarendon Press, 1969.

GOLSONG, H. *Das Rechtsschutzsystem der Europäischen Menschenrechtskonvention*, Karlsruhe: C. F. Müller, 1958.

GURADZE, H., *Die Europäische Menschenrechtskonvention*, Berlin, 1968.

JACOBS, F. G., *The European Convention on Human Rights*, Oxford: Clarendon Press, 1975.

KHOL, A., *Zwischen Staat und Weltstaat*, Vienna, 1969.

Mélanges offerts à Polys Modinos: Problèmes des droits de l'homme et de l'unification européenne, Paris: Pedone, 1968.

Miscellanea W. J. Ganshof van der Meersch, Vol. I, Brussels: Bruylant, 1972.

MONCONDUIT, F., *La Commission européenne des Droits de l'Homme, Aspects Européens*, Série E, No. 4, Leyden: Sijthoff, 1965.

MORRISON, C., *The Developing European Law of Human Rights, European Aspects*, Series E, No. 7, Leyden: Sijthoff, 1967.

PARDOS PEREZ, J. L., *Derechos del hombre en el Consejo de Europa* (preface by Antonio de Luna), Murcia, 1960.

PARTSCH, K. J., *Die Rechte und Freiheiten der Europäischen Menschenrechtskonvention*, Berlin: Dunker & Humblot, 1966.

René Cassin Amicorum Discipulorumque Liber, vol. I, Paris: Pedone, 1969.

SOHN, L., and BUERGENTHAL, T., *International Protection of Human Rights*, Chapter VII, New York: Bobbs–Merrill, 1973.

VARELA FEIJÓO, J., *La protección de los derechos humanos*, Barcelona: Hispano-Europea, 1972.

VASAK, K., *La Convention européenne des Droits de l'Homme*, Paris: Librairie Générale de Droit et de Jurisprudence, 1964.

WEIL, G. L., *The European Convention on Human Rights — Background, Development and Prospects, European Aspects*, Series C, No. 12, Leyden: Sijthoff, 1963.

WIEBRINGHAUS, H., *Die Rom-Konvention für Menschenrechte in der Praxis der Strassburger Menschenrechtskommission*, Saarbrüken: West–Ost Verlag, 1959.

See also the 'Reports of Conferences and Colloquies' in the 'Note on sources' at the beginning of this volume.

INDEX

Individual cases considered by the Commission and Court of Human Rights are indexed in the 'Table of Cases' at the beginning of this volume